SO-AHC-234

WESTERN HORSE
AND
HORSEMAN'S DIGEST

by Mark Thiffault and Jack Lewis

Follett Publishing Company / Chicago

T - 0525

THE COVER: This montage features Sam Wilson and a companion pleasure riding on the historic Hollister Ranch near Santa Barbara, California. Wilson is aboard the premier cutting horse, Two D's Dynamite. Also featured is Rusty Richards giving initial training to a new foal and sacking out a well-marked paint at his Modjeska Canyon ranch in California. Hollister Ranch photo by Mark Thiffault. Photos of Richards by Chuck Tyler, associate editor of *HORSE and HORSEMAN* Magazine.

Produced by *Charger Productions*

TECHNICAL EDITOR
RUSTY RICHARDS

PRODUCTION EDITOR
BOB SPRINGER

ART DIRECTOR
LORIE DISNEY

LINE ILLUSTRATOR
MICHELE BARBER

PRODUCTION COORDINATOR
WENDY LEE WISEHART

PRODUCTION ASSISTANT
DIANE E. BIR

QUALITY CONTROL
DONNA SUE WALKER

ASSOCIATE PUBLISHER
SHELDON FACTOR

Copyright © MCMLXXV by Digest Books, Inc., 540 Frontage Rd., Northfield, Ill. 60093. All rights reserved. Printed in the United States of America. No part of this book may be reproduced, stored in a retrieval system, or transmitted, in any form or by any means, electronic, mechanical, photocopying, recording, or otherwise, without the prior written permission of the publisher. The views and opinions expressed herein are not necessarily those of the publisher and no responsibility for such views will be assumed.

ISBN 0-695-80525-8   Library of Congress Catalog Card No. 74-27495

CONTENTS

INTRODUCTION

JUST ABOUT ANYBODY with at least one good eye has noticed something mighty peculiar in most of the cities and towns, that they hadn't noticed before to any great extent: horses are everywhere! Indeed, there are many times the number of horses alive and doing well in the United States today than even when it was the main form of transportation, or so says the U.S. Department of Agriculture.

Horsemen realize that there has been a boom in horsemanship's many facets. In fact, the horse industry has become just that — an industry with assets over the $12 billion bracket. That's a pretty healthy contribution to the economy!

Looking at results of a survey conducted in 1959, it is discovered that there were something in the vicinity of three and one-half million horses throughout the country, mostly centered in the relatively rural states. In order of their horse populations, this was the top ten in 1959: Texas, North Carolina, Kentucky, Mississippi, Tennessee, Missouri, Alabama, Oklahoma, Louisiana and Montana.

A scant fourteen years later, there were an estimated seven million horses scattered throughout the backyards and ranges of America, and the top ten listing changed drastically in content. For example, California, which wasn't even in the rankings in 1959, rocketed into second place behind the leader, Texas. Another non-ranker, Florida, muscled into the top ten, while Alabama and Louisiana dropped from the chart.

The really interesting factors surrounding the California and Florida listings were that the states do not utilize the horse primarily in an occupational manner. In fact, both coast-dwellers are more known for their temperate climes and resultant recreational atmospheres. They share similar smatterings of Disneyana, miles of warm, sandy beaches and gaggles of neck-twisting, eyeball-grabbing gals.

Just as the horse has been revamped from a worker in the majority of cases, it seems only natural that his new role as a pleasure outlet be utilized in such areas. Recreation has become big business in any state, but particularly in California and Florida, and they woo buck-spending tourists on a regular basis.

There are something like 450,000 pleasure horses in California alone today and California caballeros spend upwards of $200 million on upkeep, feed and other related items. Is it any wonder that horses and mounted riders have started popping up in places that previously were without?

The total number of horses scattered throughout the backyards and at stables of the U.S. is unknown, but best estimates currently place the population at somewhere in the neighborhood of eight million, with analysts predicting continued growth. At what point the market will reach saturation levels is uncertain, but all agree it's not within the Seventies.

The influx of owners, the great majority solidly of middle-class means and tastes, has led to the necessity of books similar to this. None is all-inclusive; such would require a string of volumes putting the Encyclopedia Britannica to shame.

Consequently to attempt adequate coverage of just one segment of the equine world is the purpose behind WESTERN HORSE AND HORSEMAN'S DIGEST. In the pages that follow, the history of the horse in general and his usage in what has come to be known as "Western" events will be chronicled, along with the training, proper care, feeding and breeding regimen. It is our hope that WESTERN HORSE AND HORSEMAN'S DIGEST not only will promote good and sound horsemanship, but also increase the pleasures associated with man and horse, a team that's been inseparable throughout recorded history.

The Authors
January, 1975

Chapter 1

HISTORY OF THE HORSE

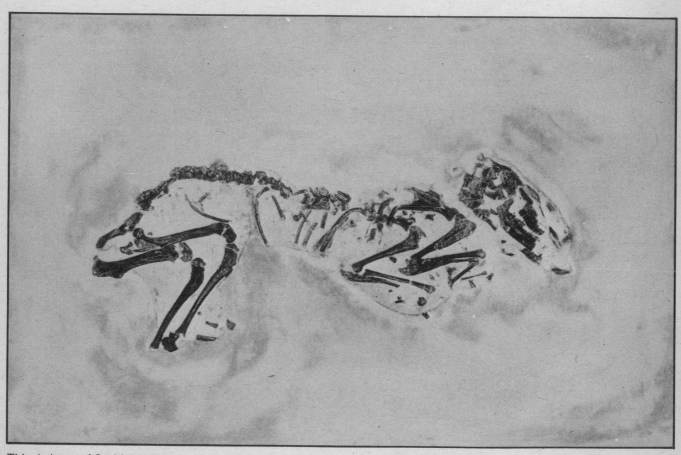

This skeleton of Orohippus was found in 1957 at Little Dry Creek, Wyoming. Retention of milk teeth denotes immaturity of this ancient relative. It's preserved as found.

Eohippus

Mesohippus

Merychippus

Many Questions Are Answered And Many Are Raised When Tracing The Species' History!

THERE ARE SEVERAL schools of thought regarding the evolution of horses through the millenia, none proved completely or concretely. While much is known of the horse's past, a great deal is left to supposition and so it shall remain; the mystery-laden fog that shrouds earth's early history has not yet been pierced by the shining flashlight of science. Until such time, man is forced to reconstruct as logically as he can the chain of evolutionary events, not unlike the archeologist does a new fossil, to the best of his deductive powers. As has been shown in history, man isn't always right.

So this chapter will proceed on the premise that much is yet to be learned of the horse's past and the events which led to his current niche in nature's scheme. New data, as it is accrued, may prove these theories obsolete or inaccurate, a circumstance that cannot be avoided. It will be up to the reader to evaluate the theories which follow, gleaned from many sources, and choose which to him seems the most logical, updating as more becomes known.

Equus caballus, the scientific term for the horse of today, can be traced back nearly sixty million years through fossil finds to the Eocene geological epoch and his commonly accepted ancestor, *Eohippus.* Translated, *Eohippus* means "dawn horse" and it's a suitable definition for this ancient relative. The line of descent preceding this period hasn't yet been uncovered conclusively, but some scientists feel *Eohippus'* ancestors range back into the Jurassic epoch — 160 million years ago — during which time fearsome dinosaurs ruled the infant planet.

Since there is a void in the horse's history prior to the Eocene, we'll begin tracing his development from that point. During this epoch, the land masses of the world were joined with land bridges. Much of the planet was covered with jungle flora today associated with limited areas known as rain forests. It was in these steamy, damp regions that the ten to twelve-inch *Eohippus* lived.

While his ancestors had five toes and a splint on the forefeet, and four toes on the hind feet, *Eohippus* was equipped with four toes on the front feet and three on the hind. This was suitable for the marshy, soggy habitat of North America, which enabled the fox-terrier-sized animal to maneuver adequately to ensure his survival from carnivorous predators that stalked the forests.

The dawn horse subsisted on a diet of soft, leafy vegetation, a fact confirmed by examination of fossilized teeth. A study of the small animal's skull by Richard Owen, England's Nineteenth Century anatomist, disclosed the eyes being rather large, filling a bony socket that was open behind and stationed near the middle of the head — as seen front to back — and not nearly as far back as in today's horse. This skull was so different than the horses of Owen's time that he dubbed the species *"Hyracotherium,"* which means "the cony beast."

Throughout the Eocene geological epoch, which lasted some twenty million years, *Eohippus* flourished on the North American continent. According to one theory, he also passed over the land bridge connecting Alaska with eastern Europe and Asia, thereby introducing the new species to these lands. The horses then spread rapidly throughout Europe and ventured into the Middle East. Unwittingly, it was the migratory pattern established during this and the following epochs that was responsible for *Equus caballus'* current existence, as we shall see.

During the Oligocene geological epoch — which followed the Eocene and lasted from forty million up to twenty-five million years ago — a tepid environment continued to exist but the horse began to change. There is some dispute over whether this change was gradual or precipitated by sudden alterations in his environment, but they took place nonetheless. Accompanying these physical changes were changes in scientific names, to positively identify the slightly different animals.

Orohippus and *Epihippus,* both slightly more advanced than *Eohippus,* lived during the Eocene epoch, with *Epihippus* surviving into the Oligocene before becoming extinct. Both horses had slightly more crested premolars and molars

Pliohippus   Equus caballus

than did *Eohippus,* and the teeth became more V-shaped. This, perhaps, was to increase chewing efficiency of the tender vegetation upon which he survived. Perhaps the jungle growths were becoming slightly tougher in constitution; man doesn't know.

During the late Eocene epoch, another offshoot of *Eohippus* evolved, termed *Mesohippus.* There were great differences between the dawn horse and this distant relative, specifically size and dentition. While *Mesohippus* fed on the jungle flora during his time in the late Eocene and Oligocene, perhaps he nibbled a mouthful or two of the tough plains grasses at the forests' edges, which triggered a biological clock to begin producing teeth slightly larger and stronger in his offspring, the jaws becoming more pronounced. His size was about that of a mature sheep, his conformation similar to a deer, and perhaps this size increase was the result of unlimited forage or the need to maneuver faster due to predation or competition for food. Again, the cause is anyone's guess.

A big difference, a hint of things to come, was the loss of one toe from the front feet. *Mesohippus* thus was able to travel faster with better footing on the somewhat drier soils he called home.

For some reason not yet explained, all of the horse's ancestors which had migrated over the land bridges into Europe and Asia became extinct during the Oligocene, while *Mesohippus* and various other equine subspecies continued to develop in North America. As of this point, more than twenty-five million years ago, there had been no movement southward into what today is Central and South America. For this science has no explanation, either.

The next link in the horse's evolutionary chain was during the Miocene geological epoch, which dates back from twenty-five million to ten million years ago. It was during this epoch that *Merychippus* evolved and he differed greatly from his forebears. It wasn't so much in size, although he was slightly larger than *Mesohippus,* but in habitat. For it was during the Miocene that *Merychippus* became a plains-dweller and this required vast changes in dentition and conformation.

This habitat switch was triggered, perhaps, by geological changes that began to shape the land masses into what we know today. Cool winds began blowing down from the northern reaches — a hint of the Ice Ages to follow — and destroyed much of the tropical rain forests, reducing them to vast plains vegetated with tough grasses. *Merychippus* was faced either with extinction through starvation or predation, or survival through adaptation. While some of his relatives within the horse family failed to make this adjustment, *Merychippus* was successful and horsemen of today owe him thanks for this.

Physically, *Merychippus* was about the size of a small pony and theorists believe this size increase came about because of his need to see longer distances in avoidance of predators on the open plains. Because he wasn't eating leafy vegetation from low trees and bushes, *Merychippus'* neck grew longer, allowing him to graze on the grasses.

But the most noticeable changes developed in the teeth and feet. Because the tough grasses he now consumed required more and stronger chewing before swallowing, *Merychippus* soon would wear down his teeth and starve if advancement didn't eventuate. Therefore, nature took over and this horse's molars and premolars — the grinding teeth — became high-crowned. They also developed extensive coatings of enamel and another hard compound not unlike cement. The jaws, understandably, became more pronounced and, in appearance, the horse began to look like a horse.

A second major difference was in the function of the feet. While *Merychippus* retained the three toes of *Mesohippus,* the two side toes had retreated until they no longer touched the ground. The central toe became enlarged and carried all the weight, as this permitted faster movement over the semi-soft, dry plains.

The horse's skeletal structure changed, also, and was markedly different than *Eohippus.* Whereas *Eohippus'* gait was rather stiff and not really extended — like man — *Mesohippus* began obtaining more mobility and *Merychippus* continued this pattern. His only defense on the plains was speed, so this change was necessary!

During the Miocene geological epoch, various offshoots

An assembled skeleton of Orohippus *(center) shows relatively small size and lack of jawbone prominence. He is shown with other animals of the Eocene/Oligocene (top left) lemur-like primate, hyena-like fisheater (left) and a rodent-like creature somewhat resembling a woodchuck with extremely large feet. Unearthed in Wyoming, this display is from the Smithsonian.*

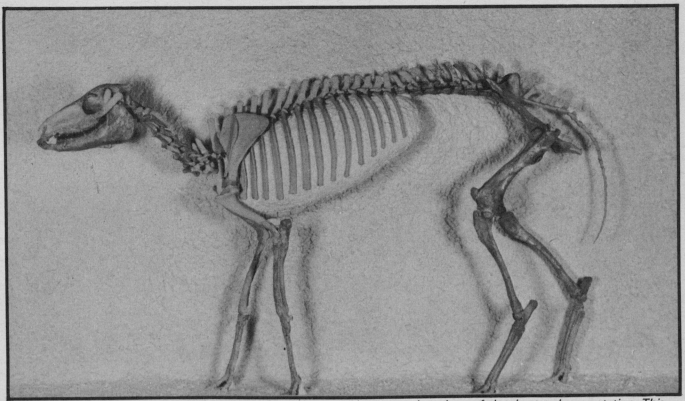

Mesohippus *was larger than* Eohippus *and had more pronounced jaws, a result perhaps of chewing tougher vegetation. This fossil, collected from the White River badlands near Harrison, Nebraska, shows only three toes on each foot instead of four.*

of the horse family — some large, some small — migrated from North America to other parts of the world, according to some scientists. They were different than *Merychippus* and, for whatever reason, became extinct.

Of note late during this epoch was the migration of one subspecies, termed *Hipparion*. After crossing the land bridge between Alaska and eastern Europe, he quickly populated Europe and crossed through into Africa. This was the first time any known species of horse had reached the Dark Continent. Perhaps he received a warm welcome from the predators present or was unable to forage on the vegetation — the strain died out.

The Pliocene geological epoch began some ten million years ago, lasting until roughly one million years ago. It was during this epoch that the equine strain refined into a rough semblance of *Equus caballus*, the horse of today.

The horse's ancestor of the Pliocene epoch was termed *Pliohippus* and he was about the size of today's donkey. He was dentally equipped to handle the grazing existence and now moved about solely on one toe, called a hoof, the other two toes having vanished. He was faster, his increased size gave him better visibility of skulking predators on the plains and he must have been somewhat more intelligent than his forebears.

It was during the late Pliocene/early Pleistocene that the horse first migrated to South America and other subspecies' migrations found the horse again invading Europe. Some branches of the equine family tree were pruned into extinction during this phase in Europe and at least one offshoot of the *Pliohippus* strain survived into the next geological epoch, the Pleistocene, before dying off. It is in the Pleistocene that we now exist, an epoch that dates back one million years.

Some mighty strange things happened during this relatively recent period in the horse's history. *Equus caballus* evolved, a slightly more refined model that increased in size, beauty, speed and probably intelligence. The last migrations were made over the land bridges connecting North America with eastern Europe, repopulating that continent, Asia and Africa. The horse also migrated into South America again.

During the Pleistocene epoch, no fewer than four times did vast sheets of glacial ice cover most of the world, reshaping the land and, as they melted — and continue to melt to this day — raised the water level of the oceans to submerge the land bridges connecting the continents.

The most efficient and cunning of predators made his emergence during this epoch: man. He preyed on the vast herds of wild horses throughout his domain and there's no doubt of his skills: at the base of a great cliff in Solutre, France, are the skeletal remains of more than 100,000 horses that Cro-Magnon slaughtered for food.

Despite this vast reduction in numbers, *Equus caballus* continued to flourish in Europe, Asia and Africa. But for some reason not yet explained, about eight thousand years ago the horse disappeared from the Americas. Did the glacial ice creeping down from the frozen North wipe out the herds? Was there some type of pestilence? Perhaps this mystery will someday be solved.

The logic of this theory of migration of the various subspecies in the equine family has been questioned in at least one of the sources researched. The reasoning is that the horse today is not a wanderer, the exception to this being the immature stallion driven from his band by the herd sire, who then wanders until he attracts or claims his own band of mares. Rather, some feel the horse stays pretty much within a specific amount of geography. It's disputable whether the stallion fights intruders to retain territoriality or for possession of the mares, however.

Following this line of thought, what, then, is the ex-

Merychippus, *the plains-dweller, had a neck reaching to the ground and teeth suitable for a grazing existence (right). It is is pictured with another animal of the Miocene epoch, an early rhinoceros. Note how* Merychippus *walks on single toe, the others receding up the leg. Its jaws are more pronounced because of improved dentition. It was found in state of Wyoming.*

planation for the emergence of identical strains on continents far removed from one another? The inconclusive answer is that the horses evolved in those areas through the natural process already outlined from *Eohippus* forward in North America. As stated at the beginning of this chapter, the theories are many and diverse; to say which is correct is not within our capabilities.

Too, there are split camps when it comes to theory on the evolution of breeds. One segment of the scientific community feels all of the modern breeds evolved from one specific strain, possibly similar to the Przewalski horse of Mongolia, the last truly wild equine. Another group feels that the modern breeds are the result of crosses between at least two and perhaps as many as six distinct strains. The most popular notion is that four different strains go into the makeup of today's different breeds, at least at some point in their dim histories.

Essentially, there are thought to have been two strains of ponies and two of horses, since there has not yet been a positive evolutionary link between pony and horse established. One pony strain is thought to have frequented the marshy, wet climes like those found in England, and this pony is small. Another is thought to be similar both in color and size (about that of a donkey) to the Przewalski horse and adapted to the cold conditions of eastern Europe and western Asia. The first strain of horse proper is thought to have been a native of central Asia and points westward, including parts of Spain. The fourth strain is thought to be native to western Asia, a fine-boned forerunner of the Arabian. Through the crossing of these individual strains, the breeds we know today supposedly developed.

Of course, man had to play a vital role in this development, but this exact time of his association with a domesticated horse is unknown. Probably, it dates back to the time when man still was primarily a hunter, over four thousand

years ago. Perhaps he discovered a horse could aid him in the taking of larger game species, thereby making him of more value than simple table fare. Too, the horse could be of assistance in carrying man's articles during the nomad's frequent moves. There also is the theory that, in defending his territory from ancient invaders, he realized the horse's value in the first primitive forms of combat. Unfortunately, man hadn't at this point begun to record his efforts in paintings or stone carvings, so this first contact aside from a predator/prey relationship is left to supposition.

It is known, however, that man began to mingle with his neighbors far in the past. Inevitably, clashing occurred when one tribe coveted the goods of a more materialistically advanced tribe. Thus, warring began and the horse became of tremendous value in this effort, right up to the second world war.

The horse in war was used in two different manners. In central Asia, the Huns and other steppes-dwelling tribes actually rode the horses. In western Asia, teams of two horses were used to pull chariots. As is logical, the latter weren't quite as nimble as the mounted rider, a disadvantage that often led to crushing defeats.

The Hittites, a race of master horsemen, utilized the information they gathered from their Asia Minor neighbors of Babylonia and Assyria on conditioning and training, in time conquering these two countries and menacing Egypt and Arabia. In fact, the first known writing dealing with horse care were five stone tablets prepared for the Hittite cavalry by Kikkulis, the Hittite king's stablemaster. After being translated, it was found much of the information still is used today!

From this lesson others learned well. History tells us of the conquest by Persian cavalrymen; of Genghis Khan and his Tartars who conquered India, China and Russia; of the Assyrians; of Attila the Hun; of the Arabs who conquered in the name of Allah; of Alexander the Great; of Hannibal and his mounted army; of the Greeks; of Frederick the Great; of the knights in heavy armor; and even of the Poles during World War Two. With the Roman legions of infantrymen excepted, it's doubtful these conquests would have been consumated were it not for the horse.

There still were continents devoid of both these wars and horses: the Americas and Australia, to name just three. It was not until the Spanish Armada ruled the seas and Spain began building her empire that the horse came back home to North America: a complement of sixteen war horses, under the charge of Conquistador Hernando Cortez, in the 1500s. Terrified Indians were no match against these mounted plunderers, so *Equus caballus* played a role in the conquest of yet another civiliation.

As history discloses, the Indians of the Americas were far from simple-minded, and soon began to covet the Spanish-Barb horses. They managed to steal a few and began breeding them, while others escaped without recapture,

beginning the repopulation of the continents. As we shall see in the following chapter, various breeds were established in North America, some through imported stock and others through selective breeding. Then there are others, like the Morgan, which seems to have started through the efforts of one prepontent mutation, the stallion Justin Morgan.

So there we have the history of the horse from the Eocene epoch to the present. We chose not to delve deeply into the exploits of warring nations and their histories with horses, since volumes have been devoted to these subjects and those interested can follow up the subject at their leisure.

But enough has been learned to show that all hasn't yet been learned about this fantastic creature. The theories advanced here are offered only as possible explanations for the horse's continued existence and it's up to you, the reader, to form your own conclusions, until such evidence evolves which proves one — or none — right.

As stated in the text, Pliohippus *esentially was the complete and known horse of today, sans a few minor refinements. Three of the Pliocene horses, unearthed by Smithsonian Institute archeologists near Twin Falls, Idaho, show state of advancement. These horses, which traveled on one hoof and well-equipped for grazing existence, lasted well into the Pleistocene epoch.*

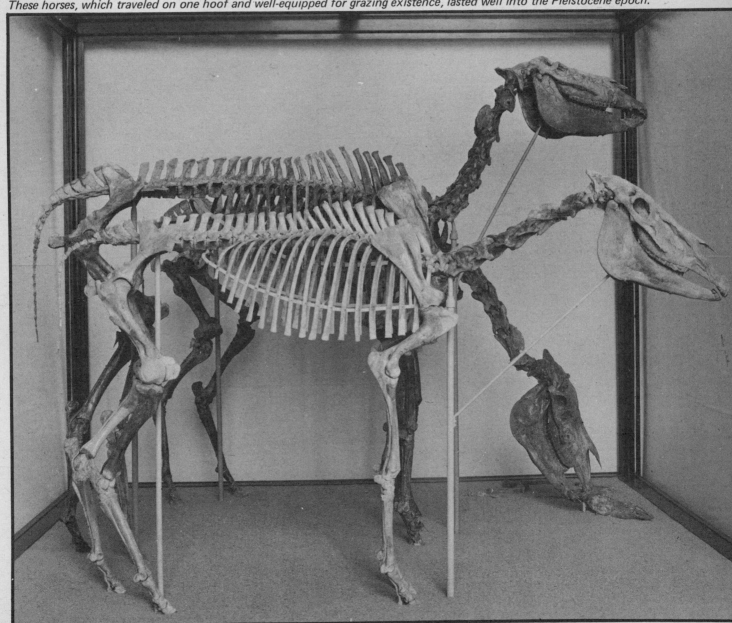

THE 'WESTERN' BREEDS OF TODAY

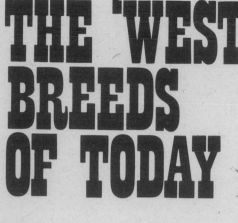

Chapter 2

THE ARABIAN HORSE

THE ORIGIN OF the Arabian horse is lost in antiquity. Many chapters have been written and serious students of the subject do not all agree as to just when and where the Arabian horse originated. But, it is accepted by all scholars, animal breeders and Arabian horse enthusiasts that the breed is very ancient and twenty centuries ago was essentially the same as we know him today.

As stated by the late Professor Henry Fairfield Osborn of the American Museum of Natural History, between 25,000 and 40,000 years ago, the Arabian horse was clearly depicted on the walls of limestone caves along with other animals of the hunt. He wrote, "In the Grotto of Cambarelles in Southern France are represented hundreds of small horses of the Arabian type intermingled with outlines of those of coarser blood and heritage, both of what we now call the Nordic type and what we call the Steppe type." Osborn went on to say that the cave drawings depicted the outstanding characteristics of the Arabian, "the small, finely drawn muzzle, pointed ears, the deep cheek, the short back, the slender limbs, the facial profile which even now remains one of the most distinctive features of the Arabian...."

Professor Osborn stated that the skeletal differences of the Arabian horse are distinguished by one less vertebra (5 instead of 6 lumbar) in the back. The foreleg, the ulna, or small bone of the foreleg, is complete, whereas in other horses it ends in a splint. There are only sixteen vertebrae in the tail as compared to eighteen in the tail of horses of northern Europe. Other skeletal characteristics are the horizontal position of the pelvis, the large size of the brain case, relative shortness of the skull and slenderness of the muzzle.

R.H. Smythe, examiner in surgery to the Royal College of Veterinary Surgeons, England, states, "The Arabian horse has usually an extra dorsal vertebra and one lumbar bone less. As each dorsal bone carries a pair of ribs, one on either side, most Arabians possess nineteen pairs of ribs instead of eighteen. This is why specimens of the breed are short-backed and well ribbed-up, almost to the flank."

The Arabian's head is a real thing of beauty, the upper

half being larger in proportion to the whole size of the horse, especially in the depth across the jowls.

The head has a triangular shape which diminishes rapidly to a small and fine muzzle, which is so small that it can be enclosed in the palm of the hand. The lips are fine and thin. The nostrils are long, thin, delicately curled, running upward, and projecting outward. In action or when the horse is excited, the nostrils may become greatly dilated.

The eyes are set far apart, and are large, lustrous, and, when aroused, full of fire. They are set more nearly in the middle of the head, with plenty of brain capacity above them.

The distance from the top of the head to the top of the eyes is often within one inch of the distance from the lower eyelid to the top of the nostril. Added brain capacity is frequently given by a slight protrusion over the forehead and extending to just below the eyes, called the "Jibbah" by the Arabs, and greatly prized.

The cheekbones spread wide apart at the throat, often between five or six inches, enabling the muzzle to be drawn in without compressing the windpipe, and permitting the animal to breathe easily when running.

The ears, smaller in stallions and of good size in mares, are pointed, set evenly together in an upright position, and of great flexibility.

The head should be lean, somewhat well chiseled, and showing energy, intelligence, courage and nobility. The neck is long and arched, set on high and run well back into the withers.

The Arabian horse measures 14.1 to 15.1 hands at the withers, although there are horses which measure above or below this height.

The animal's coat is thick, close, fine, soft, and silky. The mane and tail are long and very fine in texture.

The Arab may weigh from 800 to 1000 pounds, according to his size, but there are horses who exceed this weight occasionally.

The primary colors of the Arabians are bay, gray and chestnut, with an occasional roan and black. Common markings are stars, stripes or blaze faces, as are also snip noses, a white foot or more, or white stockings.

George Gaylord Simpson of The American Museum of Natural History states: "That the Arabian has existed and has been kept without marked change since about the time of Mohammed, in the Seventh Century, is reasonably established. It is indeed inbreeding within a relatively small stock of individually highly prized horses that has kept this ancient type recognizable and distinct for so long a time. Wherever they came from originally, the peculiarities of the desert horses of Arabia have been intensified and maintained by long inbreeding and by selection, natural and human, in an environment poor for horses and demanding toughness, alertness, and speed in those that survive."

Because the Arabian horse is a subspecies with distinct anatomical differences from other horses, and because he has been bred pure and by selection for centuries, his peculiarities are said to be "fixed." He breeds true and his qualities are "fixed"; he is a prepotent breeder when his blood is introduced into other breeds. It is from the Arabian blood on the pony and the cold-blooded species that has given rise to possibly all light horses (riding types) around the world.

There is little agreement among scholars concerning the place of origin of the Arabian horse. As a subspecies, and as the most conspicuous hot-blooded horse, the Arabian's place of origin has been identified as such widely scattered places as Siberia, Libya and India.

Professor William Ridgeway claims that the Arabian goes back to the desert regions of North Africa rather than to the Arabian Desert, the traditional home of the Arab.

Lady Wentworth writes: "Apart from Nomad traditions of the original wild horse we have the historian El Kelbi's records (A.D. 786) of the Arabian horse pedigrees which date back nearly 5000 years to the original wild horses of Yemen Hoshaba and Baz, a mare owned by Baz, son of Omain, son of Lud, son of Shem, son of Noah, circa 3200 B.C." Hoshaba and Baz were captured by Baz in Yemen in the southwestern tip of Arabia.

While its earliest habitat may be disputed, it is generally agreed that the Arabian horse as we know him was found in Asia Minor at least three thousand years ago, and on the Arabian peninsula 2500 years later. It was in the warm climes that the Arabian found a home where it remained until recent times.

Although much of what we read about the equine migrations is part legend and part fact, it is thought that the route of distribution in northern Europe was first through Greece and some of the Gothic countries. It is believed that the Romans rode Arabian horses into France, Holland, Belgium and parts of Germany.

The tremendous growth of the Mohammedan religion resulted in the introduction of the Arabian horse to North

Witezarif, ridden by Donna Fitzgerald, won an unprecedented four consecutive Tevis Cup 100-mile endurance contests (left), proving Arabians well-suited for this competition. Chris Watson and Arabian gelding, Abu Vain, jerk down a range cow during ranch horse trial at Rush Creek Land and Livestock Company, Lisco, Nebraska. The Arab truly is a versatile horse!

Africa, Spain, and France. The Moslems, defeated in 732 A.D. at Poitiers, retreated to Spain where their war horses were used to create a new breed of horse, the fine Spanish-Barb. When the Christian Crusaders landed in the Holy Land in the Twelfth Century, they found many fine Arabian horses. The Crusaders imported the Arabian into England and France.

Wherever Moslem conquests or defeats led the Arabian horse, its influence on and improvement of other breeds of horses is a matter of record.

In 1580, in the duchy of Carnida near the head of the Adriatic Sea, a stud with Spanish (Andalusian) and Arab stock was formed at Lippizza. These Viennese "high school" horses became the famous Lippizzan breed, Arabian in type but retaining the Andalusian convexity of head.

Count Orloff of Russia crossed Dutch Hart-draver trotting mares to the Arab and Barb to establish the celebrated Orloff Trotter.

In 1689, 1706, and 1724, respectively, three Oriental stallions...the Byerly Turk, Darley Arabian, and Godolphin Arabian...were imported into the British Isles where they were crossed with the Barb or Royal mares previously imported by Charles II (1660-1685). Practically every thoroughbred racing in the world today stems from one of these great foundation sires.

Not only did the Arabian influence light horse breeds, but the Percheron breed as well. The Oriental sires Gallipoli and Godolphin, crossed with French mares, are considered the most important foundation sires of the Percheron breed as well.

Nine years after the Godolphin Arabian was foaled, his first son was imported into the American colonies in 1733. Another of the earliest Arabians of eastern breeding was Lord Lonsdale's Monkey, imported to Virginia in 1747. Monkey's popularity in America is indicated by the fact that he had sired 300 American foals by the time of his death in 1754.

About 1765, the first recorded purebred Arabian, Ranger, appeared on the American scene. Later called Lindsay's Arabian, Ranger first stood in Connecticut. General George Washington, after noting the superiority of the Connecticut cavalry mounts, purchased Ranger and took him to Virginia to stand at stud.

In Bruce's American Stud Book are forty-two Arabian horses imported between 1760 and 1860. The thoroughbred breeder, Keene Richards, backed by The New Orleans Jockey Club, imported Arabians from the desert to Kentucky in 1854.

During Lincoln's presidency, two Arabian stallions were presented to his Secretary of State. Sultan Abdul Hamid II presented General U.S. Grant with two fine Arabian stallions, Leopard and Linden Tree. These two horses are listed in the Arabian Horse Registry of America's Stud Book, Vol. 5, as are five of the twenty-nine horses that were brought by the Bedouins to the Chicago World's Fair in 1893. The impression created by the Bedouins' horses at Chicago was most desirable and resulted in a wide interest in the Arabian horse. The final importation of note in the Nineteenth Century was made by Randolph Huntington of Oyster Bay, New York.

The real "breakthrough" for the Arabian horse in America took place after the turn of the Twentieth Century as a result of Homer Davenport's trip to the Arabian desert in quest of Arabian horses. This expedition led by Davenport was sponsored by President Theodore Roosevelt and financed by Peter B. Bradley of Hingham, Massachusetts. In his book, "My Quest of the Arabian Horse," Davenport describes this expedition which resulted in the shipment of

Astride Quist, Mike Fitzgerald heads for finish line after 50 miles aboard the Arab. The combination's tough to beat!

twenty-seven Arabian horses to Boston in 1906. It was the importation of these horses that stimulated a few Arab breeders in the United States to form a registry with the expressed purpose to promote increasing interest in the Arabian breed and to encourage others to import new Arabian blood to America.

Prior to 1908, Arabian horses were registered in the American Stud Book by The Jockey Club of America. However, all such Arabians were from the General Stud Book of England before importations here and were accepted by The Jockey Club on the basis of their British papers.

When Homer Davenport returned from his famous expedition to desert Arabia in 1906 with the shipment of Arabian horses, The Jockey Club said they could not be accepted in the American Stud Book except under the rules of the General Stud Book of England. Then came the thought, "Why not have an Arabian registry? Why should the Arabian have to be registered as a thoroughbred, mixed with other blood and lose its identity in the United States?"

On September 2, 1908, in New York City, the Arabian Horse Club of America was formed. The first officers were: President, James A. Lawrence (an early promoter of the Arabian horse and director of the first Arabian horse show in Cleveland, Ohio, in 1907); First Vice-President, Peter B. Bradley (breeder and importer); Second Vice-President, Homer C. Davenport; Secretary-Treasurer, H.K. Bush-Brown (famous sculptor with many equestrian statues to his credit as well as the Lincoln Memorial at Gettysburg).

The U.S. Department of Agriculture approved the Club's first Stud Book on November 12, 1909. The Club accepted for registration any purebred Arabian horse that had proof of its lineage. This included the Arabians imported from England that were in the General Stud Book of England and in The Jockey Club of America. The Department of Agriculture's approval clearly established the Arabian Horse Club's standing among breed registries. Since the Department of Agriculture recognized only one registry for any breed of animals, its seal of approval made the Club, in effect, an official national registry. Thus, all Arabian horses to be used for breeding purposes had to be registered in the Arabian Horse Club of America's Stud Book.

The Jockey Club continued to register General Stud Book (England) Arabians and the progeny of the Arabians registered in The Jockey Club Stud Book until 1943. The General Stud Book in England closed its book in 1921 to all but the progeny of horses registered in the G.S.B.

In 1969, the Arabian Horse Club Registry of America shortened its name to "The Arabian Horse Registry of America, Inc." As of December, 1973, the Registry had registered 100,000 purebred Arabians, of which approximately 78,900 were still living.

THE QUARTER HORSE

The ideal quarter horse, as painted by the gifted hand of Orren Mixer. Now strong, the breed once almost vanished.

THE QUARTER HORSE is by far the most popular using animal for horseowners throughout the United States and, in the future, this statement might be applied to other countries, as well.

In a sense, the quarter horse owes its existence to the English love of horseracing and the forested terrain of the East Coast. It was a combination of both factors which led to the breed's development.

In pre-Revolutionary America, English colonists had "blooded" running horses but the dense forests precluded racing over distances comparable to those in England. Consequently, straightaways in the neighborhood of a quarter-mile were hacked from the forest and match races between two horses run over these comparatively short distances.

Perhaps in their quest of finding a more suitable horse for this short-distance racing — but more likely because they wanted more horses — the colonists began breeding their studs to the small, hardy, Spanish-blooded horses of the Chickasaw and Choctaw Indian tribes. The result was a sturdy horse with speed never before seen over short distances; a perfect compromise, since the horse generally would perform double-duty as a work horse besides his racing role.

In a great many cases, it was this hardiness that led to the continued existence of the "Celebrated American Quarter-mile Running Horse," as he was known. It's been recorded that, following the day's labors, the horses might be fed a little Indian maize and turned into the woods to fend and forage for themselves. Only the toughest could survive, which is the way nature evaluates her handiwork.

The sport of quarter racing was the rage of the colonies throughout most of the 1600s. Near the close of the century, however, longer-distance racing began to emerge as the vast plantations were cleared of timber and planted with tobacco and other crops. The Celebrated American Quarter-mile Running Horse didn't have the staying power to compete against English "blooded" horses constantly being imported and the interest in quarter racing began to wane. This popularity decline lasted up to the Revolutionary War and not much breeding of the stout horse was conducted during those years.

Back in the 1750s, some two decades before the start of the War of Independence, a horse that would play a major role in the quarter horse's history arrived on American soil. Janus, a grandson of the Godolphin Arabian — one of three Arabian stallions imported to England to start the thoroughbred strain — was under fifteen hands yet possessed a stamina that won him numerous distance races in England before he pulled up lame and was brought to the New World by well-heeled shipper Mordecai Booth. Whatever the nature of his lameness, the change of scenery healed the condition and Janus built himself a racing reputation on this continent.

Breeders experimented with this solid horse, covering various Celebrated American Quarter-mile Running Horse mares. Janus' get possessed absolutely blinding speed over the short distances and some of his offspring also did well in the three to four-mile races.

Quarter-mile racing still was popular in Virginia and the Carolinas, so Janus was used in the stud throughout both colonies. He died at the age of 34 and is found in the pedigrees of at least six, and perhaps as many as nine, of the original eleven founding families in the American Quarter Horse Association stud book.

Following the Revolutionary War, the quarter horse, along with other breeds, went with the pioneers who conquered and settled the West. They powered the emigrant wagons, broke the virgin prairie sod, tended the cattle herds and waged war with Indians. Upon a horse's condition, his willingness and his ability depended all prosperity, and often even life itself.

The coming of the great cattle herds to the Western prairies brought the quarter horse back into his own. Long since supplanted by the distance-running thoroughbreds on large, circular tracks in the East, the quarter horse had suffered in prestige, lost to general public acclaim, though still valued and honored by many.

The range country was made for the quarter horse. In every department he filled the needs of the cowboy as a full partner in the exacting business of working the great cattle herds. For, to an unmatched degree, the quarter horse is endowed with the rare quality of cow-savvy.

Add to this rare ability the capacity for short, quick

Because of his speed and athletic ability, the quarter horse is a favorite of the barrel racer, among others.

The quarter horse still is used for racing and the world's richest race is the $1 million All American Futurity at Ruidoso Downs, New Mexico. Winner nets $330,000!

bursts of flashing speed, spirit, stamina, and unfailing obedience, and you have a picture of the peerless cowhorse.

Southwestern ranchers were quick to realize the value of the original bloodstrains of the quarter horse. Upon their working strains they infused the blood of the American thoroughbred. The strain of the colonial racing quarter horse was restored and revived. On the arid plains of the West and Southwest, short racing flourished anew. Cowboys, anxious to display their skill, contested at roundups. And, since cowboy activities consist of a team of man and horse, they used their favorite mounts in arena events that eventually became a part of stock shows and fairs.

The name, "quarter horse," was seldom if ever used to designate type or breed. Southwestern horsemen generally referred to him as "Steeldusts," "Billys," "Rondos," or "Copper Bottoms" to describe his type if not, in fact, to infer — rightly or wrongly — that he was a descendent of one of these famous foundation sires.

Until the American Quarter Horse Association was form-

ed on March 15, 1940, the quarter horse had no official name or breed registry. The early Western horseman's lack of interest in a breed registry is understandable; neither time, inclination nor circumstances in the range country were conducive to an organization to record the ancestry of a horse.

Pedigrees, other than those impressed on the minds of horsemen, seldom were used. Horses and men were judged by what they were, not by what they were supposed to be. In the first stud book published by the AQHA, W.M. French observed that, "Many an old-timer had the feeling, and was right about it, too, that if you couldn't head a steer on a horse it wouldn't help to have a paper telling how well he was bred. The West used too many horses and used them too hard to be bothered by such minor details."

Breeders used the science of practical experience which teaches that the heritability of a trait is one of the most important factors to consider in deciding upon the breeding plan that is most apt to be successful in bringing about a continuation or even improvement of a good trait.

To Billy Anson, a native of England and a renowned horseman who migrated to Texas in the late 1900s, is attributed the first serious effort to establish a modern quarter horse registry. Although Anson's efforts were unproductive in his lifetime, the flame he sparked later was fanned by willing hands.

The bloodlines of many of the best individuals had vanished prior to 1870 and the genealogical strains of several predominant cowhorse families were threatened with extinction as fewer horses were needed on the rapidly shrinking pastures of Western ranges. The relentless tide of a motorized economy in the two decades following World War I contributed further to the fear that time was running out.

Dan Casement, widely known cattleman and highly respected horseman of Manhattan, Kansas, was among the country's most avid spokesmen for quarter horses. Casement's son, the late Jack Casement, a quarter horse breeder of Sterling, Colorado, and a director of the AQHA, was equally active and effective in extolling the virtues of the breed. In fact, other than Billy Anson, Jack Casement wrote the first magazine article advocating a stud book for quarter horses which, it must be noted, he called "Steeldusts."

Among the foremost apostles — and certainly one to round up a great many converts — was Robert M. Denhardt, a professor at Texas A&M University and a prolific writer of articles for numerous newspapers and magazines.

It is remembered that Denhardt's accounts of top quarter horse bloodlines, based upon several years of travel and research, were particularly useful in spreading the gospel. In fact, Denhardt is credited with revealing the line of descent of some of the breed's most famous families. He was the first, for example, to tell of the importance of Peter McCue blood in the modern quarter horse.

The stimuli provided by these men and their friends prodded others to action. Whenever and wherever cattlemen and cowboys gathered — around branding pens, at livestock conventions, in country stores, at the crossroads — there was talk, most of it favorable, about the desirability of an outfit that could record, preserve and propagate the bloodlines of the revered, time-honored cowhorses still working on Western ranches.

Spurred by the reported success of other equine breed and color registries, Denhardt and R.L. Underwood, an oilman and quarter horse visionary of Wichita Falls, Texas, began contacting leading horsemen/ranchers in an effort to trigger a quarter horse association.

The late Jim Minnick of Crowell, Texas, was among the

first persons enlisted by Underwood. No Texas horseman was ever more respected than Minnick. He was the first inspector employed by the AQHA after its inception.

The first group discussion of an association involving several men from various regions across the Southwest occurred in 1939, at Fort Worth's Southwestern Exposition and Fat Stock Show. Among those participating in the informal parlay, in addition to Underwood and Denhardt, were John Burns, manager of the Pitchfork Land and Cattle Company, with headquarters at Guthrie, Texas; J. Goodwin Hall of the 6666 Ranches, with headquarters in Fort Worth; Duwain Hughes of San Angelo, Texas; Dean Marstellar, head of the School of Veterinary Medicine, Texas A&M University; and D.W. Williams, head of the Animal Husbandry Department, Texas A&M University.

Although the proposal to form an organization that could compile and maintain a stud book and serve those who bred quarter horses fell on receptive ears, it was generally agreed that further study should be made to more accurately reassure the patronage such a movement might receive.

It was agreed that another meeting should be held in Fort Worth during the next Stock Show and that, in the interval, proponents would do their utmost to publicize the idea of an organization and invite all interested persons to the conclave, scheduled for March 15, 1940.

Approximately seventy-five persons from several Southwestern states, including Maxie Michaelis and his wife, Helen, of Coahuila, Mexico, attended the widely publicized dinner-meeting the following evening at the Fort Worth Club.

Denhardt, in cooperation with Wayne Dinsmore of Chicago, secretary of the Horse and Mule Association of America, had prepared a constitution and bylaws following the 1939 conference and presented the documents to the assembly.

The organization, to be known as the AQHA, was to be a stock-holding, non-profit concern with a capital stock of $8000. The sale of 800 shares at $10 each would finance the concern until it could become self-sufficient through registration and other changes. Demand for stock exceeded the supply to the time the association became a membership entity in the mid-1940s, whereupon the association paid stockholders par value for their holdings.

The late William B. Warren, a rancher of Hockley, Texas, was the first president of the fledgling organization. First vice-president was Jack F. Hutchins of the Shanghai Pierce Estate in Pierce, Texas; R.L. Underwood, Wichita Falls, Texas, was second vice-president; Robert M. Denhardt, College Station, Texas, secretary; and J. Goodwin Hall, Fort Worth, Texas, treasurer.

The Association's first annual meeting was held March 13, 1941, at the Blackstone Hotel in Fort Worth. One thousand horses had been registered in the association's first year. The first stud book was published in 1941. By prior agreement, the Grand Champion Stallion at the 1941 Southwestern Exposition and Fat Stock Show was designated No. 1 in the registry. History records that the imperishable honor went to the King Ranch of Texas entry named Wimpy.

Even though the years of World War II were not conducive to many functions removed from the worldwide holocaust, the interest expressed by horsemen in registering their horses with the AQHA remained remarkably strong. Gasoline and tire rationing greatly restricted travel by automobile, but several of the increasing number of directors in various states volunteered to serve without compensation on the association's team to make inspections of horses in their respective regions.

When AQHA directors ruled that the organization should be strictly a breed registry, running horsemen, some of whom were on the AQHA board, formed two racing associations in the early 1940s. The Quarter Horse Camp Meeting Association of America was based at Stamford, Texas. The Southern Arizona Breeders Association, as the name denotes, was formed in Arizona. Neither association was expected to conflict with the AQHA. Whereas the life of the Texas racing group was brief, the pattern set by the Arizona organization resulted in the formation in 1945 of the American Quarter Racing Association, with headquarters in Tucson, Arizona.

Disunity infested the AQHA membership in the years of World War II. Differences over various operating methods, including the registration of horses, became so pronounced that one group withdrew from the AQHA to form still another organization, named the National Quarter Horse Breeders Association.

The NQHBA based its registration formula on bloodlines alone; horses were not inspected for conformation as required by the AQHA.

The chief concern of the American Quarter Racing Association was largely limited to identifying and posting records of quarter running horses.

It was possible for a horse to be registered in all three entities, but under different names in each one. That breeders, owners and buyers were confused is a gross understatement of fact.

It was under this cloud of disagreement, despair and indecision that the AQHA began its 1946 convention in Fort Worth. A miracle, or at least a miracle-maker, was needed immediately.

Albert Mitchell of Albert, New Mexico, who was present for the convention's opening sessions, had been called back to his ranches on personal business before the convention ended.

In their search for the one person who might possibly salvage the AQHA and perhaps guide it to solid footing, the organization's policymakers turned to Mitchell. Convention delegates unhesitatingly elected Mitchell to the presidency with the knowledge that his acceptance of the office with all of its responsibilities was questionable.

The quarter horse world could hardly have appealed to a more capable or a busier man than Albert Mitchell. A confidant of heads of government in this and other countries, a member of numerous commissions and boards concerned with wartime emergencies, riding and working day and night with his cowboys on the Tesquesquite and Bell ranches in New Mexico, Mitchell was not easily persuaded.

A committee, including Richard Kleberg, Sr., R.A. Brown, Howell Smith, Roy Parks and R.E. (Bob) Hooper, was instructed by the directorate to contact Mitchell following the convention's adjournment to learn if he would accept the post. Parks, named spokesman for the committee, telephoned Mitchell from a hotel room in Fort Worth.

Years later, Parks said, "Albert told me that he didn't want the job. He said he wouldn't accept it unless members believed no other way could be found to save the association. I told him we had to have him if the organization was to survive another year."

The persistence of his many devoted friends prevailed; two days following the election, Mitchell accepted the position. His reputation gave the association the esteem it needed to assure prosperity and growth.

Mitchell served three consecutive terms in the presidency — 1946, 1947, 1948 — and still another term in 1957.

Efforts to find solutions to the problems which had created three separate associations designed to serve quarter horse owners slowly resulted in victory. Amalgamation was accomplished at a meeting in Omaha, Nebraska, in the latter days of 1949. The merger, wherein the AQHA absorbed the American Quarter Racing Association and the National Quarter Horse Breeders Association, and in which the AQHA accepted horses listed in the NQHBA Stud Book, was formally approved at the 1950 convention of the AQHA in Amarillo.

Today, the AQHA is a paragon of all equine registries. With headquarters in Amarillo, Texas, housed in ultra-modern, association-owned buildings, there is a staff of over 200 men and women to serve the industry and numerous related industries.

By 1973, the AQHA had become the world's largest and fastest-growing equine registry, supported by more than 68,000 dues-paying members and more than 970,000 of its horses registered in the United States and fifty other countries.

Physically, the quarter horse is one of the most beautiful of all equines. He has a short, broad head, denoting intelligence. His eyes are soft and set wide apart. His jaws are well-developed and the muzzle is short. He has particularly small, pointed ears.

His neck is full and slightly arched at the crest, protruding from a well-muscled, deep and broad chest. His withers aren't overly pronounced, yet well-suited to holding a saddle. His back is short, his barrel large, and his hindquarters are sloping and heavily muscled.

The quarter horse's legs are flat-boned, with strong yet smooth joints and his cannons are short. His legs are kept under the body, which gives him exceptional balance at all gaits.

He has a calm, gentle disposition, a desirable mount for youngsters. His speed and sense make him a favorite of competition cowboys. He can do it all.

THE MORGAN HORSE

THE GENT WHO coined the "hindsight is beautiful" phrase must have had his tongue solidly in his cheek: It just ain't so, at least when discussing the Morgan horse breed.

The gallons of ink used for printing "facts" about the breed's history probably would make the Caspian Sea appear a raindrop in comparison. Piled one atop the other, the individual pages devoted to this topic would stretch to stratospheric heights. The black eyes, bruised knuckles and fits of apoplexy caused by arguments over the Morgan's history would make even the Tin Man wince.

And just think — all this over one small, rough-coated horse. Perhaps it's poetic justice to literally fight over this remarkable stud horse now; nobody expressed a great deal of interest when he was alive.

The whole head-scratchin' business started with the foaling of a stud colt named Figure back in 1789 or 1791, depending upon whom you believe. He was the get of a thoroughbred, True Britton (alias Beautiful Bay), and the produce of an unnamed mare of medium size, bay in coloration with black points, which traced back directly to the Godolphin Arabian, one of the thoroughbred foundation sires. True Britton, for that matter, allegedly was but a couple of generations removed from the Byerly Turk, another Arabian thoroughbred foundation stud imported to England and bred to Flemish mares. It therefore is reasonable to believe that Figure was of primarily Arabian/thoroughbred genealogy, a theory most historians grudgingly concede.

The stud colt was foaled supposedly in West Springfield, Massachusetts, but how the colt got to Vermont as a 2-year-old is another disputed area. The theory most accepted is that he traveled from his birthplace to Randolph, Vermont, in either 1793 or 1795, as the property of Justin Morgan, who either purchased the colt outright or received him as payment on a loan. As the colt wasn't even halter-broken, he traveled freely behind a stablemate hitched to the back of Morgan's wagon.

Once into Vermont, Justin Morgan kept the horse for only a short period before leasing him to a rum-swilling opportunist named Robert Evans. He was broken and put into the traces, pulling stumps, hauling logs and, in the evenings when Evans could find a bettor or two, racing against all comers for rum or money.

There is a widely circulated — and disputed — story concerning one of Figure's superequine feats of strength that bears mention. Evans allegedly boasted that the 950-pound Figure could out-pull draft horses scaling 1200 pounds, and put a gallon of rum as a wager against any takers.

The bet was that, within three pulls, Figure could haul an immense log to a specific point. Upon examining the size of the log, Evans allowed as how it was too easy for the horse and bade three more-than-slightly inebriated lumberjacks to climb aboard, thus making the load suitable to the task.

Figure reached the appointed location in just two

All Morgans trace their beginnings back to one single stallion, Justin Morgan.

mighty heaves. Evans won his gallon of rum and the legend of the small horse with heart began to grow. Whether the horse did, in fact, perform as reputed and whether Evans won his gallon of rum are open to much debate, but there certainly is no doubt about the word getting around.

D.C. Linsley, one of the few writers whose research is given more than a passing glower, described Figure — later given the name of his owner, Justin Morgan — in expressive terms after the stud's demise somewhere around age 30. He said the horse weighed in the vicinity of 950 pounds and stood somewhere around fourteen hands tall. He was dark bay in color, with black legs, mane and tail. The hair was long and coarse. He had a medium-sized head, wide at the poll, with short, pricked ears, expressive eyes and finely

Because of their good looks and fancy gait, Morgans were in demand as coach horses before the automobile arrived. They're one of the handsomest horse breeds today.

This painting of a Morgan stallion shows the conformation typical to the breed. They are used extensively by modern cattlemen.

chiseled features. He had straight, clean legs, deep muscling over the quarters and shoulders, which he surely put to the test throughout his lifetime.

Around this time in the horse's hazy history, he passed from the control of Evans back to Justin Morgan, a schoolteacher by trade. It was then that he proved himself super in yet another area: the breeding pen. Sons and daughters, all virtually mirror images of the stud, began dotting different parts of the countryside, being used as workhorses and doubling as harness horses. Demand grew as city folk in Boston and New York noticed their good looks and excellent performance.

It wasn't long before the Morgans were used in trotting races, with spectacular results. In 1850, the world's fastest trotting stallion was Justin Morgan's great-grandson, Ethan Allen. In fact, it's been claimed that no sub-two-minute standardbred miler — from Greyhound to Billy Direct — has existed that doesn't have some Morgan in him.

With the gold rush of 1849, Morgans were driven and ridden westward, where their bloodlines often mingled with breeds present. There were many attempts to breed into the Morgan attributes the horse lacked, especially leginess, which breeders thought would increase an already superlative performance on the race courses. To a point, the true Morgan was bred almost out of existence and perhaps would have been were it not for the efforts of a well-heeled Morgan fancier, Colonel Joseph Battell.

On his modest Vermont farm, Colonel Battell began breeding for the characteristics traditional in the Morgan horse. He began tracing pedigrees and did his part to help clear the mystery of Justin Morgan, culminating in the first-ever Morgan Horse Register, published in 1894.

To ensure the survival of the Morgan horse in 1906, Colonel Battell deeded the property and the Morgan horses to the United States Government. In his deed for the farm, Colonel Battell stated, "In making this gift to the United States, I am actuated in large measure by the desire to encourage the breeding of Morgan Horses and to effect restoration of their former leading position in this country, and I trust this gift of land will be used primarily for this purpose."

It was a shrewd move on the part of Colonel Battell and his wishes were carried out. The government kept the farm until 1951 and, until that time, bred, trained, sold, exhibited and, perhaps best of all, kept records of the Morgans at the farm. In 1951, the government turned the facility over to the University of Vermont, under whose care it remains today.

Present-day Morgans have few wildernesses to conquer, few wars to win. But they still accomplish great deeds, albeit less romantic. Morgan horses do range work from the Rocky Mountains of Montana and Wyoming to the plains of New Mexico. They live long, work-full lives, providing their owners with added years of productivity. They learn quickly and shorten still more the time spent teaching one to become that ranchowner's prized possession, a top cowhorse. Of late years, Morgans have been appearing in cutting contests to challenge successfully the supremacy of other breeds raised solely for that purpose.

Morgan horses are filling the show rings of the nation, competing within their breed and, almost as ably, outside it. He's a truly versatile mount.

THE SPANISH-BARB

THE SPANISH-BARB, which has made such an impact on the history of the world, has made little impact on the minds of American horsemen. Many, in fact, raise inquisitive eyebrows when the breed's name is mentioned and the number who have seen the horse is minute.

The Spanish-Barb had his beginnings in ancient Persia. Time and man spread him South and Westward into Egypt, where he became known as the Numidian horse. Centuries later, modified by both the desert environment and the needs of the people, he came under the hands of the

The Spanish-Barb, brought to this country by the Spaniards, has cow-sense developed after centuries of working bovines.

Moslems and traveled the entire northern half of Africa during the Moslem Conquest.

Raised and nurtured in the differing climes of Lybia and the Barbary States of Tunisia, Morocco and Algeria, he was called Lybian, Turkamen and Barb. Still under Moorish command, the Barb horse and his Saracen masters invaded Spain in 711 A.D. where, under Moorish breeding programs, the Barb later became the foundation for the renowned Spanish horses of the Fourteenth and Fifteenth centuries.

This is the horse that served both in Spain and the New World and it was here, the Western Hemisphere, that addi-

While his blood is found in many breeds, the Spanish-Barb isn't a large registry here. He's a game horse.

tional Barb blood was infused by the direct importation of Barb horses from Africa. Spain, all but depleting the countryside of available stock, refused to ship anymore of her famous horses to her colonists in the Western Hemisphere.

Thus, the Spanish-Barb, bred and raised in North America by the early Spanish settlers for three centuries, again played his part in the history of yet another continent. He became a reliable and capable mount for the Indians and early frontiersmen, and a superior cowhorse for the Anglo-American cattleman. For over three centuries this enduring little horse served the various inhabitants of a new country and was a dominant factor in the growth and development of the American Southwest. But the end of an era was at hand and the Spanish-Barb soon hovered on the brink of extinction.

Americans, determined to mold and shape everything different into their own concepts, began changes that would forever alter the face of the frontier. The hardy and exceptional Longhorn cattle were gradually replaced with Herefords and Shorthorns. Mile upon mile of fenceline established boundaries of the cattle empires, reducing the need for vast crews of cowboys and their Spanish cowponies. Thoroughbreds, Morgans and Hamiltonians were brought in from the East and crossed with the Spanish horse to obtain more size and speed. Competitors for the rangelands, the buffalo and Spanish-Barb's brother, the original mustang, were all but eliminated. The Indians, whose way of life differed so vastly from the American dream, were herded onto reservations and their horses slaughtered or castrated.

What, then, of the Spanish-Barb? How did this horse escape being completely cross-bred out of existence? How did this ancient breed survive at all?

Each country and each era produces its share of men who recognize and appreciate those things which have genuine value. It is due to the farsightedness and tenacity of these widely scattered individuals that several proven strains of this horse remain in America to this day. Because of their stubborn belief in the superiority of this breed over the larger cross-breds, they continued to breed, use and retain pride in the horse that had served their ancestors before them. Due to the persistence of a few, a remarkable breed has survived in quality, though not in quantity.

What factor draws people to and involves them with the Spanish-Barb? What does this horse possess that causes his owners to consider him superior to all others? Owners and breeders alike make claims for this horse; are they merely bragging or does the Spanish-Barb really have something special? What, if any, are the notable contrasts between the Spanish-Barb and other breeds of horses?

One of the more important variations lies within the skeletal structure. The majority of horses have six lumbar vertebrae, eighteen thoracic vertebrae and an oval front cannon bone. The Arabian is separated from this group, as studies by R. M. Stetcher in 1967 have shown the majority to carry six lumbar vertebrae but one less thoracic, although this genetic trait may vary. The Spanish-Barb is unusual in that he has but five lumbar vertebrae (sometimes five and a piece), seventeen thoracic vertebrae and a round, dense front cannon bone. This strong-bodied breed matures later than other breeds, but they have an exceptionally long and useful lifespan.

The exterior of the Spanish-Barb appears much the same as other breeds, but here, too, dissimilarities are found. The chestnuts of the Barb are small, smooth and flush with the leg and many times missing altogether on the hind legs. The feathering and fetlocks are quite sparse and curled tightly against the legs. Remarkably smooth gaits are consistently

Hardy and not overly big, the Spanish-Barb primarily is used by ranchers today, but has qualities for entry in a stock horse contest. His owners state he's intelligent.

inherent in this breed. The eyes are large and set well forward in an attractive head.

The average size, 13.3 to 14.2 hands, plays a vital part in his ability to perform at maximum efficiency, as the organs carrying oxygen are in perfect balance with the body and the blood circulates faster. A larger horse, having the same size thorax, has organs that must work much harder to supply the brain and muscles with life-giving oxygen that enables him to function. Primarily a thrifty, grass-fed animal with grain supplemented only at times of rigorous use, Spanish-Barbs are exceptionally "easy keepers."

These are some of the unique physical characteristics belonging only to the Spanish-Barb. There are other differences, not always visible to the naked eye, that set this breed apart.

Contrary to the general aggressive nature of stallions, Spanish-Barb studs are of a calm, reliable nature and easily handled. When in pastures or large runs with their mares, they show great concern for their foals and will come to their aid as quickly as the dam. Geldings prove quite friendly to foals and are not at the bottom of the pecking order when pastured with mares and foals. They retain many of the protective mannerisms of the stallion and are inclined to herd and watch over mares with which they are pastured.

When pastured with another breed of horse, the Spanish-Barb tends to remain clannish and once the initial investiga-

tion and acquaintance period is over, keep to themselves. Endowed with a high degree of intelligence and a sensible nature, this breed — from foal to adult — is not panicked easily. When trapped by a tangle of undergrowth, the ensnaring branches of deadwood or coiled barbed wire, they will calmly attempt to free themselves and, if unsuccessful, will patiently await human assistance. However, it is in training and use that the exceptional disposition, intelligence, inborn cow-sense and athletic abilities of the Spanish-Barb are amply displayed.

Cooperation between man and animal is essential for top performance. The physical ability to perform specific acts also is a vital factor in all the areas of work, show or pleasure, and the Spanish-Barb has the features that bring about the finest relationship between man and beast, which produce the finest results in performance. The Spanish-Barb's short back, dense bone structure and efficient size all combine to make him an enduring and highly competitive athlete. A sensitive, intelligent brain accompanied by a capable, athletic body produces an animal that gives pleasure and satisfaction to his owner.

As with any horse, but especially with the Spanish-Barb, the trainer must know what he wants and how to properly ask for it. A genuine appreciation and feeling for this breed is essential to success in training, as the Spanish-Barb is amazingly intuitive in his relationships with humans. The ability to learn exceptionally fast and a willingness to do what is asked of him by a trainer who understands his nature shortens the practice period for each phase of training. Because of his high degree of intelligence, the Spanish-Barb has a definite need for purpose of action, and daily variation and challenge in routines.

The Spanish-Barb has had a strong effect on history, to be sure. Several years ago, concerned horsemen began an effort to return the game horse to its rightful and deserving place in the scheme of things equestrian. Breeders of these horses, realizing a concentrated and united effort must be made if the original Spanish Barb breed was to be firmly re-established, decided to pool their knowledge, efforts and time. The result was the formation of a strict and protective organization, the Spanish-Barb Breeders Association, a non-profit corporation whose breeding programs are insuring the continuation of the first horses domestically bred on the North American continent. Today, the enduring, inherited qualities of stamina and intelligence, which have served man throughout the centuries, are waiting to again serve in whatever capacities are needed.

This is the Spanish-Barb; a horse of ancient heritage, a rare and exceptional animal that is once more demonstrating his worth to yet another generation of man.

THE COLOR BREEDS

AS STATED IN the chapter on breeding horses, a good horse is a good horse, regardless of his coloring. This hasn't always been the philosophy, however, as indicated by this lymric that virtually was law through the recent decades:

One white sock, buy him!
Two white socks, try him!
Three white socks, deny him!
Four white socks and a white nose,
Take off his hide and feed it to the crows!

As far back as history has been recorded, the colored breeds have been favored mounts of noblemen and even wars were fought to gain possession of them. Until relatively recent times, in fact, colored horses have been retained for ceremonial functions or as silver screen companions for the white-hatted cowboys.

Exactly what triggered this attitude change is unknown, perhaps personal philosophy or some factual basis. For example, the Bedouin tribesmen believed the chestnut-colored Arab superior to those of other colors, followed closely by the bay-colored horses. Those of white coloration supposedly were lacking in stamina and couldn't handle the exceptionally hot desert conditions. This belief hasn't been borne out in recent times, but, of course, the Arab today isn't put to the same tests as his forebears.

There are some horsemen today who feel that a splash of white extending upwards from a hoof denotes a weakness in that hoof. This loss of pigment hasn't proved to inhibit the normal function or strength of the hoof whatsoever.

Still, there are individuals who claim one breed or one color superior to all others in some given task. Presumably, these individuals could be compared with the owner of one brand of automobile: to him, no other is comparable to the make he's been buying and driving for years, regardless of proven test results. For these individuals, there's usually no way to change their preconceived notions; probably, they already have skipped this section entirely.

It is our feeling that a good horse is a good horse, whether he's bay, gray, chestnut, roan, spotted or splotched with combinations. There was, for some years, speculation that the albino horse — a pure white color — was characterized by shortened lifespan or eyesight difficulty, caused by the lack of pigment in the skin. This is a claim that the American Albino Association has been refuting continuously. We endorse the statement of the late "Sunny Jim" Fitzsimmons: "It's what you can't see that matters."

Under the color breed heading are found the Appaloosa, paint, pinto, palomino, albino and buckskin. All now have specific registries and, since the Appaloosa is largest, we'll begin by detailing its history.

THE APPALOOSA HORSE

The spotted ancestors of the Appaloosa are known to have existed in the time of Cro-Magnon man, since cave paintings in France and Spain depict galloping horses with the coat distinctly spotted; usually black on a light brown or white body. These paintings weren't made to commemorate the horse. Rather, they were magical symbols to the early hunters to aid in the taking of the spotted horses as food.

As stated in the first chapter, the exact time of domestication of any horse is unknown and the next recorded instance regarding the spotted horses was about 1000 B.C., in what today is Austria. The steppes-dwelling hordes who swept through in conquest of new territory from their Asian bases buried their dead with objects of value. Among these objects unearthed from one of the many crude cemeteries was a scabbard inscribed with a drawing of four spotted horses being ridden in line.

Dr. Francis Haines, who was instrumental in the establishment of the Appaloosa Horse Club and historian of note, found in his research the first printed mention of the spotted horse dates back to 480 B.C., in the writing of the Greek historian, Herodotus. He chronicled the ill-fated invasion of Greece by Xerxes, the king of Persia. He describes in some detail the special "sacred" horses used to draw Xerxes' chariot and implies that the spotted relatives of the Appaloosa at that time were part of a special breed reserved for the king and his high-ranking nobles. "The Persians also claimed that the greatest war horse ever known was the Appaloosa Rakush, owned and ridden by their folk hero, Rustem," states Dr. Haines.

Emperor Wu Ti, of China's Han Dynasty, learned of the beautiful Persian horses about 126 B.C. "He first tried to buy breeding stock from the Western tribes, offering large quantities of gold," reports Dr. Haines. "When his offers were refused, the emperor sent out his armies." The bitterly

The Appaloosa is one of America's most popular horses and can be found competing in the full gamut of Western events, like Western pleasure (left) or endurance competition. He was bred for work by his Nez Perce owners and he's colorful!

fought campaign dragged on for several years and, according to Chinese records, cost the lives of 40,000 men and 100,000 horses before the Appaloosas were captured and brought to China in 101 B.C. That Emperor Wu Ti wanted the spotted horses badly is a gross understatement of fact!

When in China, the emperor was so inspired that he wrote a poem in their honor under the title, "The Heavenly Horses from the Extreme West." Artists honored the horses with paintings and statues, showing beyond all doubt that they were ancient Appaloosas.

"From Persia, Appaloosas spread to the West across southern Russia, Germany and the Netherlands. By 1600, they had reached northern France. They appeared frequently in contemporary paintings of battles and hunting scenes. In 1774, King Louis XVI had a matched pair of the spotted horses to draw his hunting sleigh, with a matching pair of Dalmatian dogs to trot along behind," notes Dr. Haines.

In 1685, a spotted horse was imported to England. The breed became well-established there and continues to the present time. Early in the Eighteenth Century, some of the stock sent from England to Virginia were marked with spots on white-blanketed rumps.

His good disposition makes him well-suited to youth events like pole bending (above). He's got speed.

The rope race is standard at Appaloosa-only events (left), a holdover from the days of Nez Perce tribe.

He doesn't startle easily, even when passing porkers in a trail class (below)!

Strangely, Appaloosas never were popular in Africa, where they remain unknown to this day. The hostile attitude of the Spanish horsemen toward the breed helps explain why Appaloosas were not introduced into Argentina until 1920.

Since the Spanish weren't fond of the Appaloosa, it's only reasonable to assume they shipped large numbers to the horse-hungry settlers in Seventeenth Century Mexico. The first herds were shipped to Chihuahua either from northern Spain or Trieste, Austria.

Appaloosas were taken north from Chihuahua, probably by the Navajo Indians, and finally reached the Nez Perce country in the Columbia basin some two hundred and fifty years ago.

The Nez Perce obviously were pleased with the intelligence, stamina and colorful markings, as they chose to breed them in preference to other horses. During exploration of the West, the Nez Perce were the only tribe to have Appaloosas in number.

From about 1730 to 1830, the Nez Perce bred their

colorful horses to a distinctive type able to stand the rigors of mountain travel. They bred only the best of the animals and gelded or traded the poorer ones.

The area inhabited by the Nez Perce — the northeast corner of Oregon, the southeast corner of Washington and the bordering Idaho country — was ideal for horse production, providing lush summer range in the hills and meadows, and abundant winter range in the sheltered canyons of the Snake, Palouse and Clearwater rivers. The Nez Perce were fond of racing, with finish lines set from a few hundred yards to as far as twelve miles. Performance helped guide the Indians in eliminating the slow.

Close contact with the people of the tribe demanded a quiet, sensible disposition. This trait is common to Appaloosas today. The combination of stamina needed for racing and hunting, and disposition and good sense necessary for life around the camp tended to produce a superior horse.

One of the centers of the Appaloosa herds was the rolling hill country along the Palouse River in southeastern Washington. White settlers began calling the horses Palouses, then A Palousey and finally Appaloosa.

The other important center of Appaloosa breeding was the Wallowa country in northeastern Oregon. When the Wallowa band, under their leader, Chief Joseph, finally was driven from their homes in 1877, the large horse herd was estimated to be from one-third to one-half Appaloosas. These horses proved their worth that Summer, as they carried the tribesmen, their families and possessions across the mountains ahead of the U.S. cavalry. They dashed 1350 miles toward Canada over some of the ruggedest terrain in the West, outrunning five U.S. Army units: Were it not for a telegraph line and a handy steamer to ferry troops across the Missouri River, the Nez Perce would have made it.

After the surrender of Chief Joseph at the Bear Paw Mountains in Montana, the Appaloosa, bred to perfection by the Nez Perce, were sold and began assimilation into other breeds. This was due to the missionary and Indian Agent belief that it was sinful for any Indian to own such speedy and beautiful horses. Perhaps, too, there lay in their minds the possibility that this war might have to be repeated in the future, if the Nez Perce retained their swift steeds.

A revival of interest in Western riding horses after World War I finally led to the formation of the Appaloosa Horse Club in 1938, with headquarters at Moro, Oregon. Claude Thompson, a horse raiser and wheat farmer, started the movement. In 1947, headquarters of the club were moved to Moscow, Idaho. The club has held a national show each year since 1948.

Today, there are more than 60,000 owners of Appaloosas who have registered more than 150,000 horses. Appaloosas comprise the third largest breed registry in the world and it still is growing. The Appaloosa officially became a breed when the club's stud books were examined and recognized by the National Association of Stallion Registration Boards in 1950.

There is much confusion over the color patterns and other distinguishing characteristics of the Appaloosa breed. We first will detail differences not connected with coat coloration.

The Appaloosa is the only horse breed that has a white eyeball, correctly termed the sclera, surrounding the colored iris of the eye. Iris color varies, but for the most part is a rich, deep brown.

Another distinguishing difference lies in the Appy's striped hoof. These stripes, sometimes present on all four hoofs, are vertical from pastern to the base of the hoof wall. It should be noted that not all Appaloosas have strongly noticeable laminations. Dampening the hoof generally will make it show up better.

One of the most telltale signs a horse is of Appaloosa breeding is through parti-colored (mottled) skin always evident in the genital region. It sometimes is visible around the lips, muzzle, nostrils or eyes.

As a breed, the Appaloosa tends toward a sparse mane and tail. Some, called "finger-tails" or "rat-tails," show little more than a stump for a tail. Not all horses have this characteristic, but a larger percentage do.

Another aid in determination of the breeding of this horse is termed a "varnish mark." Most common in Appys of roan coloration, a varnish mark is a section of the coat where a grouping of dark hairs predominates. These spots usually are on the nose and face, above the eye, on the point of the hip, behind the elbow, and in the gaskin and stifle region. If a horse has varnish marks and the other characteristics outlined thus far, bet your money that he's an Appaloosa.

When discussing Appaloosa coloration, it should be remembered that no one pattern or color is indicative of the breed. The Appaloosa can run the full line of equine colors and have one of six different patterns, but the relative value of one over another is dependent upon personal tastes.

The six basic patterns are: spotted blanket, white blanket, leopard, snowflake, frost and marble. There is one void in this classification system: What about the horse that's a solid color, or that doesn't quite fit into one of these categories?

The Appaloosa Horse Club long has recognized the need for another category, one which essentially contains horses with a lack of typical Appaloosa coloring. A heading for this category is "marginal" and it contains horses showing only faint traces of the traditional color patterns, or showing none at all. Appaloosa Horse Club officials state that a horse in this category should strongly manifest other characteristics of the breed, however, and this lack of color needn't be indicative of that horse's reduced value in the stud. A well-made horse is a well-made horse, regardless of nature's fluke in not finishing with the coloring.

As noted in the chapter on breeding horses, individuals desiring offspring from their marginal animals should endeavor to strengthen the areas in which the horse is weak; in this case, color. The marginal horse should be bred to one showing a strong color marking, with the hopes the offspring will acquire the spotted markings of one parent and the good qualities of the marginal parent.

THE PAINT HORSE

There is a great deal of confusion over the difference between a pinto and a paint horse and, before tracing the horses back into history, this should be clarified.

Today's paint horse is a special kind of quarter horse with a lot of coat color. Every paint is a pinto, but not every pinto can be registered as a paint. Pintos, for instance, crop up occasionally in other breeds besides the quarter horse — the Arabian, for example — but these occurrences aren't widely publicized.

This accidental coloring, according to some breeders, is the result of what is called a cropout: After intense breeding of solid-colored horses specifically for that solid color, a two-tone horse is produced. This seems a far less logical explanation that that of scientists, who feel this colored gene is present at some point in the horse's ancestry, but has been recessive until the present. Clearly, there is still much to be learned on the subject of genetics!

Since there now are specific registries for both of the colored horses, we shall deal with them as separate entities when discussing their positions in today's horse industry. When going into the past, however, we must lump them

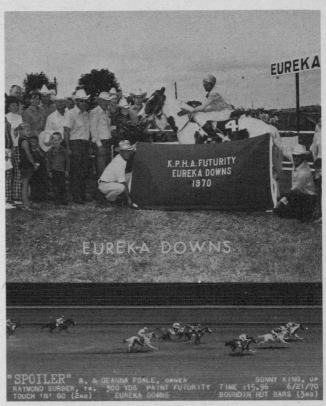

The paint horse, because of his quarter horse background, also finds favor with barrel racers (left) and competes strongly in racing. It's Patti Oswalt and Sequoyah Chief on barrels, and Spoiler with Sunny King up winning Kansas Paint Futurity.

together under the heading of painted horses, since no ancient scholars distinguished the difference.

This species of horse goes way back, almost to the beginning of recorded history. We know, for example, that painted horses existed in 3400 B.C., since Egyptians painted their likeness on the walls of tombs. Where the color came from — was it natural development of a camouflage color? Did a zebra sneak into the ancestry somewhere back in the hazy past? — can't be determined, but the spread of the painted horses is known: besides Egypt, they also were in India, Tibet and Mongolia.

Perhaps the first painted horse to be seen in the New World came with the Spanish Conquistador Cortez. At least, in the write-up of Cortez' exploits, Spanish priest Bernal Diaz described one horse so marked as having been with the entourage.

Exactly how the painted horses came to be in the New World in any numbers is unclear but, like other colored horses, they were favorites of the Indian tribes, especially the Comanches. The warlike plains-dwellers demanded a tough, intelligent horse, and this they found in the painted animals. This hardiness increased their value in the eyes of the cowboys who followed the cattle herds into the Southwest, leading to the association to which legend and song have been devoted.

Even up to modern times, the paint horse has been considered the Cadillac of the cowpoke. The derivation of both cow-sense of the quarter horse and the hardiness of his early ancestors continues to make this breed a favorite with the working cattleman.

Paint breeders today are striving for a finely featured horse whose conformation is not heavy like the bulldog quarter horse. He is long-muscled, short-coupled and, ideally, is the perfect mixture of the savvy old cowpony, the modern cutting quarter horse and the streamlined thoroughbred of today. These are the future goals of the

American Paint Horse Association, which was founded as the American Paint Stock Horse Association in 1962.

If the confusion between what's a pinto and what's a paint weren't enough, there still is the confusing matter of the color pattern of the paint: Is he overo or tobiano?

Tobiano and overo don't refer to any particular color such as sorrel, bay, black or gray, but to the location of the white on a paint horse. Neither do the patterns refer to basically white or basically dark horses as such, since there

Paints frequently are seen in the stock horse event, like Koko Bars. Is he overo or tobiano? See text for details.

Paint horses, because of their cow-sense and durability, were great favorites of early cowpokes and still today are used in arroyos of the nation. In the arena, paints like Snip Bar have put cash in the pockets of their partners, here Bill James.

are examples of both coat colors striding around America today. The difference lies in the location of the white, not in the amount.

"One of the first characteristics to look for in identifying the tobiano will be in the head, which is usually marked like that of a solid-color horse," says APHA Executive Secretary Sam Ed Spence. "It will be dark without any white at all, or it will have a blaze, stripe, star or snip. Whenever an apron face appears on the tobiano, it is often the sign of a tobiano/overo cross.

"A second characteristic to look for in the tobiano — and one which almost always holds true — is that the legs will be white at least below the knees and hocks. Very seldom will a tobiano have a solid-color leg.

"A final distinguishing trait of the tobiano is its regular and distinct spots often coming in oval or round patterns that extend down over the neck and chest, giving the appearance of a shield. The tobiano usually has a dark spot in each flank and often will have 'suspenders' — that is, a white front leg with white extending up over the shoulder and over the withers."

Overos, on the other hand, give the impression of having been splashed with white paint from the belly up, rather than from the back down, which is the case with the tobiano.

"It is rare to see an overo which has white crossing its back between its withers and tail set," notes Spence. "This perhaps is the best rule to use in determining if a horse truly is an overo, although there may be exceptions."

The overo almost never has four white legs from the knees and hocks down. Sometimes all four legs will be dark, but more often three will be solidly dark.

Another giveaway area is the head and, almost without exception, the overo will have some white present. Overo head markings generally come in bald, apron or even bonnet-face patterns.

Because of the predominately white markings on the head, cases of glass or blue eyes are more prevalent in the overo than the tobiano. This is not to infer there's anything wrong with a horse having these eyes: he's as normal as the next horse.

The overo usually has scattered, splashy markings, different than the oval or round patterns of the tobiano. These generally are referred to as calico or lightning patterns.

A final distinguishing difference involves the tail of the horse. Tobianos commonly have a mixture of white and dark hairs in the tail. The overo seldom does; it's usually either light or dark, rarely mixed.

The overo/tobiano cross is a whole 'nuther ball game, however. Sometimes both patterns will emerge in the offspring resulting from this mating. Other times, perfectly marked tobianos will appear, or perfectly marked overos.

"The most common product of the tobiano/overo cross seems to be a predominately white tobiano pattern, sometimes with overo traits about the head; that is, a bonnet face or white head with dark ears," reports Sam Ed Spence.

Of course, if this is altogether too complicated, when registering a paint horse, don't record whether he's overo or tobiano; leave it to the breed registry. After examination of the photographs, determination will be made and noted on the registration certificate.

Mrs. Rebecca Tyler of Gainesville, Texas, and E.J. "Junior" Hudspeth of Era, Texas, officially formed the American Paint Stock Horse Association in 1962. With Mrs. Tyler as the secretary-treasurer, the APSHA began registering horses in the late Summer of that year and, by the end of 1962, had more than 250 horses listed, along with some 150 members.

In 1963, the offices were moved to Amarillo under its first executive, Ralph Morrison. The year ended with 1041 numbered horses, 255 appendix registrations and a membership of almost 800.

The association continued to grow in size and prestige and, in 1965, a major step forward was taken when officers and directors of the APSHA made preliminary agreements with the officers of the American Paint Quarter Horse Association of Abilene, Texas, to consolidate the two organizations. In June, 1965, the consolidation was ratified by the memberships of the two associations, and the new American Paint Horse Association emerged. The combined membership rose to over 1300 by August, with total registrations numbering over 3800.

The Paint Horse Association has grown remarkably in the last several years, as more people become attracted to the "sports model of the horse industry," as APHA is wont to call their favorite. In 1973, for example, association growth was up twenty percent over 1972. There are more than 27,000 paint horses now registered.

THE PINTO HORSE

With all this discussion of color, let's not forget the pinto horse. "Pinto" was the first American term used to refer to pinto horses, and it comes from the Spanish word "pintado," meaning "painted." The Pinto Horse Association of America, Incorporated, an international registry, uses the term pinto because of its universal significance regarding these specially spotted horses.

"The pinto genetic factors have existed from prehistoric times, along with all other horse color traits," writes Mrs. Roxanne Greene, editor of the association's magazine. "In recent centuries, systematic prejudice has removed it from many of the so-called 'pure' breeds of horses. It appears regularly in many of these breeds because some of the pinto

Showmen of all ages can compete in the pinto Western showmanship class and build points toward championship awards.

characteristics are recessive and difficult to eliminate entirely."

Three main types of pinto horses are bred, with specific conformation traits that lend well to the performance commonly associated with the outcross represented. These are the stock type, saddle type and pleasure type. Like paints, they can be tobiano or overo.

By far, the majority of the horses are of stock-type conformation and breeding, which means they are largely quarter horse or thoroughbred in bloodlines, and Western horses in performance. The saddle type is an English-type horse with the high head and neck carriage, and animated action of gaited horses. The predominant outcross for saddle-type pintos is the American Saddle Horse. Saddle-type horses are shown in a full mane and tail, often with an elevated tail.

The pleasure type is an all-around pleasure horse for English and Western use, with good, light horse conformation and medium size. The predominant outcross for pleasure-type pintos is the Arabian Horse Council Registry Arabian, and The Jockey Club thoroughbred.

To qualify as a pinto horse, the animal's amount of white or dark color, whichever is less, must conform to one of the following size specifications: one spot of seventy-five square inches (the size of a large dinner plate); two or more spots each twenty-five square inches (the size of a large saucer); or three or more spots each fifteen square inches (the size of a man's palm). The spot requirements must be on the body of the horse, to the exclusion of the entire legs and head, and the spots must be visible to a person in a normal standing position.

The Pinto Horse Association considers these requirements liberal and instigated them for a number of reasons. First, they feel the credibility of the breed is harmed if the animals of poor color and indistinct pattern appear in the show ring or are used in breeding. Too, the small, recessive white markings are common in many breeds and are not necessarily indicative of genetic pintoism. It isn't fair to breeders and buyers of pintos to suggest that these animals are pintos or that they could transmit pinto characteristics to their offspring. Finally, the association maintains a solid-color breeding stock division for horses with pinto parentage and insufficient color for the main registry. These horses may be registered for breeding use at the option of the owner, but they may not be exhibited as pinto horses.

The association has some solid reasons for the breeding of three distinct conformation types. "Rather than develop one type which can perform any requirement in a mediocre way, the three types enable owners and breeders to work with the kind of horse they prefer, and develop individuals outstanding enough for open competition," notes Mrs. Greene. "Also, it is contrary to the theory and promotion of a color breed to specify a single type of horse, since it excludes earnest horse breeders who prefer their color on a different type. The last reason is that the oldest known

Hooper's Sir Prize is one of the best pinto cutting horses owned and ridden by Al Hooper (below). A slow, cautious horse is what trail judges like to see, so they must have been pleased with the performance of Circles J (below).

registry for pintos, The Pinto Horse Society, maintained the separation of popular types. The Pinto Horse Association is based on the PHS registry, which now is part of the PtHA registry records."

All pintos are inspected before being registered, a practice that aids in eliminating undesirable color and conformation characteristics, and is indispensable to the production of a dependable breed of animals.

The Pinto Horse Association of America, Incorporated, was formed in 1956 to carry on the registration and breeding of good pinto horses begun in the 1930s by the Pinto Horse Society. The records of the American Pinto Horse Association also were included in the registry at a later time. It now is the major and international registry for horses with pinto marking patterns.

THE PALOMINO HORSE

The origin of the palomino probably is one of the most controversial subjects one can find when attempting to authenticate the history and background of this horse with the golden coat, and contrasting white mane and tail.

The palomino has appeared in myth, legend and fact from the beginnings of earliest history. They were ridden by the emperors of China. The Greek warrior, Achilles, rode with his two super horses, Balios and Xanthos, who were "yellow as gold, swifter than stormwinds." And in Spain, it was Queen Isabella who owned many of the golden horses that became known as Golden Isabells. These

Orren Mixer creates another eye feast with this painting of an ideal palomino horse. Ancient in history, the breed is popular today and used for all manner of ceremonies.

Michele Macfarlane's Flashy Stonewall Peavine is a top parade horse (above). Danny Glisson's Oklahoma Q-Ton, international champion gelding, is superstar of breed.

Cutie's Star Bar, a palomino quarter mare, was sired by a son of immortal Three Bars. That her conformation was pleasing is blue-ribbon-obvious. Palominos must meet rigid requirements, as outlined in the text.

probably all were palominos and an American group devoted to the preservation of the mounts of Queen Isabella is called the Ysabella Saddle Horse Association, Inc.

There are several versions of the meaning of the word "palomino." Perhaps the closest association we can find of the word with the horse it describes comes from Spain. A species of grape still is grown there that is called the palomino grape, no doubt because of its golden color. Perhaps, then, we owe the origin of the name, palomino, to the Spaniards of early history.

It's been said that, when the Spanish Conquistador, Cortez, made his first journey to Mexico, he brought with him sixteen horses, one of which was purported to be a golden horse. Historians never have been able to verify that such a horse did exist and, like so many other theories

expounded over the years concerning the palomino's origin, the one concerning Cortez' palomino must be considered a piece of romantic supposition.

Perhaps, then, it would seem more practical to date the accurate history of the golden palomino with the beginning of the first organization formed for the recording of bloodlines of palominos. In the early 1930s, Dick Halliday began researching the palomino horse and, at the same time, writing numerous articles about the horses in many of the national magazines such as Colliers. Through his articles, he was able to create a considerable amount of interest in the golden horse, to the extent that, in 1936, he incorporated the first registry association for the palomino, the Palomino Horse Association. For his first horse to be registered, he chose a stallion owned by Dwight Murphy, a well-known

Yellow Straw Jr., a son of Yellow Straw, gallops alongside his bay quarter horse dam. Mane and tail will whiten later.

Glistening under a small fortune in silver appointments, Richmar's Double Eagle, a palomino American saddlebred, competes in the palomino parade horse class.

rancher in the Santa Ynez Valley of Southern California. The stallion's name was Rey De Los Reyes, and he sired many good palominos.

During the first few years of registration activity, little effort was made by breeders to breed for quality or conformation. Of necessity, many horses were registered on color only, primarily because there had been little record-keeping on the ranches of California prior to the interest created in palominos by Halliday.

"By the early 1940s, however, it became quite apparent to palomino breeders that color alone was not enough if progress was to be made in furthering the golden horses," comments Willard Beanland, spokesman for the association. "It was during this period that horse shows were being staged for palominos only and competition, together with demand for horses that would win, prompted breeders to inject the blood of already recognized breeds into their breeding programs. More and more, it became apparent that one could have the golden color in such breeds as the quarter horse, saddlebred and, occasionally, in the Morgan."

By the late 1940s, the golden color had become so popular in the saddlebred that a special association was formed just to promote them. At the same time the quarter horse was achieving its popularity with that trend, the palomino quarter horse came into its own. Today, there are thousands of palominos that are double-registered not only as palominos, but also in the breed recognized in the light horse division. Although the palomino is extensively used in English performance classes such as fine harness, under flat saddles and as parade horses, he probably is most often seen under Western equipment as a stock horse, Western pleasure, trail horse or in other Western-type competition.

At the beginning of the palomino's popularity, the golden horse found ready acceptance in all of the major parades throughout the Southwest. The Tournament of Roses Parade in Pasadena, California, long has been associated with the palomino under spectacular silver equipment. The

colorful city of Santa Barbara, California, has for many years featured the palominos in its traditional Spanish Days Fiesta Parade.

The requirements to register a palomino in the Palomino Horse Association have changed to some degree over the past thirty-five years. However, the basic requirements have remained pretty much the same.

"The color requirements are described as being that of a newly minted gold coin, with some degree of lighter or darker shades permitted," explains Willard Beanland. "The mane and tail are described as white with a percentage of dark hairs permitted. White stockings are permitted to the knees.

"One of the parents of the offspring to be registered must either be a registered palomino or registered in one of the light horse breeds as prescribed in the rules for registration. Horses with blue, moon, pink or glass eyes are not acceptable for registration. In addition, no horse whose sire or dam was an albino, Appaloosa or pinto shall be eligible for registration.

"An Associate Certificate of Registration is provided for horses of acceptable conformation and color that don't have a registered sire or dam," adds Beanland. "This ruling applies to mares only and a permanent certificate can be issued an associate-registered mare who has produced two qualified palomino foals. They, in turn, then would be eligible for a regular certificate of registration."

From the time the Palomino Horse Association first was incorporated in 1936 until 1973, their national headquarters were maintainted in Reseda, California. Over the past two decades, however, the center of palomino activity shifted from the West Coast to the Midwest and East. To better serve the majority of palomino owners and breeders, the national headquarters were moved to Jefferson City, Missouri, under the direction of Robert Dallmeyer, executive secretary.

THE ALBINO HORSE

Down through the ages, kings and other leaders chose snow white horses to carry their royal personages in ceremonial functions and in battles. Easily identified on the battlefronts, the white-horse-mounted leaders spurred flagging spirits and often turned the tides of battle. Notable among these leaders were Spain's El Cid, France's Napoleon Bonaparte and America's General and later President Zachary Taylor, along with numerous American Indian chieftains.

For some reason, within relatively recent times horsemen associated the albino, as the white horse is called, with other oddballs of nature. The word spread around was that

The American Albino traces back to one sire, Old King, and this stallion projects Morgan/Arab features of the breed (above). White horses still are seen in movies.

Snow white brood mares occupy one of several large pastures at White Horse Ranch in 1950s. The ranch is being restored after being closed early in 1960s.

31

A past grand champion performance and reserve champ white mare is Patch of Cotton, showing her skills on the barrels with owner Phyllis Macdougall sitting the run.

Snow King (above), bred by the White Horse Ranch and owned by Rose Simmering, shows grand champion form. Anderson's American Albinos (below and at top on page 33) are six-horse liberty drill and perform crowd-pleasing hind leg stand here.

the white horse was weak, suffered eyesight problems and couldn't handle the sun because of his pink skin.

The American Albino Association, founded as the American Albino Horse Club, Incorporated, in 1937 by Caleb Thompson, is out to change this belief and return the white horse to a place of prominence in the light horse industry.

The American albino traces to a single white stallion, "Old King," who allegedly was of Morgan/Arab breeding. Bought by Caleb and Hudson Thompson, "Old King" began the white strain at AAA headquarters near Naper, Nebraska, being bred to a band of Morgan mares. At first, the registry accepted only dominant white horses. In the last three decades or so, they have begun accepting off-white horses of ivory through creme coloring under a separate listing of American Creme Horses.

The American albino can be of any breed and today primarily is used as a pleasure animal. Still a favorite of moviemakers, the white horses continue to appear on the silver screen occasionally. But the AAA is a long way from having their animals readily accepted by the majority of the horsemen in the country, and perhaps this will change.

These highly trained white horses, ridden by Carley Daugherty, performed at the Tennessee Walking Horse Celebration in Tennessee. Exciting isn't quite the word!

One of the Texas White Horse Troupe's acts, as performed at Hamburg, New York, is the Indian Fantasy, in which "Indian maidens" take hurdles (right). The albino is a favorite of entertainers.

THE BUCKSKIN HORSE

The buckskin horses in America, at this time, do not belong to any one pure breed, although proponents of the buckskin feel he may well represent a specific and separate breed within himself.

Buckskin researchers feel the horse traces back to a Norwegian Dun, a horse of antiquity that favored the cold climes of northern Europe. A buckskin in color, many authorities believe he derived this color from matings with the Sorraia, the original and always-buckskin-colored horse of Spain.

It is believed that the horse imported from Spain to the New World at the time of conquest had some of the genes of the Sorraia, which still exists in Spain today. This gene continued in the offspring of horses bred in Mexico and, when these Spanish horses were bred with the quarter types brought from the East after the Revolutionary War, this could explain why there are many quarter horses of buckskin, dun or grulla colors.

The skin of the buckskin, dun or grulla always is black. The eyes are dark and rarely show a white sclera. White markings are at a minimum and, as the blood is strengthened, the white markings tend to disappear. The "Dun Factor," as geneticists call it, is equalled in strength only by the gray color gene.

This "Dun Factor" can readily be seen in the hair of the buckskin when examined under a microscope. Colors other than buckskin have pigment granules in the hair that are distributed evenly, the color depending upon density of the granules. In buckskin, dun or grulla, however, the pigment granules are located only down one side of the hair shaft, with the other side being transparent.

A description of the colors is necessary: True buckskin is a shade of yellow, from gold nearly to brown, but not to red. The horse's points (mane, tail and legs) should be black or dark brown. A dorsal stripe, following the spine from withers to croup, isn't required.

Dun ranges from yellow to pale creme, with darker points. Sometimes these points may be just darker shades of the coat color; light brown, dark yellow, etc. The mane, tail and legs must be darker than the body color. The dorsal stripe is necessary on some duns.

The grulla, pronounced grew-ya, has a smoke-colored body, often the exact shade of a mouse, with no white hairs mixed in. These are often called "blue buckskins" and a dorsal stripe is necessary always.

The final color category is the red dun. This horse has a dun body coat of flesh color or pinkish-red. His points are dark red or red mixed with black and they must be darker than the body color. Again, a dorsal stripe must be present.

There currently are two organizations registering buckskin, dun and grulla horses, the International Buckskin Horse Association and the American Buckskin Registry Association. Both are worldwide in scope.

Just about any breed of horse has been used in what traditionally are regarded as Western events, as explained in a following chapter. Those listed here are the most popular and any are capable of providing the Western horseman with years of enjoyment, no matter his event preference.

Joyce Leuthold puts buckskin champion Charge Moore through trail class at Yreka, California (left). Pretty Doll Buck, the first buckskin to earn Superior Award for more than 50 points in one class, competes with Sue Atchley on tough trail course.

This fine champion gelding, Poco Guinea, won Registers of Merit in Western pleasure, trail, Western riding and reining (above), piloted by Harry Hayes. Janet Warne exhibits Sad Song, an ABRA/AQHA registered mare that won Registers of Merit in Western pleasure, Western riding and trail. While the buckskin isn't yet a breed proper, historians feel he may represent one.

Chapter 3

LEARN TO RIDE

There's A Great Deal More To Riding Than Throwing A Leg Over, As Explained Here!

WITH THE CURRENT popularity of horseback riding, it would seem Americans are blessed with an innate knowledge of horsemanship somehow passed down through the generation since man first began his association with equines. There appears little more to the art than simply throwing a leg over Old Paint's back and cantering away.

As many would-be horsemen discover, there's a great deal more to the subject of riding, however. In this chapter, we intend to take the grounded novice, place him properly on the back of a steed and advance him to the point he's qualified to sit a Western pleasure class competently. As with any other endeavor, you get out of horseback riding exactly what you put in. With this as our guiding maxim, the first topic concerns catching the horse in a pen; the initial phase of ride preparation.

An old movie, "The Russians Are Coming! The Russians Are Coming!" was more than simply wholesome entertainment. Throughout the screen epic, the director cut to a scene in which the town drunk, out in a pasture, was attempting to catch "Old Bess" in order to make a Paul Revere-type ride warning the townspeople of the Russians' approach. He finally did catch "Old Bess" and make his ride, but not until she had familiarized him with every square foot of her pasture.

This is a circumstance not merely dreamed-up by a Hollywood screenwriter. Rather, it's an actual occurrence in the pastures of America daily, but often the would-be rider gives up in frustration before catching his horse.

Rusty Richards lives on a small, thirty-seven-acre ranch and his horses roam free over its expanse. He recalls, "My four kids, because of their love of riding, have had to become pretty capable at catching horses. In the learning process, however, each has come to me at least once saying, 'Daddy, I can't catch my horse.' Whenever this happens, the first thing I do is ask, 'Did you take a bucket of grain along?' Although I sometimes could hardly hear the answer, as far as I can remember it always has been the same: 'No.' And my response also has always been the same: 'You did it wrong, then.'

"As far as I know," Richards adds, "the best way to

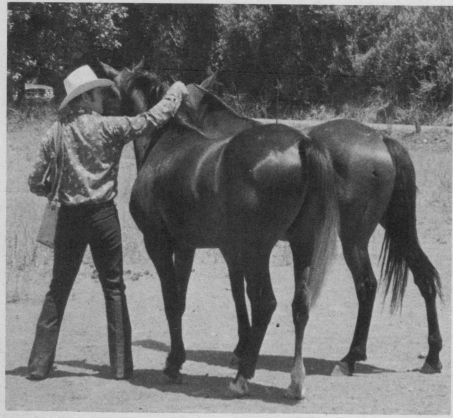

Before you can get into the mounted phases of horsemanship, you have to first catch the horse. In a pasture, this is best done by coiling lead rope and halter over arm, carrying an amount of grain in a handy bucket.

catch a horse out of a big, open field is to take along some grain in a bucket, keeping your halter and lead rope coiled up and slung over your shoulder."

Many horses will have nothing to do with you or your grain, if you try to approach them with the halter and lead rope dangling from your hand, and some even will spook if the lead rope is hanging down from your shoulder, bouncing around your knees.

Once the horse is eating grain from the bucket, slip the whole coil down your arm in such a way that it doesn't alarm the horse, then place it under his neck while reaching over the neck with the other hand. Then take the grain bucket away and lead him a few steps to let him know he's been caught. At this point, using your arms and the halter to form a circle around his neck, open the halter and slip it on him.

One word of caution: If you set the bucket of grain on the ground and let the horse eat, then lean over him to buckle the halter, he could throw his head up and hit you in the face with his poll.

Once in awhile you'll run into a horse that is very spooky about being caught and has his own bag of tricks. The way to best handle this horse is to leave a halter on him all the time. If you choose to do this, be sure the halter isn't so loose that it will snag on things. It also must not be

As the horse starts to eat, gently slip the lead rope and halter down the arm, then around his neck, using your arms to form a circle. This is simplest and easiest way.

It's a good idea to carry extra grain for other horses in the pasture and it makes it easier to catch them in future (below). This is especially helpful with spooky horses.

so tight that it will cut into the horse's head. Occasionally, someone will halter and turn out a horse that still is growing. The owners don't realize the horse will grow into the halter, until they see it cutting into his head. Consider, too, that some halters — especially cotton — will shrink when wet.

The main things to consider here are: 1. That the halter is well-fitted to the horse; 2. check regularly for halter shrinkage; and 3. if you should put a halter on a young, growing horse, adjust the halter from time to time, making sure it doesn't become too tight as he grows.

Another way to catch a spooky horse is to feed him grain from a bucket occasionally without trying to catch him, usually when you're after another horse. Take along some grain for him at this time and allow him to eat it, then leave without incident. A diving grab at the halter usually will only compound the problem.

When you do go to catch him, use a long rope with a good snap on the end. A longe line works well for this. Hold the bucket with both hands. As he reaches in for grain, snap into the halter ring with as little fuss as possible. The remainder of the rope should not be allowed to dangle, but in this case don't coil it around your body: this type of horse quite often will pull back and you could be injured.

Tuck the remainder of the rope up under one arm. If the horse does pull back, give him a little rope before trying to stop him, which gives you some leverage. Gloves are a good idea here, to prevent rope burns.

The first step is saddling is to use a thick pad or blanket of some type, positioned properly on his back. Make sure it's forward far enough to cover withers, to avoid bruising.

This technique might be useful to some, but this type of horse is not a good choice for beginners or children.

Now that you have caught your horse, take him to the area where you intend to groom and saddle him while tied up. When tying a horse, there are two important things to remember: 1. Never use a knot around the neck that can

One method of putting on saddle is shown (below). Note that cinch is tied up, as is latigo, the reasons for which are explained in text. Don't bang horse's side with stirrup.

slip and choke him. Some prefer using a strong halter and braiding the lead rope right into the halter ring; and 2. don't tie him to something he can pull over.

You'll often see horses tied by the reins, bits in their mouths, where they can and do cause serious injury. Horses have been tied to door knobs, water pipes, truck and car bumpers, and even to barbed wire fences. Of course, accidents can happen but this kind of thoughtlessness is just plain asking for trouble.

Don't tie your horse by the bridle reins and, if you're going any distance, take along a halter and lead rope. You either can put the halter on over the bridle, then tie the lead rope back to the saddlehorn, or coil them up and tie them to the saddle with the saddle strings.

When tying young horses, tie him to something strong, such as a tree limb or strong hitching rail. As a general rule, tie horses up fairly high where the rope can't slip down, such as through a crotch of a tree. However, if you are out on an overnight ride, you may have to use a picket line.

Here the horse must be tied so he can't slip up and down the line, yet must be able to reach the ground to eat. Ask for advice if needed.

Before getting into the subject of saddling the horse, let's jump ahead and talk about unsaddling, for reasons which will become clear.

When unsaddling, tie the cinch up with a saddle string. Some saddles have a rope thong which is a single leather strap, split at the end to form a loop. This can be strung through the cinch ring and the loop in the end can be placed over the horn.

The latigo strap hanging down should be secured in the

When the saddle is on, lift the pad and saddle at the fork, which prevents binding at the withers. This leads to really erratic performance, which can be dangerous to rider.

following manner: Take your left hand and pull it towards you, away from the horse. Then take your right hand and push the strap portion below your left hand up under the rigging ring. Pull the loop until the latigo is all even, as illustrated in the accompanying photographs.

Back to saddling: Be sure to use a good pad or blanket. Place it on the horse so it covers the withers. Put the saddle on by picking it up with the right hand under the pommel and swinging it up onto the horse's back. If you choose this method, be sure the stirrup doesn't slam the horse in the side or elbow.

If the saddle seems too heavy to perform this effectively, it is better to fold the stirrups and cinch back over the seat and hold the saddle by the cantle and horn, then place it upon the back carefully with both hands. Next, let the stirrup and cinch over the side until the saddle is hanging in balance, with the cinch and latigo still secured as they were when you unsaddled. Now take the horn of the saddle in your right hand and, at the same time, slip your left hand under the pad or blanket near the withers. Lift with both hands until the pad or blanket is pushed up all the way to the underside of the pommel. This is done to prevent binding across the withers as the cinch is pulled tight.

Reach over now and release the cinch from the saddle-horn, allowing it to fall straight along the opposite side of the horse. Look under the horse as you reach under and pull the cinch ring toward you to make sure it isn't twisted in any manner.

Take the tip of the latigo and insert it into the cinch ring and give it a pull. Here is one of the payoffs from the little bit of care taken when unsaddling, not to mention that you were able to put the saddle away and retrieve it without walking on the trailing latigo or being banged in the shins by the cinch ring!

A good technique is vitally important when bridling a horse. Most any horse will become troublesome if, every time someone comes at him with a bridle, he gets his ears handled roughly or gets clunked in the teeth with the bit.

To begin, unbuckle the halter and slip it off his nose while holding it with both hands to form a circle around his neck with your arms and the halter, in the same manner used when putting it on. Buckle the halter around his neck. This way, you still have hold of him when bridling.

Hold the top of the headstall with the left hand, standing on the left side of the horse. Take the right hand and reach under the neck and open his mouth by inserting your

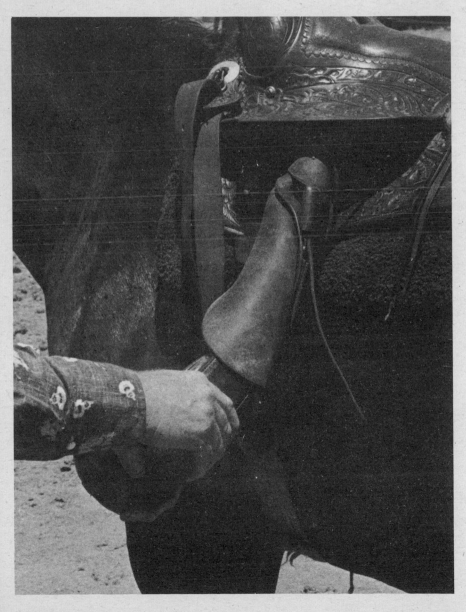

Sometimes a stirrup refuses to hang in the proper position, which can be cured by rolling the entire fender to the rear. If really recalcitrant, wet the fender and roll it up, then insert broom handle to hold it when on rack.

fingers at the corners and exerting downward pressure on the bars. At the same time, raise the bridle up his forehead with the left hand. The bit now is in position to enter the mouth.

Once the bit starts to enter the mouth, the right hand can be used to guide it and to pull the chin strap down under the chin, where it belongs. While continuing to hold the bit up firmly by lifting the top of the headstall, reach up and tuck in the ears and you've got him bridled.

Most young colts will take the bridle quite nicely at breaking time if they are approached this way. Once in awhile, however, one doesn't want his ears handled. "I've had pretty good luck with these by just unbuckling the headstall and not fooling with the ears at all during bridling. Later, when the colt is relaxed, I will try to unbridle him without unbuckling the headstall," says Rusty Richards, who has thirty years' experience with horses.

Another little trick used with good success is to put a little molasses on the bit before starting to bridle the colt. Most soon will open their mouths and reach for the bit if this method and a little patience are used.

Now that the horse has been saddled and bridled, unbuckle the halter from around his neck and get ready to mount up. Place the reins up over his neck, near the saddlehorn, and check to see that they are even. This probably seems overly basic but it's surprising how many people have gotten themselves into a real storm just by getting on a horse without checking to see that the reins are even. A well-broke horse will be apt to respond to the one-sided pull on the bit, caused by the reins being uneven.

This isn't to mean a novice should stay away from a well-trained horse. On the contrary, it's been proved that a really well-trained horse is much easier for a beginner to learn on — provided he has someone competent to help him — than on some old, sour thing that is full of tricks and

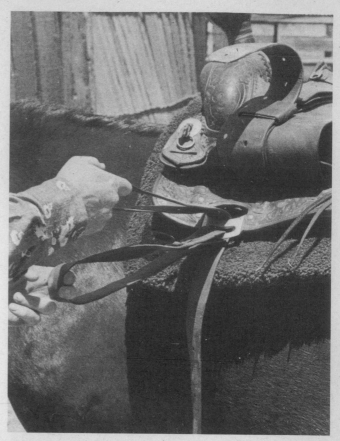

When removing tack, it's a good idea to run latigo strap through keeper. This saves treading on dangling end and, when tacking up, end simply is pulled down into cinch ring.

won't respond to cues at all. If the rider is a beginner who has bought a well-trained horse, it's a good idea to take some lessons from a professional to ensure that the horse isn't messed up.

Before going into the mounting procedures, here is a useful tip. Some saddles, especially new ones, are rather stiff and the stirrups won't hang properly. What you can do with a saddle like this is twist the stirrup toward the rear of the horse until even the fender is rolled up. This helps shape the leather in the fender so that, when the stirrup is released and allowed to unwind, it will hang in a more comfortable position. If the leather is really stiff and stubborn, the fenders can be moistened and a broom handle run through the stirrups when the saddle is put on the rack.

When mounting a horse, begin by standing alongside the horse near the shoulder. Grasp the reins — having made sure they're even — and a handful of mane about six inches in front of the pommel, then step behind the stirrup and turn to face forward. Your line of sight and the horse's vertebrae now form about a forty-five-degree angle.

Grasping the horn with the right hand while your left hand still holds the reins and mane, hop high enough to insert the left foot into the stirrup, then drop back to the ground with the right foot. Hop once more with your right foot and, at the same time, pull with your arms and rise straight up alongside the horse. Some beginners, in their

With the saddle positioned properly, let down the cinch as shown. Then reach under the horse for it, making sure it's not twisted. It then can be tightened with latigo.

Some horses are difficult to bit, because their ears are handled roughly and teeth get banged. On young mounts, molasses on bit aids procedure, as does proper application.

Remember, practice is the way to become proficient at anything, but practice in the proper manner.

There's been a lot of bunk written about cruelty to rodeo animals. In reality, the largest amount of suffering brought upon horses does not come from professionals, but rather from people who use horses for pleasure yet seem bent on remaining ignorant of even the most basic rules of good horsemanship. Don't fall into this category.

Rusty Richards, entertainer/horse trainer, relates an incident from his past that rivals the novice horseman's first ride in the saddle.

"I was working in a circus in Evansville, Indiana, that was held in a big indoor sports arena," he elaborates. "Each performance found me walking past a bunch of elephants in a hallway where they were kept prior to entering the circus ring. Not having been around elephants much, it gave me a mighty funny feeling to see them standing there weaving, untied, as I walked past. I kept wondering what was keeping them from chasing me right up — or through — the walls!

"It occurred to me that, had I been walking through a bull's pen, I would have had more control over the situation: I would have kept an eye out for an avenue of escape, such as a fence to climb or dive under. But with these elephants, I just followed the example of the seasoned veterans and walked past."

His curiosity over them grew, however, until he finally spotted the trainer and began asking him questions. His name was Jim O'Dell and he was a real hand with those elephants.

"After awhile, he got tired of answering all the questions

When ready to mount, grab handful of mane with the even reins in left hand, saddlehorn with the right. This gives a solid hold for safe mounting, should horse spook.

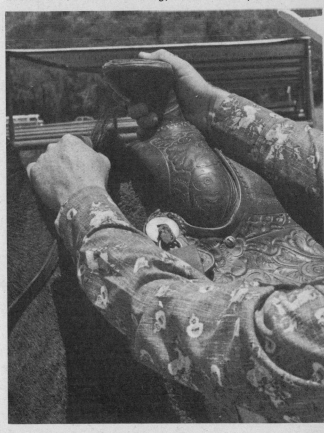

eagerness to get on, will lean over the horse which throws them completely off-balance. Once standing straight up on the left stirrup, it's an easy matter to swing the right leg over the rump and down into the right stirrup.

Use caution when mounting. Don't jam the toe of the boot into the horse's side or elbow, or he'll be put on the defensive and be wiggling around.

A variation to this mounting method is to grasp the reins and the horn in the left hand, then reach over the pommel, grasping the front of the pommel with the right hand. This is necessary when mounting a horse with a roached mane. Most horses aren't sensitive to a pull on the mane during mounting, but occasionally a horse objects. When this happens, use the latter mounting procedure and you're both happy.

There are some who just don't seem to be athletic enough to mount in either of these two fashions. Maybe the legs are too short, or the horse is too tall. In this case, grasp the reins and mane in the same manner. Then, with the right hand, twist the stirrup towards you and hold it firm while inserting the left foot. Reach for the horn or pommel with the right hand, take a hop with the right foot and follow through in the manner described for the first mounting procedure.

Some people claim they can't get on a horse without grasping the cantle with the right hand. The trouble with this procedure is that the right arm has to be moved out of the way before you can sit down. Also, you are not in a good position should the horse decide to bolt.

Left foot in the stirrup (left), the rider raises straight up and now can easily throw right leg over the cantle. Don't jam horse in the ribs with the left toe! A common form mistake of beginners is sitting as in a chair (right), on the tailbone. The pelvis should be rotated forward, which puts the horseman well down into the neck of the saddle for balance ride.

I was throwing at him. He took me over and put me up on an enormous bull elephant called Tommy. As soon as I got hold of the harness, he had Tommy rear up. It was like sitting on the corner of a building and having it tip backwards.

"A small crowd had gathered and, when I finally got down, one fellow asked for my autograph. I tried to sign it but was so shook up I couldn't even recognize my own name when I got through."

It was long afterwards when Richards realized that some people, getting on a horse for the first time, must feel somewhat like he did that day with the elephants. And it's for this reason that trainers, when teaching a complete novice riding skills, begin with familiarization. This usually consists of putting horse and horseman in a small corral and having the rider simply walk the horse.

The second step mastered is how to reverse the horse, which is done often. Most feel that, if a novice spends lots of time on the back of a gentle horse in the beginning, feelings of insecurity disappear and he'll be in a much better frame of mind to learn about form and the finer points of riding.

There are various mistakes common to beginners. One of these is the fellow who decides, "If I'm going to do it, I'm going to be in charge." He piles on the back of the horse full of determination and proceeds to try to overpower the animal. He usually will take a short, tight hold on the reins while leaning forward to watch every move the horse makes. At the same time, he will try to hang on by

squeezing the horse with his legs and heels, and his toes are pointing straight at the ground. His back is well-rounded and, as a result of all this, he ends up a classic example of terrible form. Unless he's on a very insensitive horse, there's a good chance his toes are pointing in the general direction of where he's about to land.

Since people vary greatly in build, stirrup adjustment also will vary from person to person. For example, take two people having the same height and weight. One may have long legs and a short trunk, while the other may have a long trunk and short legs. In either case, the stirrups should be adjusted so that, when the person stands with the balls of his feet on the stirrups, he should be able to clear the seat of the saddle by about five inches.

When sitting in the saddle, the stirrups should be held by the balls of the feet with the heels well down. This "keeping the heels down" seems one of the points of good form that most beginners have to work at before it feels natural.

There are two frequently seen beginner's mistakes regarding foot position. One is drawing the heels back in an effort to grip with them. As a result, the toes point at the ground. Another beginner's error comes from thinking they should pin themselves tightly against the cantle and, in an effort to accomplish this, they push their feet forward. This might look nice while walking or even on a smooth-jogging horse, but should the horse spook — or even when asking the horse to perform beyond these two simple gaits — this

Sitting right back on the cantle is another mistake, leading to an uncomfortable ride (left). The back should be arched and the pelvis rolled forward, as noted in text. Many riders have a tendency to drop their right shoulders, causing a twist in the spine. A concerted effort should be made to ride with shoulders squared, sometimes aided by this exercise (right).

position becomes a handicap to both the horse and his rider.

The feet should run parallel to the horse's sides. When the rider is sitting in good form, an imaginary line can be drawn from the tip of the knee down past the tip of the toe and, where it strikes the ground, it should form a ninety-degree angle. Because saddles are made differently, this cannot be achieved perfectly with all of them. The point is that the foot should rest in the stirrup where the stirrup hangs normally, without either pushing it forward or drawing it back.

Next comes the all-important manner in which you sit in the saddle itself. Many times beginners are reluctant to sit as straight as they should. The tendency is to sit in the saddle flat on their backsides, as if sitting in a chair. The reason the back must be straight, even to the point of keeping a slight arch in it, is due to the effect it has on the pelvic region. Keeping the spine erect and slightly arched will rotate the pelvic region forward, putting the rider down in the saddle where he belongs.

The shoulders should be squared. That is, neither slumped forward or pinned back. Beginners often tend to trail one shoulder, usually because they are unfamiliar with the proper techniques of rein handling.

Rein handling is an enormous subject that can run all the way from breaking colts to dressage. For illustration purposes, let's assume the horse you're riding is trained well enough to compete in a Western pleasure class.

The finished Western horse is ridden with one hand holding the reins. The reins are held in a full grip with the thumb on top, as if holding a pipe emerging vertically from the saddlehorn. Assuming braided reins and romal — standard equipment in the Western classes at a horse show — are being used, the reins run under the little finger and up through the hand. The romal should lay across the thumb and down the right side, where it is held in the right hand.

Beginners who have not yet gotten the feel of how to handle the horse tend to ride as if they are thinking, "I've got to guide this horse with one hand." Therefore, they reach forward with the reining hand and trail the other arm. This causes the crookedness in the shoulders and puts a twist in the spine.

Another common mistake is overreining. In this, the beginner will stick the reins way over to the left or right in order to guide the horse.

The rider must learn to "feel" the horse. Most horses appreciate light contact with the bit but they do, of course, vary in regards to the quality or lightness of the mouth and responsiveness to cues. Most horses responding poorly have hard mouths because they have been abused by riders who thought they could force a good move or stop from the horse by thoughtless, heavy-handed pulling and yanking rather than teaching the horse what is being asked of him and using the bit to cue him. A beginner must realize that rein handling is a major factor in communicating with the horse and he should be careful to never use the reins to balance himself.

To become an accomplished rider, one must learn to rate

Another example of leading with the left shoulder is shown (left). If bad habits like this aren't corrected at the outset, they become harder to break. The proper form is shown (right). Left hand is positioned above horn, reins running vertically up through it, right hand on thigh holding trailing end. The shoulders are square, back is arched, pelvis rolled forward.

the horse; to determine the time required to cover a certain distance while traveling in the different gaits. For example, let's say the horse is at a trot and begins to trot faster. He still is trotting but is improperly rated. By the same token, if he reduces his speed below that which you desire, he also is improperly rated. In this case, bring him up to speed through the use of leg pressure.

Remember, when applying leg pressure, it's just that — leg pressure, not heel pressure. With the heels kept well down where they belong, the calves will lay alongside the horse's barrel. Any leg cues that are given, such as to urge the horse forward or to side-pass, should be given with the calf of the leg against the barrel.

The finished horse we're using as an example responds to these pressures. He has learned during training that, when he does respond, the pressure is released. And when he doesn't respond, he receives a tap with the training bat. Through this simple method of disciplining, the horse becomes more and more responsive to the pressure until it's merely a cue.

During this period of a horse's training, use caution and restraint. Follow the principles of good horsemanship so the horse doesn't become nervous and try to find a way out of the pressure that's beyond the control of the rider, such as switching his tail or improper foot position, prancing and the like.

When rating the horse with the reins, the beginner must watch so he doesn't pull the horse down to a walk or stop. The rider must learn to anticipate this and prevent it by urging the horse up into the bridle by use of the legs. The horse should not be held by the legs even when urging him forward. Instead, he should be urged by gripping with the calves and then released as he moves on through his stride.

When pulling the reins to rate or stop the horse, the rein hand should be drawn straight back toward the belt buckle. The beginner quite often will get himself into trouble because he didn't adjust his hold on the reins properly. He then moves the rein hand up toward his chin and the panic sets in. Remember: keep your hands low!

This entire matter of leg pressure, a most important subject, is covered in greater detail in the chapter dealing with training horses.

Getting back to the subject of form, remember that the balanced seat is used in Western riding. Much of this already has been covered but the following is the description of a balanced seat from top to bottom.

The head should be carried back in balance above the shoulders, not tipped forward looking down at the horse.

The shoulders should be squared, the elbows held evenly at the sides. The left hand holds the reins just above the saddlehorn, the right hand holding the romal should rest on the thigh. The back should be erect, even slightly arched. The pelvic region should be rotated forward, putting you down in the saddle. The legs and feet should hang where the stirrups hang. The ball of the foot should rest on the stirrup with the heels kept well down.

This position may seem unnatural at first and therefore uncomfortable for the beginner. This is the reason that riding lessons are primarily drill.

In a sense, horseback riding can be compared to military boot camp. The first attempts at marching, or even such simple things as forming a straight line, leave a great deal to be desired. But after a couple of weeks, the entire platoon is performing these maneuvers smartly, the result of self-discipline and drill. These same two qualities can be applied to horsemanship, with similar results.

Some beginners will try to freeze themselves into the proper position and not move. This would be fine if the horse was standing squarely on level ground. But a horse

Often when backing or stopping a horse, the inexperienced horseman raises rein hand up toward the chin. The pull on the reins should be straight back, towards the belt. When out riding, the horseman should endeavor to keep proper balance and form at all times (below). A "fun" ride can be anything but if principles aren't followed!

As text notes, some riders master the proper form only when stationary, not when riding. Both horse and horseman can be helped in performance, as noted.

doesn't stay in one place and you'll want to ride him about. The horse must then move unhampered by your presence on his back and even be assisted by your controls.

What the rider must strive for when practicing is a suppleness, aided by good form, which will allow him to ride well-balanced, offering a minimum of interference with the horse's movements while maintaining maximum control.

One way this can be seen is when riding up and downhill. If the horse is climbing uphill, the rider should lean forward slightly so the pull of gravity runs directly down through his body. His head is closer to the horse's than when riding on level ground. When riding downhill, the reverse is true.

If you live in an area where there are horse shows, equitation classes and not just playdays, it's a good idea to go and watch the various riders entered. Even though you

may not be able to pick the winners, you will find that most riders in equitation classes ride with good form and you can learn by observing them. Watch the rider as he is being carried along at the canter. The horse appears to be rocking underneath him, yet the rider's body will remain fairly vertical.

"I like to encourage beginners to have their horses walk nice and bright," says Rusty Richards. "In this way they learn to rate a horse properly. I don't think a whole lot can be learned just by having a horse barely plod along under you. On the other hand, when I ask the beginner to trot, I want him to trot the horse as slowly as possible."

The slow trot is the easiest of all to sit. Even a skilled rider doesn't sit the fast or extended trot, for most of the shock is taken on the stirrups at this gait. At the slow trot, however, the shock is distributed more between the stirrups and the seat.

The trot is the most difficult gait to sit properly, so novice rider should attempt this as slowly as possible.

Proper (far left) and improper leg leg positions are shown here. The heel should be well down, toe aimed straight ahead. This distributes leg pressure evenly with the calf, which is desired. Otherwise, you might end up where right toe is pointing!

Good, properly fitting equipment is essential for any horseman — novice or expert — to get the maximum enjoyment from riding. If a novice, it's a good idea to get professional help before purchasing any tack.

Probably the nicest thing about involvement with horses is that there always are new horizons. No matter how long or how hard you work at learning about horses, and no matter what your level of achievement, you never will arrive at the static condition where there's nothing left to learn. This is one of the main reasons why horses hold a life-long fascination for so many people.

Since this chapter deals primarily with the basics of Western riding, it would be incomplete without some mention of the use of the hands, seat and legs, commonly called the "aids."

We already have presented a capsulated version of the manner in which a horse learns to respond to pressure applied by the rider's legs. To get into this subject a little deeper, let's talk about the manner in which the aids are used in getting the horse to side-pass.

At this stage of the horse's training, he usually is in a training bridle such as a snaffle bit or a hackamore. These tools are used so the young horse can be given a direct cue which is easy for him to understand. The direct cue simply is pulling his nose in the direction you want him to go, using one rein.

Throughout this chapter, it has been assumed that you are riding a horse finished in the bridle well enough to be entered in a Western pleasure class. This kind of horse works off the indirect cue, or neck rein. To get a better understanding of why the horse responds to the aids, let's regress to that point in his training where he first learns to respond to cues that produce lateral movement, or side-passing.

This phase of a colt's training is begun after he already has learned to move out in response to pressure from the rider's legs. Since the colt never has been asked to perform this maneuver, he must be taught what we are asking of him. This is done in stages.

The first stage is getting him to move his rear end around the front end. To accomplish this, use a snaffle bit with reins about seven feet long and one-inch wide. Cross the reins in front as you sit in the saddle, so the tail end of the right rein hangs down the colt's left shoulder. The tail end of the left rein hangs down his right shoulder.

Holding the reins with both hands, knuckles up and palms down, slide down the left rein a little and pull his nose slightly to the left. At the same time, close the left leg against his left side, applying pressure with the calf of your leg, still keeping your heel down.

The colt often won't move until you bring the tail of the rein hanging down the right shoulder across in front of you and give him a tap on the left haunch. As he gives way behind, release the pressure of the leg and square him up. Give him a pat on the neck as a reward. During this movement, more or less stabilize the front end with both hands to keep him from moving forward. The whole procedure then is repeated on the right side, causing the rear end to rotate to the left.

Most colts will learn in a short period that, when pressure is applied by the rider's leg, he is to step away from it. Again, remember to go slowly and not overwork him, or you may sour the colt and make him switchy.

Once the colt has learned to give way behind and the hindquarters can be rotated around the front, the rider uses his outside leg to keep him from stepping out as the forequarters are moved around the rear end.

Once the colt has these two stages down fairly well, he is ready to learn the side-pass. At this point, the colt is given simultaneous cues. The direct cue from the hands asks the colt to move his front end to the left. At the same time, the cue to move the rear end to the left is given by the rider's right leg. As a result, the colt steps to his left behind and in front at the same time, and you have lateral movement.

Since the manner in which leg pressure in used in controlling the rear end of the horse has been explained somewhat, this next subject might cause confusion.

This refers to the use of pressure from the rider's inside leg. That is, the leg on the same side as the horse is turning. These two factors seem to contradict each other at first glance. However, the most successful trainers are those who have integrated the use of inside and outside leg pressures. pressures.

Perhaps the best way to illustrate this would be to give some examples where inside leg pressure is used in training. One is in getting a horse to free up. Occasionally, someone has a horse that has gone stale on them. Quite often, these are horses that have had good training at one time, but have developed bad habits because the persons riding them were lacking in ability and knowledge; in fact, they were the causes of the problems.

What happens is they see a horse performing in a reining or stock horse class, or a top barrel racing horse, and figure it looks easy. It does look easy. In fact, the better the horse handles, the easier he makes it look.

These people figure, "All I've got to do is get after Old Blaze and make him hurry, and he can do that, too!" At this point, they go home and get out the whip and spurs, and Old Blaze begins to find out what trouble really is. The more the whip and spurs are used, the more confused he becomes until he finally begins to buck or rear up in desperation. Our unskilled rider, in trying to make him drop in the turn quicker, usually will move his reining hand over farther than he should and begin to work over the outside of the horse with the whip and outside spur, thinking this will cause the horse to turn fast in order to get away.

It just doesn't work that way. What usually happens is that the excessive use of the whip and spurs on the horse's side will cause that side to freeze up. With his side tensed, the horse then will move his head toward that side, which is the opposite direction to which the rider is trying to go.

A spoiled horse should be taken back through the basics. Put him in a snaffle bit and use quite a bit of inside leg in order to get him to easily move his head in the direction you want him to travel. This helps to free up the horse and get rid of the spine stiffening that was caused by his unskilled rider.

Perhaps you have an old, gentle saddle horse that goes along pretty well, but will cock his head in the wrong direction when you try to neck rein him. Try using some inside leg pressure, even when just walking; it helps.

If you ever have been to a professional rodeo, you undoubtably saw the girls' clover-leaf barrel race. A top barrel horse will move around a barrel in a quick, fluid motion. He looks as if he is bending around the barrel, which, in fact, he is.

Two of the main ingredients in this kind of a turn are skilled, balanced riding and use of the inside leg. The girls in

The running martingale, shown on the horse at left, is a definite training tool and shouldn't be used by inexperienced horsemen. It can create problems.

the Girls Rodeo Association make this event look easy, but if you've ever been to a gymkhana where every gunsel in town is trying to run barrels, you soon realize that these girls are skilled horsewomen.

People often say that horsemen are born, not made. This, of course, cannot be true because the statement implies that there is no necessity for improvement. Some people do seem to have a more natural feel for horses, but there is no substitute for a desire for improvement.

Funk & Wagnalls, the dictionary folks, define the word "horseman" as: "One who rides a horse." Perhaps a better definition would be, "One skilled at getting horses to do as he asks through understanding and knowledge."

Rusty Richards relates an incident that graphically shows the difference, involving a horse trainer by the name of Billy Bushbaum. "The incident occurred at a rodeo in Burwell, Nebraska. Billy was there with a horse he called Mr. Nifty. He would set up a curb ring like the type used in circuses and work Mr. Nifty at liberty in that ring. The horse was beautifully trained, performing many intricate maneuvers easily. He even did the capriole, a movement perfected by the Lippizaners of the Spanish Riding School that consists of a leap into the air with kicks out behind with both hind feet cupped upwards.

"Just after Billy and Mr. Nifty entered the arena, something spooked the horse and he took off. Billy began walking towards him, speaking softly. Several times, just as Billy was about to catch him, he whirled and ran to the other end of the arena.

"The whole thing didn't take all that long, but it might have seemed an agonizingly long time to Billy. The announcer tried to cover up as best he could by saying things like, 'It can even happen to the best' or 'Whenever you are working with an animal, there always is the chance something might spook him,' and other such comments, all of them true.

"Billy continued to walk slowly toward Mr. Nifty, trying to soothe him. Finally, the horse stood his ground and Billy walked up to him. He then gave him a pat on the neck and stroked him gently once or twice, speaking softly the whole time. He then turned and walked toward the ring with the horse right on his heels. As they got to the ring, Mr. Nifty hopped in and Billy put him through his paces, finishing with the capriole. Needless to say, the crowd went bananas, and Billy and Mr. Nifty took a well-deserved bow.

"It's been my frequent observation that, when a horse gets away from someone who has to chase it before making the catch, the result usually is that the horse gets a kick in the belly or a few severe yanks on the mouth, or is whipped and yelled at. How well do you think Mr. Nifty would have performed if, instead of settling him down, Billy had chosen this abusive treatment instead?

In schooling a horse to side-pass, he might not respond to leg pressure at the outset. In such case, he often will move out promptly when lightly tapped on the haunch with trailing end of reins, at the same time giving the leg cue.

This is a good example of a horse properly executing the side-pass maneuver. He's given the leg cue with right leg to move hindquarters to the left, at the same time being given rein cue to move to his left. The side-pass can be invaluable aid.

"I think Billy Bushbaum is a horseman, not just by Funk and Wagnalls' definition, but by any definition."

To be a top horseman, you first must recognize the need for the proper administration of both discipline and rewards. Both should be done thoughtfully in planned anticipation of the result. Too much of either while neglecting the other will lead to a spoiled horse.

Some general information about leads is needed. If a horse is cantering in a left-hand circle — counterclockwise — he should be reaching the highest with the two inside legs — the left fore and hind. He then is said to be in his left lead, the proper lead for a horse traveling in this direction.

If he's traveling at the canter in a right-hand circle, he should be reaching the highest with his inside legs, the right fore and hind. This is said to be the right lead, the proper one for a horse traveling in this direction.

The flying change of leads and even departure into the correct lead is complex. Most horses ready for the show ring, however, will take the proper lead by simply urging them into the canter with the outside leg, the leg closest to the rail. Until you get used to leads, it's a good idea to have someone watch you. They can tell if the horse is in the correct lead and you don't have to bend over and be looking.

It is possible for a horse to be in a different lead in front than in back. The common term for this is cross-firing. If you have any difficulty whatsoever in getting your horse to take the proper lead, have a professional assist you. It beats ruining the horse.

Even if you aren't interested in riding in horse shows, knowing how to ride well and having a horse that is well-trained is advantageous. Just the fact that the horse understands you, for example, is a mighty nice thing. So many horses spend their lives being yanked and pounded,

Side-pass skills enable horse and horseman team to go through gates without dismounting. After side-passing to gate, it's opened (left) and leg cues direct horse into the opening. He then side-passes to left for closure (below). This is just one skill the horseman can learn for a most enjoyable relationship with his animal. See text for more.

becoming only mediocre forms of transportation. This is a shame since, with just a little effort in the direction of learning about and understanding horses, both the horse and owner would be a lot happier.

Besides the fact that he is happier, the well-trained horse is a pleasure to ride. He handles with ease. You can get the mail out of the mailbox without getting off his back, open and close gates without dismounting; through proper use of the aids you can hold him over on the side of the road when traffic approaches.

These are but a few of the advantages that belong to the skilled horse and horseman. There is plenty to learn; the basics of Western riding is a good beginning.

Chapter 4

HINTS ON HORSE BUYING

There's A Lot More
Than Meets The Eye
When Buying A Horse,
And Here Are Some
Useful Tips!

WHEN IT COMES to horsetrading, offering the age-old advice, "Caveat emptor: Let the buyer beware," is sound. This is not to mean there aren't honest people engaged in the business, but with others you'll need to put your wallet in your boot and tuck the pants leg securely over the top!

When looking at a horse with the idea of buying it, you first have to know what you want and it's not every horse-trader who is all that interested in filling your every need; after all, he's simply trying to sell a horse.

Undoubtedly the biggest and most frequent mistake that's made is when the novice, without a sound knowledge of horses, attempts to buy a horse on his own. Rather than give a complete course in what makes a good horse, we suggest that the prospective buyer have a knowledgeable professional horseman accompany him. You probably can't get a veterinarian or even a qualified horseman to go around looking at horses as often as you may want to, but after you find the horse you feel is just right, call in an expert to join you in final approval.

While this chapter will deal with the proper selection of a mount, another area bears mentioning that often is overlooked: Are you willing to meet the responsibility that goes with owning an animal to put under that brand-new saddle? Before you go charging off with checkbook in hand, there are some questions you should ask yourself.

Why do you want to buy a horse? Where are you going to keep him? How much is he going to cost? You need to know the answers to these questions before you start looking for that first horse.

Although horses can — and often do — exist in accommodations varying from backyard junkpile corrals to palatial stables and huge pastures, there are minimum requirements for a healthy and useful horse that can't be overlooked. He needs food, shelter, equipment, shoeing, medical care and room for exercise.

As a general rule, the average horse that does not have access to pasture will consume the equivalent of his own weight in hay each month, which means that the average riding horse requires about six tons per year. He may also require grain, depending upon the quality of the hay being fed and the work he is doing. For example, a mature saddle horse being ridden a few hours each day may require from four to twelve pounds of grain daily in order to maintain good condition. He needs to be fed at least twice a day unless he spends all of his time on grass pasture and should have clean water before him at all times. Local feed stores can estimate the cost of feed and grain in your community.

Your horse will need protection from the hot sun and severe storms, and must have a comfortable bed for sleeping. A box stall ten by twelve feet that opens into a corral at least twenty by eighty feet is adequate, but the larger the accommodations, the better. Fences should be constructed of lumber or woven wire, never barbed wire, and built in a way that the horse can't hurt himself on it.

The type and quality of equipment that you buy for your horse will depend on his use, as a riding horse or work horse, and the size of your pocketbook. You can estimate the cost of equipment by visiting the local saddle shop, which sells all sorts of stable gear, or by looking through a catalog.

Your horse will need exercise every day, either by running in a corral or pasture, or by working under saddle or in harness. His feet may need attention every month or two, either by trimming or shoeing. Consequently, the availability of a good farrier is important. In many parts of the country, the ground is such that horses may work barefooted and need no shoes. In other parts of the country, many horses must wear shoes continuously if worked. A set of shoes should never be left on a horse longer than six weeks without removal and/or resetting or replacing with new ones, if the old ones are worn out.

In most parts of the country, horses should be vaccinated annually for sleeping sickness and tetanus, and for other diseases in some areas. Horses, like people, occasionally do get sick and need a doctor. Your veterinarian can advise which vaccines should be used in your area.

If you can afford a horse, then the next question is, "Why do you want a horse?" Once you know what you intend to use the horse for — working, riding, or show — you can visit people or stables who own that type of horse and learn more about it. One thing to remember is that if you want to participate in horse shows, you should buy a horse of a breed and type that is shown in your community. Otherwise, there will be few, if any, shows open to you for participation.

Two common mistakes many beginners make in looking for a riding horse are to start looking for a stallion or a young, vigorous 2, 3, or 4-year-old. Stallions, with very few exceptions, are never pleasant riding horses, good pets, or easy to handle. The young horse, like the young child, is full of vigor and vitality, quite playful, and sometimes uncontrollable, no matter how pleasant his disposition or how willing he may be. He also must be trained by an expert, a service which may cost from $100 to $200 a month and take from twelve to fourteen months.

The best horse, then, for your first horse, is an older horse that is more settled in his ways, well-broken and quiet. He will be safer and will be more fun to ride or handle. The bargain for the real beginner frequently is the horse up to 16 years old that has been and is well cared for. He will work under saddle willingly and safely until he is about 20 years old. Economics and safety usually indicate that you should look for an older, well-trained horse.

While you still are looking at horses, and especially if you are buying for a young person, you should visit with your county agent, agricultural extension office, 4-H clubs, pony clubs, or other riding groups in your area. If there are any state or local breed associations in your area, their members will probably invite you to their monthly meetings, if you show an interest.

Too, much can be learned by attending regular clinics held by veterinarians or others knowledgeable in the field, which might be held in your area. Some of these have slide presentations which depict explicitly conformation faults and it's here the adage "A picture is worth a thousand words" really comes to the fore. You can't learn about conformation faults through simply reading books such as this; you need to see the faults to readily recognize them.

Where do you look for a prospective horse? As stated earlier, you first must establish the purpose for the horse you intend buying. Is he to be a roping horse? Is your interest centered around the show ring? Will your mount simply be a hacking horse?

To a great extent, the proposed usage of the horse will have bearing on where to look. For example, quite a few top roping horses have come off the quarter horse tracks of the nation. They might be plenty fast for roping, but they didn't have the staying power to cut it against their speedier peers.

But a horse coming off the racetrack generally isn't a good mount for the newcomer to riding who simply wants a saddle horse. A racehorse, because of the thoroughbred blood in him, is more high-spirited and nervous than horses used only for hacking, and consequently wouldn't be a good choice for inexperienced horsemen.

Quite a number of horses are sold at auctions, some good and some bad. The trouble is that there's little time to make a decision on the relative value of the horse and whether he's completely normal. There have been recorded cases of horseowners drugging outlaw horses to make them docile as sheep. It's when you've got him home in the pen and the drug's worn off that you discover the truth.

Because you're taking your chances at an auction, the prices generally are lower than purchasing from private parties.

The bigger national auctions and shows, often held concurrently, are different matters, however. At these sales you can be pretty sure everything's on the level and that there aren't any goats in the bunch. Because of the national scope, you can expect to spend a goodly amount of cash at one of these sales.

There are other horse sources closer to home. One of these is the aforementioned horsetrader. Most are honest,

A veterinarian can be an invaluable aid when purchasing a horse, since he's trained to spot equine trouble areas.

decent men who make their living selling livestock. This reputable trader is the one with whom to do business, accompanied by a knowledgeable horseman. If there's any doubt over the integrity of the horsetrader, do your business elsewhere.

By far, the bulk of America's horses that change hands are sold by private parties. If a trainer is approached by a prospective buyer, but doesn't have any stock interesting to the latter, he won't hesitate to refer the buyer to another individual or make the deal personally. In either case, the buyer is expected to pay a finder's fee, which only seems right if he turns up a horse you desire. After all, he found what you wanted.

Another way to find prospective horses is by cruising through areas with a heavy density of horses. Keep your eyes open for horses. If you find an interesting horse, inquire whether he's for sale. If so, you might consummate a deal on the spot, or perhaps the owner can refer you to another location.

Newspaper and magazine classified sections also are good places to hunt for horses. Patiently checking the advertisements and following up on those sounding good often results in a horse in the trailer.

In buying a horse, never rush into the deal. Spend lots of time looking around, checking and seeing the horse work. Don't get anxious — like the kid with the fever to buy his first car — because you might invest unwisely. The slow, cautious approach also puts you into a stronger bargaining position, which can equate into a lower price!

And don't be afraid to bargain with the owner. It seems traditional that haggling takes place prior to a sale. Many owners automatically price a horse higher than they figure he's worth, so they can come down in price. If the buyer is

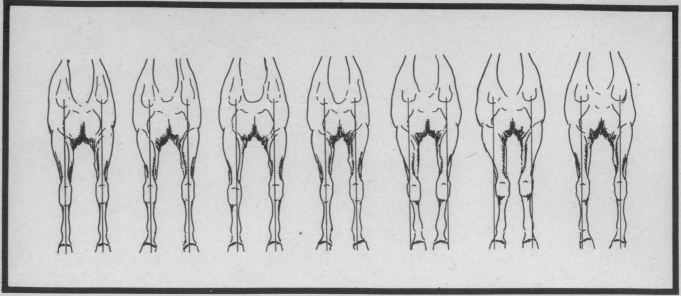

When viewed from front, line from point of shoulder should bisect knee, cannon, pastern and hoof (left). From left are: toes out; bowlegged; narrow chested with toes out; base narrow, stands close; knock-kneed; and pigeon-toed horses.

willing to pay the initial figure, so much the better for the seller.

In selecting a horse, beyond soundness and health, there are three things to consider: disposition, conformation and breeding. The logic of this order of importance can be seen by looking at it in reverse order.

Suppose, for example, that the horse had an impressive pedigree and beautiful conformation, yet you couldn't get near him without danger of being bitten or kicked. Or suppose there is a good pedigree with bad conformation faults. (This isn't likely, but does happen.)

On the other hand, if a horse has a terrific disposition, you might forgive some faults in conformation, if not too serious. If the horse had a great disposition and beautiful conformation, yet the breeding was not too fashionable, he still may be considered.

If a certain horse has good conformation and seems to have good sense, the next question would be, "How is he bred?"

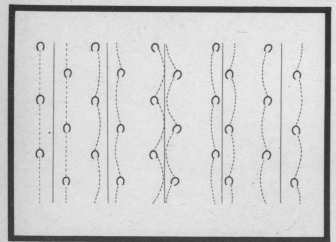

From left: Normal foot moves in a straight line. "Base-wide" feet have slight inward arcs. Splayed feet have a more exaggerated inward arc. "Base-narrow" feet have slightly outward arcs. Pigeon-toed feet have a more pronounced outward arc. These are as seen from above.

This is not to say that only horses with champions in their pedigrees have the potential to become champions, but it can be a useful tool to aid in your search for just the right horse for a certain purpose.

Say one does not want a great athlete, but merely a nice, gentle pleasure horse. Usually, with grade horses there is no pedigree kept on them. Many times, however, one can inspect the immediate parents. If possible, find out all you can about the sire and dam. Frequently, the mare will be there on the premises. Ask to see her and inquire as to her disposition. Get all the history on her that you can. If she is a sour old biddy, then her foal has a better than average chance of inheriting some of her traits.

Many times the sire will be a registered horse, which gives you more to go on; but don't take that as a sign that everything is perfect on the sire's side. Check him out, also. See if you like him; again, considering disposition, conformation and breeding.

If you are looking for that stock horse or quick reining horse, remember that a stock horse is asked to get his hind feet under him, hold and slide, so he is going to have to be physically equipped to do it. He should be a reasonably square horse with good, straight legs and a strong back, especially across the loins. He must be strong in the front end, also, but the legs should be pinned on properly. Don't mistake a wide, massive chest with the legs coming straight down from the outside corners and a wide, flat area between them with a good front end. On the other hand, legs that are pinned too closely together don't make a good front end, either.

Ideally, the muscles between the front legs, in the region of the chest, should meet or nearly meet, then slope down to the legs so that when one looks at the horse from the front, these muscles form a wide, upside-down V.

Watch for a cow-hocked horse. A cow-hocked horse, when viewed from the rear standing as square as he can, has a greater distance between his pasterns than between his hocks. In other words, the cannons are not parallel.

Most Arabian horses toe out slightly behind and tip in a little at the hocks, but the cannons do parallel each other like a figure eleven when the horse stands straight. This tipped-in, toed-out position can give the illusion that the horse is cow-hocked, however.

A steep, short-pasterned horse should be avoided, especially if one is going to be riding him any distance. Such horses tend to have a short, choppy gait and little shock absorption in the pasterns. They are rare, but a horse that is too long in the pastern is somewhat handicapped, but not quite as undesirable.

Look for good withers on a horse, as mushy, mutton withers will not hold a saddle properly and will affect the horse's ability to perform.

A horse that toes-in on the front feet, although it is a fault, is not nearly so dangerous as one that toes-out, called splay-footed. These horses will wing out when they travel which puts some added stress on their joints, but the feet are carried well away from each other and they are not apt to stumble because of interference.

A horse that is over at the knee (when viewed from the side, the knee appears to be bent slightly forward) is not perfect, but he is far stronger and much less apt to break down than a horse that is back at the knee or calf-kneed.

A horse that is sickle-hocked, though imperfect, is preferred over a horse that is too straight in the hocks. The sickle-hocked horse, when viewed from the side, has his feet up underneath him, almost directly below the hip bone.

A horse can be measured for straightness in the rear end by placing a plumb bob or a straight edge at the hindmost point of the buttocks. If he is standing with the cannon perpendicular to the level ground, the plumb bob or straight edge will run down the back of the cannon.

Most people like a horse that isn't too fleshy in the throat latch, yet still has a well-developed neck. The neck should be well arched and the underline should have little or no bulge. The neck is the balancing arm of the horse and those that bulge downward at the throat usually flex at the withers and carry their heads up in your face.

Finally, take a close look at a horse's eyes. It has been said that they are the windows to the soul and just as a kind and gentle eye can be spotted easily, a wild-eyed, rather distant look usually means trouble.

If you are waiting to buy until you find an absolutely flawless horse, we're afraid you are in for a long wait. We have yet to see the horse that is perfect.

Far too many people place a great deal of importance on the color or beauty of a horse, many times overlooking some of the faults heretofore outlined. While a pretty horse is desirable, this factor shouldn't overrule common sense in the selection of a mount.

No matter where you decide to buy your horse, you, or whoever is going to ride him, should go to the place where he is stabled and ride him several times to insure that he is the type of horse you want and that he has the disposition and character that are compatible with the rider's.

You will need to talk to the veterinarian you have selected to look after your horse. He will be able to inspect the horse and advise you whether he is sound, serviceable and free of disease. The veterinarian can probably also give you an evaluation of the animal's temperament, usefulness and worth. Usually, the veterinarian who specializes in equine practice has a good knowledge of most of the horses in the community and is in a good position to advise. (There are a large number of veterinarians now who specialize in the care and treatment of horses.)

There are several tricks used by unscrupulous horsetraders that bear mention. It is hoped they will avoid the purchase of a bad horse and lead to eradication of the practices, which are nearly as old as horses, themselves.

One of the oldest tricks is termed "bishoping," named after an Anglican bishop in England who devised the practice. Specifically, it denotes the filing down of a horse's teeth to make him appear younger.

Unfortunately, not all horsemen have their new purchases examined by a veterinarian prior to purchase and end up with a goat. If inexperienced, seek professional help.

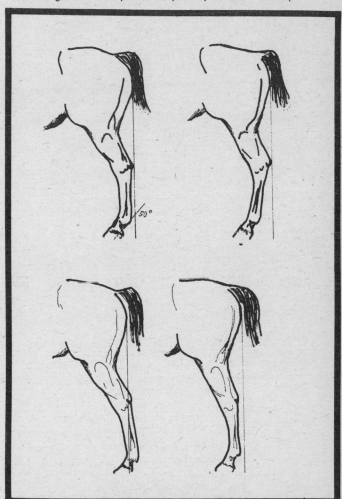

Ideal hind leg position forms 50-degree angle (top left). Horse at top right stands under. Horse at lower left is camped out, horse at lower right has legs too straight.

Closely examine the feet of a prospective purchase. If shod, check the shoes for any corrective work applied. As noted in the chapter on corrective trimming and shoeing, much can be done to improve a horse's gait. If the horse is barefoot, look for any rasp marks to indicate filing to overcome a defect. See if there are cracks in the hoofs, or whether mud or grease has been applied to hide an underly-

Pulling a hind leg forward and up allows the prospective purchaser to examine the frog and check demeanor of the animal. Pay close attention to his feet and legs always.

ing problem. It's best to know of any faults in this region prior to getting him home.

Many horses with mild lamenesses appear normal after a short period of exercise, so beware of any horse that's lathered when shown to you.

Often an untrustworthy seller will attempt to engage in a friendly toast or two prior to examination of the herd. Should the buyer indulge, he may end up with something less than the horse of his dreams. Stay sober!

Be suspicious of any seller who continually interrupts a buyer when examining horses, or one who allows other distractions like dogs underfoot to break the chain of concentration. If he tries to move you along quickly, chances are there's a major fault he doesn't want you noticing.

While it may be difficult, try to determine if a horse has been drugged. Usually a veterinary surgeon can spot this, but sometimes extensive laboratory tests are required. It's enough to skip the horse if there is suspicion he's been drugged, either to tranquilize the animal or pep him up.

It's common practice with some nefarious traders to stuff sponges well up into the nostrils of a horse that roars or has the heaves. This tends to mask the condition and close examination of the horse's nostrils should be undertaken.

If a horse is prancing boldly around his pasture with tail raised, make sure this is his normal demeanor and not the result of ginger applied at the dock of his tail.

One of the surest signs that all isn't right with the world is when the seller tries to arrange the sale at sundown. By so doing, it's possible for him to mix the herd and present the same individual several times. Many faults are hidden by the

fading light that would be readily detected earlier. Too, the seller often can get away with selling a blind horse. It's impossible to wave the hand near the eyes and expect a reaction after dark, or to see if the animal blinks. In sunlight, a horse turned facing the sun invariably blinks if his eyesight is normal. Beware one that doesn't.

Though it's hard to believe, some sellers will dye the hair of their horses to the specific color the buyer prefers if discovered in advance, or he may ask the buyer to return the following day at which time he'll have "just the horse." Usually, this horse is one of the crop rejected the previous day, whose hair coat has been dyed the desired color.

Here's the final checklist before you definitely buy your horse:

Is he sound, serviceable and free of disease? Does he respond properly to bridle and saddle when ridden and to halters and lead shank when on the ground? Is he safe for the rider or for the purpose intended?

Can he be loaded and transported in a trailer? Does he have any special peculiarities? If it is a mare supposed to be in foal, do you have a veterinary certificate certifying that she is in foal or that she has had a veterinary examination?

Do you have a bill of sale? If the horse is to be moved across a state line, do you have a health certificate where required by law? If the horse is reported to be and is purchased as a registered, purebred animal, is the animal effectively registered and do you have the papers?

One last caution, especially if you are buying a riding horse: Older horses, like older people, are more fixed in their habits, good or bad, but are more predictable and dependable than youngsters. Pick an older horse that has habits and traits that you like. Then you know what you are buying and what to expect of the animal.

Actual riding gives insight into the horse's experience and past training. Take things slow and gradual (below).

Before heading out into the hills on an unfamiliar horse, check his abilities and disposition carefully in the ring. This could save you serious problems.

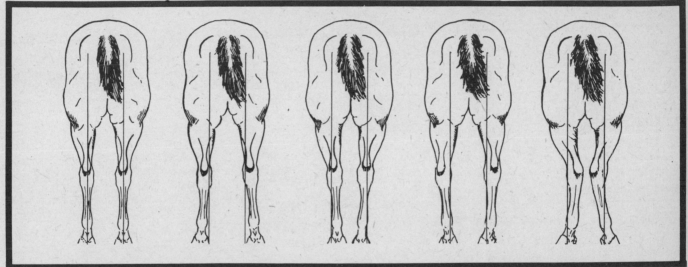

Ideal conformation (from left, above) shows vertical line from point of buttock bisecting hock, cannon, pastern and foot. A horse standing wide breaks this, as does horse standing close. Bowlegged and cow-hocked horses are next seen. Avoid them. Forequarter leg position (from left, below) is ideal, forming 45-degree angle. Camped under, camped out, knee-sprung and calf-knee conditions should be shunned. Try to buy the best possible horse affordable and recall the responsibilities!

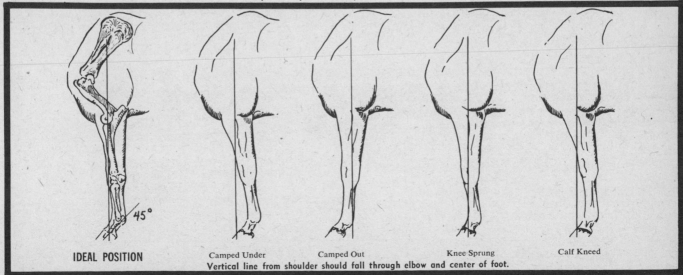

IDEAL POSITION   45°   Camped Under   Camped Out   Knee Sprung   Calf Kneed

Vertical line from shoulder should fall through elbow and center of foot.

Chapter 5

TACK TIPS FOR WESTERN RIDERS

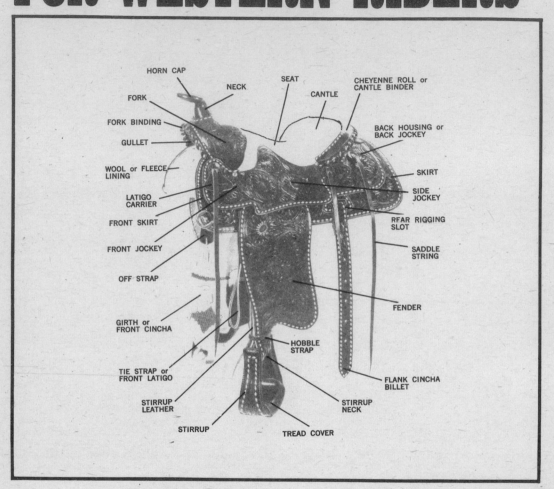

- HORN CAP
- NECK
- SEAT
- CANTLE
- CHEYENNE ROLL or CANTLE BINDER
- FORK
- FORK BINDING
- GULLET
- BACK HOUSING or BACK JOCKEY
- WOOL or FLEECE LINING
- SKIRT
- SIDE JOCKEY
- LATIGO CARRIER
- RFAR RIGGING SLOT
- FRONT SKIRT
- SADDLE STRING
- FRONT JOCKEY
- OFF STRAP
- FENDER
- GIRTH or FRONT CINCHA
- HOBBLE STRAP
- TIE STRAP or FRONT LATIGO
- FLANK CINCHA BILLET
- STIRRUP LEATHER
- STIRRUP NECK
- STIRRUP
- TREAD COVER

Both Saddle And Bit Date Far Back, And Here's Their Place In Horsemanship Today!

1500: Spanish War Saddle   1700-present: Mexican Vaquero Saddle   1800: Early California Saddle

WHILE ONE CAN hardly say that the saddle is as old as the horse, perhaps it would not be amiss to state that the saddle is nearly as old as the domesticated mount.

The Greeks, Romans and even the Mongol hordes all had saddles of a sort, as they rode across Europe and Asia. The Crusaders of the Middle Ages weighed their horses down with tack that made it easier to stay aboard in spite of the heavy armor and the armament.

Introduction of the saddle to America came in the form of the Spanish war saddle of the Sixteenth Century, when Cortez and others passed through Latin America and the Southwest plundering the Indians of anything valuable. The Spanish war saddle also seems to have been the basis of the modern stock saddle, although it has gone through numerous changes and modifications in design.

The Spanish saddle of the colonization era had a high, swept-back fork and a wrap-around cantle, both designed to add to the rider's security. According to Phil Livingston of Tex Tan Western Leather Company, who has made a study of the development of the modern Western saddle, the tree was of wood covered with leather, velvet or — in the everyday version — ordinary cloth.

"The rigging was in the centerfire position, midway between the fork and the cantle. A breast strap and breeching or crupper helped to hold the saddle in place both fore and aft. The stirrup leathers hung directly behind the fork, as they do today, and the rider rode with long, straight leathers as did his knightly forebearers," Livingston says.

This saddle, incidentally, bore unmistakable similarities to the Moorish-designed saddles, a result of three hundred years of domination and occupation of Spain. "In many ways, it was a modified combination of both African know-how and the Crusader's saddle of Europe," Livingston adds.

Actually, the history of the Western saddle began in 1519, when Hernando Cortez unloaded his sixteen war horses in the vicinity of what today is Vera Cruz. Later, as the Spanish began to colonize Latin America and the Southwest, missions stretching across southern Texas, New Mexico, Arizona, and the entire length of the Pacific Coast were established. In time, each of these missions had its own cattle herd and the men responsible for overseeing them began to adapt the Spanish war saddles to their own immediate needs. There have been numerous changes down through the centuries, dictated by the old "form must follow function" creed familiar to all designers.

For example, the Mexican vaquero saddle, developed about 1700, has changed little in design in nearly three hundred years. Virtually the same saddle that was employed before the Revolutionary War is being used today by Mexican cowboys. The main modification has been in the shape of the saddle horn.

In the beginning, the Spaniards attempted to work cattle with a pike or lance, astride the war saddle, but it wasn't long before someone discovered the lariat and found that it provided a good deal more latitude.

This, however, proved that some sort of snubbing post had to be developed as part of the working equipment. "The high front of the old war saddle was whittled down, a horn fashioned and the cantle or back shortened to allow freedom of movement," Livingston reports. "The general outline of the modern stock saddle had come into being."

As suggested, today's Mexican vaquero rides a saddle that is three centuries old in design. The rig, or rings to which the cincha or belly band attaches, has been moved forward from the center position to be directly under the fork.

"Tapaderos, or stirrup coverings, protect the rider's feet from brush and cactus. These taps, which completely enclose all but the back of the foot, bear a remarkable resemblance to the profile of a pig, hence the name 'hog snout' style."

According to Livingston's research, "From the early Mexican saddle evolved two different, yet remarkably similar saddles. These two were the result of the spread of the Spanish colonization in both the Southwest and California."

From this originated what came to be called the California saddle, which had a heavy impact upon development of the Western saddle. This particular style, according to Livingston, reached the height of its development in the 1850s and resulted in the hackamore system of horse training, the spade bit — which will be discussed later — the rawhide riata and numerous other pieces of horse and cattle-handling equipment which became peculiar to the cowboy and still are in use today.

The tree of the California saddle was of native wood, usually covered with rawhide for additional strength. The horn still was a part of the tree. The rigging, still single, was changed to what is termed three-quarter position. The mochilla — or tree covering — was removable and behind the cantle was an "aquera," removable from the rest of the mochilla.

"This was designed to protect the dress of the caballero's senorita when she rode behind him," Livingston reports, adding that "even in those days, courtship was not always under the watchful eyes of the parents."

1800: Santa Fe Saddle   *1850: Early Texas Saddle*   *1870: Texas Trail Saddle*

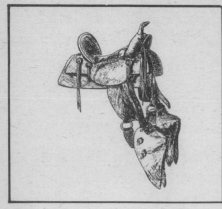  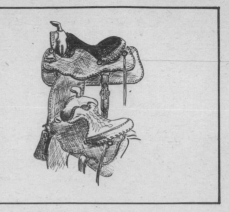

1870: Late California Saddle   1895: Swell Fork Saddle   Today's Saddle

The stirrups were carved by hand from local wood and usually were covered by a modified tapadero, allowing only toe room in the stirrup.

The Santa Fe saddle was developed about 1800 and was a modification of the early California or Spanish saddle. Many of the newcomers to the West still rode flat, English-type saddles, but soon came to realize the advantages of the wooden tree. The style developed by and for these newcomers was derived from its popularity with the early Santa Fe trade. Soon it was "ridden from border to border and from the Mississippi River to the Pacific Coast by trappers, explorers and pioneer cattlemen. The drawings of both Charlie Russell and Frederic Remington frequently depict this saddle."

Again, the wooden tree was covered with rawhide for reinforcement. The rigging varied, being installed to the buyer's preference in the three-quarter, Spanish single position or even as a centerfire item.

"The curved mochilla of the Spanish saddle was changed to a square shape, although the pockets on each side of the fork were retained. The fork and cantle were left bare," Livingston says.

The large, flat horn and the cantle with handholds cut into it were distinguishing characteristics of this saddle. The stirrups usually were of wood in the California design, but without tapaderos. Occasionally iron rings were used, but these were found to be too cold on moccasin-covered feet.

"Texas was the first area to feel the impact of Anglo-Saxon tampering," according to Livingston. "This, coupled with the thick brush of the area and Yankee 'hurry-up' ways of handling cattle, developed a new type of equipment. The short, grass ropes and system of tie-to-the-horn required a stronger saddle.

"Following the Civil War, the trail herd era also continued the modification of the traditional equipment of the vaquero. Liberal dashes of American inventiveness brought about new developments as the situation demanded.

"California, cut off from the rest of the continent by deserts, continued to develop along Spanish lines, although the equipment, methods of handling stock and the very way of marketing beef continued to change."

As a result, two distinct styles of saddles and even styles of horsemanship developed, each peculiar to its own side of the Rocky Mountains. It was not until the beginning of the present century that the two began to merge.

The early Texas saddle, developed about 1850, was pretty much a copy of the Santa Fe design, but was modified for use in the south Texas brush country. The Mexican vaqueros preferred to dally their riatas with a quick turn around the horn, holding one end with a cow on the other end. The Texans, however, simply tied the end of their grass lariats to their horns, saving a lot of wear and tear on the hands.

As a result, the tree still was made of wood, but an iron horn was bolted to the fork. Rawhide, sewn on while wet then allowed to dry and shrink, formed a strong, elastic covering around the entire tree. This same system still is used today in many instances, despite the development of high-impact plastic trees.

The Texas saddle incorporated the first full double rig, using two cinchas. Purpose of this was to hold the saddle in place in spite of the jerking experience when a heavy steer hit the end of a rope.

"The cantle and fork were also covered with leather," according to Livingston. This helped to protect the wood from the elements and to prevent warping. A permanent mochilla covered the seat and formed a skirt. This style still is made today in limited numbers with what has come to be called the "Mother Hubbard skirt."

"On the stirrup leathers, an appendage called a fender had made its appearance and served to protect the rider's legs from horse sweat. The stirrups were made of flat pieces of wood, steamed, then bent to shape."

But even the Texas saddle was open to change to meet requirements. The Texas trail saddle was developed in the 1870s, when millions of Texas cattle were being driven north to new ranges or to railheads for shipment to Eastern markets. The result was a saddle that combined what cowboys considered the best features of both the earlier Texas models and the Santa Fe saddles.

An "A" fork boasted a bolted-on steel horn that had a large flat cap on this style. There was a fairly low cantle and large, square skirts. The full double rigging was developed for strength and allegedly is called Sam Stagg rigging after its designer.

"The rig strap ran up from the ring, around the horn and back down to the ring on the opposite side," according to Livingston. "Then it returned to the spot from which it came.

"The rear rigging went completely over the bars behind the cantle in a similar way. Both front and rear were tied together by a strap still found on all double-rig saddles.

"The square skirts went completely under the tree, were lined with woolskin and were held in place by strings that went completely through skirts and tree. Fenders were, by now, an accepted addition to the stirrup leathers."

Again, the stirrups were of steamed wood with a broad tread, looking much like those on a modern roping saddle. Because of the brush problem, the Spanish tapadero had been reintroduced for use on the long trail drives.

After the discovery of gold in California, the Texas influences began to be felt on the Pacific Coast. The steel horn was added to the early California saddle.

From this development came what was known as the late California saddle, appearing initially about 1870. The earlier California style was modified so that the steel horn was pitched back, making it ideal for the roper who dallied his rope. The cantle was higher and boasted less slope than that of the Texas style of the same era, however. The fork and cantle combined to offer a deeper seat, making it popular when bad horses were being handled. This was the forerunner of what is known as the swell fork saddle.

Adhering to Spanish tradition, the rigging usually was in the centerfire position, although versions appearing in the Northwest featured the three-quarter version.

The skirts usually were square, lined with wool to help hold the saddle blanket in place. Large saddle pockets could be attached behind the cantle. Tapaderos, often up to twenty-eight inches in length for the fashion-conscious, were installed over oxbow stirrups.

The swell fork saddle made its appearance just before the turn of the century, appearing in the late 1890s in the Northwest.

"It rapidly became a favorite wherever big, rank horses were ridden," says Livingston. "During the heyday of the swell fork, some saddles spread up to twenty-two inches! Today, it is seldom that one is seen which will exceed fourteen inches. It is no wonder that slang terms for these saddles were 'freak' and 'bear trap'."

The tree usually was fashioned from willow, cottonwood or even pine, with a brass or iron horn screwed to the fork before the entire tree was covered with rawhide in the traditional wet method. The cantle was high and dished deeply to offer more security over the wide fork and short seat. The most popular rigging was the three-quarter style.

"The leather covering was in the style of the late California saddle," according to Phil Livingston, "with a one-piece seat and front jockey. This did away with the old eight-string seat. For the first time, the stirrup leathers, which went over the tree bars, were concealed under the seat cover."

Oxbow stirrups were used, since they made it easier to stay on a hard-bucking horse. Today, the professional bronc rider and trainers of cutting horses ride a slimmed-down version of this stirrup, taking full advantage of its design to do their job.

Today's Western-styled saddle continues in the honored tradition of form following function, although major changes are being made continually, depending upon possible use.

In today's era of the show ring and competition events, certain situations require special designs — at least variations on the traditional. There are frequent changes in fork width, height of the cantle, horn style and position of the rigging, all made to meet the requirements of the specialized jobs for which saddles are used today.

According to Livingston, "Ornamentation continues to become more and more a part of the workday saddle look, with hand-tooling or embossing of the leather, color, buckstitching and even silver trim being used. Beneath all of these changes, there is, however, the same basic saddle which was used when horses first came to the American continent in the early Sixteenth Century."

How does a saddle manufacturer know, when he introduces a new design, that he is making what the public wants and, perhaps more important, something that will be properly functional?

Most saddlemakers, of course, have years of experience and think they know what is functional; after all, they've been in the trade long enough that they should know the requirements.

But Big Horn has taken a different tack in recent months. They have assembled a performance board and are getting the advice of this contingent of experts.

Big Horn's Performance Rating Board is composed of professional horsemen representing the five performance events: reining, barrel racing, roping, cutting and Western pleasure. Each is a recognized expert in his or her particular event.

These board members test Big Horn saddles in their respective fields, checking out performance suitability, durability, handling features and workmanship, according to Bill Diekroeger of the saddlery's parent company, Outdoor Sports Industries.

Following each test, an eight-page evaluation report is filed by the individual doing the test work. Based upon these reports, Big Horn approves — or may modify — each saddle to meet the style requirements of these experts.

According to Diekroeger, "each saddle is shipped to the board member from the Big Horn production facilities in Chattanooga, Tennessee. No saddle tested is given special treatment beyond the normal inspection program.

"Saddles are tested in actual situations over an average of thirty days. All of the tests are conducted by the board members individually." At the same time, the board members are not endorsing the saddle, he insists, "simply conducting the tests."

Each of the individuals involved, of course, has his own ideas as to just what the saddle for his event should include. For example, Joe Lott, who checks out cutting saddles, says:

"A top cutting saddle is well built. I don't want to be ashamed of how my saddle looks, but in cutting, a horse wins points on the way he works. The right fit of a saddle is important.

"The fork and swells need to be moderate — semi-round. I like the square, comfort-type cantle with just enough height, say, three to 3½ inches. The seat should be rough-out with a low front. The gullet should be man-sized.

"Dee rigging is handier for someone who rides several horses daily. I like a large, square, sheepskin-lined skirt, with rounded corners to distribute my weight and hold the saddle in place. I like narrow, laced-leather stirrups and Blevins buckles. The fenders have to be attached well. Single-ply fenders have less bulk at the stirrup top and across the bars.

"My saddles must have a real Cheyenne roll, small and neat. The horn cap should be stitched on a long, narrow horn, or stitched and covered in rawhide on a small, round horn. My preference runs to welted swells.

"Even though design isn't crucial, I like a little silver on the cantle and maybe on the front of the fork. Neat tooling, not overdone, helps. I just won't ride a saddle with a dude look. The saddle has to look professional."

Lott, who operates out of Oxford, Florida, is a professional member of the National Cutting Horse Association, working both as a rider and trainer. His nationally ranked horses have included Official Notice, Billy's Whizzer, Kitty Holly and other top winners. He conducts his tests under both ranch and arena conditions.

Margaret Clemons of Kersey, Colorado, is a professional barrel racer. As two-time president of the Girls Rodeo Association and a contestant at major rodeos across the country, she has plenty of opportunity to try out new saddles. A nurse by profession, she also trains barrel horses and operates barrel racing clinics.

She feels that "a good barrel racing saddle is tough. It has to be able to stand up under the beating a professional gives it. But it shouldn't be tough-looking. A saddle's appearance won't affect the stopwatch, but the way a saddle looks is some indication of the built-in quality.

"Toughness and good looks have to be combined in a lightweight saddle. Weight is critical. I like saddle and pad to weigh under twenty-five pounds, lighter if possible, and a tree that fits properly over the withers and across the loin with rounded swells and a Cheyenne roll on the cantle.

"A flatter seat front is best and a roughout seat helps. I like a contoured seat with deep leg cut, narrow in front and with a slightly dished cantle. The horn cap should be tapered for better grip.

"A saddle with rigging in the skirt works fine, with the lightweight skirts lined with wool. I like cutting horse stirrups — they're narrower — and narrow stirrup leathers not too thick across the bars. The wider fenders will prevent leg pinch.

"I want my stirrups set forward and the leathers made to stay in place. Skirts should be contoured to reduce weight and to prevent any restriction of the horse's loin muscles. Most important, the saddle has to fit me and my horse, so that we both can perform at our best."

Ernie Taylor of Hugo, Oklahoma, the 1973 Rodeo Cowboys Association world champion calf roper, operates a roping school at his ranch where students receive thorough instruction in calf, steer and team roping. It is here, under ranch, school and RCA-arena conditions, that Taylor conducts his own tests.

"Strength, fit and design are the key points a roper looks for in a contest saddle. A roper's saddle is nearly as important as his horse and his skill," Taylor contends.

"I like a bullhide-covered tree — never seen a tree that's any stronger. The saddle fit comes from the tree. The bars should seat low on a horse's back, with a wide spread to the bars. The swells and the cantle should be low enough to let the roper come off the horse without interference. I prefer a wide gullet and slight leg cut.

"The cantle's Cheyenne roll should be strong. A wide roll is not necessarily a good one. A good horn angle is about eighty-five degrees, with horn cap and neck rawhide-wrapped. I find the smaller cap size better for me. The fenders and stirrup leathers should be hung forward, over the front dee. And, I must have dee rigging over the bars, with three-inch rear billets and a wide flank cinch.

"Lightly padded seats are good. I prefer the screw-type rosettes for saddle assembly. Color and tooling design are intended to help the saddle's appearance. They won't help your time.

"Saddle parts should fit together without producing bulges. A good fit between parts indicates good workmanship. My students know I demand good saddle fit to a horse's back. Without fit, you don't have anything going for you — including your rope horse."

Jim Willoughby of LaPorte, Indiana, is a professional performance horse trainer. He trained and rode both the world champion open stake reining horse at the Quarter

Horse Congress and the National Reining Horse Association futurity champion. His reining horse experience and reputation have been built over more than twenty years as a trainer/exhibitor, with wins in most of the nation's leading shows.

He insists that the saddle must allow communication between rider and horse. Natural balance is important, as is freedom of leg movement by the rider. "I like a professional appearance in the saddles I use, including quality tooling and finish. Fit of the tree to the horse, particularly across the withers and over the loin, is critical to good performance. Generally, I prefer a quarter horse spread to the tree bars, with a wide gullet. The fork and swells should be no more than medium width, not too high. I like a comfort-type cantle with a moderately deep contour, slightly higher than that of a roping saddle. And I like square skirts — less roll and more contact.

"Weight is important, but only to prevent restriction of action and excess load on the horse; for instance, single-ply fenders rather than heavy two-ply types. I prefer a narrow cap, long-angle horn. Leg cut? I'm critical about it. Deep leg cut worked into the saddle seat is much better than overhanging, big-ear type swells. Proper leg cut will maintain rider position, which is very important in maximum performance. The closer the rider is to his horse, the better he can sit a competitive reining horse."

Greg Whalen and his daughter, Debbie, are professional trainers of four American Quarter Horse Association (AQHA) champions, four AQHA youth activity champions and many fifty-point performance horses. The Whalens, of Aptos, California, specialize in Western pleasure horses and are the only father-daughter combination on Big Horn's Performance Rating Board, testing Western pleasure and Western equitation saddles.

Greg Whalen reports: "We look for saddles with overall quality and coordinated appearance for our Western pleasure horses. Good leather, deep tooling, unique design and natural-looking finish add to the impression a rider has to make. The saddle has to fit. The bars should be wide enough to prevent pinching the withers. We like an equitation-type cantle with enough contour to keep the rider in the seat. A high-rise seat front helps the rider sit upright. Padding makes seats more comfortable, of course, and the seat should be narrow enough to provide leg control comfortably.

"The back cinch and rear billets should be removable for those who like to ride without them. We like sheepskin skirt lining for long life and horse comfort. For the show ring, we use a pliable latigo rather than a stiff leather billet in the off-side front rigging to center the cinch.

"An equitation rider needs the wider stirrup to help control excess foot motion. We like three-inch stirrup leathers with a single-ply fender. Screw-type rosettes are best. They're easier to keep clean, look better and don't have strings that flop when you ride.

"The amount of tooling and silver trim is not as important as the overall quality appearance and proper fit. These are the real keys to point-winning performance."

The subject of bits is dangerous ground, indeed, as no two professional trainers seem to agree upon the type of bit and exactly how it should be used to get the most out of a horse.

Today, there is an endless variety of bits — curbs, snaffles, spade bits and hackamores — available. With each seems to go a great deal of information and an equal amount of misinformation. However, there are some basic facts concerning the bit and its uses that every horseman should know and recognize.

The bit, as such, dates back to the era before Christ and

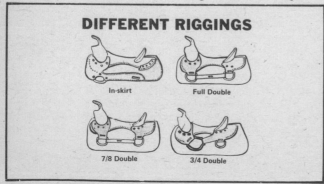

DIFFERENT RIGGINGS

In-skirt

Full Double

7/8 Double

3/4 Double

the snaffle bit used today is not all that far removed from what was used 2000 years ago. In fact, the design of that time is much the same as the familiar O-ring bit used by many English riders today.

Such bits were forged by hand and lacked many of the refinements found in today's smooth-to-the-mouth products. In fact, some of the bits used by the Romans and the Greeks were downright torturous. Later, in England, the curb bit came into being and was even more harsh, as a result of the long shanks hanging from the mouthpiece.

The Spaniards also were renowned for harsh bits, as were the Moors of the Sixteenth Century and before. The Spanish introduced the spade bit — or the version of the time — also bringing to American shores the rawhide bosal, which has changed little if any in design in the past four hundred years!

The use of the bosal or "jaquima" was introduced by these early Californians, eventually creeping into use in Texas and throughout the Southwest as a result of the work of Spanish and Mexican horse trainers.

Many trainers today still use the bosal for early training, but more tend to use the snaffle bit in early phases. The spade bit was replaced by the curb style. Today, the California horse trainers still tend to rely upon the bosal and spade bit in keeping with their Spanish forebears, while other areas lean toward snaffle bits, followed by curbs. One reason, of course, is the fact that the bosal and spade bit can require up to five years for a horse to be trained properly. With those seeking to train and turn over horseflesh as a business, that's just too long a time.

Like people, horses seem to work better under some circumstances than others and this includes the selection of a bit for the horse. The conformation of the horse's head has much to do with what type of bit will work best in training or handling him, for there are seven different points of pressure that can be used.

The first of these points, of course, is the tongue and it was on this that the American Indian tended to concentrate. In place of a bit, most of the tribes simply used a strip of rawhide for what they called a war bridle. The rawhide was put through the horse's mouth, under the tongue, then tied to the lower jaw. Depending upon what type of bit is used, the amount of pressure received on the tongue will vary.

Along the side of the tongue is another control point known as the bars. They are the flesh-covered jawbones sans teeth that separate the front incisors from the rear molars. The bit's mouthpiece fits between the two sets of teeth. The flesh covering the jawbone at the bar is sensitive, but the feeling can be deadened by overly enthusiastic jerking or pulling on the bit.

The lips play an important part when using a snaffle bit, for they have a thin layer of skin that is sensitive to pressure. There are bits that will pinch or cut the lips at the corners of the mouth and these should be avoided.

The groove on the underpart of the horse's head — just behind the lower lip — is called the curb groove. Again, this area is sensitive and can be used in control, especially with the curb bit.

The horse's nose is important with the bosal, the mechanical hackamore and some types of curb bit headstalls. The last often features a nosepiece that exerts pressure when the reins are drawn. The sensitive nose will respond to various types of inducement. For example, some horsemen favor a sheepskin pad over the nose, but this does not offer nearly as much control as braided leather. There are even those who favor a wire or cable nosepiece, although our feeling is that these verge on the inhumane.

However, it should be pointed out that, the wider the

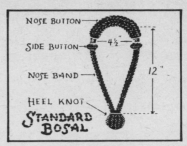

noseband, the more widespread the distribution of force, thus reducing the effectiveness.

The underside of the jaw is still another point of sensitivity. The flesh covering this area is thin, which also makes the area subject to injury. This point is used primarily in training a horse with a bosal or hackamore and those that are extremely heavy should be avoided.

Finally, there is the poll — that area atop the head that is directly behind the ears. Most horsemen think of this as nothing more than the area holding the headstall, but this also is a control point and can be injured if one tends to jerk on his bridle reins. In fact, this is the theory behind the one-ear bridle: it tends to distribute part of the pressure ahead of, as well as behind, the ear.

There is a certain charm of nostalgia and, if you will, expertise connected with the Spanish spade bit, but the average horseman will do well to forego using it. As indicated earlier, it can take years to train a spade-bit horse properly and not everyone has the tenderness of hand required to handle a horse properly when carrying such a device.

Instead, the Western horseman is more likely to find his horse trained with the snaffle, the curb bit or what is called the mechanical hackamore — not to be confused with the Spanish hackamore or bosal.

The snaffle usually is chosen as the first bit in which to train and work a young horse. Many trainers use the ordinary D-ring snaffle, inexpensive but effective, in their initial training. With a jointed mouthpiece between the rings that holds the headstall and reins, it is exceedingly mild and is not likely to injure the horse or damage the bars of the mouth.

There are more severe snaffles, of course, including one of twisted wire and even one that has several links of chain as a mouthpiece, but we'd prefer to forget these except in special cases; as the average horseman is not likely to run into those contingencies, the less said at this point, the better.

The snaffle works on the corners of the mouth and does not touch the bars, although the mouthpiece tends to draw together in its two pieces, acting upon the tongue. The snaffle should not affect the jaw, curb groove or the nose, although it can act upon the poll if the headstall is fitted improperly.

In choosing a snaffle, one should consider just what he wants it to accomplish. For example, a mouthpiece with straight sections will exert great pinching pressure on the tongue when drawn back with the reins. The smaller the diameter of the mouthpiece at the ends, where joined to the rings, the more severe the action on the tender corners of the mouth.

Again, trainers tend to differ in their approaches, but we feel that the ideal snaffle bit has a joint in the middle that cannot close so much that it actually pinches the horse's tongue. The diameter also should be large enough that it is not excessively severe on the corners of the mouth.

In introducing a young horse to the snaffle for initial breaking, some trainers cover the mouthpiece with leather or a length of rubber or plastic hose. The pinching action is reduced and the bearing surface of the bit, itself, is increased. This, in turn, reduces the severity at the corners of the mouth, too, offering a cushioning effect on the horse's mouth.

The curb bit — in its various configurations, good and bad — affords a good deal more pressure on the horse's head and mouth than the snaffle.

With the curb in the mouth, the bit is used as an axis upon which to exert pressure on the curb groove and on the poll. According to bit designers, most curb bits have a leverage ratio of two to one. This means that a draw on the reins of two inches will cause the curb strap to tighten an inch, as well as the same distance for the headstall.

The bit's cheeks have lengthy shanks, the headstall being attached to rings at the top of the shanks, the reins to similar rings at the bottom. The mouthpiece may incorporate the snaffle design, be straight, curved or have a port.

The curb strap passes from rings at the top of the bit — often those holding the headstall — under the curb groove, thus furnishing the necessary pressure when the reins are shortened.

The curb bit brings pressure to bear not only on the curb groove, but on the tongue and bars as well, if designed properly. The severity of the pressure depends largely upon the length of the shanks and the tightness of the curb strap. As indicated earlier, most trainers favor using the curb bit after a horse first has been broken with a bosal or snaffle bit.

Curb bits come in just about as many configurations as there are designers. Most have their own ideas as to what works best and it usually is up to the individual trainer to make his selection and determine what will work best on a specific horse.

These bits, for example, are available with fixed mouthpieces or in a loose jaw style. On the former, the cheekpieces are welded or even bolted directly to the mouthpiece, allowing no movement of either.

The loose jaw style, dating back to early Spanish designs, allows the cheekpieces to move since they are mounted to the mouthpiece by means of swivels at each end.

The loose jaw style is favored by most trainers and knowledgeable horsemen, as it is less severe in the horse's mouth. Also, it promotes flow of saliva and allows the horse to work more naturally. Incidentally, in recent years, some curb bits have been fashioned of aluminum. We don't recommend these, as they tend to hang incorrectly in the horse's mouth and, because of their light weight, react too severely on the bars.

Trainers contend that the loose jaw bit gives better control, allowing them to work with the fingertips, using minimum pressure on the reins, the swivel action doing much of the directing.

But the mouthpiece is the most controversial part of the curb bit, affecting two points of control as it does: the tongue and the bars.

A straight bar mouthpiece will put more pressure on the tongue than on the bars of the mouth, as the tongue tends to lift the bit off the bars completely when there is no pressure from the reins. Thus, the action on the tongue is rougher than it would be with a low or medium port bit.

Incidentally, among the unknowing there is a sad misconception here. Simply because the bar is straight, many neophytes automatically assume it is the least harsh of the various styles.

As mentioned earlier, the smaller the diameter of the mouthpiece, the more severe it can be in the horse's mouth. The low port mouthpiece has become one of the more popular styles, since it creates almost equal pressure on the bars and tongue. Thus, it is not overly harsh on the bars,

not deadening the nerves or reducing overall sensitivity.

With a high port bit, the tongue still is in contact but the greater part of the pressure is on the bars. However, in selecting such a bit, be certain that the edges of the port are smooth so there is no irritation to the tongue. The high port mouthpiece, incidentally, does not work against the roof of the horse's mouth as some horsemen think. The port would have to be more than four inches high before this would happen.

The snaffle-type curb bit is entirely different from the true snaffle and the knowledgeable horseman recognizes the difference. When you attach the snaffle to shanks and use a curb strap, you are working with an entirely different tool than the simple snaffle attached to D or O rings. The Western curb bit with a snaffle mouthpiece is considerably more severe. When the bit has a curb strap as well, it can mean severe control since there is great pressure being used on the shanks to pull the mouthpiece into what amounts to a nutcracker action on the tongue. Again, diameter of the mouthpiece can mean a great deal in determining severity.

The cricket bit is gaining in popularity across the country as there is better understanding. In the past, many felt this was a severe bit but, if designed properly, this becomes a misconception.

Most crickets are of copper, which tends to increase the flow of saliva in the horse's mouth. Incidentally, there are those who favor copper-plated mouthpieces in any kind of a bit over chrome or iron, for the same reason. When the mouth is dry, it soon becomes insensitive.

More important, perhaps, is the fact that the cricket acts as a plaything for the horse, similar to a pacifier for a baby, as the animal rolls his tongue over the movable piece of metal.

However, to serve this function, the cricket — in fact the entire mouthpiece — must be designed correctly. Some past designers have made the port high and narrow, only a small cricket fitting into it. The ideal is for the cricket to be placed low in the port, almost centered on the metal bar that extends to the cheekpieces.

At the other extreme, the port that is too high and has a small cricket placed high in the loop will tend to pinch the tongue, at the same time decreasing pressure. As a result, it becomes an irritant rather than an aid.

The spade bit still is popular on the West Coast, although we feel there are a good many more of these bits than people who know how to properly use them.

The spade bit, derived from the old Spanish design, has a port that will measure as much as four and one-half inches in height. It usually has a good deal of copper incorporated and often will use a cricket to help soothe the horse. The port — or spade — is meant to help in training the horse to flex at the poll and maintain his headset properly. However, the same can be accomplished by putting the horse in double reins and tying the reins to the saddle horn for an hour or so over several days.

Again, if the bridle is adjusted properly, the spade should not work on the roof of the mouth.

Less severe is the so-called half-breed bit, which has a copper-covered port and is about two inches high. It also has a large copper cricket that works against the tongue. As the top of the port is covered with copper, the cricket — usually serrated — cannot come in contact with the roof of the horse's mouth.

The question that most new horsemen ask is: "What kind of mouthpiece should I use on my horse?" That's up to the individual and only he can make the determination, but a good deal of consideration should be given to whether he has what horsemen call "good hands."

A good rule is to use the mildest bit in which a horse will

work well. At the same time, as a horse grows older, he sometimes becomes insensitive to a specific bit and it becomes necessary to increase the severity just a trifle.

Another consideration involves selection of the proper curb strap for your horse. There are any number of types and styles, but they break down into three basic designs. Perhaps the most popular are either single or double links of flat chain, which afford the greatest amount of control. The single-link type is the more severe and tends to pinch the tender skin of the curb groove. A plain leather strap comprises the third type and, since it has smooth surfaces, is the least severe.

Another type combines a leather strap in the center with single links of chain at each end, while another alternative has leather at the ends, buckling to the bit, with chain in the center.

There are those who suggest a chain bit be covered with a piece of rubber hose, but it would be equally as simple to use the leather strap. Severity of the strap depends largely upon its length. The shorter, the more severe the fulcrum action on the bit. All too often, when an inexperienced horseman has trouble finding a bit that works well on his horse, he discovers it isn't the bit at all that is creating problems; the curb strap is too short or too long.

This chapter would not be complete without discussion of the hackamore. First, there is a great deal of misunderstanding as to precisely what is a hackamore.

Actually, the hackamore originated during the Spanish era and incorporates the bosal of braided rawhide with a rawhide core. Length and width are selected to be in proper proportion to the side of the horse and the stiffer the bosal, the more control it provides.

At the end of the braided section is a heavy knot of rawhide called the heel knot. To this is attached the mecate or horsehair reins, while the noseband is attached to a standard headstall or perhaps just a strip of latigo leather to form a headstall. The mecate usually is long enough that, when rigged properly, it affords a pair of closed reins as well as a lead rope, the end of which can be tied to the saddle or even looped and tied around the horse's neck.

The rawhide bosal acts mostly on the lower part of the jawbones which have only a thin covering of skin, bringing the nerves close to the surface. These bones, if you will look closely at your horse's head, tend to jut out just above the chin, then taper towards the throat.

Since the bosal can be quite severe, one problem, of course, is that a quick or hard jerk can cause the hard rawhide to break the skin.

That, in turn, leads to another problem; or an extension of a problem mentioned in connection with the spade bit. While one can buy a bosal in almost any tack shop, there are few people who know how to use it properly. In fact, this is rapidly becoming a lost art, trainers tending to introduce a young horse to the snaffle bit, bypassing this part of training.

The other segment of this discussion encompasses the so-called hackamore bit or mechanical hackamore. Serious horsemen who understand the use of the bosal tend to think of this item of tack as a vise into which one is putting his head and they aren't entirely wrong. In untrained hands, it can create problems. Also, there have been versions of this rig that border on the inhumane, incorporating rigid nosebands of aluminum or alloy pipe, pieces of thin cable, et al. We even know of one man who wrapped the noseband of a mechanical hackamore with baling wire with the idea that this would help him control a rank horse.

But before we get into how the mechanical hackamore acts on the horse's control points, perhaps a description is in order for those unfamiliar with this tool.

The noseband is somewhat shorter than that on the bosal and is attached to long-shanked cheekpieces much like those on a curb bit. A strap running beneath the jaw connects the two shanks, which is held on the horse's head by a standard headstall. There is no mouthpiece and it is the long shanks that bring about the pressure.

For what it is worth, this device is not allowed in most events recognized by the American Horse Shows Association, with the exception of gymkhana contests. However, it is popular with ropers, cutters, barrel racers and pole benders, all of whom want to allow their horses maximum freedom of their heads.

Many riders — including the idiot who wrapped the noseband with wire — think that the primary pressure point is the nose. Actually, it is the underside of the horse's jaw. The jaw strap here is critical, riding several inches higher than does the curb strap on a curb bit. It reacts upon the sensitive nerves along the jaw. Again, there are those who use a chain rather than a strap, resulting in maximum severity.

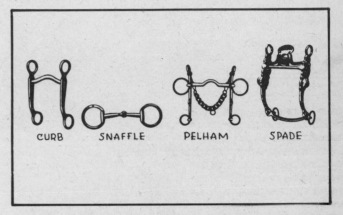

CURB   SNAFFLE   PELHAM   SPADE

This is not to underemphasize the importance of the noseband. The size and texture of this part have much to do with the manner in which the horse reacts. As might be surmised, a thin, small-diameter noseband results in greater force being exerted on a smaller area and therefore is more severe. As a result, many riders favor a flat piece of heavy leather — sometimes reinforced with several thicknesses — over the nose.

If your horse tends to throw his nose up, it may mean that the noseband is too severe. If using a braided rawhide band, it might be better to try the flat leather type.

Another type of noseband looks much like the braided rawhide version at first glance, but actually is a laced type with a piece of spring steel woven into it. Thus, with barrel racing or gymkhana horses, even when the rein is loose, there still is pressure on the nose.

The ideal hackamore, we feel, has a four-to-one ratio. The shanks are long enough and the chin strap set so that a four-inch draw on the reins means that there is one inch of tightening on the chin strap and the noseband.

But a word of caution: The nerves that are used in controlling a horse with the mechanical hackamore are subject to deadening, as are the nerves in the bars of the mouth. Too much severe treatment simply will deaden these nerves. Never jerk on a hackamore with both reins at the same time to punish a horse, although there are good trainers who advocate jerking first one rein, then the other, giving a see-sawing effect as punishment.

But the key term with the hackamore again is good hands. It takes careful handling and tack to get the best out of a horse with either the bosal or the hackamore bit.

Good hands can be developed in time, but don't ruin a good horse while you're learning!

BASIC HORSE TRAINING

Chapter 6

There Are Many Training Procedures
And Here Is One!

EVERY HORSEMAN has his own unique method of starting a horse. There is no absolute best way, but with this in mind, this procedure may help those still searching for a workable technique.

Each year thousands of potentially great horses are ruined, because their owners insist upon a do-it-yourself training program. Ray Doering, a prominent horse trainer from Tucson, Arizona, once said, "The cowboy is the most imitated person in the world." Truer words were never spoken. It seems that anybody who puts on a big hat and a pair of high-heeled boots is transformed miraculously into a dyed-in-the-wool cowboy. Nothing could be further from the truth and this is something we all should keep in mind.

The most crucial period of time for a horse in training takes place from the first saddling until he is green broke. "Green broke" means able to walk, trot and canter as well as turn, stop, back and be trustworthy in general. From this stage he is ready to go into specialized training.

It is assumed that by 2 years of age a horse is halter broken and broken to tie. This is where we will begin.

GROUND WORK

It is extremely important throughout the whole training period to "keep your cool." Patience is the most important quality of any horse trainer, as he must keep in mind that this is a confusing period for the young horse. He is being made to do many things that are both frightening and senseless to him. If, at any time, you become frustrated with him, stop right where you are and take a five-minute break. After you have cooled off and collected yourself, go back and pick up where you left off.

The average age at which a young horse should go into training falls somewhere between 2 and 4 years. The best guide as to when to begin is the size of the horse. If the horse is small or thin-legged, he is apt to be 3 or 4 before he can be started without any chance of injury. On the other hand, if a horse is large and big-boned, he can be started safely at 2 or 2½ years of age.

There is research being done on the epiphyseal line of the horse's leg bone which someday may lead to a definite time at which each individual horse can be safely started; however, until such time, we will have to rely upon general appearance.

This will be a light period of training for the horse, so it is usually unnecessary to increase his feed. If he does start dropping weight, you can increase his ration slowly to keep him in good condition. There is no set rule for feeding a horse in training. This area is best summed up by the age-old quotation, "The eye of the master fattens the stock."

To begin training, you will need a stout halter with a six-foot lead rope and an old saddle blanket. Take the horse to an area that is isolated from other horses and people. This will help you maintain his full attention.

The first operation will consist of the "sacking out" procedure. A box stall makes an ideal place to work. Back the young horse into a corner so he cannot move either backwards or too far from side to side. The only way that he can move now is forward — and you are responsible for blocking that exit.

While holding the lead rope in your left hand and the saddle blanket in your right hand, approach the horse slowly. Rub him around the head and neck with the blanket, then over the front part of his body. He is likely to shy away at first, but as he discovers that no harm is being done him, he soon will settle down. Continue rubbing him with the blanket until he stands quietly, pausing often to pat him on the neck and constantly talking to him in a soft and soothing voice. Although a horse may not understand what you are saying, he does understand your tone of voice.

After you have acquainted him thoroughly with the blanket, begin to flop it against his shoulder; slowly and softly at first, then a little harder as he begins to settle down. Continue this same procedure over his entire body including his head, stomach, legs. It is important to move around and do both sides. After about ten minutes, either lay the blanket down or drape it over his back and handle his legs, lifting them and setting them down. When you finish this, pat him on the neck and put him away. Continue to sack him out until he will stand quietly, while you

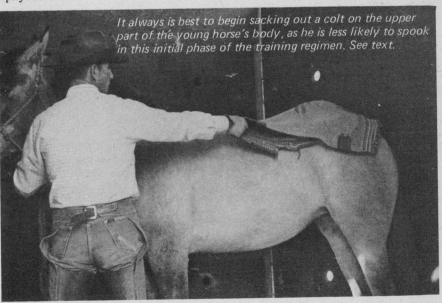

It always is best to begin sacking out a colt on the upper part of the young horse's body, as he is less likely to spook in this initial phase of the training regimen. See text.

When ponying the green horse, do it from the back of an older horse that doesn't rattle easily. After dallying the rope, leave a foot of slack but not too much. You don't want the horse to become entangled, nor to try climbing in your lap!

Many things can be taught by ground driving the young horse. He should be put in a light bosal and the reins run back through the stirrups, which are fastened together with rope. In initial driving, keep some slack in the lines, if possible.

When ready to mount the horse, hold both the mane and reins in the left hand, the horn with the right. Stay in close to the horse when putting the foot in the stirrup, which keeps you in position should the horse begin wiggling around.

flop the saddle blanket over his entire body. This should take three or four days with two twenty-minute sessions each day.

The next operation will consist of saddling and, again, a box stall makes an ideal place to work. For this, you need an old saddle that can be banged around. Put a saddle blanket on, then lift the saddle on slowly, being careful not to let the cinches fall down and startle him. Cinch it up snugly, then continue with the sacking out procedure. When he stands quietly, flop the stirrup leathers against his sides, slowly at first, then more vigorously as he settles down.

Take the saddle on and off several times, each time putting it on a little more quickly, until he allows you to toss it on without flinching.

The last time you put it on, lead him around the stall, turning him sharply in both directions. When you are finished, leave him alone in the stall with the saddle on for a couple of hours. This should be done for another three days, once each day. On the seventh day of the training period, slip your foot into the stirrup and ease your weight onto it, stepping down often. When he stands quietly for this, ease up into the saddle and sit for a few seconds, shifting your weight from side to side. Do this at least a half-a-dozen times, then put him away.

He now is going into his second week of training and should be ready to be ponied from another horse. You will need a fenced area, such as a riding ring; a helper; and an older horse that handles well and doesn't rattle easily. It is best to use a gelding for a snubbing horse, as you will have your hands full without having to fight him, too.

Saddle the young horse in the box stall and have your helper hold him, while you get mounted on the snubbing horse. The snubbing horse should have a saddle with both a front and rear cinch and, if possible, a breast collar, as there may be a lot of pull put on it.

Have your helper lead the young horse out of the stall and hold him, while you dally the lead rope around your saddle horn. It is important that you dally and not tie to the saddle horn, so you can get loose quickly if you get in trouble.

Leave about a foot of slack between your dally and the halter, so the young horse can keep his balance. If you have too much slack, you run the risk of getting tangled up in it as well as allowing the younger horse a running start at you. It is advisable to carry a dogging bat during the ponying period, especially if you are working with a young stallion. A few sharp thumps will change his mind quickly about chewing on your horse's neck or getting up in the saddle with you.

Lead the younger horse to the fenced area and walk him for about five minutes, going in both directions and turning often. Be sure to keep him right alongside of you. If he starts moving too fast, make a small circle away from him to slow him down. He is likely to balk at first, so your helper may have to work behind him to keep him moving. When he begins to walk out well, proceed to a jog, then to a canter, turning and stopping often. The ponying operation should last for three days with a twenty to thirty-minute session each day.

The young horse is now ready to be ground driven. For this period of training, you will need a light bosal and a set of driving lines. The driving lines can be made out of either leather or nylon and should be at least twenty feet long, with large, heavy snaps on the ends.

Take the young horse to the fenced area with his saddle on. Put the bosal on and tie the stirrups together beneath his heart girth with a short piece of rope. If the bosal has a metal ring plaited into it, you can snap the driving lines to the ring. If not, you will need large-enough snaps to go around the sides or cheeks of the bosal.

When you have fastened the driving lines to each side of the bosal, run each line through the stirrup on its respective side. Have your helper stand at the horse's head, while you move the lines to the rear of the horse and coil up the slack. The young horse shouldn't be bothered much by this step, if you have done a good job of sacking him out.

You should be positioned about ten feet behind the horse with a line in each hand. Hold the lines at chest height and wide apart. Try to keep enough slack in the lines so they form an arch from the stirrups, down to the horse's hocks, then up to your hands. When you are in position,

have your helper move away from the horse's head and you are ready to begin.

Use your lines in a slapping motion against the horse's rear to make him move forward. Keep him going in a straight line by anticipating his turns. If his head starts to swing to the left, straighten him up by tugging on the right line and vice versa. You will find that it is easier to work along the fence at first, until you gain control. Try not to pull on the horse's head any more than necessary. Use your wrists to pull and slack, pull and slack, until you gain the response you are after. A steady, hard pull will only make a young horse fight you.

Make the horse walk around the fenced area for about five minutes, stopping every forty or fifty feet by tugging at

When backing the horse on the driving lines, he is cued by a pull on the lines, while keeping head looking directly forward.

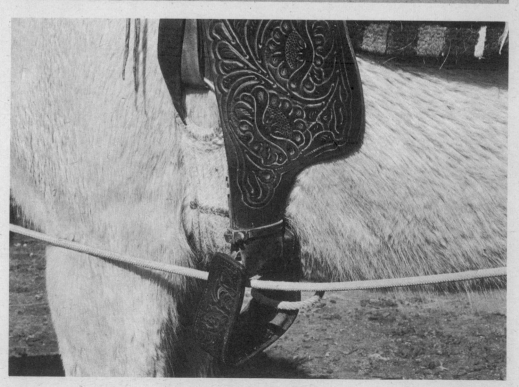

This close-up shows how the stirrups can be fastened, with driving line running through.

his head and saying, "Whoa." Each time you stop, make him stand still on slack lines for a few second before proceeding. He soon will begin to associate the word command, "whoa," with stopping and will require less and less pressure to stop.

After you gain a good response on stopping, start working him on turning. When turning, turn into the fence. This will prevent him from making a large circle. Begin your turns from a stopped position until he catches on. Tug at the line on the fence side and give slack to the other line. As he is making a turn, you should move in a semi-circle away from the fence and come in behind him as he completes the turn.

Be careful not to fight him if he refuses you. Be patient and continue to use the pull and slack method and he will respond before too long. As he moves in the direction that you are calling for, slack up on his head. When he starts to work well on his turns, speed him up by slapping him on the rear with the slack line as he turns into the fence. When he catches on, start the whole process over again at the jog.

Backing on the driving lines may take a little longer than stopping and turning. Start from the stopped position and use the pull and slack method. When you get the young horse to take one or two steps backwards, stop and let him stand. Don't expect too much at first. You may find it necessary to tug on one line, then the other, in a see-saw fashion to get him to move backwards. You should use the word command, "back," each time you tug on his head. After he has moved backwards a couple of times, move him forward and work on turning or stopping for a while.

As he begins to back more easily, work on backing him in a straight line by keeping his head straight.

You can do this by tugging a little harder on the line that his head turns away from. You must be careful to work only a short while on each operation. After you have worked on turning a couple of times, work on his stop or his back, then come back to turns. Too much time spent on just one operation alone can easily cause a young horse to sour and begin to fight you. The ground driving period should last for about four days, with a thirty-minute workout each day.

The young horse now has been in training for eleven days and is ready to be worked on a longe line. Working on the longe line will teach the young horse to walk, trot and canter. He also will begin to pick up his leads during this period. You can use one of your driving lines for a longe line, but in addition, you will need a long buggy whip.

Again, take the young horse to the fenced area with his saddle on. You can use either a bosal or a halter on his head. It is best not to tie the stirrups together during this period of training, as they will flop against his sides and serve the same purpose as the sacking out period.

Snap onto the bosal with your line and move to the center of your imaginary circle. Use your buggy whip by snapping it on the ground to get the horse to move forward. If he breaks out of a walk, slow him down by pulling his head to you. As you make him walk in a circle around you, remain stationary and don't walk with him. Start with a small circle, then let out more line as he begins to catch on. Keep him out the length of the line as he works. When he has made a couple of circles in one direction, turn him toward you and go the other way. Stop him often by pulling his head toward you and saying, "whoa." Make him stand still, while you walk up and scratch his forehead, then return to the center of the circle and start again.

When he begins to work well at the walk, put him into a jog by snapping the buggy whip on the ground and follow the same procedure used at the walk. When he is working well at the walk and jog, go to the canter. Maintain control at all times, keeping in mind that the canter is a slow, collected gait, not a run.

Once the young horse is working well at the walk, trot and canter, it is time to start working on his leads.

To get him to take the right lead, you may find it necessary to have a little slack in your line when he breaks into a canter. If he picks up the right lead, keep him going, but if he starts out in the wrong lead or switches to it, stop him immediately and start again. Don't continue to let him work in the wrong lead. After a while, he will begin to pick up the correct lead automatically and will stay in it.

By the end of three days on the longe line, at thirty to

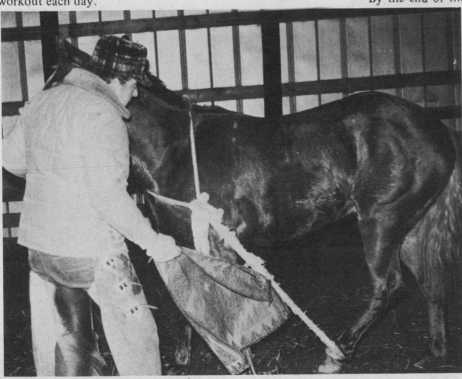

Where circumstances warrant, trainers frequently hobble horses during the sacking routine. They soon get the idea they won't be hurt by the floppy, burlap sack.

During a stop, slack in reins should be taken up with wrists. Using entire arms is a mistake seen commonly with novice riders.

forty minutes per session, the young horse should be working at a walk, trot and canter as well as taking the correct leads and working on a slack line. He should also know the word command "whoa" by this time.

The young horse has now been in training for two weeks and the period of ground work has drawn to a close, although throughout the training period you may want to put him back on the driving lines for a brush-up.

IN THE SADDLE

The young horse, when entering his third week of training, is ready to be ridden. It is advisable to use a saddle that is light, but comfortable to sit in.

Put the bosal and saddle, with pad and blanket underneath, on the horse and lead him to the ring. It usually is a good idea to longe him for five or ten minutes before you

During initial mounting — and throughout training cycle — move slowly so you won't frighten the still-green horse.

get on. This will give him a chance to loosen up and settle down.

After you have longed him, remove the longe line and adjust your cinches, then move him a few steps to untrack him. Tie the lead line of the bosal to the front tie string of the saddle, leaving enough slack so the horse can move his head in any direction without receiving any pull.

Hold your reins in your left hand and ease your foot into the stirrup. On a rank colt, hold the mane and reins both in your left hand. Slowly put your weight onto the stirrup and slip up and into the saddle. Talk to the young horse constantly in a soft voice and be careful not to make any fast movements that might startle him.

When you are well seated, with a rein in each hand, ease him forward by squeezing with both calves. Use whatever pressure is needed to gain a forward movement. Keep your hands about twelve inches above the saddle horn and about eighteen inches apart. A young horse will learn to work by watching your hands. Always keep plenty of slack in your reins and use the pull and slack method to turn, slow down, or stop. Remember that light hands are a horseman's greatest gift. Use only your wrists, never pull on a horse's head with your arms.

Begin by walking along the fence in one direction for about five minutes, stopping every so often by tugging on the reins, shifting your weight slightly back and saying, "whoa." After five minutes, reverse and follow the same procedure in the other direction.

Now dismount and mount several times, making the horse stand still as you do. Ten to fifteen minutes of riding is plenty for the first day.

On the second day begin the same as before, walking for several minutes in both directions and stopping often. After about ten minutes, ease the young horse into a slow jog, first in one direction, then in the other. Make him work on slack reins, using the pull and slack method to keep his jog slow and easy. After ten minutes of jogging, put him away.

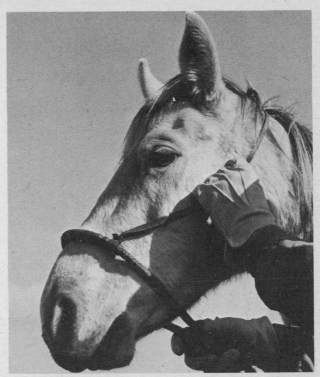

Of course, the proper tack is required before any time is devoted to schooling the new mount, as is the in-depth knowledge of what's required. Have both — or headaches!

On the third day of riding, work for five minutes at a walk, for five minutes at a jog, then ease him into a slow canter. Don't be concerned about correct leads yet, as this will come later. You are just getting the young horse used to carrying a man's weight at different gaits right now.

Working a horse on the longe line until he learns the proper gaits is followed by teaching him to pick up the proper leads. Don't let him work on the wrong lead. If he picks up the wrong lead, stop him, then start him up again.

Canter in one direction for about one minute, then walk and jog for a few minutes before reversing and cantering in the other direction. Remember to work on slack reins. After twenty to thirty minutes, put him away.

On the fourth day you can dispense with longing and go right to work. Always begin by walking for several minutes to give the horse a chance to loosen up. Follow the same procedure as on the third day, only do more turning and stopping. When you make a turn, use the pull and slack method and be patient. It is a good idea to turn into the fence to keep the young horse from making a large circle. Shift your weight slightly in the direction of the turn.

On the fifth day, begin with your regular workout in the ring for fifteen minutes, then leave the ring and ride around at a walk for another ten minutes. It goes without saying that you should avoid roads with traffic or any type of activity that might excite or scare the horse. Keep in mind

rope to a solid post. The other end was tied around the horse's neck. Once rigged up, he would put the horse into a dead run and yell "whoa" at the instant the rope came tight. He put one heck of a stop on the few that lived.

While you are working on the stop, be careful not to stop in the same place twice. Stopping at the same place more than once can cause the horse to begin to anticipate your cues, which is to be avoided.

Begin by stopping at the walk; then as the young horse begins to respond, work at a jog, then at a canter. Every time you make a stop, make him stand still for several seconds before proceeding. Pick an imaginary spot about twenty yards ahead of you and cue for the stop when the horse reaches it. This allows for a premeditated stop. Spur-of-the-moment decisions by the rider will only lead to confusion on the part of the horse.

Four cues must be given at the same instant to gain a

The direct rein method is used to first teach a horse to turn from upon his back, which leads to a knowledge of the neck reining.

that your horse is not broke yet and may try you at any time. Stay awake.

On the sixth day, work in the ring at the walk, trot and canter. Spend most of this session on the areas in which you are having trouble. After thirty minutes put him away.

The seventh day is a day of rest. Leave the horse alone and let him think about it.

STOPPING

The horse now has been in training for three full weeks and it is time to concentrate on stopping, turning, leads, and backing.

For the next three weeks, the young horse should be worked for thirty to forty-five minutes each day, with one day each week off for rest. During each workout it is important not to work on any one thing for more than a few minutes at a time.

For example, work on stopping for a couple of minutes, on turning, on leads, then come back to stopping. Too much time spent on one operation easily can cause a young horse to sour and begin to fight you.

Come back to trouble areas more often. Stopping is one of the most important areas of concern. A horse should stop with his rear legs well underneath him. If he is to accomplish this, the cue to stop must be applied while his front feet are off the ground. You can do this by looking down between his neck and your hand — keeping your eyes on his lead foot.

We once heard of a fellow who would tie a hundred-foot

good stop. The verbal command, "whoa," should be said as you shift your weight slightly back and your feet are shifted slightly forward. At the same time, your wrists should flex to tug on the bosal. In some cases you may want to turn the horse's head slightly into the fence, to use it as an aid in stopping.

A bull ring is an ideal place to work a young horse on turning, but if you do not have access to one, be sure to use a fenced area.

To turn properly, a horse must work off of his rear legs. That is, he must keep them stationary and use them as a pivot point.

As in stopping, there are four cues that must be given at the same instant to gain a good turn. Shift your weight slightly onto the stirrup that you are turning towards. At the same time, push into the horse with your off knee and pull and slack with the lead rein, while you bear into his neck with the other rein.

You should start your work on turns from a stopped position. Set the young horse up by taking one step back and applying the four turning cues together gently. Pull and slack to get him to move his front end around, while keeping his rear legs in place. Be patient and work slowly until he gets the idea.

Next, proceed at a walk along the fence. Stay far enough away from the fence so the horse doesn't hit it when he turns, but close enough so it can be used an an aid in preventing too large a circle.

When you start getting a good response at the walk,

proceed to a jog, then on to a canter. Canter slowly out away from the fence, then make a circle back toward the fence by putting tension on the lead rein with the pull and slack method. Make your circle come back along the fence which will act as an aid, and proceed in the same direction.

As the young horse begins to get the idea, start to work him on a set up and turn back. Begin at the walk stage and then come to a stop — take one step back and turn him around.

If a corner is available, ride from the center of the working area straight into the corner at full speed. As the young horse approaches the fence he will begin to shift back and forth, deciding which way to go. It is important to apply your cues at an instant when his front end is off the ground to get him to pivot on his rear end.

If you have trouble with this method, ride him in a circle which comes along the fence at one point. As you are com-

Leg cues must be mastered before a horse is capable of performing rollbacks (above). He here is being set up for rollback. Teaching young horse to get on proper lead, use same spot in fence for giving the cue (lower right).

ing into the fence, catch him with his front feet off the ground and cue him to change direction. This time, break the rule and use a hard pull on the lead rein. After two or three times he should begin to anticipate your turn with your weight shift.

While you are working a horse along a fence and using it as an aid, a young horse often will try to turn the tables and rub your legs on it. You can quickly change his mind if you have a catch rope handy. You will have to get off the horse for this old Indian trick. Tie one end of the catch rope onto the bosal and feed out about thirty feet. Spook him down the fence, then hip lock him two or three times by taking one wrap around your seat with the rope and sitting back on it hard. He will soon learn to give to your tug on the rein.

LEADS

The longe line period should have acquainted the young horse with his leads; however, you still will have to spend some time brushing him up on them as you go along.

There are three cues that should be given at the same instant to start a horse into the correct lead. Again you will be using the fence as an aid.

Hold the rein that is on the fence side snug enough so the horse's head is cocked slightly into the rail. Urge the

horse forward by squeezing with your leg closest to the fence and, at the same time, shift your other leg forward, putting your weight on it. When all of these cues are given at the same time, the young horse will naturally lead with the inside leg to catch your weight and keep his balance.

A young horse often will switch leads while you are working him. When he does, stop immediately and start again in the correct lead.

There are basically two types of lead changes: the flying change, which comes from a figure eight; and the natural

Some horses are more adaptable to learning slide stops than others. This facet of training is somewhat advanced.

change, which comes from a change of direction. The flying change is beyond the realm of green-breaking, but you should be concerned with the natural change.

To get a young horse to do a natural change, begin by cantering along the fence in the correct lead. Make a slow turn and cut across the working area, staying in the same lead. As you approach the opposite fence, turn in the other direction and at the same instant cue the horse for the correct lead in the new direction. He should change leads naturally to catch your weight and keep his balance.

Handling a horse's feet each time he's ridden does more than get him used to humans; it also makes all farrier attention much easier — a real bonus!

BACKING THE YOUNG HORSE

Ninety percent of backing is taught with driving lines. There are three cues given at the same time to get a horse to back. The verbal command, "back," should be given, as you squeeze with both legs, and use the pull and slack method on the reins.

If you have trouble getting a young horse to back up, put him back on the driving lines until he gets the idea, then get back on him and start again. Don't expect too much at first. It is important to remember that one or two steps backwards is plenty for a young horse. If you ask for too much too soon, you will only make him fight you.

Walk down the fence line, stop, then back one or two steps and stop again. Wait a few seconds, then more forward again.

Keep him in a straight line when you are backing by tugging a little harder on the rein so that his head swings away.

Never "pull" a horse backward by sheer force. Just be patient and be satisfied with a couple of steps. A fast, straight backup will be taught to him somewhere beyond the green-breaking stage.

Some trainers prefer to put the backing maneuver on their horses from the saddle, skipping the ground driving procedure. This calls for the proper use of leg pressure and a goodly amount of patience.

When in the training ring, begin by taking up the reins, which sets a barrier for him with the bit. While triggering the reins lightly with the fingers, squeeze with both legs, at the same time shifting your weight slightly backwards.

At this point, if the horse gives way even a step, reward him with slack reins and release the leg pressure. Be satisfied the first day with a small step or two, then follow this

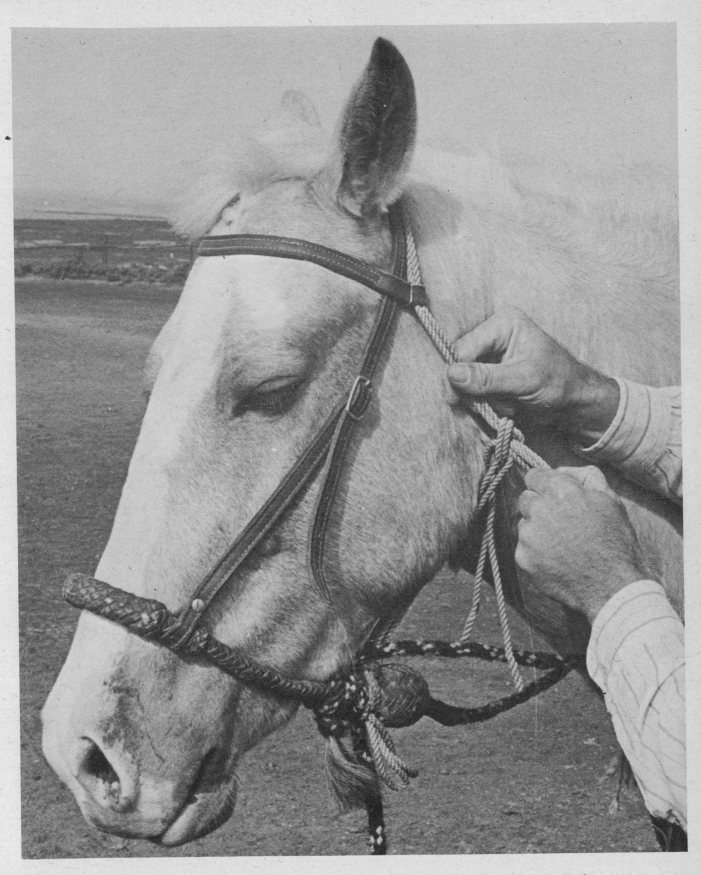

Throughout the entire training cycle — and throughout his lifetime — the proper fit of the hackamore is of great importance, if the horse is to react properly to signals which are transmitted through it. Check it frequently.

the next day with several steps willingly. Don't overback him or he'll learn to stick. Spread his backing training over several days.

If you have an older horse that absolutely refuses to step backwards, put him in a corner of a high board corral and ask him to back. Hold his head in the corner by using a snaffle bit or hackamore of the braided rawhide type. If he refuses to back, get after him pretty good with the bat. This leaves him the choice of staying where he is or backing out.

This set of circumstances usually will cause an old, spoiled horse to take a few steps backward, possibly for the first time in his life. Remember that this is not the procedure that should be used on a young horse that doesn't know what you're asking.

These two methods are fine for teaching a horse to back on cue while being ridden, but there are times when the horse is required to back without the horseman being up; for instance, out of a trailer.

Teaching a young horse to back from the ground is easy for most horseowners. After you have taught him to lead and he's accustomed to being handled, stand in front of him, facing him. Take the lead shank up close to the halter and ask him to back by a tug toward his chest. At the same time, take a stiff whip or stick and hold it across in front of him.

If he doesn't back readily when you ask him to with the tug, give him a light tap on the chest with the whip or stick. Don't hit him hard — remember, you're just teaching him what you want. Don't expect too much of him at one time. If you get a little back out of him, reward him with a pat on the neck and give him slack.

The verbal cue, "back," is given each time the horse is asked to back. He soon will learn the meaning and, after he gets the hang of what's being asked, will back readily down trailer ramps, away from water troughs and the like.

While you are riding the young horse regularly for a six-week period, you should be working at gentling him from the ground, too. Handle his legs every day, picking them up and holding them for several seconds before setting them down again. It is advisable to have the young horse shod with light training plates before you begin riding him. Keep him off rough ground and clean his feet daily. If his feet get sore, you will lose his full attention quickly and he will begin to fight you.

Keep his back well padded while you are riding him and watch for cinch sores and skinned places. A little Vaseline on skinned areas will keep the flies from making them worse and also will help the hair grow back quickly.

Spend some time teaching him to load into a trailer and haul him around the ranch a little bit.

Hobble him every so often, using a good set of hobbles that are double stitched, with floating D rings and sheepskin lining.

Spurs are a great aid if you know how to use them properly, but they can work to your disadvantage if you do not. Use them if you know how, leave them hanging on the wall if you don't.

Have your veterinarian give the horse a health check before you begin the training period. Make sure he has a tetanus shot, as minor injuries are common during the green-breaking period.

When you finish working him, make sure he is cooled out well before you put him away. If you are in a cold climate, you will have to walk him out. If you are in a warm climate, tie him up and hose him down with water thoroughly, then you can leave him tied until he dries off in the sun. The latter method has several advantages. Not only does it mean less leg work for you, but it also cleans off loose hair and dirt and serves much the same purpose as does sacking him out.

Getting the young horse out from the training pen is good therapy both for horse and horseman. While this won't, in most cases, entail punching cattle during roundup, it's the change of scenery that keeps the horse from getting stale and sour.

At least one day each week, you should ride him out of the ring. Not only does this break up a monotonous routine, but it also gets him used to various situations.

Be patient with him, but let him know that you are the boss. Don't be afraid to discipline him, if he has it coming. There is nothing more frustrating than a spoiled horse and nothing more disgusting than the person who spoiled him.

Don't be afraid to ask for help if you run into difficulties. When a problem arises that has you stumped, go ask for advice from a reputable horseman who has made a success of himself in the profession of horse training. At the same time, beware of the advice given by the non-professional.

This six-week period of green-breaking will have an effect on the horse for the rest of his life. If he goes on to be a finished horse, he will spend a year in the hackamore, six months in a snaffle bit, six more months in a grazing bit and another year in a spade bit. All during this three-year period, someone will be either praising you or cussing you for your work.

Always be willing to learn. If you are in the horse business for a hundred years, you will still be learning when you finish. Remember the saying, "Trust the man who is searching for truth — but beware of the man who has found it."

The most important thing to remember while training a horse is that a horse has a concentration point. You can only work him for a certain period of time, which varies with every horse; then he will tire and begin to fight you. The best way to ruin a horse is to push him past his concentration point. You will never, under any circumstances, do anything but harm by doing so.

If you can honestly say to yourself that you are capable of green-breaking your horse with the procedure described, then get after it; but if you are not yet experienced enough to do so, for the sake of your horse, admit it and send him to a qualified horseman.

As stressed throughout this chapter, each horse is an individual and his training should reflect this individuality. To expect one green horse to perform in the manner of another is neither sound nor productive. Do it right, or don't do it!

Chapter 7

A: Barrel Racing Fundamentals

The Ladies' Counterpart To Men's Rodeo Events, Barrel Racing Is Demanding Of Both Rider And Horse. Here's How To Train Both, From Someone Who Knows!

UNLIKE MOST PROFESSIONAL barrel racers, Jann Kremling, of Enumclaw, Washington, has never purchased a seasoned barrel horse. From the beginning, she's preferred to train her own.

Moreover, the personable, gray-eyed brownette received her own barrel seasoning where it counts — on the dollar road. Her first public set of barrels was not in gymkhana, junior rodeo or other for-fun contesting, but as a full-fledged competitor in the Washington State Barrel Racing Association many years ago.

Northwest champion three years in a row — in 1969, '70 and '71 — she had no problem maintaining position in the elite Top fifteen of this country's professional barrel racers in 1971. With 5111 GRA points, she finished eleventh in the nation for that year, her first season. At the same time, she picked up the coveted West Coast Golden State Rodeo championship, a trophy saddle, buckle and $1000 Olympia Brewing Company award: a memorable start for her first year on the circuit.

Despite her youth, Jann Kremling already is widely recognized in professional rodeo as a top horse hand. Stock contractor Cotton Rosser was so impressed by her ideas on conditioning that he put her in charge of his entire saddle string, a position she held throughout the grueling 1972, until after-the-season finals.

Jann travels with her husband, Tom, also a working member of the Golden State organization, and their youngsters,

Rebecca Sue, 4, and Trevor Scott, 2. (Tom, a former RCA bull rider, now contests as a steer wrestler. He was Northwest Rodeo Association steer wrestling champion in '69, '70 and '71, bringing home the second family championship honors for those years.)

With this type of background, it's easy to see why we chose Jann Kremling to shed some light on the intricacies of barrel race training.

Born and raised in Palm Springs, California, Jann began riding at age 2 — "strapped to the back of a gentle donkey in the desert on family trail rides." Riding over dry desert country, the tiny lass developed an early confidence in herself and her mounts that she has never lost over the years.

"In barrel racing, your horse is — at the very least! — seventy percent of your run," Jann maintains. "If you can't place your confidence in your horse, you might just as well not bother."

Which is exactly why this pro trains her own mounts, preferably starting at the beginning of their weight-carrying careers, at approximately age 2.

"I've been lucky," she admits. "I learned horse care and psychology — and I think they have to go together — from two experts. Woody Anderson, now training horses at Yakima Meadows, learned from Rex Ellsworth, one of the all-time most famous thoroughbred trainers in the world. I think Woody is an expert's expert on training and conditioning. The

During her days with the Golden State Rodeo string, Ms. Kremling participated in opening ceremonies (right). She later was charged with care of saddle horses (below).

other man was my dad, Virgil Studebaker, who has done everything with horses that can possibly be done.

"Dad knows more about how to get the most out of your horse than any other person I ever met. For instance, I was 'down' going into Reno in 1972 and couldn't put my finger on what was wrong. Well, Dad watched our run one day, then came right up to me and said 'Throw away your bat. That horse doesn't need it.'

"We both believe that a bat is a good attention-getter, but if you've already got your horse's attention, you're not going to get any more speed just by dusting at him with a bat. I was nervous and wasn't observing my horse as much as I should have been but Dad saw, right off, what was wrong. My horse was being over-ridden with that bat and it was throwing him off. I threw away the bat, placed in both go's, and won second money in the average."

Jann, who started barrel racing at 9, is a dyed-in-the-wool quarter horse fan.

"My dad bought his first quarter horse to ride in the mountains, an old 'logger' to trail ride and cruise lumber. Then it became the old story of someone coming up and saying 'Bet my horse can outrun your horse.' After that, match racing became a way of life, just naturally working toward faster and faster horses."

Her first barrel horse was Fairy Flicka, a Hancock-bred mare. Two other favorites were King Coke and Foxy Coke, Waggoner-bred geldings that were deemed the two top Washington State barrel horses in 1965. Jann used her own methods of training on all three, and "not one had been around a barrel once when I started them.

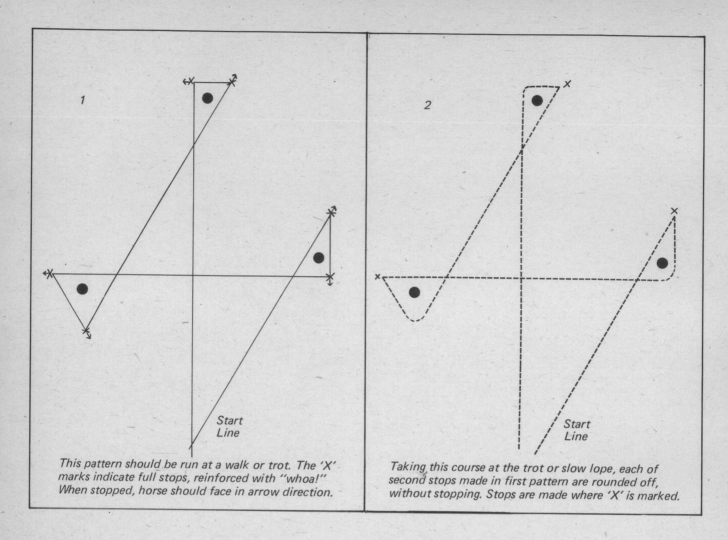

1

Start Line

This pattern should be run at a walk or trot. The 'X' marks indicate full stops, reinforced with "whoa!" When stopped, horse should face in arrow direction.

2

Start Line

Taking this course at the trot or slow lope, each of second stops made in first pattern are rounded off, without stopping. Stops are made where 'X' is marked.

"My dad always provided horses for me," she recalls, "and sometimes I was riding up to fifteen a day in various stages of training. But we both feel this is where you get your know-how: through actual experience with many different animals."

Three other special mounts stand out in Jann's memory and she and her dad raised them all. Rainier Frosty was 1962 Northwest Running Quarter Horse of the Year and Jann trained her out of the starting gates at the tender age of 14. She was a little older when she trained Rainier Misty, the 1969 Washington Barrel Racing Association Futurity champion. Rainier Janyre was both 1972 Washington State barrel racing champion and 1972 Northwest Junior Rodeo barrel racing champion, with two sisters riding the buckskin mare to the respective titles. Jann trained on her for six years before selling her and still admits a special fondness for the home-bred mare.

"If I had to make a choice between demonstrated speed and what I think is top breeding, all other things being equal, I'll take the breeding every time. Speed is great, but triple-A time on a track doesn't provide any incentive to turn. Controlled speed is what I want and I just think you get a better horse with the better lines."

Zantanon, Oklahoma Star, Grey Badger II, Joe Reed and Wimpy are Jann's ideas of oldies but goodies; names she likes to see in her horse's pedigree..."the more the better and as close-up as possible. When the blood is there, it's there and performance almost always follows."

Ms. Kremling's current number one barrel horse is Barbird Cee, an 11-year-old stallion and one of the last sons of Barred. A grandson of Oklahoma Star, Barbird was born on the Chowchilla ranch where Barred died. In race training at 18

months of age, his heels were cut down and he was considered lamed for racing.

"They couldn't see much future for a horse that might not run, even after a long and expensive layoff, so I got him for a fraction of what I think he was worth. I rested him till he was 2, then started him real slow on the barrels. He had his first race at 2½ and, until late 1972, was never crippled, dead lame or laid-off for any other reason."

At the December National Rodeo Finals, however, Jann and Barbird ran into trouble when the stallion slipped momentarily on his first run, slightly twisting his right front leg. Jann rode him four more times, "slightly sore, but perfectly willing."

On the fifth run, however, possibly protecting a touchy front leg, Barbird fell with his rider. He got up again and finished his run with what turned out to be "a pretty bad sprain."

Borrowing a friend's roping horse and a green colt "that had galloped around the barrels a total of four times in his life," Jann finished the finals to protect her standings. Needless to say, there were no more barrel points after Barbird's injury.

"Here he is, 11 already, and he's only got eighteen colts on the ground," Jann says. "But we feel there'll be time enough for that after he's retired. He's never been in a halter class and, while he lacks only one point of ROM in barrel racing, he's never campaigned for AQHA points at all. The only times he's even been entered in quarter horse competition is when I could use an AQHA show as exercise or practice for his next rodeo run."

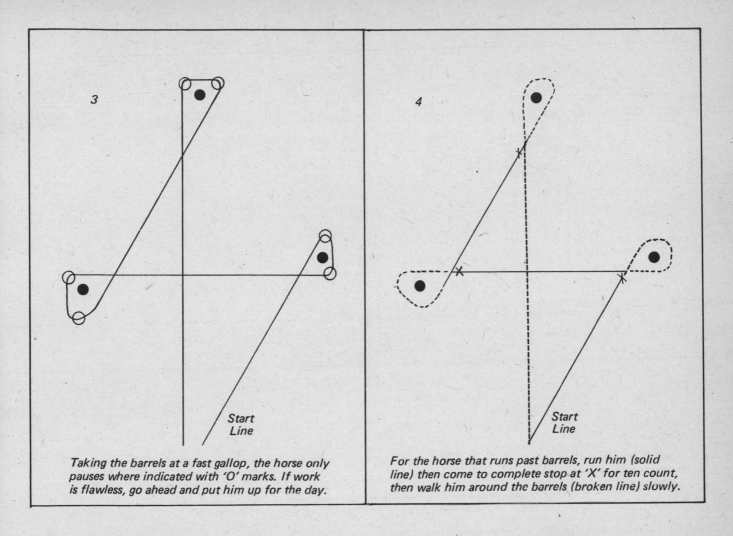

3

Start Line

Taking the barrels at a fast gallop, the horse only pauses where indicated with 'O' marks. If work is flawless, go ahead and put him up for the day.

4

Start Line

For the horse that runs past barrels, run him (solid line) then come to complete stop at 'X' for ten count, then walk him around the barrels (broken line) slowly.

Barbird has also been used, occasionally, for bulldogging, but "only in an emergency."

"His job is barrel racing, which he knows and does well. You never know how many races a good barrel horse has in him and one more run at the end of his career means more to us than building his 'dogging ability today."

This is not to say that Jann uses the stallion exclusively on barrels.

"Sometimes, even though he's a stallion, Barbird doesn't get high enough. Actually, he adapts so well to everything, he tends to get bored. So I do different things with him to keep him interested in life."

On the circuit, Barbird's exercise is varied, a 1½-mile gallop one day, a two-hour walk the next. Figure eights in the arena are also utilized "and, if I can find open pasture for a trail ride, this is even better."

Long-trotting is Jann Kremling's favorite conditioning tool. "I think it's the best all-around exercise for endurance, lengthening the stride and building muscle.

"I believe in natural physical fitness," she says. "Nothing you can give a horse or do to him will result in his running faster than his peak natural ability."

As she sees it, however, her job is to bring a horse to this peak ability through training, then keep him there through natural care and animal psychology.

She does admit to feeding Ewing's Formula 707, believing that vitamins are "nature" and that sometimes diets need this boost. She might also slip a dab of honey into Barbird's morning rations, if he's making an afternoon run. "He likes the taste and I think it gives him immediate energy. It's like an

athlete munching a candy bar just before a race. It doesn't increase his natural ability, it just gives him an extra little pickup that allows him to run up to it."

Jann, who views rodeoing as a business, sums up her widely acknowledged preoccupation with care and feeding principles by saying "I believe that if I take care of my horse, he'll take care of me moneywise."

She doesn't believe in "luck," meaning "superstition," and feels that in barrel racing, at least, "you make your own luck."

"I don't know if I'd enjoy any other aspect of rodeo as much," she admits. "I do think reputations are made or broken on 'the luck of the draw' in all the standard men's rodeo events. In barrel racing, it's just you and your horse. And that's the way I like it."

The following — with accompanying diagrams — shows her unique approach to pattern training, "after a horse is green broke and handling nicely.

"I start pattern training in exactly the same way for every horse I ride. It may not be the best method, or the fastest. But it works for me. So far, I've seen no reason to change, so it's what I have to recommend if someone is starting a new horse.

"I usually set the barrels in the standard cloverleaf, preferably at GRA-prescribed distance apart. However, if you have to set up a short course for one reason or another, go ahead. After all, at this stage, you are not training your horse so much to the barrels as you are using them to train him to be responsive to rider command."

This is the keystone theory to all of Ms. Kremling's training ideas: First and foremost, she wants an obedient horse.

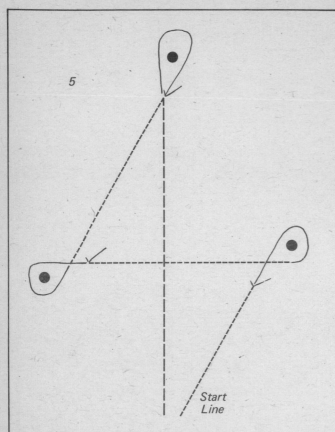

5

Start Line

A horse that knocks over barrels should be walked (small broken line) till position marked by "tick," then run around barrels, trotted off course (large broken line).

"To a certain degree, a top barrel horse learns to rate his barrels, judge his own momentum and compensate for the condition of the arena grounds. But if for some reason I want to stop a run in mid-gallop, I want my horse to set down and stop. Some horses are so busy running pattern that they forget they have a rider.

"No matter how good a horse might be, sometime or another he's going to make a mistake in judgment. That's when he has to be able to rely on his rider. If that rider is just a lump on a running machine — or if the horse has been allowed to become used to running pattern only, that's when a problem begins to develop.

"Horses are creatures of habit. And they're smart enough to pick up on the easiest way of doing things, all by themselves. One uncorrected mistake leads to another and, by the time a horse has done his own thing two or three times, it's already become habit.

"That's why I approach pattern training the way I do. My goal is not just training a horse to the barrels, which, after all, are just three inanimate objects. I want him tuned one hundred percent to his rider's wishes. He has to want to do what I want him to do when I ask it. And I think my way of approaching the barrels — the very first time — starts him out in this direction."

Jann starts with "the very minimum of what I can put on his head," often a Sleister hackamore. A Tex Rudolph hackamore is her favorite working headgear. Once in awhile, she finds a horse that seems most willing in a rubber bit or racing snaffle, "but never anything stronger. After all, if you start tough, where do you go from there?"

By the time she is ready for barrels, Jann already has spent a lot of time circling and figure-eighting. But now the most unorthodox aspect of her pattern ideas comes to the fore. Although aiming for a smooth-working run, the young trainer teaches her horse initially to think of the barrel course as a series of stops and go's.

At the start line, Jann begins when she is sure she has her mount's attention. She starts walking the course, until her horse's hips are at the far rim of the barrel, then brings him to a full and complete stop on the voice command of "Whoa." She then turns and walks to the same position on the other side of the barrel and stops again, saying, "Whoa." Turning, she walks a direct line to the second barrel and repeats the procedure, then on to the third. That's six full stops and seven starts on the course, with nothing but walking between.

The accompanying diagrams show the progress of this stop and go training. The speed at which this training progresses varies with the ability of each individual horse.

"Some young horses are ready to eliminate the second stop after a couple of approaches. With others, it might take a month. This is where horse and rider rapport comes in. The smartest horse is not always the most willing and I base my progression of training on his willingness to obey, not just on his ability to remember where he stopped the last time out. It's something the trainer has to feel for himself and it's hard to describe."

To illustrate:

"Many seasoned barrel horses develop the problem of running by the barrels. Now these horses know how they've been running the pattern, sometimes for years. They know where they're supposed to start their turns, but they're so full of run that their momentum is carrying them right on by the barrel. They've made an error in judgment and, by the time it's happened a couple of times, they've lost their willingness. They're still smart and they're still pattern-wise. But they need to get back on the track of instant obedience when the rider feels she has to take over. They've got to develop the want-to again, the desire to please the rider instead of only anticipating the barrel course.

"I might start such a horse at a run, stop him dead-still three horse-lengths before the barrel, make him stand, then walk him around the barrel and take off again at a dead run for the second barrel, where we'll stop and repeat the procedure before going on the third barrel.

"I'm a great one for voice commands and I reinforce and exaggerate that first stop with a big 'Whoa.' It gets his attention back again and he's standing there wondering what's next. A few more times and his willingness is back, and hopefully with it, his ability to put you back in the money."

Stop-and-go is also helpful to a horse that's developed the habit of knocking over his barrel. With such an animal, Jann would begin at the walk until she is three horse-lengths from the barrel, "then barrel around the barrel." She'd then walk to the next barrel and repeat. The problem soon takes care of itself.

On any "kindergarten" try, however, Jann walks only, uses all the stops and starts with the traditional right-hand barrel. (If later she decides he'd run better with a left-hand approach, she will stop at whatever stage he is in, go back to the beginning and start over, at the walk, with the full stop-go approach from the other side.)

A first-time-ever green barrel horse may be puzzled by this strange new procedure, but he is invariably interested in what is going on. She has his full attention and interest and he has just completed his first barrel run — at a walk. From now on his progress as a barrel horse will be up to him.

Usually only a few walks of the course, making a virtual triangle at each barrel, with full stops at each corner of the triangle but the last, will prompt Jann to eliminate the second of each pair of stops at each barrel. To do this she generally goes to the trot, depending on her horse. She now trots to the first stop position, halts, then turns for the second barrel, with only a slight hesitation at the rounded-off angle where she previously signaled the second stop. By now, most horses are ready to turn willingly at their former No. 2 stop position. But Jann still comes to a full halt with each horse at the No. 1 stop at each barrel, feeling this vital step necessary to concentrate the horse's immediate attention on the job at hand, the "turning" of the barrel, which by now has become a familiar landmark on his three-barrel run.

"I never take a horse more than once around a barrel," Jann says. "Always stay on pattern and make the complete circuit each time, but use your stops as you feel them to be necessary. You've seen some trainers running up to and around a barrel five or six times before going on to the next barrel. I don't agree. I think that all they're doing is fooling themselves and making their horses mad. A mad or bored horse is never a willing horse, so I think they're just defeating their own purpose.

"I'd much rather walk up to that barrel I'm having trouble with, come to a full stop and show the horse the barrel. This gives him a chance to rest until he gets there and puts him in a better frame of mind. It also gives him a chance to prepare himself for what he has learned comes next, some cue from his rider that will tell him whether he is to remain standing or he is to proceed around the barrel. I guess you could say it is focusing the horse's attention on the rider, not on the barrel. A horse standing dead-still is not going to be worrying about anything in the world except what's next, because he can only think about one thing at a time. So what can you lose except time and how can you do anything but benefit from his increased attention?"

Jann Kremling starts her first bona fide run at the barrels only when her horse works smoothly at the trot, with or without that first-position stop at each barrel.

"With most horses I eliminate all stops at the trot, progressing through only the slightest hesitation to a smooth working trot all the way."

On the first actual run or gallop, she works at the slowest lope her horse will maintain, putting him through the course without any stop at all, but maintaining the same triangular pattern around each barrel with only the slight hesitation necessary to turn at the "corners."

She is careful to observe whether he works smoothly and willingly, or whether he seems to be fighting the program.

"If I feel it's necessary, I will then stop him from the gallop in the first position, then proceed again," she says. "Or if I really feel he's not quite ready for loping the barrels, I'll go back again to the trot or walk and start again on the basics, with both stops at each barrel if necessary. Each horse is an individual and some will pick up quickly what another might take a long time on. But there's one thing I've found common to all horse training: You've always got the upper hand, if you are forcing him to think. With my approach to pattern training, I believe there's little opportunity for him to start operating so mechanically — or so fast — that he is not permitted the necessary thinking time so vital to the learning process."

After her barrel horse has learned the basics of willingness and pattern, Jann Kremling begins work on phase two, getting the most speed possible without sacrificing the willingness. This marks the beginning of a long seasoning process, which in her estimation, takes a minimum of four years; two years' basic training and two years of hauling down the road.

"Out in actual competition you come up with experiences you'd never meet in strictly a training environment. Back on

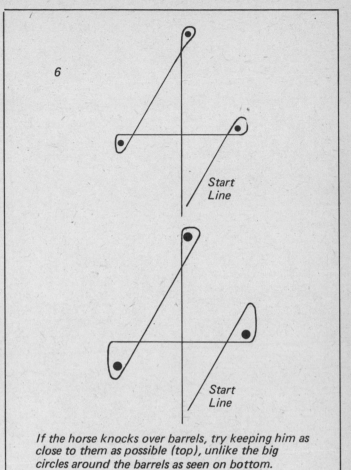

6

Start
Line

Start
Line

If the horse knocks over barrels, try keeping him as close to them as possible (top), unlike the big circles around the barrels as seen on bottom.

the ranch you can hang bunting and flags around the arena and turn on the radio full blast to get your horse used to noise, but how do you prepare for that first on-the-spot emergency other than coping with it when it arrives? How do you get a horse used to traveling one hundred miles a day without doing some hauling? How do you know he'll adapt to a different taste in his water bucket without giving him a change of water? No matter how well he's educated at home, he has to go out and start doing before he can be considered a seasoned horse.

"A lot of girls' horses refuse to go into an arena or they run over anyone in their path going out. Maybe a rider is careful never to figure-eight in the arena while the barrels are up. To me these are clues that the seasoning process is not over. If I want to exercise my horse in the arena while the barrels are set up, I will. I want him trained enough to do what I want him to do. It all goes back to training to rider command. If you're approaching things right, you're going to make him do what you want him to do, no matter where he is or what's going on around him. And you have to give him lots of opportunity at different experiences to learn that what you say goes, no matter what."

On reining: "I do change hands, sometimes. If I feel I should two-hand a horse to the barrel, I use my active hand to lead him or guide him around the barrel, not to pull him around. After all, my object is always to show him what I want. If he does not oblige, and I'm pretty sure he knows what I want, it's time to correct him. He won't learn anything if you haul him around by the head, except, perhaps, more resistance the next time."

At Travis AFB, California, rodeo, Jann Kremling is awarded diamond-studded wristwatch for top score.

On rein length — "It depends somewhat on the individual horse, but I never want my reins so long that I have to gather them. I guess most people would say I use a fairly short rein. But when my horse is all set up for backing I want my hand to barely touch my stomach. A lot of barrel racers use longer rein, gather and let go for control. I only want to get into my horse's mouth when necessary and I want to be able to do it instantaneously, something that's not possible when you've got too much rein in front of you."

On surging — "To me, this means a horse's habits have not been formed yet. He's unsure of himself, the pattern or his rider's wishes. I'd go back to an earlier version of my training pattern, slow down and re-establish what I thought he had already learned."

On rider balance — "I guess I differ with some of the other leading barrel racers in that I put my saddle high on the withers and strive to keep my balance over the front end of my horse. Some girls sit back more, but I guess I lean more toward the thoroughbred people's beliefs on riding balance. I firmly believe that all running ability, balance and control is at the front, not in the hindquarters as is commonly supposed. I guess that's why I seldom sit down in the saddle when making a run. I want to be over the center of the action, not somewhere behind, just being a drag."

On leads — "I never worry about throwing a barrel horse into his leads. This is a natural thing and, if a horse is ready for barrel racing, the proper lead will be second nature."

On spurs — "I have never used spurs for speed, only for turning. Actually, if you think you have to use gimmicks — a bat, spurs, buzzer, tack collar or other device — it means you're not getting the most out of your horse by using two things you ought to develop more: the ability to observe and common sense."

Becky Carson is another top barrel racer, shown here winning the National Finals in 1973. Note how horse is bending around barrel in display of controlled speed.

These photos were taken at 1972 Travis Air Force Base rodeo in which Jann Kremling won the barrel racing event. But photos were taken a day apart, illustrating how closely her form is repeated in each performance.

On correction or punishment — "People might get the idea that I am very easy-going with my horses, which is true to a certain extent. But I want full control of and respect from my horses, and if a hard spanking with a bat is what it takes to gain this, well, then, that is what that horse will get. But it has to be done just at the right time and not often. Do it once and make it count! I might spank a young horse if he needs it, but then I find he doesn't need it when he's older. It's like disciplining a child. If it's done right and at the right time, the lesson is learned and the discipline doesn't need to be repeated."

The best advice she ever received that she would like to pass on — "If you can, learn with the best. If you have a problem, go to someone who is winning right now. Ask her to watch your run and ask for advice. Everyone wants to be a winner, and almost every winner is proud to be asked for ideas. After all, the whole world is filled with ideas, and if you're ever going to really form any philosophies for yourself, you don't want to miss out on at least hearing what the best have got to say."

B: TRAIN THE ROPING HORSE

The team roping heading horse requires schooling different from a heeling horse, which is trained much the same as the calf roping horse. Team roping horses, because of the large steers, are generally bigger than calf horses.

MANY OF THE top names on the roping circuit don't train their own horses; many simply don't have the time necessary to finish a horse and rely instead upon a handful of individuals for their horses. Mike Nelson of Dayton, Oregon, is one of that handful.

"Horses are individuals," says the 30-year-old horseman, "and it's up to the man making them to recognize that fact. Each horse is different and needs a different type of handling than any other. Many trainers don't recognize this fact and consequently turn out horses that will never be top quality. You can't follow a set pattern for making horses; not for roping or any other activity."

Even using this methodology, Nelson feels that there has never been nor will ever be a perfect roping horse, one without a "hole" in it somewhere.

"A hole is a flaw," he explains, "and every horse has one. It might be that another calf horse runs faster than this one; another might stop harder; another might stop straighter. Each horse has something done better by another horse, but it's just something you have to live with. A horse is only capable of so much."

In selecting a good calf roping prospect, Nelson feels that one breed is better suited than any other: the quarter horse. "I've seen horses of every breed, color, size and demeanor that have worked well in the arena," he says, "but quarter horses are best suited physically.

"I look for a horse that is athletic or has athletic potential. Athletically inclined humans can perform more demanding tasks than a old fat man and I feel this also applies to horses."

Nelson looks for speed in his horses, because of its paramount importance in the arena. "At small calf ropings, it's not unusual for the best time of the day to be thirteen seconds," he explains. "But at big rodeos where all the top names are present, a roper must get down into the eight or nine-second bracket to win and a ten might not even place. For this reason, a good horse has to be fast."

The conformation of a horse also is important. "A calf

The Calf And Team Roping Events Are Competition Favorites. Here's How To Train Your Equine Competitor!

This heading horse is driving well on the left lead, arcing the steer into a good target for the heeler. When the heeler has caught the hind feet, the heading horse is faced as noted in text, then continues to back until flagged.

roping horse must have the hind legs well under its body to be able to stop hard," says Nelson. "This is an attribute the top horse must have; to be able to jerk a calf off its feet. This saves the roper lots of time, because if that calf gets to its feet, it can beat you."

Leaving the box fast is of dire importance and Nelson feels that a long hip aids in this. "The sooner a horse can get out of the box and to the calf, the better the time should be." As a final requirement, he demands that a horse have kind, soft eyes, indicative of its temperament.

Once Nelson has a prospective calf roping horse on hand, he begins the actual training routine. Initially, he rides the horse for a few days, checking over his reactions to given commands and his temperament. When he is satisfied, he turns loose a three hundred to four hundred-pound calf — one that is pretty well roped-out and that won't run too fast — in the arena. Mounted on the horse, he then tracks the calf.

"Tracking is nothing more than following behind the calf as close to it as possible," Nelson explains. "This serves a variety of purposes, only one of which is familiarizing the horse with a loose calf in the arena. It also teaches him the position I want him in; that of being as close behind the calf as possible and gets him used to following the calf in different directions."

The position of the horse in regard to the calf is easy to understand, when it is remembered that tossing a loop straight down over a calf is much more accurate than trying to reach out with the rope. Also, it gives the horse a little longer to get set low in the dirt when stopping, thereby increasing the amount of force jerking the calf backward.

"I continue tracking until I think the horse has had enough or he begins to tire," Nelson says, "then we go to the box (staging area for horse and rider prior to chasing a calf during competition) and rest; let our hair down a bit. This is of extreme importance, for the horse gets used to being relaxed in the box. Then we'll go back out and track some more, always returning to the box to rest.

89

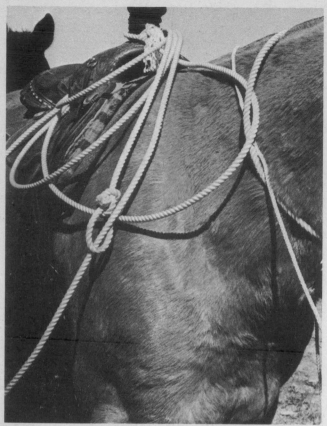

The rope encircling the horse's neck keeps the grass calf rope from slapping the horse, which could lead to serious problems. The jerk line also is run through the neck rope.

"I work the horses on a left lead," he comments, "which means that a horse's initial forward movement comes on the left side; not unlike a person striding forward with the left foot. I assure that a horse starts this way by physically moving it to the left with my right knee."

Nelson connects jerk line to the bit shanks on his new trainees, line running back through a pulley on horn and into his belt. This keeps horse backing during run.

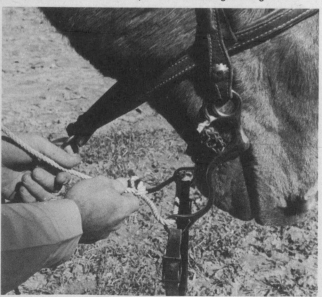

"I'd guess that ninety percent of all horses lead to the left naturally. A horse will stop hardest on a left lead and, if done properly, a horse can gain one entire stride with a lead change in the arena. This gets too complicated to explain; most ropers can't do it, anyway!"

Another added advantage of starting a horse on the left lead is that it might save the rider being slapped with a ten-second penalty for breaking the barrier — a rope stretched across the box, which releases when the calf reaches a certain distance down the arena. The barrier is connected to the chute wall on the rider's left and heading for that juncture often results in the horse's arrival just a split-second after it is released. This results in a faster take-off.

During the initial tracking sessions, Nelson carries a nylon rope. While resting in the box, he will rub the rope all over the horse, getting him used to its presence, until the horse no longer is surprised or frightened by its sudden appearance. After the horse has settled into his tracking role, Nelson will twirl the rope over his and the horse's heads, so that the horse will come to recognize it.

After the horse has made substantial progress in the initial phase, Nelson rigs a breakaway honda in his rope and, during tracking, throws his loop over the calf. At the exact instant he pitches his slack, he stops the horse and makes him back up a couple of steps. The breakaway feature allows the rope to snap apart when it tightens around the calf's neck, so that little pressure is put upon the calf or the horse. "I'll repeat this procedure five or six times in succession, each time making the horse back a couple of steps," says Nelson. "After each throw, I stop the horse and let him think about what has transpired. We then will go and rest in the box."

Often a young horse will get angry during the process and Nelson sometimes will leave the calf and ride the horse casually, or put him up for the day, if progress was satisfactory.

"If he's an old horse that knows better, I'll climb his frame — give him some discipline," he says. "A young horse doesn't know any better, but disobedience from a horse that does is intolerable."

After a week or so of working with the breakaway honda, teaching the horse to stop and back a few steps each time, Nelson will begin roping "solid."

"I use the old, roped-out calf for this step, in which my rope doesn't have the breakaway feature. This gets the horse used to the snap and jerk that occurs when the rope pops tight. This old calf isn't running too fast or hard, so the force isn't too great."

Nelson continues to make the horse stop and back at the proper time, to further reinforce in his brain what he is expected to do. "A horse learns by repetition, so this is a natural step," he adds.

If everything progresses properly, Nelson will continue working the horse in this stage, until he gets bored and wants to move on to something better. "Just like a person, a horse gets bored if he does the same thing, day in and day out. He starts out with great interest in what he's doing as he progresses up the steps, but this wanes, if he continues on the same stage for a great length of time."

Nelson next will buy a few good but small calves that will run like those to be found in arenas during ropings. During the first week of running them, he will use a breakaway honda again.

"I also start working the horse from the box," Nelson says. "This adds a new dimension to the routine and means more interest for the horse. He has to work harder to catch the calf and I make him really stop hard and get back

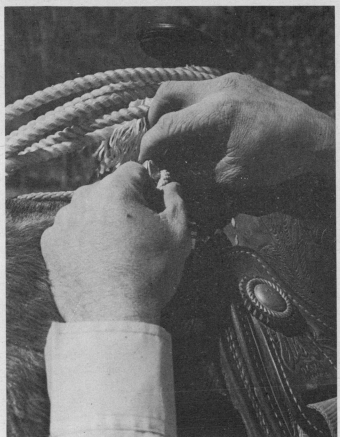

As noted in text, pulley is attached to the horn and jerk line feeds through it (left), then is attached to the belt (right). This tool produces a continual backing cue while roper runs to the calf, keeping pressure on the line. This avoids bad habits.

quick. As of this point, I still haven't gotten out of the saddle and tied any of the calves."

In this stage, Nelson works the horse toward leaving the box at its extreme left, where the rope connects to the side of the calf chute. "I try to get the horse close enough to the box that my knee will hit the latch," says the stocky horseman. "This gets him in behind the calf that much quicker. Saving time is the name of the game in roping. It also helps to avoid breaking the barrier."

In this stage, as with the others, Nelson returns to the box for rest periods. He continues to surround the box with the aura of relaxation, of letting down. This pays big dividends when pressure is at its peak.

When he feels that it's time, Nelson begins actual roping and tying of the good calves. As he throws his loop, his mount stops hard and begins backing. Before the rope snaps taut, Nelson already has bailed out of the saddle and the jerk gives him extra speed. "I can really fly down the rope when it happens," he says.

Upon reaching the calf, which should still be on the ground, he flanks it or lifts it off the ground — and drops it on its side in the dirt. Nelson then ties the animal by one front and both hind feet. During the entire period, the horse must be applying continual pressure to the rope, almost to the point of dragging the calf backwards.

"I try to make the horse work hard and fast and stop straight behind the calf. By stopping straight, it means I can get off the horse and to the calf more quickly. If the horse angles to the left when stopping, it means I have to go around or under his head to get to the calf. This takes time

During initial roping, breakaway honda is used. This is made by using a ring and baling wire, as shown. When the rope comes tight, the honda breaks apart.

Calf roper must flank beef before tying (left), not too easy with big calves used today! It saves time if the calf is down on arena when roper approaches.

Once calf is flanked, roper straddles prostrate critter and positions feet with legs and hands. Pigging string is in mouth.

Feet properly positioned, roper begins tying quickly. If horse is keeping pressure on the line, it keeps calf from fighting (left).

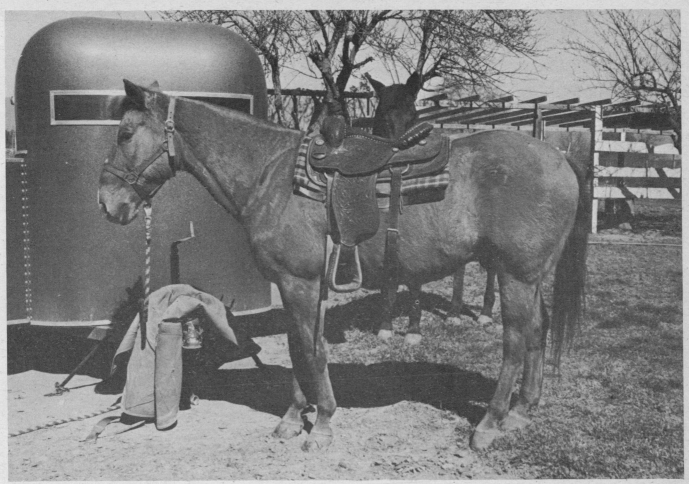

Nelson's "Hog" may not be beautiful in appearance, but he's won a pile of money. Note how the gelding keeps his hind legs beneath him, even when standing on a slope. The quarter bred animal has the good speed required to get to the calf fast!

With the winning times measured in tenths or hundredths of a second, it's easy to see why this roper is grimacing as he hurries his tie. A well-trained horse sure helps!

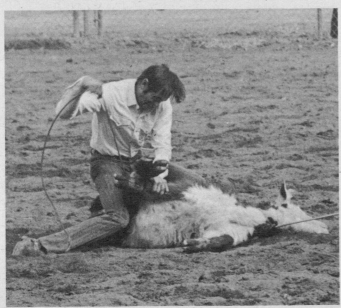

and could cost money. If he angles to the right, I won't be able to get under the rope to flank the calf."

According to the horseman, a roper knows everything has been done right when, as the rope pops, it develops a visible arc. "This means that the horse is stopping so hard that the calf is actually jerked backwards, sometimes head-over-heels," he explains. "This action will drop a calf on the dirt, saving the roper time.

"A calf can beat you, if it regains its feet, because it's going to be running around the arena at the end of the rope. This means that the roper must give chase, get a good hold on it, then go through the motions. It saves much more time if the calf already is down and not fighting you. It then can be picked up, dropped, then tied. A calf on the ground can't whip you."

Nelson demands that his horses "work the rope," which means that the horse pops the rope and continually backs. Sometimes a horse will stop all right, but won't take up the slack, enabling the calf to regain its feet.

"When this happens, I resort to a jerk line," explains Nelson. "A jerk line is a piece of rope attached to the bit of your bridle which then runs back through a pulley on the saddlehorn into my hands or belt. I use a fifteen-foot line, which enables me to stand in front of the horse — off his back — and communicate orders he is to perform."

Nelson usually enlists the aid of a burlap sack filled with sand. Tossing his loop around the gunny sack, he stands near the sack and pulls the jerk line. The horse starts backing, pulling the sack, which simulates the weight of a calf on the ground. He continues the procedure until the horse is cured and will work the rope.

As the horse improves in performance, Nelson gets some big calves and runs the horse on them. Here the horse learns that he really must lean on that rope to stop the calf clean and must run just that much faster to catch it.

When he feels confident that the horse has covered the rudiments of calf roping, Nelson will haul him to small jackpot ropings and rodeos, where the entry fees — and winnings — are small; experience is the goal here.

"I always use a jerk line during these first money ropings, because I don't want to give the horse the chance not to work. A top calf roping horse may have a flaw or two, but he must perform with consistency. If he messed up one calf, it could cost money and he might learn a bad habit or two. After he has been seasoned, I dispense with the jerk line, but not until he has proved himself."

There are numerous factors that can inhibit a horse's performance in the arena.

"If you arrive at the arena the day before you are to rope, you have to watch where you tie your horse for the night. For example, if you fed and watered him near the holding pens for the cattle — usually at the opposite end of the arena from the starting box — the horse might just feel that place is home and charge right past the calf you're roping in the arena to get there. What you must do, therefore, is tie the horse near the box at night, so he will continually try backing up to get to that spot when you're roping.

"Another factor is hauling two horses in a trailer," Nelson adds. "They get used to one another and, upon arriving at the arena, if you separate them, each will whinny up a storm looking for his roommate.

"If you're roping on one of the horses and have tied his roommate at the far end of the arena from the box, the horse you're riding will be concentrating on getting close to the other horse, instead of on the business at hand. I tie the other horse near the box somewhere, so that the horse will continue backing toward the area after the calf is roped. There are many such factors that come into play!"

Nelson trains his team roping horses identically through the first stages, altering the routine when finishing the training and according to the future job of the horse: heading or heeling. "Some horses are capable of going both ways in competition, but I feel most do one of the jobs best," he says.

"When tracking calves — not steers — in the arena, I favor tracking slightly off to the left of the calf and behind him if the horse is to be a heading horse. When the rope tightens, the steer's head will be turned to the left, so this is the logical position for the heading horse.

"For a heeling horse, I use the same positions as for a calf horse: directly behind the calf or off to his right slightly. The whole routine for a heeling horse is identical to that of a calf horse."

The most important technique a heading horse must master is quartering — when he stops, he gets into the ground at a forty-five-degree angle away from the left side of the steer, which breaks its momentum and cocks its head. Done properly, this results in a steer that arcs gracefully as the horse turns him up the arena, providing a better target for the heeler.

"Team roping is supposed to be exactly what the name implies: a team effort. The job of the header is not simply to catch the horns and duck off, letting the heeler fend for himself. Just about anybody can rope a set of horns, but it takes an artist to catch those feet and he needs all the help he can get."

Teaching the quartering technique is much like training a calf horse to stop and Nelson again resorts to the breakaway honda on the end of a twenty-foot rope. As the slack is pulled, the horse is angled to the left at forty-five degrees and stopped. This is mastered before moving the horse out into the arcing phase. When the horse stops in proper position, a slow moving calf is roped hard and fast, getting the big horse used to the slight jerk.

Nelson then moves to the arcing phase, using a twenty-five-foot rope. As the horse buries up following the slack being pulled, Nelson spurs him out of the stop after a moment and the calf then swings gracefully. The horse may be confused the first couple of times he's spurred forward, since he hasn't done this before, but Nelson says they catch on quickly. The extra five feet of rope — about one stride — gives the horse a chance to regain his composure.

When arcing has been learned, the horse must be taught to "face," keeping tight pressure on the rope all the time. The steer aids in this, since he's fighting to get back to the safety of the holding pens at the rear of the arena.

"Facing is turning the horse to face the steer, after the heeler has caught the feet," he says. "This stretches the steer as required until the flagman stops the clock."

The heading horse is pulling the steer on the left lead, driving with the right legs. To get him facing the steer, he's spurred in the right flank with the right spur, at the same time being spurred in the heart girth with the left spur. This physically moves his head around in a circle to the right, at the same time pushing the body against the rope to keep it tight. Once facing the steer, he's cued to back continually.

When the entire procedure is mastered using small calves, the size of the calves is increased to get the horse used to the harder jerk. He also begins leaving from the box, in the same manner as for calf horses and patience is used to thoroughly school the horse in all the fundamentals.

It's at this stage that Nelson begins dallying the rope, instead of having it tied to the horn, and this is one of the hardest tasks for a roper. "They're worried about catching a finger or thumb in the rope, which can be severed when the rope comes tight," he says. "The chances of catching a finger or thumb in the rope are improved, it seems, when the roper looks down at the horn when dallying. He doesn't need to, since he unconsciously knows where it is."

When the team roping horse works well on the large calves, the progression is to steers, roping a few at a time. This should not present undue problems if he's been schooled properly and, if so, he should be regressed into the basics. He then is hauled, like his calf roping counterpart, to small ropings for familiarization under competitive conditions.

Team roping is slowly replacing calf roping as the favorite roping event, because it's not as demanding and can be practiced in more parts of the country. Calves are expensive and relatively fragile compared to steers. Too, wives, girlfriends and youngsters can rope along with dad, leading to total family interest in the sport.

But calf roping still is strong in most parts of the country. It's hoped this section gets you into the line at the pay window, no matter the event.

As his figure eight loop wraps around this calf (above), the horse already is hitting the brakes. A good, hard stop transfers most of the shock to the calf. While the rope is arcing (below), this horse is not stopping straight and roper had to run around the left shoulder then under rope when moving toward calf. Time expended for this easily could cost money!

C: REINING HORSE TRAINING

This Truly Is An Advanced Equitation Event
That Requires Special Schooling!

KEITH MOON, an American Quarter Horse Association judge and trainer of ten AQHA champions, could be termed qualified to discuss training techniques for reining horses. Odd as it may sound, Moon calls reining "dressage for the stock horse."

"A reining horse has no outside stimulus to aid his performance. I mean that, unlike the cutting horse which has cows, the barrel horse that has barrels or the hunter or jumper that has the fences, the reining horse — like the dressage horse — has only the subtle cues from his rider to achieve a good performance. A good performance in a reining class is dependent upon a horse responding to only the slightest cue from his rider and the horse has to respond immediately and correctly to this cue for the go to be a winning one.

"Essentially, a reining pattern consists of many of the tests — although they are altered slightly — that a dressage horse would have to do in an exercise," continues Moon, a native of Rochester, Minnesota. "For example, a spin in a reining class would be similar to a turn on the haunches in a dressage class; our sliding stop is just a refinement of the immediate stop a dressage horse has to make from a canter; and in either activity, the horse has to make flying lead changes."

Moon adds that, because of the similarities between dressage and reining, trainers in both activities face a common problem: how to keep the horses from getting bored. The method Moon uses is to do plenty of trail riding with his horses.

"The reining horse is a highly schooled stock horse," Moon says, "so one of the problems is to keep him sharp. One of the best ways to bore a horse is to keep him in the arena and run patterns with him. I only put a horse in the arena to sharpen him up. For example, if he has a particular area where he is weak — like rollbacks — I'll put him in the arena and do some rollbacks with him, until I have the fault corrected. The basic day-to-day work, though, I do on the trails.

"A typical work outside for one of my reining horses would be something like this: I'd probably lope him along for awhile, then do a 360-degree spin. Then I'd probably lope him another two hundred yards and ask for a slide stop. I might go off and lope circles and perhaps lope on a straight line for a hundred yards, then make a flying lead change.

"One thing I do once the horse is trained — by this I

mean he can rollback, slide stop and spin 360 degrees fairly proficiently — is never to work a reining pattern on him between shows. All this does is make him less sharp for the reining pattern he will have to do at the show. I expect that a good dressage trainer would say the same thing: 'Never work a complete exercise between shows'."

Like a dressage horse, a polished reining horse does not just suddenly burst on the scene. A lot of time and effort go into training before the horse can even be listed as a good prospect. Moon uses a process of elimination to determine which of his young horses will go on for the high schooling required of a reining horse.

"Actually, I start all my young horses the same way," Moon explains. "Those horses that stay nice and relaxed, have a nice way of going with a soft trot and a slow lope, stay as pleasure horses. Those that seem to have a little more desire — a little more competitiveness — we try as reining horses. If this horse is handy about lead changes and seems to be in control of his feet most of the time, then we definitely start to think of him as a prospect."

To start his young horses, Moon begins the serious part of breaking when the horse is between 18 and 20 months old. "We start by just bringing the colt up to the barn and getting him accustomed to being handled. When he is fairly quiet about being handled and knows what it means to stand in the crossties, we start breaking him to saddle. When we saddle the colt for the first time, we put him in the crossties and put the saddle blanket on him. We just rub it around until he decides it isn't going to hurt him. Then we saddle him, but we don't cinch the saddle up tight, just sort of snug.

"If you cinch the saddle up tight the first time, a lot of colts will fly back into the crossties and get cinch bound. They get in the habit of going backwards every time you cinch them up. I believe in going as quietly as possible with these young horses. If you can make breaking a pleasant thing, you are less likely to get a sour or frightened horse as your finished product. Besides, it saves a lot of wear and tear on the trainer if he has a willing horse to work with, not one that he has to fight every step of the way."

Once Moon has his young horses used to the saddle, he takes them out in the arena with the saddle on, but only a halter on the horse's head, starting the horse's lessons on the longe line. He teaches the horse to walk in both directions before he goes to a faster gait. Moon does not use driving lines — not because he doesn't think the method

A proper rollback is demonstrated in above illustrations. The horse is running in the proper lead (1), then comes to a balance stop (2). He then pivots 180 degrees on the hindquarters, over the hocks (3) and breaks quickly out of the rollback into a run on the proper lead. Many riders overlook balanced stop, turning the horse in a small circle instead of a rollback.

works, but because he has never used the method.

"Once I get horses going pretty well on the longe line, I take them out in the arena and work them enough to get the edge off on the line. Then I just walk up to them, put a foot in the stirrup and ease onto the colt. Most of them, if they are handled a lot, don't fuss at all when you do this. If they do fuss, I get back down off them and work some more on the longe line. Then, I stop them again and try to get on them. This might go on for two or three days.

"Patience is the key here," Moon adds. "When I feel that the colt is relaxed with me sitting on his back, I move him off a couple of steps and, if he stays relaxed, I move him off a few more steps. If he starts to act shook, I get off and work him some more on the longe line."

Moon starts riding his colts with only a halter. He feels that they can't get too far away in the arena, so the threat of a runaway is minimal. After he has ridden the colt two or three days with just the halter, he switches to a bosal for about thirty days. During this period, after Moon finishes riding the horse every day, he puts a D-ring snaffle in his mouth and stands the colt up in a bitting rig.

Moon uses rubber reins on his bitting rig. These are not the rubber-covered leather reins one would see on a race

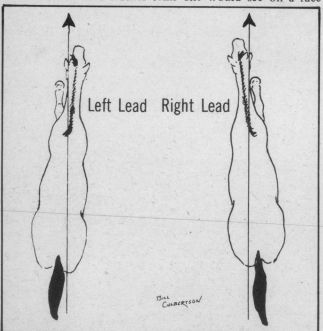

The differences between right and left leads are shown in this illustration. Note the body position changes that are relative to the horse's travel on different leads.

horse, but are actually stretchy, rubber reins. With a rig like this, when the colt hits the bit, he is not hitting an immovable thing. The rubber in the reins will give to the motion of his head just like your hands. According to Moon, a bitting rig like this has a tendency to produce a horse that is a little behind the bit all the time, but he likes his reining horses to be that way.

When Moon does get around to riding the colt with a bit in his mouth, he uses the D-ring snaffle for a considerable period before he switches.

"Actually, I teach the colt to do just about everything on that D-ring snaffle. He has to stop, turn and back well before I go to anything with any curb on it. I teach my colts to turn by using a direct rein. For a long time, I ride them two-handed. Then, gradually, when I apply the direct rein to make them turn, I also start applying the indirect rein on their necks to start them neck reining. Pretty soon, they are switched from turning on a direct rein to turning on a neck rein and they don't even know that the switch has occurred."

When Moon is working his young horse to the left, he likes the horse to be looking left and vice versa. He also uses his legs a great deal in riding. "I am a firm believer in the use of legs rather than the overuse of hands," he says. "A horse that is totally responsive to legs and takes most of his cues from the rider's legs turns in a much smoother and more sophisticated performance. I want my horses so that I seldom even have to touch their mouths to get the job done. Lots of young horses are a little goosey to leg pressure, but you just have to keep after them, using your legs lightly, until they get used to it.

"I never ride a young horse with spurs," notes the AQHA judge. "As a matter of fact, I seldom ride any of my finished horses with spurs. The only time I use them is when I get a horse that absolutely refuses to move. Fortunately, individuals like this are pretty rare. Most horses are pretty sensitive. Of course, I apply all my leg pressure in the cinch area or slightly behind the cinch. The horse isn't quite as goosey in this area as he is ahead of the cinch in the shoulder area or far back of the cinch on the ribs. In those areas, he might just drop his head and buck you off.

"When I want a horse to turn to the left, in addition to the light neck rein, I use my left leg just back of the cinch," explains Moon. "This displaces his rear end slightly and he moves away from the pressure and bends around your leg. This makes a much prettier turn than tearing his head off."

Since many of Moon's horses do not become reining horses but stay as pleasure horses, one of the earliest things he teaches them is how to back well, back quietly and back straight. Moon does this by stopping the horse squarely and letting him stand for a minute. Then, he puts pressure on

Wally Moon's method of mounting a green horse is to insert a foot in stirrup and climb on after longeing, demonstrated by Frank Fitzpatrick.

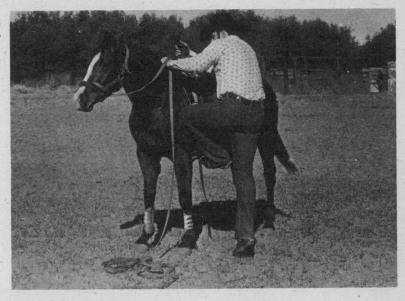

If horse offers resistance when being mounted for the first time, rider dismounts and longes horse further. There are no problems here (left).

If everything proceeds smoothly, the rider then throws his leg over green horse slowly (right). After sitting for awhile, the rider then dismounts.

Frank Fitzpatrick hits the binders on this young mare, which Moon would classify as well on the way to being finished. However, before a horse gets to this stage, it must be brought up gradually through a familiarization process with humans.

the reins to make the horse tuck his head and he also applies pressure slightly with his legs. He feels that, if you apply too much pressure, you are just driving the horse up into the bit. If you use subtle pressure with both your hands and legs, the horse usually will give. Even if it is only one step, if the horse does it freely, half the battle is over, this trainer contends. One step easily leads to two, three, four or however many you want. Doing it freely, of the horse's own accord is really the key, according to Moon.

"You have to get the horse's head set correctly, though, to make this method work. Lots of horses, if their heads aren't set right, will throw their heads up. When they do that, you aren't going to get anywhere, so you might as well move off and try again later in the lesson. By setting a horse's head, I mean that when I put a little pressure on the reins, I want him to flex at the poll.

"You have to keep the same amount of pressure on both sides to keep the horse backing straight," Moon comments. "This is not as easy as it sounds, because most people are right or left-legged, just like they are right or left-handed. Unless you are conscious of it, you naturally apply more pressure with the strong side."

When Moon starts his young horses for the first month or two, he only rides them about fifteen or twenty minutes at a time. He feels that the horse's attention span isn't much longer than a half hour and he likes to put them away with some of their mental freshness remaining. "Boredom is one of the toughest things a trainer has to combat — both his own and the horse's. I think an arena is a fantastic place to break a colt, but after you've got him going, get him out of there. Get in the woods, the fields or along some quiet road somewhere and let him look around. If you do this, the horse won't get bored even after you have him trained completely. A change in environment does wonders for the mental attitude of a horse."

One of the big problems that Western horse trainers face these days is getting a horse used to working in company. The sizes of the group classes increase every year. For a young horse to be removed from working in the relatively isolated environment of home to the chaos of the show ring often is a considerable shock. Moon solves this by using his young horses to pony other young horses.

"Once I have a young horse fairly well broken, I use him to pony my really green horses. I get some young horses that aren't broken at all and they have to be made fit for halter. Some of these colts are too young to be broken, anyway, so I just use one of my young trainees to pony these halter horses. Ponying gets a horse used to another

Moon does most of his initial schooling on the longe line and doesn't use driving lines because he's never had experience with them. Prior to mounting, he schools vigorously — to get the edge off of them — on the longe. Patience is the key.

horse close by him in a hurry, so he doesn't get upset when another horse bumps him or steps on him, as frequently happens in a lot of these crowded pleasure classes."

Like most quarter horse trainers, Keith Moon frequently is called upon to prepare horses for halter classes. As a showman and as a judge, he has a few things to say about the way halter horses are prepared and the way they must be kept in order to have any chance at a ribbon.

"I really don't like to see a horse as fat as most halter horses are," he says. "When I get these horses for training after they have all their halter points, the first thing I have to do is make them drop three hundred pounds or so.

"I think judging standards for halter classes should be changed. Actually, it is for the benefit of the horse. Think of the damage that carrying all that extra weight must do to the green joints of those young horses. It's no wonder we have leg troubles!"

A lot of quarter horse people tend to blame the increase in leg troubles in quarter horses to the steady influx of thoroughbreds being crossed into the registry. Moon admits this might be part of the problem — thoroughbreds being notorious for bad legs — but he does not feel this is the major cause. As indicated, he blames the excess weight the

horse carries at a young age and the fact that he is called upon to perform at an earlier age.

"In a way," Moon declares, "we are getting more and more like the racehorse people. Many of them would rather not race their 2-year-olds. They recognize that these horses are too young to handle that kind of strain, but there is so much money on the line that they can't afford not to race the babies.

"With the demand for good, young pleasure horses and reining horses increasing every year, we are inclined to push these young horses and show them before they should be shown. Also, there is the pressure of making an American Quarter Horse Association champion as fast as you possibly can, so the horse can enter the stud or the brood mare band and get in production."

Of the ten AQHA champions that Moon has trained, several had a considerable amount of thoroughbred breeding. Although he is not at all opposed to this practice, he does have a few words of caution.

"One thing I think should be considered carefully in this practice — although I believe the thoroughbred influence is a good one — is to watch the temperament of this crossing. We have some lines of quarter horses that don't seem to

When riding, Moon initially uses two-handed direct rein (above left), at the same time applying slight neck rein pressure. This speeds changeover to neck rein. In schooling for rollbacks, Moon often uses circular pen (right). After riding trainee into barrier, he reins back through, working horse off haunches. Jim Willoughby (below) has trained this horse to perfection.

have their brains too tightly wrapped up and I know that there are thoroughbreds with this same problem. For example, there is a famous line of thoroughbreds that had all the speed they would ever need, but a lot of them never made it at the track because trainers couldn't convince them to run the right way. By the same token, I know a few quarter horse lines like this — horses sire offspring that are hotter than firecrackers and aren't at all sensible.

"It doesn't make sense to breed a screwy quarter horse to an idiotic thoroughbred. You are asking for a heap of trouble. But if you take a good-dispositioned quarter horse and breed it to a good-dispositioned thoroughbred, you probably have a good thing. Thoroughbreds are big horses, but are unusually handy for their size. Also, adding thoroughbred to quarter horse gives you the long and free-striding horse that produces the smoother-looking ride that the judges seem to favor in the pleasure classes. Frankly, I have no quarrel with mixing thoroughbreds and quarter horses as long as the mixture is controllable."

So Moon keeps right on being successful at training his pleasure horses and his reining horses despite his slightly radical ideas. He has reached the point now where many of the offspring of champions he has trained are coming to him for training. He allows that this is a nice position to be in.

When horse is fairly well trained, Moon uses him to pony other green horses. This gets him used to being jostled and bumped in crowded classes without coming unglued (right). It also helps halter-break young stock, saving much of trainer's time!

D: TRAINING THE TRAIL HORSE

THE WORDS, TRAIL HORSE, bring to mind different things to different people. To some, it means maneuvering a horse through some difficult obstacles in an arena. To others, it is a ride alone to communicate with nature. Still others might think of an organized three-day ride with campfires and singing. Still others see an endurance race or a trek into the Grand Canyon.

Regardless of which way you use a trail horse, it takes a lot of preparation to maximize your enjoyment with him.

Assuming you are just breaking a young horse and intend to make a trail horse of him, he has a lot to learn before he will make a good one.

He must possess some inborn characteristics, such as good general conformation; especially straight legs and feet. A horse that toes-out, for instance, is liable to stumble. A horse with a shoulder that is too steep is limited in his length of stride and, as a result, his feet must strike the ground more often in covering the same amount of distance.

Disposition also is of prime importance in selecting a trail horse prospect. In order of importance are disposition, conformation and breeding. This logic is apparent when you look at these in reverse order. Suppose that you had a horse with a great pedigree, but crooked legs. What if he had a great pedigree, great conformation, but he was so bad that you couldn't get near his pen or he'd try to hurt you?

much pressure to apply to the reins to keep his head in set and still keep him walking. Try, however, to not hang on his head.

Instead, learn to anticipate his breaking into a trot and give him just enough pull through the reins to prevent him from breaking.

You can learn this technique fairly easily and will find it rewarding to discover that old Lazy Bones really can walk out after all. Most lazy horses are caused by lazy riders.

But there is the horse that will not walk at all. This may

To Avoid Unhappy Incidents, There Are Skills To Be Mastered Which Are Outlined Here.

Ideally, the horse should possess all three qualities, although most of us ride something less than the perfect horse. Beyond this, the horse should be sound and healthy, of course.

As for disposition, it is not enough that a young horse comes over to you and hangs his head over the fence to be petted while you are looking at him. This is nice and we'll give him credit for it, but it is not the total picture. There are horses that are friendly around the corral, but when you saddle them up and get on to ride, they are loaded with bad habits!

Some young horses are sweet to be around on the grounds, but as soon as they are in unfamiliar surroundings, they come unglued and spook at every little thing. Of course, all young horses have to become acquainted with the world; that's just a part of training. What we are saying is that your first impression will not always give you the whole story, as far as disposition is concerned.

If your horse is going to be a top trail horse, he must have a good way of going. That is, he will have to walk out at a good pace. Some horses walk out naturally and, in others, the walk has to be developed.

If you have a horse that mopes along and doesn't walk out well, that doesn't mean he must always be that way. In another chapter, we have discussed some basic principles on the use of the legs.

If your horse responds well to leg pressure, he will move out when you squeeze him. If he does not, pop him with the bat or popper and he will soon learn to take action or that the bat will follow. Use judgment here and be sure you are communicating to him what it is you want. If you overdo it, you may get him to move out but, at the same time, you might start him on another bad habit.

Hold the bat so that the butt is up by your thumb and the rest runs down through your hand and along the horse's shoulder.

Urge him to walk out with your legs. If he does not respond, give him a flick with the bat. Do not hold him with your legs; just squeeze and release. Don't let him loaf even a little bit. Remember, you are not pleasure riding now; you are training him. As you are urging him to walk in this manner, you will have to keep him from breaking into a trot, using your hands.

To do this, he first must have his head set; that is, he must flex at the poll and be up on the bit. You may need a running martingale at first. Since all horses do not have the same lightness of mouth, you will have to determine how

or may not be easy to cure, depending on the cause. If, for example, he is a horse whose owner liked to race him against other horses in the neighborhood, most likely the run has come down on him hard and he may be difficult, if not impossible, to cure.

Now, if the horse is simply responding to a piece of equipment that is pinching or rubbing him, the cure is easy.

If you add up the many different causes, with the many types of individuals, you can see that we can only offer some general information without analyzing the problem with each horse.

"As often as not, when someone has come to me with a horse that 'will not walk,' I can get on him and have him walking before he has gone a quarter of a mile. This is a good indication that the problem lies with the rider, not the horse," according to one top trainer.

Over-control is a fault common with people whose horses don't seem to do anything right. Quite often this is someone who never has learned to ride properly and is gripping the horse with his legs, hanging on his head. Spend a little time just sitting on the horse, the reins loose. Then ride him some, with much the same attitude.

Some nervous horses will need to be regressed to the point that they almost are starting all over again. If you are starting out with a new horse, remember that gaining his confidence at the start is important, especially with the young horse.

A major part of horse training is getting the horse psychologically prepared to learn. This can be quite a different thing with each individual horse.

If working with a young, flighty filly that has been out in pasture all her life, then psychologically preparing her to learn would consist largely of grooming, handling her feet and just letting her know you don't mean to do her any harm. You might even be a soft touch for a carrot or a handful of grain.

On the other hand, if working with a spoiled, older horse that comes with his teeth bared and he thinks of himself as being the teacher instead of the pupil, psychologically preparing him to learn would consist of something like tying him down and sitting on his head for awhile for the professional trainer.

By the same token, even with the bad actor, don't abuse him and still try to convey to him that you mean no harm, trying to gain his confidence all the while.

Every good trail horse should be well acquainted with

Prince Tazzraf, a 5-year-old Arabian stallion, executes the side-pass properly, well aware of the pole beneath him (above left). Hobble breaking should be done by a professional and is a good trait for the trail horse (above right). Should there be trouble, he can be restrained in this manner. A good trail horse must be watchful of surroundings, but not spooky (below). By first mastering the skills he'll need in the arena, he then will respond properly when out in nature's hills.

the trailer. In the show ring he sometimes will be asked to demonstrate his willingness to load and unload properly. If you don't want to show him, you still will want to take him out looking for new trails to ride.

Every good trail horse has to understand the use of leg aids. It is a must! Aside from being asked to side-pass the horse over a pole or a chalk line in an arena, think of how valuable this control is when riding along a roadside with a car coming. The horse can be held by your hands and legs at the side of the road. With the leg aids, you can open and close gates without getting off your horse, or guide your horse while backing.

If your horse does not understand leg aids, you haven't got a trail horse.

Using the hands and legs to communicate with the horse is probably never better demonstrated than when you see a show horse back through an L, a course laid out in the shape of that letter. The horse must be quiet and responsive to your cues, called aids. When you first begin acquainting him with the L, walk him in and stop him. Don't try to give him everything at once. Look for any opportunity to let him know that he has done something well.

Developing a quiet, confident attitude in your horse will come only through correct communication with him. Give him lots of room, at first. Make the L quite large. Just back him in, stop him and let him stand there quietly awhile. When you back him in and around the corner, it is best if you look at one side of the L only, rather than shifting around, looking from one side to the other. If you feel you should look to the other side, try not to shift around too much in the saddle, as such movement could be mistaken for a change in cue.

On a trail ride, you can't always count on having a suitable tree handy at every rest stop and, when working your trail horse in an arena, you can just hobble him while you are moving and setting up new obstacles. Hobbles also can constitute a safety factor for your horse. Once he understands the hobbles, he will carry this knowledge with him wherever he goes. It could save his life or prevent a serious injury, should he ever be so unfortunate as to get himself tangled in wire or some other hazard. But if you are not skilled at training, do not try to hobble break your own horse.

Teaching your horse to be unafraid of water may take some doing. We know of one mare, about twenty years ago, that would not cross the stream that ran through on her owner's place. The way her owner finally got around this was to take her up the canyon and cross the bridge. (Luckily, she was not afraid of that.) He then rode her back down the canyon, on the other side of the stream until she was looking right across at the barn.

"I worked her for awhile, on the other side, until she was a little tired and starting to think of the nicer things, like getting cooled out, rubbed down and turned out. She now had a motive for stream crossing and it didn't take long for her to bail right in. Once she got her feet wet, she was water broke," remembers the trainer.

With a young colt, some riders use either spurs or a bat to make him go up to some object that has spooked him. This is a mistake. There is a time and a way to get your horse used to things, but not by forcing him up to and making him stare at everything that scares him.

If you ride a good, balanced seat, you will find that a horse can whirl around and spook fairly hard, yet not be tough to sit on. Make it a habit to use good form whenever you ride and, if a colt spooks with you, pretend he didn't. Through just using a colt, he will usually get over these things on his own. If, instead, you make an issue of them, you may be compounding the problem.

It is a good idea to take a halter and lead rope whenever you take a horse out on the trail. Some experienced trail riders put it on the horse, along with the bridle and tie the lead rope back to the saddle. This way, if you have to tie

him up, you can do it right. Tying a horse with the bridle reins is a bad practice. Not only is it a way to break reins or a headstall, but the horse can injure his mouth easily.

A top trail horse has got to have a lot on the ball. Not only must he possess the talent, but that talent has to be developed through a lot of patience and hard work. All of this is not without its reward, however, and there is a lot of pleasure in teaching him well.

Thus far, we have covered the training of the horse for trail work, but there are some requirements for humans who want to take to the wide, open spaces on the back of a trusty mount. These rules best can be described as simple etiquette and following them can make your rides — especially if there are several horsemen in the group — a good deal more enjoyable, not to mention safer.

While most of us tend to think of trail riding as a Western-oriented pursuit, there are plenty of participants along the bridle trails of the East and especially New England. As such trails are likely to be better used and more crowded than many of those in the West, we asked Phillip M. Perry to check it out for us.

It's a sunny autumn day and several horse lengths ahead of you a rider disappears over the top of the hill as the trail winds through a cool hemlock forest. This is the life, you say to yourself. There's nothing like a trail ride to get a person away from the problems of life.

Suddenly your mount bolts from the path and, catching you off guard, bucks at the side of the trail while tossing his head in the air and emitting a long, drawn-out whinny. As you attempt to muster your injured horsemanship enough to save the situation so that you don't end up with your rear end down, you observe the instigator of this crisis. An equine bandit gallops past you down the hemlock road, its rider wide-eyed and wondering what to do.

Anyone who has taken part in trail rides for a number of years can recount similar tales of chain-reaction frenzy. This particular story illustrates at least two examples of bad trail etiquette. There's a good possibility that, had the "rules of the road" been observed, the situation above would never have happened.

Right off the bat, we have a rider who is reveling in the wonders of nature. That's fine, unless the reverie becomes so deep that the rider forgets what he is doing. As a result, he allows his horse to step into a groundhog hole or onto a bottle, precipitating a crisis that will affect other members

When teaching a horse to back through an "L" course, careful use of the aids plus patience are of primary importance (left). Start with a wide "L", then decrease as the horse negotiates the obstacle properly. Every horse should be a good traveler, but this is especially important for the trail horse, who sometimes must be hauled to the site of a competitive trail ride.

Crossing a creek the first time can be traumatic, and again patience is a requisite. The text details a trick that can be employed successfully.

When a horse is over his initial fear, he shouldn't hesitate to wade right in, perhaps pausing for a drink at the time (above). Walking along a creek bed teaches the horse to control and be conscious of his feet, since the footing is uneven or slippery (right).

A horse cannot be expected to work properly if insects constantly bother him, so a repellent around the eyes helps keep his mind on the horseman.

of the ride. Too often riders slouch along in mindless innocence, like drivers on a super highway.

Next, we have the galloping horse from the rear, caused we might assume by shying from a fluttering piece of paper. Did the rider slow his horse at the first sign of shying, encourage him with soft words, even dismount and lead the horse by if necessary? Perhaps, like other inexperienced horsemen, he urged his unwilling mount on with a kick and a cluck.

Finally, the approaching rider did not warn the horseman in front of his approach. This is necessary and good equine etiquette at any speed, but in this situation it might have saved the day. If he had signaled the horseman up front, that rider could have pulled his horse over to the side of the trail, then turned the horse around so that he would be facing the oncoming horse. This is good practice to combat all kinds of approaching phenomena, such as cars and trucks, if you are riding on a highway.

On the brighter side, the first horseman was following some distance more than the recommended one-horse length on the ride. It's safe to say that, had he been following closer, he would have disturbed the horse in front of him, and so on. And, by the time the second horseman had passed the first at a gallop, he managed to bring his horse to a halt by yanking hard on the right rein, thus forcing the horse to circle.

As this story shows, poor trail etiquette can ruin a ride and can even dry up your plans for future organized trail

As noted in Chapter Four, proper unsaddling can save much hassle when it's time to saddle again. The latigo strap is run up under the rigging dee (left), then it's end can be dropped through cinch ring and pulled when saddling next time (above).

109

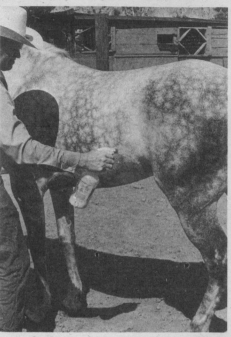

There are many repellents on the market to protect the horse during a trail ride, and a dousing prior to heading out is a good idea (below).

Riding through the country is a good boredom reliever both for horse and horseman and saves souring a horse. To avoid having it become a nightmarish outing, though, the horse needs to master certain skills, outlined here.

rides. That's because trail etiquette really involves three attitudes: one expressed toward your fellow riders, another expressed toward your horse and a last expressed toward the landowner through whose property your ride passes.

The attitude toward fellow riders begins with distance. Keeping a full horse's length behind the horse in front of you will avoid the dangers of kicking and resultant injury and/or confusion. Also, it means that any sudden actions on the part of your mount will not be transferred to the horses in front of you. Keeping your distance also means your mount will be expected to find his own way along the trail, instead of blindly following the horse in front of him.

For example, the horse before you may see a pothole dug at the side of the trail, but may walk over it, taking care not to step into it. Unfortunately, if your own horse is too close to the horse before him, he will not get a chance to see that hole before it's too late to avoid injury.

Judy Foster, a resident of Westfield, Massachusetts, has been on many rides and has a particular gripe about some people.

"We have a rule in our own club," she says, "and we try to make it clear to each person who goes on a ride with us. You'd be surprised at the number of people who don't understand that, when a horse becomes pals with another horse on a ride, it's hard to tear them apart. So we insist that either these pals stay together or, that when they are trained to stay apart, they do so without disturbing the other members of the ride."

Ms. Foster adds that, when horsemen try to break horse friendships formed during the ride, their mounts often become restless and jumpy, which unfortunately influences other horses. This club insists that if two horsemen want to get the horses separated, they first drop to the rear of the ride and force their horses to walk some distance apart until they are used to the idea.

"If we don't do this, we're always running into the horse that continually passes everyone else to get up to his friend. Then, his owner holds him by the side of the trail while the others go by again."

Judy Foster also points out that one horseman is always assigned to wait with the last horseman of the ride who is responsible for closing the gates along the trail. "We do this for two reasons," she says. "First, if the gate man is injured or has trouble with the gate, there will be someone else there so he won't be left alone. Secondly, the additional man keeps the last horseman from galloping to catch up with the group. Too often this results in a group of startled horses when the last horse rushes up on them."

When passing another horse, always pass to the left of that horse and let the horseman know you're passing. Avoid clucking to your horse or using the whip to get him into passing gear. This will do the trick, but may also cause the horse you're passing to move faster, much to the regret of the rider. Use leg pressure to move your horse to action.

Naturally, the more riding experience you've had with your horse, the more you know how he'll respond to any number of trailside stimuli. As a spokesman for the Farnam Companies wrote in *"Understanding Horse Psychology,"* a horseman should eventually understand all the "factors which affect a horse and make him react the way he does; to see with his eyes, hear with his ears, feel with his skin, think with his brain and love with his heart."

The first principle of prevention is anticipation. How does your horse respond to a strange-shaped stone, a narrow bridge, or a family group of hikers with a noisy child? How about a fluttering piece of paper coming toward you on the trail? A soothing word of encouragement can avoid a scene. If necessary, pull the horse over to the side of the trail while other horses pass a strange object. He may be encouraged to go on.

"We always try to think ahead of the horse," points out Judy Foster. Thinking several steps ahead can avoid a leg injury caused by your mount's failure to see a hole in the trail or a runaway horse caused by a barking dog.

Once again, failure to do this is bad trail etiquette, because it can encourage other horses to act up, making you and your horse unpopular companions during the ride. Every horse seems to have his own outward signs just before he does something out of the ordinary. For instance, a horse who is about to shy to the side of the trail may tip his ear just prior to doing so.

By skillful application of the reins, you can stop trouble before it starts and make the ride a pleasant one for everybody.

A horseman's attitude toward his horse really begins just prior to the ride, itself. Whether for competition or pleasure, preparation of the horse for the ride can insure that he behaves himself during the course of the next few hours.

Brushing the coat under the saddle smoothes out the hair and makes the saddle more comfortable for the horse. A horse that has his hair going the wrong way under the saddle or that has some small foreign object between the saddle and the fur can start getting jittery during the ride.

Check the shoes, too. A loose shoe which falls off during the ride can cause erratic behavior disturbing to other riders and horses. An extra pair of horseshoes in the pack will spare you troubles later on.

Checking the strength of the reins is another pre-ride must. If there is a weak spot in any of the horse gear, that part of the gear may break during a crucial moment. A frightened horse, galloping away at full speed and tossing his head, might break the reins if there are any weak spots.

Mosquito and bug repellent should also be applied before the ride. A horse "bugged" during the ride can approach the uncontrollable and ruin the ride for others.

The major problem facing private landowners who let you on their land is liability. Who pays if a horseman gets hurt on their property? This one fear often prevents landowners from opening up their land.

However, many states are currently revising their landowner liability laws. Since 1967, over half our states have adopted more lenient statutes which place the burden of responsibility on the user rather than the landowner.

As these laws take effect, it is hoped a greater number of landowners will open their land for group trail rides. This increased opportunity, of course, brings with it greater responsibility. Landowners will be watching to see if riders treat their property correctly.

Bradford Millar, a landowner in West Swanzey, New Hampshire, has long upheld a tradition of allowing horsemen to pass through his property. "As a matter of fact, I've had no trouble with horsemen," he claims. "Groups are even better than individuals; maybe that's because the person in charge feels a personal responsibility toward leaving the land as he found it."

Without doubt, landowners like Millar are a boon to horsemen. How can we make sure their land remains open?

First of all, permission should always be granted by a landowner before the horse group takes off down-trail. Using psychology when approaching the landowner can work wonders. Point out to him that your group has been in existence for some time, if it has. If possible, give him the names of other landowners who have let your group use their land. Perhaps he will want to check with these people to see how the property fared.

By all means let him know that you will take personal responsibility, as leader of the group, for making sure everyone cleans up after themselves and leaves the property as they found it.

Riding over the landowner's property without permission will only anger him and produce an immediate "no" when you seek permission at a later date. When you do receive permission, try to get tips on any dangerous or bad parts of his property. Is barbed wire fencing strung anywhere? Is there swampland on the property? Hidden potholes?

In preparing for the ride, someone should pack away several plastic bags for holding the trash you accumulate along the way. These bags are waterproof and lightweight.

During the day of the ride, keep away from cultivated fields, or ride along the uncultivated edge if you need to. Make sure the last rider closes the gate properly behind him. When tying horses, keep them at a distance from valuable trees, shrubs or flower beds.

When the ride is over, someone in the group should review the scene and remove any ribbons or signs you have employed to mark the way. These devices are especially popular for competitive trail rides. At this time, the ribbon gatherer can check the property to make sure no trash has been left behind.

Good attitudes toward these three key elements — the horse, fellow riders and the landowner — can spell a successful ride during which nobody is hurt or bothered by thoughtless conduct. Trail ride etiquette is more than a set of empty formalities. In the final analysis, it's a genuine part of the true horse lover's mentality.

3: TRICKS OF TRICK RIDING

YOU'RE SITTING THERE, watching a rodeo, with all its colorful spectacle and razzle-dazzle. A series of bronc riders have finished doing their thing and the announcer's voice blares over the public-address system, booming to hollow echoes, announcing that Miss So-and-So will give an exhibition of trick riding.

There's a flash of color at the performer's entrance and suddenly, with a mounting crescendo of drumming hoofbeats, a horse is thundering around the course, its lithe young rider performing a series of heart-clutching gyrations, defying the laws of gravity — not to mention common sense — from every conceivable place except seated in the saddle.

It's a fresh, bright change-of-pace and you're left not minding the hot sun or the settling clouds of dust; not quite as much, at least. Crowds love the trick riders, as do the rodeo committees, for the spicing of color, glamour and showmanship they provide. Trick riding is offered as pure entertainment — a holdover from earlier rodeo traditions — rather than as a competitive event and this helps to keep the performances from becoming dull and stereotyped.

Bonnie Happy and Danelle "Danny" Connelly — aged 20 and 19, respectively — are professional performers in the specialized field of trick riding. Step-sisters, they often perform as a team, working out of San Luis Obispo, California.

The girls caught their first fascination for trick riding from Connie Griffith who, with her husband, Dick Griffith, operates a school for trick riding in Palmdale, California. Bonnie, who terms Ms. Griffith "the best woman trick rider in the world," used to cool-out the Griffith mounts after Connie had performed. Both girls studied trick riding during the various seminars held by the Griffiths at times when regular schools are not in operation.

Bonnie first took up trick riding early in 1969, Danny about four or five months later. Both were attending high school at the time, Bonnie a junior and Danny a freshman.

It's the usual situation of having to learn to walk before you can run and one of the early exercises consisted of pacing along behind the horse, both of the student's hands grasping the croupers — two sturdy, thong-wound loops attached to the cantle of the highly specialized saddle that is a basic necessity for trick riding — with the feet following the hind feet of the horse at the walk and trot.

The purpose of this exercise was to acquire familiarity with the cadence and timing of the horse at the slower paces. Yes, you're right: There is a considerable hazard of getting your toes stepped upon.

"That does tend to accelerate the learning process," Danny notes.

It Doesn't Look Easy — And It Isn't —
But It Makes For Spectacular Horsemanship!

Danny Connelly shows one of the training steps for would-be trick riders: developing a sense of pace and rhythm by pacing behind the horse, holding the croupers. There is a danger of stepped-on toes, which postpones further training! Always use caution.

Danny: "Just about the last thing you want is to come unglued and have to exit to a chorus of snide comments," (above). Bonnie: "It doesn't take long to find that strong muscles can keep you from getting hurt, or worse."

Likewise early in the curriculum, Dick Griffith prescribed a regimen of sit-ups and push-ups, intended to strengthen and tone up those muscles vital to safe and successful trick riding.

"Ordinarily, most girls do not wish to appear unusually muscular, but it doesn't take long to find out that muscles can keep you from getting hurt or worse, so you begin to see the exercises make a lot of sense," Bonnie observes.

Both girls are unanimous in emphasizing that learning trick riding should never be viewed as an interesting do-it-yourself project. You need competent, professional instruction, the proper saddle and, of course, the horse is of crucial importance, too.

The trick riding saddle is an extremely specialized item of tack, with loops, straps and croupers located where needed. Likewise, it's designed to remain firmly in place during all of the various maneuvers. You can't afford to have it slip loose while you're dangling head-down, doing the Cossack Drag at full gallop!

Bonnie bought her saddle from Connie Griffith, who had built it from scratch for her own use. Danny's saddle once was used by Pat North, a woman who did trick riding with Bonnie's mother. In loose, ballpark figures, one can expect to pay upward of $600 for a used trick-riding saddle. That assumes one can be found for sale and the estimate doesn't include decorations; merely the functional saddle.

"Even if you manage to find a good saddle and prepare to buy it," Bonnie cautions, "you should have it checked over first by a good saddlemaker who is familiar with the requirements for trick riding."

The problem of acquiring a suitable mount for trick riding is as bad as finding the saddle, quite possibly worse. Both girls favor the quarter horse as the ideal choice of breed for the purpose; very nearly the only choice they'd consider acceptable.

"The horse has to have the strength and stamina to carry you easily," Danny explains. "He has to be level-headed and stable in temperament but, at the same time, you don't want a dead horse, the kind people buy for small children, one that wants to settle back to an easy jog or walk."

Trick riding calls for a saddle that is highly specialized to stand the unusual stresses without shifting or breaking

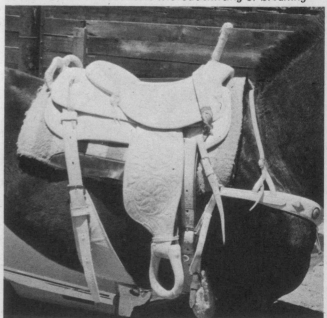

This sheepskin-padded loop around the right ankle is all that holds the rider during such tricks as the Cossack Drag.

The reasoning behind this viewpoint becomes crystal-clear when you consider that the horse is completely on his own during the time the tricks are being performed. The reins are joined together with a single strand of leather extending beyond the juncture by a foot or so. This single strand is used as an impromptu quirt in getting the mount to a full gallop. At that time, the reins are released to hang loose on the withers as the rider goes into her routine.

The size of the horse will be dictated by the size of the rider to a considerable extent. The tricks you plan to do are a further factor to consider. For example, if the rider is small and planning to do a considerable amount of ground-work, a large horse would be a poor choice.

The two horses with which the girls commenced their trick riding careers were about 12 at the time and it became necessary to retire them after a few years and begin hunting for replacements. It was a long and anxious operation.

You can't really try out a prospective purchase, since it's most unlikely that he will have the necessary training. It's extremely rare to find a trained trick-riding horse for sale.

The reason is simple: Even though Danny or Bonnie were to stop doing trick riding, it's unlikely they would be inclined to sell their present mounts.

So they spent a lot of time, covered a lot of miles and finally settled on their choices, with fingers firmly crossed. Danny's is a 7-year-old gelding she called Jumbo Jack, the name being whimsically lifted from hamburgers the girls ate at a franchised stand the day they found him. Bonnie's 8-year-old mare is called Hotcakes, inspired by a Carly Simon record she enjoyed especially.

Both mounts are black, with white blazes on their face and white stockings all around. The girls regard this as the ideal coloration from a standpoint of putting on an attractive appearance and setting off the performer's colorful costume.

Training the new mounts to adequate standards of performance and reliability was quite an operation, loaded with tension and suspense, because it was but a matter of a few short months before the start of the new season and they had to come through...or else!

During training, the person holding the flag line has an important responsibility. If handled improperly, serious injury can be dealt to trick rider, as Danny discovered!

"A real go-for-broke proposition," Danny recalls, "just about the last thing you want is to come unglued part-way around the track and have to walk off with a few thousand spectators watching you and making snide comments!"

Fortunately, both Hotcakes and Jumbo Jack made their debuts without unfortunate incidents, though neither is up to the quality of the retired mounts with which the girls launched their careers.

"Give 'em time," Bonnie says, "they're both coming along nicely, I'm happy to say."

Preliminary training of a new mount is a matter of patience and repetition, to a large extent. You have to build up the horse's confidence, helping to assure him that all the odd activities on the part of the rider won't hurt him. With the two new horses, it just seemed that everything fell into place all at once but, until that time, you just have to keep repeating until they commence doing what you want correctly.

One vital phase in training a new mount is to program him to follow a predictable track around the course, almost like a locomotive running on rails, maintaining his pace without need for further directions. A flag line helps to accomplish this. It consists of a long string, decorated with triangular plastic pennants in red, white and blue. This is strung along the first straightaway and someone must stand there and hold the flag line at the first turn.

If the horse is the most important ingredient in a successful performance, the person holding the flag line at the first turn ranks second by no more than the thinnest of slices, the girls agree.

Danny had somewhat traumatic proof as to the truth of that a couple of seasons ago. The girl holding the flag line thought the horse was going to come uncomfortably close to her, so she shook the flags at him to make him shy off. The horse shied with such vigor that Danny's leg was broken in six places.

"Make no mistake," Danny recalls, "the person holding the flag line on that first turn is darned important. They have to know what to do to help you, if you should need help, and they have to know what not to do, too!"

When in the training ring, the girls may perform the given trick somewhat more slowly while familiarizing the mount with the routine. However, in performing before a live audience, every effort is made to put the horse at a full gallop and training concentrates upon his maintaining that gait.

"Not only does it look more showy and impressive," Bonnie notes, "but it's actually safer and easier at a full gallop."

"Smoother, too," adds Danny.

The tricks can be divided into two basic categories: strap tricks and groundwork. Bonnie — unlike most girl trick riders — does a considerable amount of groundwork, while Danny has a general preference for the strap tricks. The difference lies in whether or not the rider touches the ground during the course of the trick.

Strap tricks include the Fender Layout, in which one foot is held in the stirrup, with the knee tucked up under the fender, one hand grasping the saddlehorn, with the body and the free foot extended parallel to the ground. The horn of the trick riding saddle is longer and smaller in diameter than the horn of a conventional Western saddle, and usually is wrapped with rawhide thongs to afford a better, more secure grip for the hands.

The Full Fender is similar to the Fender Layout, except that both arms are extended fully, parallel to the ground, and the rider does not hold the horn with one hand.

"This is somewhat more difficult than it looks," is Bonnie's comment and, quite certainly, it looks difficult enough for any reasonable requirement.

In the Hippodrome, the rider stands erect, leaning forward slightly, with feet about three-quarters through straps across the upper surface of the front of the saddle. The knees are locked and the weight is forward. The faster the horse goes, the more the rider can lean forward.

In the Cossack Drag, one foot is inserted through a

As with other types of horsemanship, good grooming is an essential form of stable management for the trick riders. In fact, proper grooming might be even more important: Should the horse be distracted in any way during a performance, barreling along at full speed, the trick rider could be killed! It is necessary that before-and-after grooming practices be performed.

The Full Fender (above) requires strength in the legs and ankles to retain position on the galloping horse with hands free. Practice is essential for Danny Connelly. One of the most difficult tricks is making a circle around the horse's neck and Bonnie Happy isn't satisfied Hotcakes yet is ready for this. She here swings below the neck during practice (below).

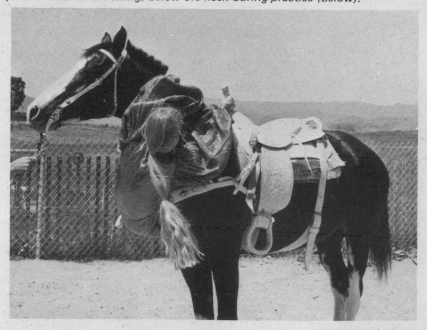

sheepskin-padded loop on the far side of the saddle and the rider hangs head-foremost. Usually, the rider's right foot is in the strap as she hangs down the left side of the horse. The free leg is extended skyward, with toe pointed, while the arms are disposed of in a manner as graceful as possible under the circumstances.

With her original horse, Bonnie used to do the trick in which she goes down beneath the horse's neck coming back up the other side and returning to the saddle. To the present, Hotcakes has not had sufficient training to justify

returning this particular trick to the performing repertoire.

It's not too common for girl trick riders to attempt the around-the-neck trick. For one thing, it takes long, strong arms and it entails an obvious hazard, should you lose your hold at the bottom of the loop and drop beneath those hammermill hoofs. The strategic time to perform the around-the-neck trick is during the turn, so that you would be thrown clear — hopefully! — should you lose your hold.

It goes without saying that weight control is another vital factor. The rider gets into unlikely positions, then must return to conventional riding position with one arm or leg.

"The less you weigh," sighed Bonnie, munching grimly on a diet biscuit and hating it, "the easier it is to maneuver with the muscles you have."

Both girls are professionals, as was noted earlier and are members of the Rodeo Cowboys Association. A condition of their membership is that they cannot perform in rodeos that are not RCA-approved. Usually, they operate as contract performers, making their arrangements directly with the rodeo committee in the given city. Shortly before the start of the new season, they write to RCA headquarters in Denver, Colorado, for a list of the committees and their addresses in the towns scheduling RCA-approved rodeos for the coming season. They go through the list and send letters to the selected committees and, if the committee is interested, back will come a request for the girls to submit contract forms for approval.

The potential payment for performing is $75 per performance — each — as a general estimate. Considering that it hardly takes much over a minute from start to completion, at first hasty glance that may seem to be a fabulous return, based upon terms of hourly scale.

Counterbalancing the tinsel glitter of $75 for a minute or so of performing is the matter of providing transportation, lodging and other expenses for themselves and their mounts; not to mention the difficulty of finding suitable mounts, the financial risk of buying them with no guarantee that they'll work out, the long and arduous program of training the horse and maintaining the rider's keen edge of perfection.

"And having to settle for one of these darned diet crackers when you'd a whole lot rather have a nice plate of spaghetti!" Bonnie footnotes.

Both trick riders sometimes team up during schooling phases of new horses (right). The equine requirements of a trick horse are many. The Fender Layout (below) is another of Danny's strap tricks, not quite as difficult as the Full Fender. Maintaining a sleek, graceful appearance is mandatory.

119

F: WESTERN COMPETITION

There Are Other Events Which Are Popular, From Western Pleasure To Ring Spearing!

EVEN TODAY, THE Western horse is thought of as a tool rather than a toy by the working cowboy...but truth of the matter is that there are a lot more horses today than working cowboys.

The days when a cowboy had to train his horse for cutting, reining and roping still exists, of course. There still is some of this activity but, for that matter, the Pony Express still is in operation. In Texas, one community has developed an annual event — running mail between two towns by horse simply to prove that they can out-deliver the U.S. Postal Service. They have proved their point rather consistently, but we doubt if that means the Pony Express is going to replace the United States Government's efforts.

Much can be said of the Western horse and the cowboy.

In the interests of economy for the most part, ranchers and cattle raisers have developed systems that make highly trained horses a less necessary part of their environment than in the past. Instead of two men roping a calf and leading it to a fire to be branded, dehorned, castrated and vaccinated, ranchers tend to run the animals into chutes, the whole operation being accomplished without the use of either horse or rope. To add insult to injury regarding tradition, the wood fire has been replaced by an electrically heated branding iron!

However, the arts of cowboying have been retained and even improved upon to a great degree in the show ring, the rodeo ring and in recreational aspects of horsemanship. In fact, today's horses have been trained to the point that the average top stock horse undoubtedly can out-perform any working cowhorse that ever was trained to chase cattle, with rare exceptions.

WESTERN PLEASURE

In an effort to keep the Old West alive — at least, to retain the training and horse traditions of the past — the American Horse Shows Association as well as the various breed associations place emphasis on a show ring class called Western pleasure. At this point, it probably is the most popular event in Western-oriented horse shows, but contrary to that fact, it is more complex than the uninitiated onlooker may realize.

While this class can be termed rather simple, it does incorporate all of the basics of Western riding. Horses are shown at the walk, jog or trot and the lope, going both ways in the ring, using a reasonably loose rein. The judge also may require that horses be made to back in a straight line.

Under AHSA rules, the class is judged sixty percent on performance of the horse, thirty percent on conformation and ten percent on appointments. The horse must be shown with a stock saddle and the rider must wear a Western hat, cowboy boots, shotgun chaps and carry a rope or reata on his saddle. Permitted in this type of competition are curb, snaffle, half-breed and spade bits as well as chain curbs. While some horse associations do allow one to show his horse in a hackamore, it is not accepted under AHSA rules.

Performance of the horse is reflected, of course, in the performance of the rider. The winner usually is one who seems to move his horse effortlessly about the ring. The horse moves at the proper speed, the rider never having to fight him down, he always is on the right lead and the rider is in full charge at all times.

Theoretically, one should be able to compete as well in a standard, working stock saddle as in a silver-mounted, custom-built creation but, alas, this is not the case. The mark for appointments often carries more than ten percent weight, the increase being created in the judge's mind when he is dazzled by the wealth being displayed by an owner intent upon winning. We don't mean that one can buy a blue ribbon by slinging a silver-mounted saddle on Old Nellie, but judges are human and tend to look closer at horses whose owners think enough of them and their talents to lavish expensive gear upon them.

The advice offered by Dwight Stewart, a trainer and showman for more than forty years, is sound: "The rider's personal attire should be such that it adds to the overall picture of the horse, but it should not overshadow him. A rider could wear clothes that call attention to himself rather than to the horse, but the faded jeans, sweat-stained hat, short-sleeved shirt and no chaps does not add up to a favorable picture to the judge."

In the matter of performance, the AHSA suggests that, at the walk, it should be a fast walk and the average judge adheres to this, choosing this horse over a plodder. The book calls for a "reasonably loose rein," but the rider who is going to win doesn't do it with flopping reins. Instead, this rider maintains light contact with the horse's mouth through the reins, maintaining control.

Dan Lopez puts the Appaloosa Ditto Sid through trail class at past world championship show. Nearly every breed is entered in this competition, which is outlined here.

TRAIL CLASSES

This class, under American Horse Shows Association rules, might be considered an extension of the Western pleasure class, although it can do much to prepare a horse for actual trail work.

The rules are much the same as for the pleasure horse classes insofar as the way the reins are handled, work on the rail and appointments for horse and rider. The AHSA rules call for six obstacles, three of which are mandatory. The first requires the rider to open, pass through and close a gate. The handle on the gate must be at least forty-eight inches above ground level and the rider is not allowed to lose control of the gate. The rider must also ride over at least four logs, then across a wooden bridge.

Among the optional obstacles are a water hazard; hobble and ground-tie the horse; back the horse through a course composed of logs shaping an L; put on and remove a slicker; carry an object from one part of the arena to another, dismount and lead the horse over a series of obstacles. These cannot be more than twenty-four inches high nor less than fourteen inches. Although it is not included in youth activity classes of the American Quarter Horse Association, another demand is to send a horse freely into a trailer. The rider may be required to dismount and mount from the off or right side of the horse, too.

The AHSA rules state that the horse shall "perform over natural conditions encountered along the trail," but there are those who have pushed this to the limit. In fact, one show manager several years ago tied a live bear at the edge of the course. No one, however, completed it. It is not at all unusual for goats, sheep or burros to be tied to the bridge or for crates of chickens or other fowl to be placed in close proximity. This may be a true test of the horse's versatility in the eyes of some, but we doubt that one is going to find many sheep tied to bridges — let alone bears — along the average trail.

There is a fallacy among some horsemen in feeling that a trail horse is a reject — one that couldn't make it in Western pleasure classes. Actually, the good trail horse must be able to do everything that a Western pleasure horse can do and a good deal more. Disposition is perhaps the most important facet involved, however. The nervous horse or one that is too young and inexperienced has no place in this class.

As suggested earlier, the horse actually is a shy creature that needs direction. He may readily take one obstacle and balk at another for no apparent reason. The horse should be trained with the idea of reality in mind. How will this animal react if he is on a trail on a dark night?

Thus, judges eye with a degree of jaundice the horse that hurries across the obstacles in the course, seeming to ignore them, not watching where he is going. Instead, the judge prefers a horse that takes its time, puts its head down and inspects the obstacles, then picks its way with care. The horse also must have full confidence in his rider and move out when directed, not refusing an obstacle.

Perhaps the toughest obstacle — rather than the bear, which verges on the ridiculous — is the water obstacle. This is particularly true with a horse new to the class — especially when the water is muddy — for the horse cannot see the bottom of the pool or puddle.

The obvious answer is a lot of homework with the horse before ever getting close to the judge. One can train the horse for water by starting him out in shallow puddles, then advancing him into deeper water as he finds it will not hurt him.

In teaching the horse to walk across the logs, it is best to start with a single log. When he learns to negotiate it without kicking it all over the arena or stumbling over it, add a second log. Most courses include more than the minimum four logs, so more should be added as he develops his talent in this department. Perhaps a series of a dozen logs should be used for such training. These should be at least ten inches high so that the horse learns to pick up his feet and they should be staggered in distance so that the horse learns to actually negotiate the logs, judging the difference in distance, rather than simply moving across predetermined distances between.

In teaching a horse to cross a bridge, the easiest way is simply to lead him across it a few times, then mount and ride him across. Of course, this may not help when he comes to a bridge of a different size or color than what he has been used to, but in time he'll learn to take all such obstacles, if proper patience is shown.

As suggested, homework before one ever enters the show ring is the answer to most of the problems. If one practices putting on and removing his slicker in his home training area, the success of this maneuver before the judge is going to earn points. Another favorite is for the rider to be required to carry a bucket full of rocks. Getting the horse used to the noise from this is a must. One also may be required to drag a log or even a sack of tin cans across the arena and home training can prepare you for this.

Most trail horse judges will call for the horse to show how well he ground ties. When split reins are used, they simply are dropped to the ground, while the rider walks away. Under AHSA rules, if closed reins are used, the horse must be hobbled. Again, teach the horse to stand hobbled before you ever get into the show ring, or you may find yourself with more problems than you want. The horse may panic in strange surroundings and throw himself in his fright, unless previously indoctrinated.

Opening and closing gates is covered elsewhere in this book, along with techniques for trailering and backing a horse through an L course.

THE REINING HORSE

While techniques of training the reining horse are covered elsewhere in this volume, little has been said about the reining contest, which is a feature of almost all approved quarter horse shows. While the reining horse can be developed into a highly trained, push-button type of responder, the requirements of the contest as set forth by the American Quarter Horse Association make it possible for most horsemen to compete.

Basically, the event is designed to show how well the horse can rein, change leads, stop and be handled with smoothness by his rider. There is a designated pattern that must be ridden for the judges and the greatest problem, we have learned, lies in the fact that many inexperienced riders seem not to be able to follow this pattern. In view of this, most judges will have an experienced rider go through the pattern at least once before judging begins, thus showing the less experienced what is expected. This usually is known as "setting the pattern."

The arena must be a minimum of 50 x 150 feet in size, with each horse being judged, according to the AQHA, on "the neatness, dispatch, ease, calmness and speed with which it performs the pattern. Excessive jawing, open mouth or head raising on stop, lack of smooth sliding stops on haunches, breaking gaits, refusing to change leads, anticipating signals, stumbling or falling, wringing tail, backing sideways, knocking over stakes or kegs, changing hands or reins or losing stirrup, or holding on, or two hands on reins, or any unnecessary aid given by the rider to the horse (such as unnecessary talking, patting, spurring, quirting, jerking on reins, etc.) to induce the horse to perform will be considered a fault and scored accordingly. Horse shall rein and handle easily, fluently, effortlessly, and with reasonable speed throughout the pattern."

Below are listed the actual AQHA rules, accompanied by a chart showing the pattern that must be ridden:

THE AQHA REINING PATTERN

PATTERN INSTRUCTIONS

Run from 1 to 2 at full speed and at least 20 feet away from any existing fence or wall.
Stop and back.
Settle horse for 10 seconds.
4 & 5, Ride small figure 8 at slow canter.
6 & 7, Ride large figure 8, fast.
Left rollback over hocks. Upright markers are mandatory at points marked X on pattern.
Right rollback over hocks.
Stop.
Pivot left.
Pivot right.
Walk to judge and stop for inspection until dismissed.

Failure to follow and execute the pattern as set forth will be considered a fault and scored accordingly.

Scoring will be on the basis of 60-80 with 70 denoting an average performance.

In case of doubt, a judge may require any contestant to repeat his performance of any or all the various parts of the pattern. A judge, also, shall have the authority to require the removal or alteration of any piece of equipment or accoutrement which, in his opinion, would tend to give a horse an unfair advantage. Any inhumane equipment will be scored accordingly.

A (quarter horse) show may have up to three approved reining classes. If three reining classes are to be held, they should be the following:
(a) Senior Reining (5-year-olds and older, all horses must

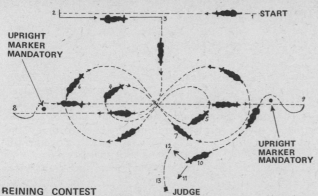

REINING CONTEST

The horse competing in the AQHA reining pattern (above) must be highly schooled as cues are given subtly by the rider. Follow the judge's instructions to the letter!

be shown with a bit.)
(b) Junior Bit Reining (4-year-olds and younger, all horses to be shown with bit.)
(c) Hackamore Reining (4-year-olds and younger, all horses to be shown with hackamore.)
If two reining classes are to be held at a show, they should be the following:
(a) Senior Reining (as specified above.)
(b) Junior Reining (4-year-olds and younger, horses may be shown with either bit or hackamore at the discretion of the exhibitor.)
If only one reining class is to be held at a show, it should be the following:
(a) Reining (all ages — horses 5 years and older must be shown in bit; horses 4 years old and younger may be shown in either bit or hackamore at the discretion of the exhibitor.)
In straight hackamore classes, two hands may be used. In combined bit and hackamore classes, only one hand on reins of bit or hackamore.
For hackamore reining, horses will be ridden only with a rawhide braided or leather braided or rope bosal. Absolutely no iron will be permitted under the jaws regardless of how padded or taped.
For bit reining, horses will be ridden with grazing, snaffle, curb, half-breed, bar or spade bit. However, no wire curbs, regardless of how padded or taped, or no chin strap narrower than one-half inch, or no nose bands or tiedowns will be permitted.
Chain curbs are permissible but must be of the standard flat variety with no twist and must meet the approval of the judge.
Horses, 5 years old and older, must perform in the bit reining class.
A rider may ride only one horse per reining.

THE CUTTING HORSE

The cutting contest began, as did most Western-oriented events, in actual ranch practice since it often was necessary to cut specific animals out of a herd for treatment or preparation for marketing. In fact, some of the top cutting horses one can find are not on ranches or even in the show rings of this country. Instead, they are found in the various stockyards around the nation, where cutting cattle virtually is an around-the-clock occupation for experts and their horses.

However, since the National Cutting Horse Association was founded in Fort Worth, Texas, in 1946, this work has developed into a sport. Oddly enough, there are those who contend that, in terms of the actual value of the horses and the money invested in training facilities across the nation, cutting may be the greatest economic expenditure in the horse field today!

To the uninitiated, cutting appears an uncomplicated form of competition, with the rider taking his horse into a group of cattle, moving one animal out of this herd, then allowing his horse — working on a loose rein — to keep this bovine opponent from getting back into the herd. In most competitions, the horse and horseman work for 2½ minutes and are scored by two judges, both mounted or stationed on opposite sides of the arena.

There also are two turn-back riders, to keep the animal cut out of the herd facing toward the cutting horse, giving the horse the opportunity to work on a loose rein in keeping the yearling from getting past the horse and back into the herd.

The judges are scoring the horse, not the rider. In fact, any help from the rider damages the horse's score. The rider can quit a specific cow or steer without penalty — if he's in command at such time — riding back into the herd for another. If he tries to handle more than two — three at most — in his allotted time, chances are he is spending more time in cutting animals out of the herd than in allowing his horse to perform.

Judges, though, are impressed when a rider goes deep into the herd, bringing out a specific animal, then working it. Usually, this is the first animal worked, since it takes less time to take those from the outer perimeter, when time is growing short.

According to most judges, they favor the horse that keeps his head low, literally looking the cow in the eye. A horse that tends to charge the bovine is scored down and judges prefer that the horse be corrected on the spot rather than allow a bad habit to develop. One problem, especially with stallions, is that they often try to bite the yearling and are penalized for this unnecessary roughness by the judges.

For the uninitiated, the judging rules of the National Cutting Horse Association are as follows:

1. A horse will be given credit for his ability to enter a herd of cattle and bring one out with very little disturbance to the herd or to the one brought out. If he (or his rider) creates unnecessary disturbance throughout his working period, he will be penalized.
2. When an animal is cut from the herd, it must be taken toward the center of the arena. If it goes down the arena fence, that is all right, but the horse never should get ahead of the animal and duck it back toward the herd to get more play but should let the turn-back man turn it back to him.

In cutting, only the horse is judged, not the tack, other appointments or the rider. The text gives NCHA rules.

3. A horse will be penalized two points each time the back arena wall is used for turn-back purposes; the back fence to be agreed on and designated by the judge or judges before the contest starts; meaning the actual fence only, no imaginary line from point to point to be considered. If any of the contestants voices an objection, before the contest starts, the judge or judges shall take a vote of the contestants and a "back fence" acceptable to the majority shall be designated and used.

4. If a horse runs into, scatters the herd, lanes or circles the herd against the arena fence while trying to head an animal, he will be penalized heavily.

5. If a horse turns the wrong way with tail toward animal, he will be disqualified for that go-round with no score.

6. A horse will be penalized one point each time he is reined or cued in any manner. If he is reined or cued several times during a performance, he will be penalized each time. When a horse is picked up hard with the reins and set over, or reined, cued excessively, or spurred in the shoulder, a heavier penalty will be marked against him.

7. For riding with a tight rein through a performance, a penalty will be given; for part of the time during a performance, less penalty.

8. If a horse lets an animal that he is working get back in the herd, he will be penalized five points.

9. When a horse heads an animal and goes past it to the degree that he loses his working advantage, he will be penalized each time he does so. If a horse goes past as much as his length, he will be assessed a heavier penalty. Unnecessary roughness, such as a horse losing his working position to paw or bite cattle, will be penalized.

10. If a contestant quits an animal he is working when the horse is out of position, or the animal has an undue advantage of the horse, he will be penalized three points.

11. A judge marks from sixty to eighty points. An average performance should be marked around seventy. A judge should be careful not to mark an average performance too high because the next horse that shows may put on a top performance that deserves five or six points above average, and if the average performance was marked seventy-five, that would leave no room to give the top horse the credit he deserved above the other.

Winning points will be based on a horse's ability to work cattle and the amount of play he gets from the animal during the performance. In other words, if a horse gets good play and shows plenty of ability to cut cattle and the judge thinks he deserves a seventy-eight marking, but he assessed a three-point penalty against him for reining, the judge would mark him seventy-five.

STOCK HORSE

Again, drawn from the training afforded working cowponies in the days when moving cattle was a way of life, the stock horse routine is a series of maneuvers developed by the American Horse Shows Association. Included in the routine are figure eights, with the judge telling you how many he wants to see. Other maneuvers required are three runs down the length of the arena, slide stops, turns and at least one backup.

In making figure eights, the horse is required to change leads on both front and hind legs. The horse normally will change automatically with the forelegs when the shift in weight occurs, but changing with the hind legs may take more time and training. It is this instant perfection that the judge seeks.

Many riders stick close to the rail and use it as an aid in handling the horse in lead changes. The judge recognizes this fallacy and will mark down the rider who tries such a gimmick. Stay clear of the rail, well into the open area of the ring.

Judges have their own preferences and one should listen intently to each judge's instructions. Of great importance is

the size of the figure eights he desires. If he tells you to use the full width of the arena, use it; don't attempt to impress him with your horse's versatility by making short, tight loops. If you are having difficulty in getting the horse to change leads, don't use the romal or your spurs forward of the cinch. Either calls for sure disqualification by the average judge.

Most judges will ask for two figure eights, which are not difficult to count, but if he wants more, be sure to count them off. Too many or not enough also can count against the rider.

A fault shown by most riders is overuse of the hands in making figure eights. Maintain the hand position over the horn as much as possible, directing the horse by twisting the wrist on the reins and by use of the leg aids, which will be discussed in greater detail. Don't lean with your body,

George Texeira rides pinto Mighty Warrior in Western riding and stock horse events, both tough classes due to increased participation and number of fine show horses.

but sit in the center of the saddle, keeping all of your movements to a minimum, attempting your best to appear a part of the horse.

In making the run at speed the length of the arena, be sure to stay clear of the rail. A minimum of ten feet usually is safe, even if the judge orders you to follow the rail. With this much room, you have space in which to make your turn and stop at the end. If crowded too close to the rail, you are looking at problems when you get to the end.

Assuming your horse is properly trained, he should recognize the cues for slide stops or whatever they are called locally. For the rundown, the rider should jog to the spot where he will begin his rundown. He also should have selected the spot well in advance where he intends to stop. In this way, he doesn't find himself suddenly at the end of the arena, jerking on the bit to bring his horse down.

When ready to stop, one shouldn't put too much weight on the stirrups, as this tends to pitch him forward in the saddle. Even if this happens, incidentally, don't grab for the saddle horn, for touching any part of the saddle during the stop means you're disqualified.

Instead, when the rider reaches the selected spot where he intends to stop, he positions himself in the saddle, rolling back on his tailbone. Thus, when the horse allows his rear to drop for the slide, the rider drops with him, rather than being left standing in his stirrups wondering what happened to his balance.

If the horse has been properly trained, the signal that forward motion is to cease is when the bit begins to come back in his mouth. There are too many riders who grab the bridle at the stop point and all but jerk the poor horse off his feet. The horse doesn't like it and neither does the judge.

Once the horse has stopped, the rider has to make his turn-around. The judge is watching this, so it becomes important.

First, be certain the horse has come to a full stop. It is surprising how many riders turn their horses before the stop is completed. When this happens, the horse does not have all four feet directly under him, so he is off-balance and the turn appears ragged.

In the turn-around, always turn away from the nearest fence. In making the turn, use your leg aids, making the horse move away from the pressure. In reining him around, keep him on his back legs so the turn will be smooth and appear reasonably effortless.

In the turn-back for the second run, make a 180-degree turn. Many riders make a ninety-degree turn, start the horse running, then have to straighten him out.

In the second rundown, always follow your previous tracks and stop in approximately the same spot. Judges resent seeing a long run and stop the first time, followed by a short, choppy run with a stop halfway down the arena. They tend to feel the rider is dogging it.

Following this run, again give your horse the chance to get his feet back under him, then back him straight back — as much in his earlier tracks as possible — for at least a dozen feet. Keep him straight and don't let him veer to one side or the other. Inasmuch as backing is a horse's least natural action, accomplishing this well speaks highly of the horse's training and of your own talents as a horseman.

If the horse has been trained properly, the best method for this long back is a gentle pull and release, repeated several times during the backing. This causes the horse to drop his head into the bridle and look good in performing the movement.

The finale for the stock horse routine comes after backing. The judge will instruct you either to ride forward for the offset or to carry it out immediately after you have stopped backing.

The offset is nothing more than a ninety-degree turn in each direction. A bit of speed in this maneuver helps to impress the judge and a touch of the spur can help, but simply use it to signal the horse, not jabbing him to the point that he becomes unruly. Through this, the rider should again attempt to appear to be a part of the horse, using as little movement as possible in execution. Keep your head up with eyes looking straight ahead.

ENDURANCE RIDING

As an outgrowth of trail riding has come the endurance contest, which becomes a test of man and animal. Probably the most grueling of these is the one-day, hundred-mile Tevis Cup ride, which more properly is called the Western States Hundred-Mile One-Day Trail Ride. It extends from Lake Tahoe to Auburn, California, and covers some of the ruggedest country to be challenged by the pioneers of a century ago. The Western States Trail originally extended from the gold fields of California to the silver mines of Nevada.

Purpose of this ride, the sponsors contend, is educational as well as sporting in that the studies and records of a committee of examining veterinarians are made available to all other veterinary surgeons as well as doctors of medicine. They say it also is adding information to the best breeding of the utility horse.

Every rider who completes the ride is awarded a belt buckle or plaque, but the top prizes are the Lloyd Tevis

Endurance rides draw all manner of competitors, even show business personalities like Clint Ritchie (above).

Memorial Cup, awarded for the best performance in time and display of horsemanship, and the James B. Haggin Cup, which goes to the equine entry among the first ten finishers that's in the best physical condition at the end. Tevis was a pioneer president of Wells Fargo & Co., while Haggin was president of the Anaconda Copper Company during its formative years.

This is a killer ride with vet checks along the way. If either horse or rider is in bad shape, they are disqualified. Incidentally, over the long haul, Arabian horses have made the best showings.

While there are any number of these endurance rides, the rules varying, it was Massachusetts' Bay State Trail Riders Association that came up with a concept that features standardization for trails competition.

According to Ed Whalley, one of the founders of the competition, "Some of us had been reading quite a lot about how ridiculous trail classes can get and the thought struck us: 'Why not get the horses out of the show ring and into the field?' So we came up with the idea of field trials for trail horses. Ring classes just don't bring out the best in either horse or rider; often they are just another chance to repeat the same performance for another crack at an award and many horses pinned by judges in the ring are the worst laggards out on the trail.

"What we wanted was an event that would demand a reasonable degree of conditioning in the horse, boldness and judgment on the part of the rider to be able to demonstrate his fitness, and a method of evaluating the performance that would be completely objective.

"We also wanted an event that would be less time-consuming than endurance rides and, if possible, one that would have enough fast-paced action to attract public attention and justify coverage on the sports page. We also wanted it to prove something about a horse in a way that would have an impact on his value. We feel that the Bay State Field Trials concept meets all of these requirements."

As for the standards, Whalley explains that "we think a good trail horse should meet old cavalry standards of four miles per hour at the walk, eight at the trot and twelve miles per hour at the maneuvering gallop. The horse ought to be able to demonstrate this over a measured course, regardless of the style of tack his rider prefers."

Under these standards, the horse should be able to jump at least two feet — preferably three; take a sand slide; jump a ditch; and wade as far as necessary, or swim if necessary. The horse should be able to walk across a plank bridge; be trained for his rider to open and close gates; and be able to take care of himself on rough ground at gaits faster than a walk.

"He ought to be able to do all this with loaded saddlebags, slicker and a full canteen," Whalley explains, "and his rider should have the horse sense to get the best out of him on a given course without killing him."

Each rider is given a record card and he is timed from start to finish, each minute serving as a point, with fractions included. For example, a horse that finishes the course in fifty-eight minutes and forty-five seconds has a score of 58.45, unless penalty points have been added.

Each horse is given three attempts to take each obstacle under the eyes of a judge, who adds penalty points for each refusal. Points also are added for not meeting the minimum speed standards on the measured course. There is an optional way around each obstacle if the horse refuses, but the clock is running all the time.

"The horse that gets added points on the measured speed course has the chance to make them up on the trail between obstacles," Whalley explains. "The name of the game is to keep the total score as low as possible. In walk zones, a good, fast horse is an asset. In free speed zones, the agility and condition of the horse, and the skill and judgment of the rider will tell. And best of all, no single judge is called upon to make a subjective evaluation of the performance."

As for the course, insofar as possible, all of the obstacles are of natural construction, while the trails offer a variety of footing and openness. They are genuine trails, incidentally, rather than maintained bridle paths.

"The length of the course should be no longer than necessary to bring in the required variety of obstacles, but it should be of sufficient length to insure that riders starting at brief intervals will not be subject to bunching up at the obstacles or interference on the trails between them," Whalley advises.

Under the plan laid out by the Massachusetts group, the maximum recommended distance is five miles. The course should include a measured distance on a linear or circular track for the speed checks. It should have free speed zones between obstacles and a mandatory walk zone through barnyards, on macadam roads or wherever the trails committee wishes to impose the walk.

The course, incidentally, consists of a quarter-mile at the walk, which should be accomplished in 3.45 minutes; a quarter-mile trot, which should take no more than 1.52; and an equal distance at the gallop or lope, which should be done within 0:56.

Obstacles, as set up by the Bay State group, include a natural log or stone jump — or jumps — about eighteen inches high; one or more sand slides ten to twelve feet in length, at an inclination of about forty-five degrees; and a ditch or ditches approximately four feet wide and deep enough that a jump is required.

"The sides of the ditch should present no hazard to the horse and permit the rider the option of walking through," Whalley explains.

Also included in the trails course would be a water obstacle such as a creek or pool through which the horse must wade to continue on course; a plank bridge suitable for ordinary traffic, but no teeter-board; and a gate, which the horse must negotiate with the rider opening and closing it, as he passes through. Another must obstacle is a pile of junk such as one might encounter in a wooded area today; a wrecked car will do for this. Included is the mandatory walk zone on paved roads or in a populated area and, at the end of the course, there should be a jog zone so that the horse is exercised prior to his soundness check.

Stewards in the walk zone will disqualify any horse whose rider violates the walk rule. The course includes all of the obstacles of the required degree of difficulty laid down in the specifications for the trial being offered, but safety must be considered. There will be no free-roaming tigers along the trail, for example.

In regard to actual judging, Whalley's group recommends keeping things simple.

"Stewards in the speed-trial areas add the required points to the tally of the horse not meeting the minimum standards. The recommended penalty is one point — equal to one minute — added for each of the gait standards not met. Stewards at the obstacles add one point for each balk committed at their obstacles, while those in the mandatory walk zone — as mentioned earlier — disqualify any horse not kept at a walk."

Under the concept created by the Bay State riders, any steward is empowered to halt the progress of any animal in obvious distress or any rider engaged in unsportsmanlike conduct. And any horse whose temperature, pulse and respiration readings do not return to normal within the specified time will have his listing stricken from the official order of finish.

Under the rules, incidentally, each horse's temperature, pulse and respiration would be taken at the start and one hour after completion of the day's trial. It is recommended that a veterinarian be on hand for the trials, too.

FUN AND GAMES

The Encyclopedia Britannica defines Gymkhana as "a display of athletics and equestrian events originated at military stations of India. The word apparently derives from the Hindustani 'Gend-Khana,' meaning 'ball house' or 'racquet court,' and the Persian 'khana,' 'house.' The first syllable of 'gymnastics' is substituted for 'gend,' implying athletic competition.

"Outside India, amusing races were added. Thus gymkhanas now include varied competitions, some serious and some funny, on foot, on horseback and on bicycles.

"Gymkhana, introduced at the University of Illinois in 1933 and continued at Florida State University about 1945, is a group-recreational activity combining gymnastics with showmanship."

So much for the encyclopedia definition.

Actually, gymkhana, as such, in equine circles boasts some events from the Indian version, more out of the Old West, where cowboys gathered to contest, and perhaps even more of recent innovation, created as a means of relieving boredom with the show ring.

Several of the events that started as gymkhana events have gained stature on their own and have been included as standard rodeo events in many instances. Among these is barrel racing, discussed at greater length in a separate section.

There isn't room to discuss all of today's gymkhana and so-called Playday events, as many horse clubs and even associations have devised their own and there are literally hundreds of events and variations. Thus, we will concentrate on two of the more universally popular events.

POLE BENDING

This event appears to be second only to barrel racing in popularity in Western riding competition. As in barrel racing, a horse with a good rein is a requisite.

Ideally, one needs six poles, which have been set in broad concrete bases. This makes them stable, but still movable. Rules vary, of course, regarding the number, length

Pole bending, next to barrel racing, probably has the most competitors of all gymkhana events. Size of either horse or horseman doesn't matter, only their time!

and diameter of the poles as well as the size of the concrete base. Most associations, though, require poles that are six to seven feet in length, measuring no less than one and one-half inches in diameter. These are set in one-gallon cans of concrete. Some organizations, however, require a base with a maximum diameter of fourteen inches and require that the poles be painted white. As suggested, ground rules change from locality to locality, club to club.

Again, rules vary widely in laying out the course. However, for the sake of standardization, we suggest six poles at intervals of twenty feet, although some organizations specify twenty-one feet, others thirty feet for no particular reason that we can determine.

In the twenty-foot configuration, the six poles can be set over a distance of 120 feet, which fits nicely into the average show ring. The first pole, incidentally should be twenty feet from the start/finish line.

The event is run in two manners. The first is to start as the horse crosses the starting marker. The horse gallops to the nearest pole, rounds it, then passes between the rest of the poles, alternating sides. The horse makes a full circle of the last pole, then begins to alternate passing sides again, weaving between the poles. The rider makes a full circle around the last pole, then races back across the start/finish line. Stopwatches in the hands of the judges have been used to determine the elapsed time. Most contests utilize three timekeepers. If there is any discrepancy between their times, they are averaged.

The other method is for the horse to start, being galloped or run to the most distant pole, turning, then beginning to weave his way along the course. When he reaches the pole nearest the finish line, he makes a complete circle of the pole as in barrel racing, then threads the poles back to the opposite end. This sequence also would have the horse passing the poles on the opposite side from his first run. When the rider hits the last pole, he reins to the opposite side from his initial run to the end and races his horse the length of the course, back to the finish line.

Depending upon ground rules, if the rider touches a pole with his hand or horse — or knocks it over — the penalty can be either disqualification or a loss of time. In most clubs, the rider is allowed to brush the pole so long as it is not knocked over. Deviation from the prescribed course also can result in disqualification.

Most organizations allow the rider to start the course from either side and either Western or English tack are allowed, including hackamores.

A good pole-bending horse must display quick rollback capabilities at both ends of the course, meaning he must react from both sides. This means a good deal of patience and training on the part of the rider, although there are horses that never are able to accomplish this specific maneuver with any degree of speed and efficiency.

No matter what the distance between the poles, the horseman should learn to set a rhythm for himself and the horse, as he reins his way through the series of obstacles. One should determine the number of strides it takes the horse between poles before leads are changed. Handling the reins too roughly can cut down speed and disturb the horse. One should learn to run the race with smoothness, depending upon the horse's training, signalling him with leg cues and by leaning in the saddle to indicate direction to be taken.

The best results in this type of race will be a combination of training and timing, with a well-practiced rollback at the end of the course.

RING SPEARING

Perhaps requiring a better eye than better horsemanship, this event is a standard at most action-oriented horse events. The event originated during the days of the Round Table — about 1100 A.D. — when the knights of yore illustrated their prowess before their leaders and their ladies.

The use of the lance in combat dropped after the introduction of firearms, although jousting with blunted lances continued well into the Fifteenth Century. Even as late as the middle of the last century, lances were issued as part of the equipment of cavalry units in the armies of Britain, Poland, Mexico and a host of other countries.

In today's horsemanship events, rules for ring spearing again tend to lack standardization and there appears to be no national standard for this type of competition, with no standardization as to the length of the spear, diameter of the target rings, length of the course, et al. However, the basic concept hardly can be changed: that of a galloping rider using a lance to spear a suspended ring.

The California State Horseman's Association has developed a set of rules that might well serve as a starting point for those interested in pursuing this activity. These basics say that:

"Three standards are placed one hundred feet apart. The starting line is one hundred feet from the first standard, making a straight course of three hundred feet. There shall be a minimum of two hundred feet after the third standard to allow sufficient distance to stop the horse safely.

"The bottom of the ring shall be seven feet from the ground, on a four-foot arm extending out from the standard far enough to give clearance to the horse and rider. A number eight or number ten wire should hold the ring clip to give minimum wind interference. Rings should be two inches in inside diameter. Spears shall be a minimum of six feet long, the handle and guard a minimum of three feet from the tip.

"Time is taken at the starting line and as the horse's nose passes the third standard. Rings must be on the spear after the course is completed. A minimum of three scoring runs for each rider should be made. In scoring, lowest gross time for a rider determines the winner, with a five-second penalty for each ring missed or dropped."

CAUTIOUS CURES FOR PROBLEM HORSES

Chapter 8

IF YOU'VE BOUGHT AN OUTLAW, GET RID OF HIM — BUT IF HIS VICES ARE MINOR, HERE ARE SOME METHODS TO USE!

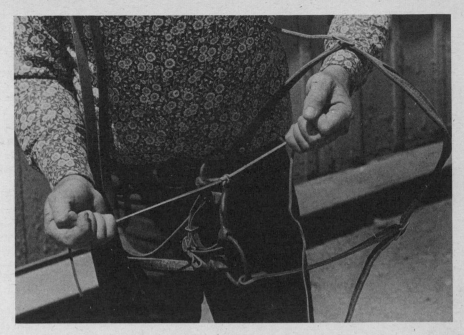

Young horses that put their tongues over the bit can be cured by a simple leather thong arrangement. It's tied to the snaffle (right), then runs over the nose and connects to headstall. This lifts the bit high enough that the colt can't possibly get his tongue over it. This is shown on the following page.

IF YOU HAVE a horse with a likable personality, one that does most of the things you ask him well, you are a lucky person indeed.

In opening the subject of problem horses and discussing some of the retraining techniques, it is important to mention that horses are individuals. They vary in their personalities and in their physical abilities just as people do. In the same way that some people are versatile and can do many different things quite well, some horses have this same gift.

There was one horse named Famed Cake Mount that left the track to become a great reining horse. Another horse, the Arabian stallion, Karrouf, won the dressage and hackamore classes in the same show, attesting to his versatility.

Twenty years ago, trainer Rusty Richards bought a weanling colt from Jackson's Arabian Horse Nursery. "His name was Baarhan and, in the 9½ years I owned him, I can honestly say that he taught me at least as much as I taught him, which was quite a lot.

"I roped on him, cut cattle on him, worked him at liberty; he was featured in an episode of the hour-long color television series, "The Tales Of Wells Fargo," as the blooded horse necessary to the improvement of a herd. Baarhan was ridden, at one time or another, by such celebrities as Burt Reynolds, Robert Fuller, John Mitchum, Jill St. John, John Huston and about six young officers from a Japanese Square Rigger, in their dress whites. He was well-mannered and had a way of trying to please."

After nearly ten years, Richards sold Baarhan to Curley Walter, who began training him as a jumper and he took to it like a duck to water. During the short time that he was shown, he never was less than fourth. His jumping came to an abrupt end when he came down wrong one morning and broke a coffin bone. After a year's layoff, he was sold to a family. They had him gelded and their teen-age daughter began showing him.

In 1968, he went to the Nationals and ended up one of the top ten in the United States. In 1969, he won the Legion of Merit and was reserve champion of the United States. He was a versatile horse, but it would be a pipe dream to expect him to race with Secretariat or to perform like the great bucking horse, Descent.

On the other hand, not all horses are capable of this kind of versatility.

"One of the first things I do, when someone sends me a new horse for training, is to try to figure him out," Richards says. "I take notice of such things as the look in his eye when I walk up to him. I watch to determine whether his attitude is one of distrust, fear, aggressiveness, friendliness or even indifference.

"Usually, I catch a new horse, lead him over to my tack room, offer him a little grain, then brush him with a soft brush.

"In fly season, I cover him well with repellent. During his first couple of days with me, I will forgive him for quite a few things that he may do wrong, such as looking around and not standing still. I wouldn't allow the horse to make a serious mistake like attacking me — biting, kicking or striking — but I will tolerate things he might do as a result of nervousness due to his new surroundings and lack of confidence in me and in himself."

Since we are talking about problem horses, let's take a new horse that introduces himself by trying to bite.

Richards says, "I may or may not be able to break him of this, depending upon what caused him to do it in the first place. If he is a young stud colt, used to rough and tumble games with other stud colts, all I have to do is to get the idea through to him that I am not another colt and that he must have respect for me or he will lose."

One gimmick Richards uses to break a colt of biting utilizes a cork with a needle run up through it, the needle point protruding through the cork about one-quarter inch. The trick is to place the cork in a strategic position so that the colt will run into it when he tries to bite you. Do not stab him with it. Stand at his shoulder where you are an easy target. Fold your arms, holding the cork, virtually inviting him to let himself have it.

This method requires a lot of patience and probably won't work in every case, but it has been used with a good deal of success. In the meantime, use any other opportunity the colt may give you to let him know that you disapprove of his biting, such as a good sharp jerk on his lead shank.

If you ever happen to be standing with a whip in your hand when the colt tries to bite you and you decide to hit him with it, it is better to let him have a good one then let him alone, than it is to pick at him.

Another kind of horse where this method might work is

the crank. A crank is a horse that has either inherited a nasty disposition or has learned to bluff his handler by backing his ears, nipping or kicking.

But a word of caution: If you have come upon a genuine outlaw, you'd be better off looking for another horse. However, few people ever see a real outlaw. Most of the horses we think of as bad are those that have learned an assortment of bad habits through inadequate training procedures or naturally poor dispositions, yet are not vicious enough to be called outlaws.

Take the horse who gets his tongue over the bit. This occurs occasionally, when introducing a young horse to the bit. As soon as you see a horse start this, it is best to take steps to prevent him from getting his tongue over the bit at all. The method Richards uses is simple and has worked well.

Take a piece of leather boot lace or a soft-lay nylon cord and tie it to the center or link of the snaffle bit. Bridle the horse and bring the leather string or piece of cord up over the horse's nose. Tie a knot, then run the rest of the line up and tie it to the forelock. If your horse doesn't have a forelock, you can tie into the headstall up between the ears. This makes it difficult for him to get his tongue over the bit and will discourage him from trying in a short time.

After a week or so, try him without the string. Watch to see if he carries the bit properly. If he starts to put his tongue over the bit again, put the string back on him for a while longer.

For horse prone to nibble on trainer out of boredom or bite out of habit, the pin-in-the-cork trick is used. The pin's point extends past the cork and it's held near the spot a horse frequently bites (below). This cures condition quickly!

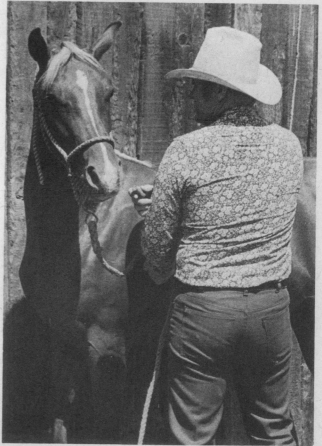

130

The needle and cork arrangement mentioned on opposite page is shown (far left) with another useful tool: a 2-1/2-inch ring. The lattter is used for heading and tailing problem horse.

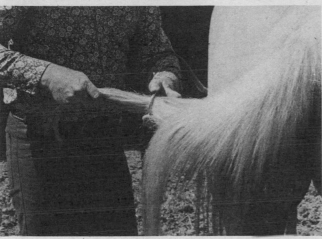

The first step in the heading and tailing routine is to put the ring into the horse's tail. Use enough hair so the ring won't pull out a hunk, making horse more than unhappy!

Follow the instructions for knotting the ring in the tail, which should resemble knot (below) if tied properly. If the horse truly is a bad actor, don't stand behind him!

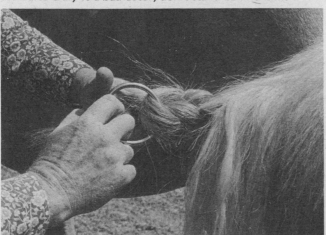

"Now and then, a horse will be brought to me that has a bad attitude and is liable to do almost anything, in the way of a vice. My approach to this type of horse is to try to change his attitude to one of cooperation," says Richards.

This can take considerable doing, but there is no other way but to put pressure on him. There are several ways to take control of a horse like this: a casting harness, a running W or hobble breaking. These three devices do require experience to apply them, as they deal with total immobilization of the horse and can be dangerous to both horse and handler.

Richards uses these methods and feels that they are musts with certain horses but, in the interest of minimizing the possibility of injury, he starts with partial immobilization. In many of the less severe cases, this is all that is needed to start a new and favorable attitude; in every case, it is valuable.

"To accomplish this partial immobilization, I lead the horse to the breaking pen, then tie a 2½-inch ring into his tail. Be sure, when you tie the ring into the tail, that you use a big enough hank of hair so that he won't rip it out of his hair. I then run the lead rope back through the ring and pull his head around to the side just far enough that he can't get it straight. Then I secure the lead rope to the ring and release the horse.

"Many times, as you try to tie the head back to the tail, the horse will spin away from you. I simply stay with him, until he stalls long enough for me to get the rope tied. It is not necessary — or even desirable — to tie his head back to his tail. Just tie his head far enough back that he can't get it straight. In this position, he is free to chase his tail and that's about all. If he is really spooky, he may go at it for awhile, but you'll find he will not go far."

Be sure you have the horse in a good, safe enclosure, as there is a possibility he may become dizzy, lose his balance and fall. Avoid barbed wire altogether! Make certain that you have safe ground in your breaking pen. Most horses will stay on their feet with no trouble. But about the time you start to count on it, one will go down and you'll be glad you've taken precautions.

Now that you have him head-and-tailed, take a big burlap sack and rub him with it. If he is real spooky, take hold of only one end of the sack and bring it up in a sweeping motion, letting it brush him softly.

When sacking out a horse, the object is not just to

immobilize him then scare him as much as you can, when he can't move. The purpose is to acquaint him with some spooky things, while reassuring him as much as you can.

At first, the horse may not give you a chance to reassure him. When this happens let him chase his tail and, at the same time, look for every opportunity to brush him with the sack.

Eventually, the horse will slow down and allow himself to be rubbed with the sack. As he is beginning to settle, continue to gentle and soothe him by rubbing and talking to him.

Another good tool to have on hand is the rub-rag. This is a soft towel used for rubbing down horses. Rub it all over the horse's neck and head. Be gentle with him, but continue to rub.

Sacking out is one phase of a horse's training to which one should give quite a lot of time per session. Stay with him till you can see some progress, then cool him out and put him away. Repeat the whole process for several days.

If your horse should stick on you and not want to move out of his tracks, take the sack and move to his blind spot. This is around behind him and somewhat to the opposite side to which his head is tied. Stepping into the blind spot and moving the sack will make him want to see you and, as a result, he will chase his tail some more.

Watch your horse's eye. What is going on in a horse's mind can be seen through this little window. If you have not yet developed the technique of reading horses through the expression in the eye, you've been missing a valuable tool.

To learn to read the expression in a horse's eye and interpret what is on his mind, simply observe as many horses in as many different situations as you can. Before long, you will discover how expressive horses really are.

At any rate, the horse will wind down and become less and less sensitive to your movements and sounds. He will become more willing to stand his ground and allow you to rub him all over with the sack.

What is happening is something more than just getting a horse to stand still, while you touch him with a burlap sack. In fact, it is a start in the development of a whole new attitude in the horse.

Some examples of this would be changing fear to confidence, unwillingness to willingness, unruliness to calm obedience, sourness into sweetness and sometimes even hate to love.

Not every trainer uses the exact same methods to train horses. Although the methods do vary, the principles do not. If you go about treating vices without discovering their causes, you are treating a symptom, but ignoring the disease.

Richards recalls walking into a stall with a young stallion he was breaking. "He had seen me coming, yet shied away. He then ran out of the stall and into an adjoining paddock. My first inclination was to work him a little extra that day and get some of the silliness out of him. Yet, as I caught him up, the thought crossed my mind that this was not normal behavior for this colt.

"I decided to pass for the day and try again the next. When I went to get him the next day, I discovered a large swelling in his chest: a dry land abscess. It is easy to imagine what might have happened had I decided to go ahead and work him the previous day. I would only have been abusing a pretty sick horse.

"A young mare was brought to me that was so loaded with vices she looked almost hopeless. Several attempts had been made to break her and all of them had ended in failure. She was a pretty mare and quite well-bred.

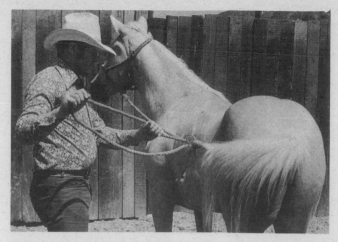
With the ring tied into the tail the lead rope then is threaded through the ring. Remember to tie up excess rope, to avoid having the problem horse tangle himself.

If the horse starts to spin when tying his head back, stay with him until his head has been tied back only far enough that he cannot get it fully straightened. Take your time.

Although partially immobilized, the horse still can move around in front of the trainer, as illustrated below. Now shake the sack at him to get him moving. He'll catch on.

Move around the horse while waving the sack at him, brushing him with it all over. He'll try to move so you must stay with him. Don't stay in one spot too long.

If the horse should stick and not move when sacking him, move to his blind spot and continue brushing him with it. He'll want to see what's happening and begin to move.

"After working with her for a while, I discovered that she had what amounted to a split personality. When I went into her corral to catch her, she seemed a sweet young filly. But as soon as there was any pressure whatsoever, she became an explosive, dangerous animal.

"I completely immobilized her with hobbles and sacked her out. She held her ground yet never appeared to let down and relax. My brother-in-law, Frank Fitzpatrick, has a big, stout roping horse and it occurred to me that it might be a good idea to have him pony her for a while. I saddled the mare and handed the lead rope to Fitzpatrick, who made a couple of laps around my arena fairly smoothly. I decided to get on her and ride her while he ponied her.

"She went along pretty good for a couple more laps, then came apart. She bucked so hard that it took all I had — and a lot of luck to boot — to stay on. She finally stopped, made a couple more smooth laps, then tried more bucking.

"The next day, Frank took her around without the saddle for a few laps with the pony horse. I stood at the rail and watched, wondering what it would be like to not feel sore again. As she jogged along beside the pony horse, she seemed real antsy and upset. She sort of danced along, now and then switching her tail, occasionally casting off urine."

Richards kept remembering how sweet she seemed when he walked up to her in the corral. Finally, the right question came to mind: Could there be a physiological disorder underlying her psychological problems? He called a veterinarian, who gave her a thorough examination and sent a urine sample to the lab. The result showed she had a urinary infection. After treatment, the vet re-examined her and found her to be clean.

Richards regressed the mare almost to the point of starting all over again. Although this mare had been sick, she also had tasted success in bucking people off. Surely she associated these battles with pain and discomfort that she didn't understand.

The trainer put her on a longe line and worked her until she would walk, trot and stop on verbal command only. When he started to ride her, he gave her only short workouts and was able to successfully saddle and ride her every day for a couple of weeks without a lot of excitement. She finally began to let down and her confidence began to grow.

Fortunately, the cause of every vice will not run as deep as was the case with this mare. Take, for instance, a horse that switches his tail. Most people know that excessive use

While brushing him with the sack, use a soft voice to let him know he's not going to be hurt. This soft voice will tend to calm his fears and will increase effectiveness.

Once the horse appears somewhat calmer, gently brush his head with the sack, then rub it all over him while talking softly. He soon will realize the sack's no danger.

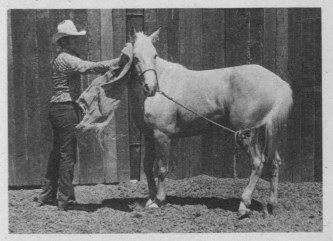

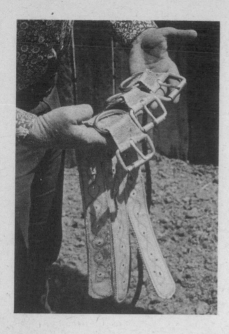

Hobble breaking is not a task for the amateur. A professional will select the proper hobble for the job (far left), then put it on at about hock level, slipping it down to the hoof. This is done to minimize chance of receiving a nasty kick in the head (right)!

of spurs and whip can make a horse switch. It doesn't necessarily follow, however, when you run into a switch-tailed horse that you have come onto a horse that has been pushed too fast and has become a chronic switcher. It may be that some part of the equipment is the culprit.

Some horses will switch, for instance, if the bit doesn't fit right. A loose-jowled bit can pinch a horse's lip and cause head tossing, shaking of the head or switching. A chin strap that is too loose and has become dry and hard also can pinch a horse's lip and cause him enough discomfort that he may tell you about it by switching and head tossing.

Keeping your cinches clean is important. Sometimes, even though you have been careful, a horse will develop a rash from the cinch. There can be many kinds of skin disorders, so either leave treatment to a veterinarian or check Chapter 10 for cause/cure. Some trainers have good luck at keeping horses that have developed a cinch rash in training, without getting them switchy, by covering the rash with Vaseline and using a woolskin-covered cinch.

Head-tossing has many different causes. It can be caused by equipment. It also can be caused by improper handling of the reins or it may be extreme nervousness. In any case, there are several choices as to what can be done.

Richards is not totally against the idea of using a tie-down on certain horses. If, for instance, it is a horse that is quite set in his ways and is just being used as a saddle horse, it probably would be better to find him a bridle in which he is comfortable and fit him with a tie-down in such a way that he can be useful. As a trainer, however, he doesn't see a tie-down as a cure. In fact, many horses that have been tied down get worse when the tie-down is taken off.

Varying degrees of success can be expected in effecting a cure of the head-tosser, depending upon how deep the cause.

Let's take the other extreme and talk about the young horse you want to put into the bridle. All too often this is a horse that someone else has broken. He doesn't handle himself too well and his head position is bad. On this horse, Richards probably would reach for a running martingale.

Although a running martingale does tend to make a

The hobbles then are attached to the front legs in position shown (left). A sturdy rope is run through the back ring and leg pulled forward before rope is attached to front.

When he realizes that his mobility has been impaired, most horses will lunge forward in an attempt to break the bonds, some even learning to run in hobbles (below).

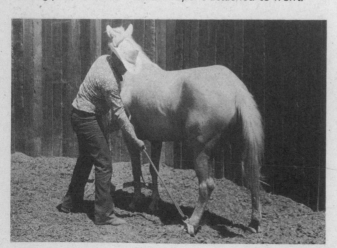

A roomy area with plenty of soft dirt
is required during hobble breaking,
as the horse could fall and be injured.

A switchy horse is seldom cured of the condition, although
some trainers report decent results by tying the tail to the
saddle during workouts. More detail is to be found in text.

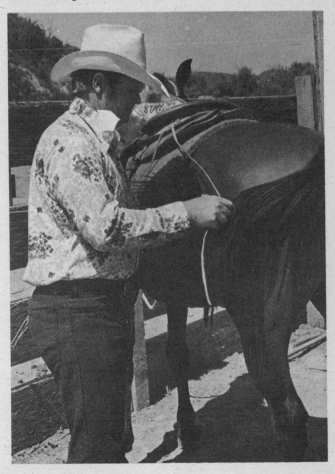

horse a little heavier on the bit, you still can keep him fairly light while using it, if you use a good technique in handling the reins.

Sometimes horses will sour if drilled too much in an arena. It is a good idea to take almost any horse out and ride him in different surroundings.

For instance, if your horse has just begun to switch, after you have checked to be sure that nothing about your equipment is bothering him and if you have used a good fly repellent on him, take him out into some new country. A change of scenery quite often does wonders for a horse in training.

If you have a young horse in the snaffle and running martingale when you take him out on the trail, you will find it fairly easy to steady him and guide him around spooky obstacles.

In regard to rein handling and teaching a horse to position himself, put the horse in a position where he just about has to turn to move properly. A wall of a breaking pen is ideal, but just about any wall or high fence will work.

One big advantage of a breaking pen or round corral is that you have the horse's complete attention. If you should ever decide to build one, make it so that a horse cannot see out of it.

Another vice found in some horses is cinchiness. It is usually the result of a young horse being put under saddle too fast and with a poor technique. It is possible for a horse to be cinchy even though he has been handled properly, but in a majority of cases they are just horses that were rushed into the saddle and cinched too tight.

"I don't know any cure, but I do know cinchy horses that still are useful horses. This is because their owners understand the problem and take precautions to minimize the danger," Richards says.

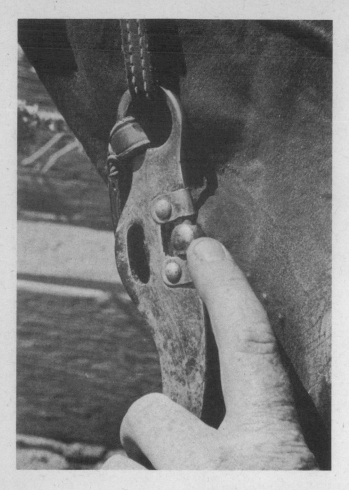

A cinchy horse will usually either run backwards and fall, or rear and throw himself over on his back after being cinched up. Sometimes he will lock-up and not want to untrack (take a step). When one does this, he usually is about to turn over.

The biggest tool in minimizing the dangers with a cinchy horse is knowledge. It does make a difference to the horse-owner, for instance, to know that his horse is just responding to a pressure that frightens him and sends him out of control, rather than to think that his horse is wanting to turn over, in order to drive his rider's head into the ground.

A cinchy horse should be taught to longe; he should be

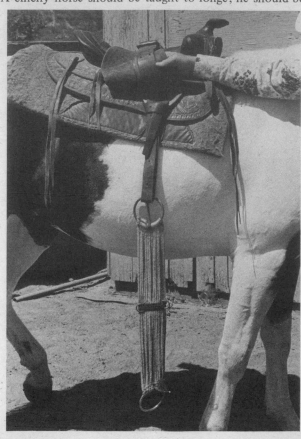

Many times tack is to blame for erratic behavior on the horse's part, like a badly worn, loose jowled bit (above). This can pinch the horse's mouth. The saddle (right) has almost centerfire rigging, determined by position of D ring in relation to saddle fork. No matter the rigging, a good cinch is a requisite for good equine performance.

Watch for a dried-out chin strap, since this can irritate the sensitive tissues beneath the chin. Before corrective work is done to horse, check his tack!

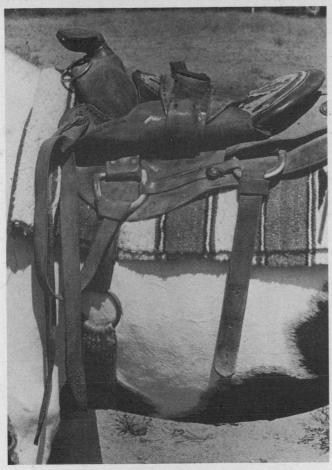

This saddle has seven-eighths rigging, as determined by D ring position. Have the right rigging for each horse!

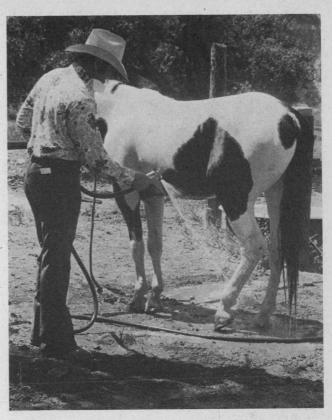

A kicking horse can cause injury at any time so it's wise to "kick" the habit. Spraying the hooves with water will sometimes cause a kick, whereupon water is shifted to other hoof. This gets the horse to know futility of kick.

cinched loosely at first, then he should be asked to move out on the longe line. The cinch should be tightened a little at a time and, after each tightening, the horse should be moved out on the line. Be sure he is moving out freely after the final tightening and before you get on him!

An important thing to remember with any horse, but especially with that cinchy one, is to have a saddle that fits him comfortably.

Kicks like this look spectacular in the rodeo arena, but not in the backyard. Follow text instructions to cure a kicker. It's dangerous and time-consuming always.

One of the more common problems experienced by some new horseowners is kicking. All too often a buyer will come home with his new mount only to find that he either kicks the side out of the stall or does his best to remove the owner's head.

We have suggested earlier that one's first horse, at least, should be gentle and well-mannered before you graduate to something more lively.

How does this apply to the question, "How do you know that a horse won't kick you?"

The only way that a novice can learn to understand the moods and attitudes of horses and hence be able to predict their actions is from horses, themselves.

Once one gets to know a good, gentle horse, he can generalize to a degree, applying what has been learned to other horses.

The knowledge required to interpret an animal's attitudes and thereby be able to predict his actions cannot be gained merely through reading or through explanation. You have to observe the animal firsthand.

We could tell you, for instance, to watch a horse's ears, for when they are back, he may be apt to kick. To say this, however, could be misleading. Although it is true that a horse usually lays his ears back when he is about to kick, he also turns them back to keep the wind from bothering them; to listen to some sound behind himself; because of an annoying fly — or just because he feels like it.

As with any vice a horse may develop, before you can effect a cure, one first must learn the cause.

The proper method of approaching a kicker to handle his feet is shown (right). Both hands glide over the animal's back, working to the rear.

There are many reasons why horses become kickers. Some can be broken of kicking with little effort, while others may be chronic kickers that will take watching all their lives. We have seen horses, for instance, that were so bad about kicking that they could not be shod without a side line or tied down completely.

We suspect that most of these horses were not handled as foals until their feet needed trimming badly and, perhaps, not until they had grown quite large. Then, either their owner tried to trim them or they called a farrier and had them trimmed...but with difficulty!

You are not hiring the shoer to train your horse; only to trim him. If you have not handled your foal's feet at all and call the shoer when he needs trimming, don't be surprised if the foal does not stand well when the shoer goes to work. Most farriers will take time with the foal to get him started right, but it really is unfair to ask your shoer to do this without some compensation and he should be told beforehand that a foal has not been handled.

Too often, people breed a mare and spend nearly a year in happy anticipation, until the foal finally arrives. Then, as soon as the newness wears off, the foal is turned out to spend a couple of boring years becoming large enough to be useful. If you live in an area where a lot of people keep horses for riding, you have probably seen this happen.

If you breed your mare, keep in mind that you are assuming responsibility for this new foal for several years and, when that foal cuteness wears off, he still will need your care and attention.

Horses sometimes are prone to kick because they are cranks and never have been taught to respect people. One likes a horse to think of him as someone upon whom he can count and have confidence. At the same time, the horse must remember that to bump into or step on you is a definite social error.

Sometimes, however, a young horse will lack confidence in himself and, as a result, when someone or thing frightens him, he will try to climb into your pockets. Horses that have been taught good manners while on the lead shank or any time they are being handled are happier horses because of it!

If, for instance, you should see someone with a horse

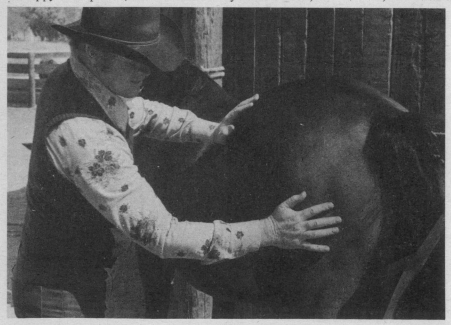

Hands maintain a firm contact on his body as they slide over the rump and begin down the leg. The left hand is kept on the horse's hip here, to aid in forcing weight off the left hind leg.

that has not been taught good manners, you will notice that this individual seems to be picking on the horse constantly in an effort to defend against this mount's unruliness.

It is much better to let a horse know that you represent something like a brick wall — you will do him no harm if he doesn't run into you! Get the idea across to him that, if he does run into you, he will lose by getting a good crack across the chest with a whip or training bat. With such firmness, he will come to respect your presence more and more in his own pursuit of happiness.

Usually, after a horse has been busted good once or twice, he will get the idea. Then you can spend all your time being good to him and he will stand with a slack lead rope. This has to be a happier situation — for both you and your horse — than a lot of wiggling around and continuous picking at him that only seems to make him worse.

"One of the best tools in my bag of tricks for the kicking horse is a regular garden hose," Rusty Richards has found. "Many times, when a horse comes to me with a kicking problem, I find he has not had his feet handled much and is jumpy about being touched below the knees."

This kind of horse often will get into all kinds of trouble when someone suddenly wants to clean out his feet. It is in such a situation that these horses learn the bad habit of kicking. If they are not straightened out carefully, the habit can be run deeper and deeper.

"I take the horse to a good spot near a faucet and turn the water on with pretty good force through a hose. Adjust the stream with a nozzle so it will not hurt him, but still be felt readily. I then run the water on his legs.

"When he kicks with one foot, I just switch the stream of water over to the other leg. Usually the horse will kick with the foot that the water is touching. By alternating back and forth between one leg and the other, he eventually will learn the futility of kicking and begin to stand his ground. I repeat this process on the front legs and, if the weather is warm enough, then spend time washing down the whole horse."

There are several advantages to this procedure. For one, there is not much danger of being kicked and, at the same

The right hand then continues down the leg to the fetlock. A horse generally will shift the weight off this leg right away but if not, left hand pushes, forcing the shift. The leg is then pulled straight upwards without incident.

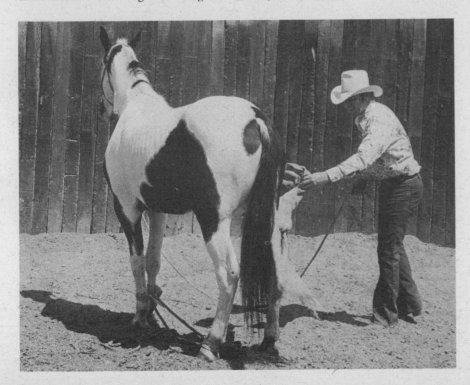

When using hobbles to discourage a kicker, the back foot is tied longer than for regular hobbling. Should he kick when sack is waved, he can pull front feet out from under himself. As horses can land on a trainer, this should be done by a horseman schooled in the usage of hobbles.

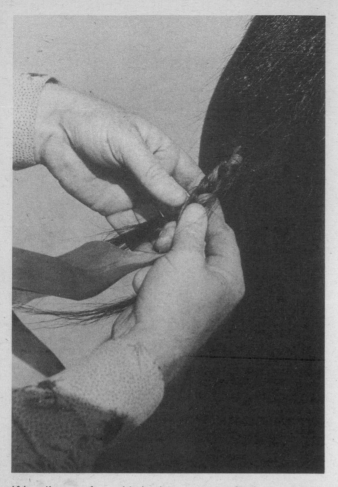

If heading out for a ride in the company of other mounted riders, the rider of the kicker always should braid a red ribbon into the horse's tail This alerts other horsemen.

time, the horse is being touched on the legs, whether he likes it or not.

"The idea that I'm trying to get through to the horse eventually is that it is not so bad to have his legs touched and handled. This acceptance is not something that you should expect to get across to him in a hurry, but I find this an excellent way to begin."

Keep in mind that the force of the water should be just strong enough to let him know he is being touched, yet not so strong as to cause the horse any discomfort. When running water over the rest of his body, reduce the pressure in order to achieve a calming effect on him. This can offer another advantage in gentling horses, as the feel and sound of running water does have a soothing effect on them.

Work a little each day at picking up the feet of this type of horse, but the proper approach, both for safety and for making progress, is of prime importance.

If you have a chronic, old dangerous kicker, you had best leave him to the experts. However, if you have a fairly young horse that is picking up this habit, perhaps he can be helped.

At this point, the method is quite the same as for a young foal. Always start by rubbing the horse down with the hands, along his neck and about the withers and shoulders, then working down the front leg. Here is a chance to give him back his leg before he tries to take it away. If he does take it away, persist until you can keep it a second or two, then let him have it back.

When moving for a back leg, rub your hands along the body, grooming toward the back of the horse. Standing by his left hip, facing rearward, rest the left hand on the hip bone. With your right hand, groom down the haunch, along the side and rear of the gaskins and finally over the hock, then down the cannon bone. With the right hand on the cannon just above the pastern, pull the leg forward, while pushing the horse slightly off-balance with the left hand. Again, all you want is his leg for a second or two and the chance to give it back, before he tries to take it away.

By having your left hand on his hip, you are in good

If riding a kicker among other horses, take measures to keep from getting in range. Sometimes others fail to see the red ribbon, leading to pure havoc!

balance so that, should he kick or take his foot away, you can support yourself against him.

With many horses, this giving-back technique will get across the idea that nothing fearful is going to happen and eventually they will allow you to handle their feet.

In the case of a horse that kicks at his tail or is prone to kick at anything that touches his back legs, put him into the hobbles, then hobble one back foot to the front two. This must be done in a safe place with deep, soft ground. Leave the rope that connects the back foot to the front hobbles longer than if hobble breaking, then brush his back legs with a burlap sack.

If the horse kicks, he has a good chance of jerking his front feet out from under himself. He will not do this too many times before he stops to think about it. Once he has had this lesson, the same gentling techniques are used until, hopefully, he lets down.

Some horses that never would kick a human are bad about other horses. These horses, however, can be dangerous to other people with whom one might ride, not to mention their mounts.

One fairly standard practice with this kind of horse is to tie or braid a red ribbon into his tail before going out to ride with other people. This is simply to remind them of the danger. If you ride a horse like this, you must realize that the responsibility for the safety of others is yours. Keep an eye out for other horses and riders, making sure you are at a safe distance. Having your horse respond well to the leg aids is helpful in positioning him, incidentally.

Above all else, remember that proper handling when the horse is young is the best way to avoid picking up bad habits or vices.

The round bullring is an ideal spot to work with a horse during correction of problems or initial schooling, since the absence of distractions forces the horse's attention solely on the rider. This attention is required for any schooling.

Chapter 9

INTERNAL & EXTERNAL CARE

A Healthy Horse Is A Happy, Useful Animal. Here's How To Keep Him That Way!

As WITH OTHER chapters of this book, it is impossible to devote space to discussing all aspects of internal and external horse care, as the list of maladies, diseases and injuries sustainable by a horse is enough to choke his owner! Therefore, the most frequently encountered problem areas will be touched upon, with the recommendation that further study on these subjects be undertaken at leisure.

As mundane as it sounds, grooming is of major importance in the horse health world. Not only does grooming improve the appearance of the animal, but also removes external parasites, aids in the control of internal parasites, removes sweat and other excretions, improves circulation, stimulates tissues and helps rid the horse of unneeded winter hair during the spring thaw. Also, frequent and proper grooming is much like regularly servicing an automobile; the owner can discover maladies early, before they do serious damage to his equine form of horsepower.

Grooming is a daily chore requiring at least a good half hour of the horseman's time and some specialized, inexpensive tools. These are a sweat scraper, a grooming or rub rag, towel, rubber comb, curry comb, body brush, dandy brush, soft-bristle brush, mane and tail comb, hoof pick and a set of electric clippers. By far the most important tool a horseman can bring to the task is old-fashioned elbow grease — plenty of it.

The type of grooming given to a horse daily will depend, to some extent, on the section of the country and time of year. Especially in cold climes, for example, a horse with heavy winter coat won't be bathed as often as during summer months, unless the horseman wants to spend extra time at his task to ensure thorough drying by hand to prevent

chilling which can lead to respiratory problems, among others.

For the most part, a horse is groomed only slightly before working. Usually this calls only for brushing before tacking up. This removes any foreign matter on the coat which could irritate the skin under the saddle or cinches and ensures the hair is lying flat in the proper direction. Start at the neck near the head on the left side of the horse and brush away all dust and foreign matter, progressing backward to the croup and hind legs before moving to the right side and repeating the procedure. Pay careful attention to the withers and back, where a burr or thistle will gouge the skin after application of the saddle and a rider's weight.

After a work, it is essential that a horse be cooled thoroughly before beginning any grooming. The easiest way to accomplish this cooling out is to walk the horse back to the barn from the exercise area and, if the horse has worked hard, a twenty to forty-minute walking stint is required. If additional walking is required, remove the tack, go over the horse with a sweat scraper to whisk away excess moisture

There are many styles of grooming implements on the market today, one of which is the shedder/scraper/trimmer shown here. Used properly, they help horses.

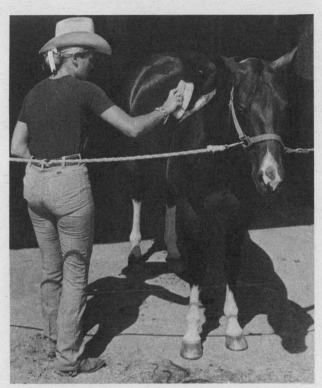

Beverly May puts elbow grease behind body brush when grooming Mighty Warrior, a Pinto champion (left). A curry comb was used previously, to loosen dirt (above).

from the coat, mop up the remaining moisture with a rub rag or grooming cloth, then blanket the animal if weather requires it and walk him until the chest is cool to the touch and his respiratory rate returns to normal. The chest is the last area to cool and, when no longer hot to the touch, the animal can be watered. If watered while hot the horse can founder, which will be explained in another chapter.

When cool, the groomer first should remove all excess dirt and mud with the rubber comb, metal curry comb or stiff dandy brush. The latter has stiff bristles some two inches long, attached to a wooden or plastic spine with some type of hollow middle for easy handling. Again starting on the left side directly behind the head, brush the hair toward the rear with firm strokes. If using a rubber comb, groom in circular fashion which will loosen deep dirt. Move from the neck down to the chest, shoulder, withers, down the foreleg to the knee, then over his back, croup, belly and hindquarter, going down to the hock. This is repeated on the right side of the horse with the same implements and, if dirt still remains on the coat, go over the horse again with the body brush, which has fairly stiff bristling with a loop of some type for solid hold.

Some horsemen feel the curry comb should be used only to clean the bristles of the body brush, which it does admirably. It shouldn't be used on the head or legs below the hocks. These areas have little fatty tissue or muscle between the skin and bone, making them extremely sensitive. Grooming these areas with the curry comb could lead to some interesting — and unwanted — rodeo-type action when the metal teeth dig in. Instead, use only a soft-bristle brush, rub rag or towel on these areas.

The mane and tail require attention next. It's hard to

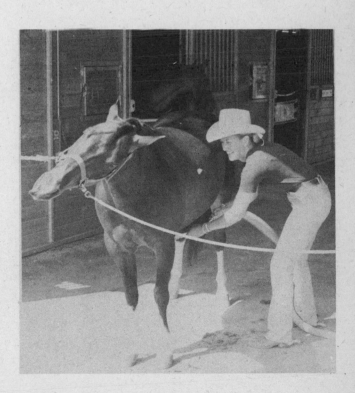

Some larger stables make good use of vacuum cleaners, with fine results. This horse enjoys the belly-rub action! Simpler implements are available to horsemen with a more limited income, though, and do the job admirably.

Once tangles have been removed with a mane and tail comb, Beverly May favors a woman's hair brush for final separation of hair. The text gives more details.

believe the incredible tangles and snarls which can develop, often with burrs or foxtails thrown in for good measure. The metal mane and tail comb has been designed specifically for this task and, with a little patience, it doesn't take long to have the individual strands separated and hanging properly.

To avoid pulling hairs from the mane and tail, begin by applying the comb at the bottom of the mane or tail and work upwards. Sometimes a squirt of tangle remover or coat conditioner will help and, when finished, brush with the body brush. Use care when attending the forelock: hold it suspended above the poll when brushing because the poll is sensitive.

Because germs can accumulate on grooming implements, it's a good idea to disinfect them at regular intervals. This is especially important if more than one horse is groomed with the same tools, as often is the case in a stable. A mild disinfectant will kill the germs on your implements. The rub rags and towels should first be soaked in a disinfectant solution then washed, which also keeps their appearance pleasing. Like any professional craftsman, it's always more of a pleasure to work with the proper tools in good condition.

There are times, like directly prior to an upcoming show, when a bath is in order. There are several schools of thought regarding proper bathing procedures, but most

The wise horseman keeps all of his grooming tools and aids in a box like that pictured below. This saves time and money, as tools don't become lost and always are at hand. Prior to heading for a horse show, other items can be added to the box.

A hoof pick is inexpensive protection against hoof disorders like thrush. Used from heel to toe, it removes dead sole and built up materials. Daily use means a healthy hoof.

trainers rely on the garden hose with a sprayer nozzle and a bucket of suds. Others use a series of buckets and a sponge. Whatever the method, remember that a horse's hair differs little from a human's. Washing removes some of the natural oils — in horses, the sebum — which gives the coat its sheen and this should be replaced during washing, generally by the use of a lanolin-containing shampoo. Never use a harsh detergent for the chore; it could damage the skin or irritate the eyes. Stick to the shampoos specifically manufactured for equines, of which there are many.

Once the horse is wet, apply the shampoo with the hands, some type of sponge or a brush. Apply it all over the horse's body in much the same sequence as brushing, only start with the head. Work the shampoo into a rich lather, paying particular attention to the mane, tail and forelock, before rinsing. Wash all the suds from the body and remove the moisture with the sweat scraper. Complete drying with the rub rag or towel or, if it's a warm day, the horse can be placed on a walker to drip-dry after scraping. If the weather is cool, he should be blanketed with a cooler.

The feet need daily attention, also, and should be clean-

Depending upon the weather and time of year, horses should be bathed with regularity. The shampoo used should have some type of lanolin base, which replaces the coat's natural oils removed during shampooing.

ed with the hoof pick. Always work from heel to toe when cleaning, to prevent puncturing the frog. A good cleaning alleviates the possibility of thrush to a large extent and brings to light any other foot problems, such as dryness. Check the fit of the shoes when cleaning and whether the horse is due for a trim.

These are the basics of good grooming but, as in most other endeavors, there still are some extra steps which can be taken to improve the horse's appearance further, so vital when showing or selling the mount. The first of these involves clipping the unsightly hairs from the muzzle, eyes, ears and fetlocks, and functional trimming of the bridle path, or top of the mane at the poll across which a strap of a halter rests.

Trimming the hairs from the muzzle is an easy and straightforward procedure, less complicated than around the eyes. Most right-handed horsemen hold the mount's eyelid closed with the thumb of the left hand (vice versa for southpaws), which serves two important purposes. It keeps the horse from shying suddenly and perhaps damaging the eye with the clipper blades, and prevents him from blinking his eyelashes into the clippers, resulting in an unusual appearance.

There are several schools of thought relative to trimming the hair inside the horse's ears and center around the problem of insects. Trimming the hair growing inside the ear avails the ear canal to easy access by insects and horsemen favoring this look must keep the ears constantly protected with an insect repellent where insects are prevalent.

For the best fetlock appearance, clippers should be booted down, or used from the knee down to the fetlock and not vice versa. There should be no sign of the clippers having been used by this procedure. The only hair booted up is around the coronet band on the hoof — take care not to injure the pastern.

Clipping the bridle path is necessary but the length of the trim is disputable. On the average, most horsemen trim somewhere around three inches, which is wide enough to handle most halters and bridles. This is a matter of personal preference, as is roaching the horse's mane.

If the mane isn't roached — trimmed short its total length — most horsemen like to have it even; the same with

Some horsemen feel "booting" a horse's legs downward, using clippers from top to bottom, results in much more pleasing appearance. Boot up at pasterns, to avoid injury.

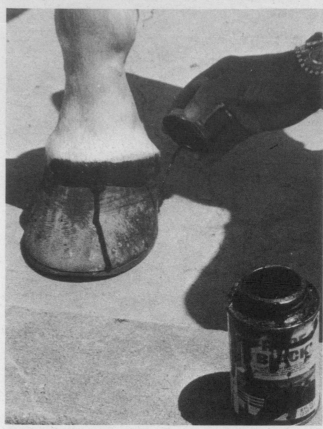

Blacking agents like Farnam's Hoof Black are employed mostly by show horsemen. This gives the hoofs a pleasing appearance — which can mean blue ribbons in the ring!

Some horseowners like the hair trimmed away from inside the ears, as Beverly May does (above). Once clipped, use insect repellent; ear canal now is open.

Clipping a horse's eyelashes must be done with caution, for a slip could result in eye injury. The lid should be held closed with the thumb during clipping procedure.

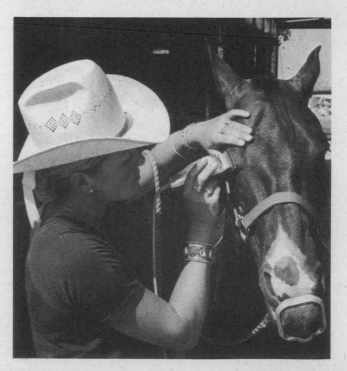

the tail. This is accomplished by pulling a few too-long hairs with the thumb and index finger of one hand, while pushing the surrounding hairs of the mane or tail toward the roots with the other. A short, snappy pull removes those too long or unsightly. Don't remove more than a few

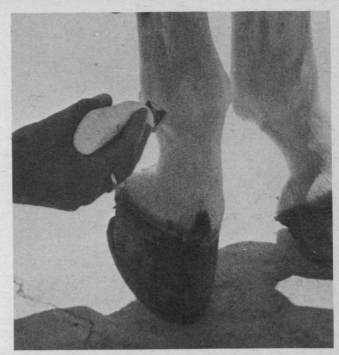

A horse sporting long muzzle hairs can be less than attractive and can be a fault in the show ring. It often takes time for a horse to become accustomed to vibration on his nose, but Mighty Warrior has no complaints (left). Any discolored or dark spots on this show horse's white stockings are touched-up with white shoe polish. This extra step aids appearance.

strands with each pull, for the mane or tail will become sore. The tail usually reaches the hocks, seldom farther.

Sometimes a horse's mane won't lie properly. This can be rectified by braiding the mane on the side the horseowner desires it to hang, the weight ultimately training the hair. When unbraided or if the problem isn't too severe, the mane can be sponged with water on the side desired to aid in holding it properly. If the mane is really stubborn, some horsemen use dowels or broomsticks some two feet long, attaching them directly to the hair. The weight trains the mane.

The last chore in grooming is to sponge the eyes and nostrils with plain water. Grooming is an endless procedure but, as noted at the beginning of this chapter, is good for the horse in more ways than one!

But grooming won't remove all the causative elements of horse ailments and, because of the variety, we will break them down into five categories for thorough examination: Internal Disorders, External Disorders, Parasitism, Diseases, and Poisoning. This simply is a loose grouping, as some maladies are either dependent upon or affect more than one category.

All horsemen should be able to distinguish between a horse in good health and one that isn't, confirming his

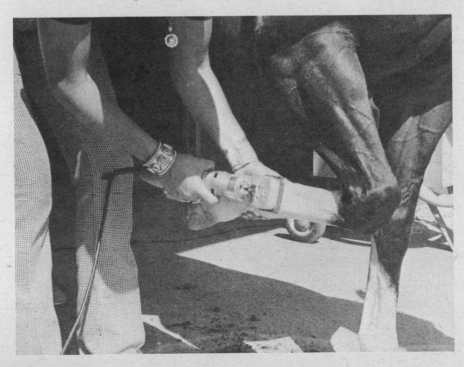

This top groomer from Mission Viejo Stables in California prefers letting a horse's white stockings grow out well before trimming for a show. Ms. May feels this results in more silvery-white look. The clippers are variable speed.

Natural sheen in manes and tails is enhanced through use of such products as Grand Champion spray (left). Most now favor the even mane when the hair isn't roached.

suspicions with simple checks. Most people instinctively recognize something wrong with their animals when behavior alters considerably.

Healthy horses appear alert, interested in what's going on around them. Their eyes, which can tell a horseman so much, should be bright, clear and wide open, except when resting. Another good indication that a horse is healthy is his appetite — he'll eat the bottom out of a bucket! If he stands with his head down, ears drooping like a mule, eyes partly closed and dull in appearance, he favors one of his limbs or quits eating, something is wrong. Before calling the veterinarian, run these simple tests which may help with his diagnosis.

First, take the horse's temperature, which requires that a horseman have a good-quality rectal thermometer on hand. The normal temperature for a horse is between 99.8 and 101 degrees Fahrenheit (37.5 to 38.5 degrees Celsius) and, if the horse is over or under this mark, jot the results down for passing to the veterinarian.

The procedure for inserting the thermometer is first to shake it snappily to drive all the mercury to the bottom, just as performed on TV medical programs. The thermometer is coated with a lubricant such as petroleum jelly, then is inserted into the anus. After one to two minutes, the thermometer is removed and the results noted.

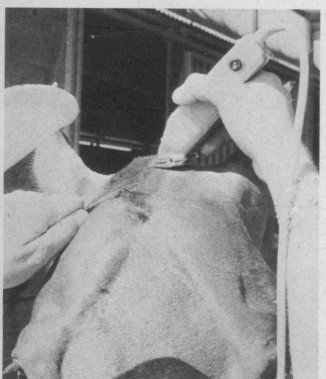

The clipped length of a horse's bridle path is a matter of personal preference, but should be long enough to accommodate horse's halter. Use sharp clipper blades.

The amount of hair left in forelock is determined by the shape of the horse's head, specifically width. A thin forelock enhances the width of the head, what judges like.

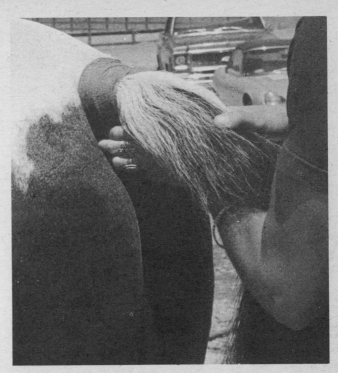

Wrapping a horse's tail is usual procedure prior to shipping or hauling, the proper way shown in the four photos on this page. After intial wrap, here using Velcro-backed Vetrap by 3M Company, is started at the base of the tail, it is wound progressively down the horse's tail. This serves to protect the tail's root, along with fending off any excrement stains.

The horse's anus must be tightly contracted to take a correct reading. If it isn't, the recorded temperature will be lower than it actually is. And because the temperature in other parts of the body differ, the rectum is the only location in which the casual horseman can take a reading. If the anus is not contracted tightly, this fact also should be passed to the veterinarian.

Another function which bears examination is the breathing rate of the horse and this should be taken when he is resting, not active or excited. This can be determined most

The wrap should be overlapped slightly as it is affixed around the horse's tail and the end result should approach that seen below right. Care must be taken, however, to avoid wrapping the tail too tightly: this cuts off vital blood circulation to tail.

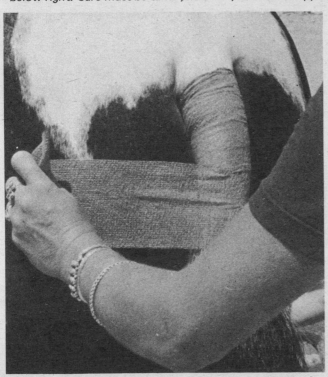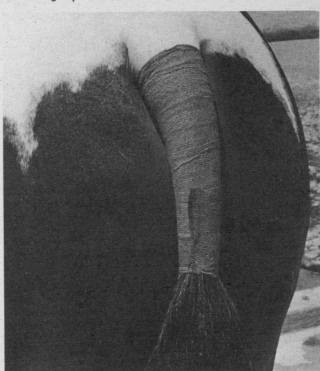

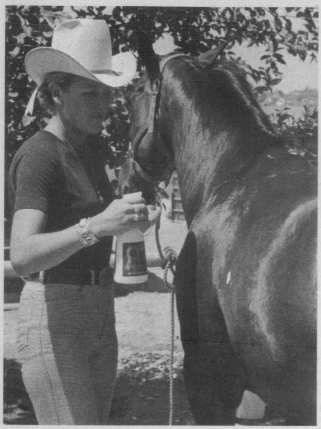

easily by watching the flanks as they swell outward with each inhalation. Count the number of breaths he takes in thirty seconds, then multiply this number by two to give the total for a minute. Horses at rest generally take between eight and sixteen breaths per minute. The rate of foal respiration is naturally higher. Note the rate for the vet.

The pulse rate is checked easily by gently pressing the large artery under either side of the horse's jaw. It should be measured with the second finger of either hand for fifteen seconds, the total being multiplied four times for one minute's total. The average rate of heartbeat is between thirty-six and forty beats per minute and, if the horse is ill, it may either be lower or higher than this group. As with the other readings, note the results for the veterinarian.

Much can be told about a horse's physical condition by his mucous membranes, specifically the eyes, nose and mouth. When the horse is healthy, the tissue around the eyes is moist and pink, denoting proper blood circulation. If the tissue is pallid, this could denote an anemic condi-

Show horsemen frequently apply some type of coat conditioner to the hair, which brings up gloss. Ms. May here uses Dazzle, which is applied to wet horse.

A horse's skin sparsely covered with hair should not be overlooked. Vaseline or Johnson's Baby Oil has found acceptance and keeps the skin shiny, prevents drying. Use it around eyes, muzzle, on rump, etc.

A dab of Vaseline on spots over which tack fits can be beneficial, especially if some form of minor irritation is present. Make sure the tack properly fits the horse.

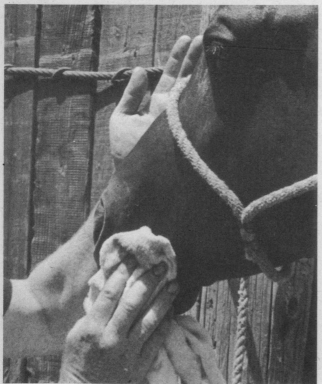

tion, hemorrhage in another part of the body or congestion of the abdominal organs, among others. If the membranes are yellowish in color, the horse may have liver problems; if red, they're inflammed. Should they be dry to the touch, the horse probably has a fever.

Examine the feces of the horse, along with his urine. If there is a change in consistency from normal, note the difference. If the urine changes color from normal, note that, too. The only exception to the latter is in some of the northern Midwest areas. Because of pigment in the urine, it assumes a reddish coloration when contacting snow on the ground which some horseowners claim resembles blood. If the animal does urinate blood, inform the veterinarian of the fact upon his arrival or when contacted by telephone.

No matter the ailment or its severity, always consult professional advice. The following diseases, their causes and symptoms are to be used solely as guiding and informative compilations and never do they supercede the advice of your veterinarian.

An improperly bridled horse, or one working with ill-fitting equipment, is less than pleasurable to ride or show. Assure chin strap is soft, pliable, not pinching.

The appearance of Mighty Warrior is a credit to Beverly May's ability, which isn't above that of any horseman. No matter whether for show ring or pleasure riding, a horse should be groomed properly and adequately. For his efforts the horseman derives another benefit: his horse will have better overall health. His parasite load can be reduced considerably by grooming.

A: DISEASES

This happy mare/foal team have overcome the possibility of infection and death by numerous equine diseases up to this point. To keep this scene from assuming one of those on the following pages, the horseowner should follow instruction in text.

Unfortunately, despite all of science's efforts, diseases plague the American horse population. A surprising number of these diseases could be eradicated, since serums have been developed which guarantee immunity against them. However, there always remains a certain percentage of horseowners who fail to have their horses immunized, which leads to continued affliction.

The most common diseases encountered will be covered in this section. These include: distemper, equine infectious anemia, colds and influenza, equine viral arteritis, equine viral rhinopneumonitis, *Salmonella abortivoequina,* equine encephalomyelitis, leptospirosis and periodic ophthalmia, tetanus, malignant edema, piroplasmosis, chronic pulmonary emphysema, colitis X, neonatal pyosepticemia, viscosum infection and neonatal isoerythrolysis.

DISTEMPER

Equine distemper, also known as strangles, is a disease prevalent where horses gather in large numbers — at race tracks, big stables, showgrounds — and is caused by *Streptococcus equi,* a bacteria. It affects weanlings and yearlings as much as older horses, but most are exposed to and are immune by the time they are 5 years old.

Generally encountered in early Spring when the weather is wet and cold, strangles strikes horses with resistance lowered through fatigue, exposure to rapid changes in temperature or stabling in drafty, cold facilities. Strangles spreads rapidly by direct contact with the mucousal secretions of an infected horse, or indirectly through water troughs, grooming tools, blankets and feed boxes or mangers. There also is a possibility of transmission by the horseowner.

The symptoms of strangles usually appear five to six days after contracting the disease and initial signs are a fast-rising temperature which peaks at around 104 to 106 degrees, increased and/or difficult breathing, general depression and the horse goes off his feed. The nasal passages will become inflamed and dry, and a clear, watery discharge begins some two to three days later. After several days, the discharge thickens and the amount increases, which leads to breathing difficulty, coughing and snorting.

At the same time, the lymph glands at the base of the lower jaw at the neck begin to swell, which may cause the horse to hold his head abnormally high, the neck outstretched. The lymph glands will become abscessed and, as the swelling continues, eventually the skin surrounding the area will rupture, or be surgically opened, releasing large quantities of thick, creamy pus. Unless there are complications, the horse generally will begin improving as his temperature drops. The fatality rate for horses infected with strangles is only about two percent.

As noted, complications are infrequent. These include the formation of abscesses in the lymph glands of other areas, including nasal and abdominal regions. The secretions draining from the nose may progress into the throat, causing breathing difficulty but rarely requiring tracheotomy to prevent suffocation. Sometimes when the lymph glands rupture, small amounts of pus are inhaled into the bronchial tubes or lungs proper, which can lead to pneumonia or pleurisy.

To hasten recovery, the horse should be isolated and placed in a draft-free stall protected from the elements, and have complete rest. Fresh drinking water should be available at all times and he should be encouraged to eat by frequently offering small amounts of appetizing, easily swallowed feeds. The veterinarian will treat him with antibiotics such as penicillin, tetracycline and chlortetracycline, or various types of sulfa drugs.

To prevent reinfection or the spread of strangles, the horse's bedding should be removed and burned, his equipment thoroughly disinfected and the stable kept clean. When the horse has recovered, the stall should be completely disinfected. A good vaccine is available.

When infected with strangles, caused by a bacteria, horses are generally debilitated. The lymph glands at base of lower jaw (circled) swell and later rupture.

EQUINE INFECTIOUS ANEMIA

Equine Infectious Anemia (EIA), also known as swamp fever, once was found predominantly around swamps but now is found just about everywhere. It is a serious ailment and if the horse doesn't die, his usefulness is at an end.

The EIA virus is present in the horse's blood consistently, although it has been isolated in milk, urine, semen, feces containing blood and nasal secretions. It is transmitted by biting horseflies, mosquitos and use of unsterilized instruments, especially hypodermic needles. Bad outbreaks have been caused by repeated usage of unsterilized needles.

Once contracted, the disease can take one of three forms, with symptoms usually developing from seven to twenty-one days after infection: acute, subacute or chronic. In acute cases, the horse's temperature skyrockets up as high as 108 degrees Fahrenheit, he sweats profusely, is depressed, won't eat, his head hangs low, he loses a great amount of weight, rests his weight on the hind legs, gets progressively weaker and dies. Subacute cases begin in the same manner, but for some reason the febrile attacks decrease in intensity and frequency after three to five days. The horse may suffer repeated attacks and, if spaced relatively close together, the animal dies.

Cases where the attacks are spaced far enough apart to keep the animal alive are termed chronic. The horse suffers intermittent fever, weight loss, lack of appetite, diarrhea and may be anemic, although in some cases the red blood cell count is normal. The average mortality rate is somewhere between thirty and seventy percent.

A problem with swamp fever is that it cannot be diagnosed readily by a veterinarian. An old way of testing was to inject blood from horses suspected of infection into test horses and observing the results. If the test animals showed symptoms of the disease, it then was assumed the horse was indeed infected; this procedure took approximately two months and was done only when numerous horses were involved.

The U.S. Department of Agriculture and all states now recognize the "agar-gel immunodiffusion" (AGID) test, often called the Coggins test. It now is official and widely used. A small blood sample is taken by a veterinarian and submitted to any of several USDA-operated laboratories for analysis.

It is safe to suspect Equine Infectious Anemia if some of these symptoms become apparent or, if for no apparent reason, several horses exhibit other-than-normal behavior after introduction of a new horse to the premises. Because there is no vaccination available or workable treatment, there is little a horseowner can do but have the test performed on the suspect horse. If the results are positive, have the animal destroyed, the carcass either burned or buried well below the surface. To do otherwise simply endangers the other horses around the infected animal, which remains an active carrier for years.

The best way to avoid the disease is to have all horses tested and require tests on all horses admitted to the farm. A good insect control program should be implemented, especially during Summertime when mosquitos and other biting insects are at peak numbers. Finally, a horseman who does his own doctoring should ensure his surgical instruments are sterilized after usage on each horse; boiling in water for at least fifteen minutes will kill any germs and bacteria. Also, since the virus may be contained in the body secretions and excretions, disinfect all equipment and facilities coming into contact with that horse.

COLDS & INFLUENZA

As with humans, horses suffer from these illnesses which cause more discomfort than serious problem. The cold is the least serious of the pair and usually makes its appearance in Autumn and Winter, or strikes foals within the first few months of their lives. The symptoms are markedly similar to human colds, with fever lasting a few days, watery nasal discharge which thickens later and an overall not-so-hot feeling. The cold, unless complications arise, generally runs its course in four to five days. Complications, especially in foals, usually affect the respiratory tract, setting the system up for pneumonic infection.

Equine Influenza, commonly called "the flu," is somewhat more serious, especially for younger horses which seem more susceptible to catching the *Myxovirus*-caused ailment. Basically, there are two types of flu present in the United States, dubbed A-1 and A-2, and older horses are affected usually by A-2. Young foals and older animals with low resistance levels are susceptible to both, however.

The symptoms of influenza, which spreads rapidly from horse to horse through direct contact or in the air, appear some two to ten days after infection. The horse's temperature rises rapidly to between 102 and 106 degrees and the fever will last up to a week. Accompanying the febrile reaction are nasal discharges, constricted nasal passages and, dependent upon the horse's usage, a cough. In working horses, the cough generally is frequent and loud, while it may not be apparent at all in brood mares or other non-working horses.

In common cases involving older horses, the treatment required is complete rest for a week to ten days, whereupon the malady disappears. Young foals which catch the virus will be treated by the veterinarian with various antibiotics and other supportive care. It's rare that horses expire because of influenza; those that do usually are young foals which develop pneumonia.

The best way of preventing the spread of disease is through sound, sanitary animal management. Horses shouldn't be kept in one large group on the same pasture. Rather, by segregating them into small groups spread over the premises, it often is possible to contain the respiratory disease should an outbreak occur. If a horse comes down with the ailment, isolate it from others and, when recovered, clean and disinfect all equipment and surroundings.

The horses, too, can be protected from *Myxovirus* influenza through innoculations currently available. Two shots are administered over a two-week period. Annual boosters then are required and should be given before the approach of Autumn. It's true that the horse will become immunized to the respiratory disease after infection, but why have him suffer through it?

Vaccines have been produced and are effective against nearly every disease mentioned in this chapter and conceivably could one day result in total eradiction. However, not all horsemen follow the example of the young horseowner shown below.

This sketch illustrates a horse exhibiting symptoms of equine viral arteritis. Head hangs low, he's oblivious to his surroundings, there's swelling in legs, elsewhere.

EQUINE VIRAL ARTERITIS

When this respiratory disease first made its appearance, it was confused with equine influenza and some of the symptoms are markedly similar. But through research, it was discovered that viral arteritis — also called pinkeye, shipping fever, stable pneumonia and epizootic cellulitis — is caused by a virus different from *Myxovirus*, the cause of influenza.

In most cases, equine viral arteritis isn't fatal, although it has caused abortion in pregnant mares, which makes outbreaks of this disease a real threat to breeding operations. It usually is noticed after introduction of a new horse to the premises and is highly contagious through direct contact.

Generally, an infected horse shows visible signs of the disease some two days to a week after contracting it, ushered in by a fever between 102 and 107 degrees. The white blood cell count drops and the horse becomes depressed, head hangs low and some swelling is encountered in the legs, tendon sheaths or teats. The horse is completely oblivious to his surroundings and the membranes around the eye become inflamed, hence the colloquial term pinkeye. The cornea may become clouded and insensitive to light, and these symptoms usually appear two to five days after the onset of fever.

In all but severe cases, these symptoms persist for ten days to two weeks, whereupon the animal recovers. In severe cases — which usually lead to death — the horse may have persistent signs of colic, diarrhea and respiratory diffi-

Veterinarian Bob Hunt takes a horse's temperature with a rectal thermometer. Each horseman should have and know how to use a thermometer for early warning signs.

culty. As noted, however, mortality is relatively low and most deaths occur as the result of abortion.

As there is no vaccine currently available to guarantee protection against viral arteritis, protection lies in proper stable management. This includes the isolation of any new horses for at least three weeks. If a horse does exhibit symptoms of the disease, he should be isolated in a draft-free stall and given complete rest until symptoms abate, then for another two weeks or so. When completely recovered, the horse should be brought back to usefulness gradually. The stall and equipment used on the animal should be thoroughly disinfected. A program of insect eradication should be implemented.

RHINOPNEUMONITIS

A far more serious threat to breeding establishments is Equine Viral Rhinopneumonitis (pronounced rye-no-new-mon-itis), often called rhino or EVR. Each year during late Fall, Winter and Spring, this killer takes its toll on the foal crops in breeding farms and it appears rhino will be with us for an indefinite period.

Essentially, it is a disease that attacks the respiratory tract of young animals and pregnant mares, transferred through direct contact with carriers or their airborne respiratory secretions. It also can be transferred through contact with a fetus aborted because of the disease.

Young horses in their first exposure to the disease generally show a temperature of between 102 and 107 degrees some one to seven days after contraction. He will appear run down, go off his feed, have a cough and suffer constipation which sometimes is followed by diarrhea. The disease usually will run its course, barring secondary infections of the respiratory tract.

In the case of pregnant mares, however, usually these symptoms aren't present and the horseowner won't know his mare is infected. It's possible for the mare to abort from three weeks to five months after contraction, but most abortions occur between the eighth and eleventh months of

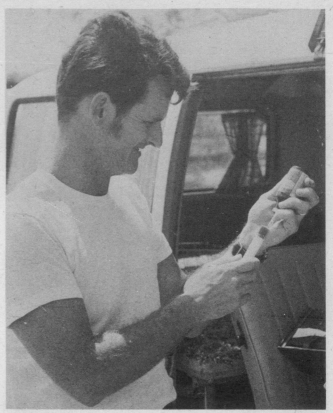

When measured against the costs of post-infection care and supportive treatment, inoculations are dirt cheap! Veterinarian Bob Hunt prepares an injection for tetanus.

pregnancy. The only way a horseowner can positively identify the cause of abortion is to have a veterinarian examine the aborted fetus; the blood of the mare after abortion shows no signs of EVR.

Though infrequent, diseased foals sometimes are born following full-term gestation, but generally they die hours or a few days after foaling. They are weak and often have pneumonia. Sometimes a veterinarian can save the foal provided diligent care is provided.

A mare which has aborted is not affected in producing other foals, although it is possible to become reinfected with EVR. It is true that horses contracting and recovering from the disease have a high immunity rate to rhino during the next several months but, after this period wanes, it is possible to contract the disease again. It appears that older horses, which have been infected several times, have higher antibody counts.

As noted, there isn't much that can be done once the horse has contracted rhino. But a new vaccine developed by Norden Laboratories, dubbed "Rhinomune," now is available. Very effective, it is entirely safe to use at any time; there's no danger of it starting an outbreak.

Another abortion-causing disease that rates only passing mention — since no cases have been diagnosed in the United States in the last twenty-five years — has the scientific handle of *Salmonella abortivoequina*.

This disease is contracted through ingestion of pasture or other feed materials which have been contaminated by con-

The "Rhinomune" vaccine developed by Norden has been a blessing to breeders and farm managers. It provides long-sought protection against deadly rhinopneumonitis.

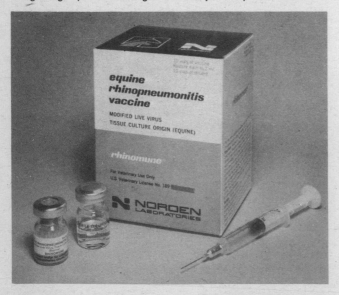

tact with the aborted fetus, afterbirth or fluids. Also, a mare following abortion may have a vaginal discharge which contains the *S. abortivoequina* bacteria. Therefore, following abortion and positive identification of *S. abortivoequina* by a veterinarian, the mare should be isolated until all signs of vaginal discharge have disappeared.

This disease is found in Canada, South America and other countries. It is plausible to assume it could be reintroduced into the United States, an event we hope doesn't materialize.

EQUINE ENCEPHALOMYELITIS

Often called sleeping sickness, there are three types of encephalomyelitis which can affect U.S. horses: Eastern equine encephalomyelitis (EEE), Western equine encephalomyelitis (WEE) and Venezuelan equine encephalomyelitis (VEE). EEE and WEE get their names from geographical prevalence: EEE in Eastern, Atlantic Seaboard and Gulf Coast states, and WEE in Midwest, Southwest and Western states. VEE is so named because it first was recognized along the Venezuelan/Colombian border.

VEE really made only one strong showing in the United States, back in 1971. Until that time, few cases had been reported in Florida and Louisiana. But a combination of excessive flooding, a bumper crop of mosquitos and constantly northward movement of the disease from Central America provided the needed factors for a bad epizootic, in which thousands of horses in the Southwest died. The Department of Agriculture released a supply of vaccine to the stricken states — which were quarantined — and the spread of VEE was checked. Since early 1972, no cases of VEE have been reported within our boundaries.

Despite all the attention VEE gained through nationwide media exposure, its cousin killers are responsible for more deaths *each year* than VEE caused throughout its outbreak. EEE and WEE epizootics appear each Summer, as wild birds migrate northward. The infected birds then are bitten by one of several strains of mosquito, which spread it to horses upon biting the latter. In no way can EEE or WEE be spread from horse to horse or from horse to man; the horse is not a carrier or a threat to health. VEE can be spread by mosquitos from horse to horse and from horse to man, however.

Of the two, grim horse-harvesters, Eastern equine encephalomyelitis is the more deadly. Nearly ninety percent of horses contracting the disease — which also affects man — die within a short period. The mortality rate for WEE is substantially lower: between twenty and fifty percent.

Symptoms of both diseases include fever, incoordination, a depressed condition with little appetite, drowsiness (hence the name sleeping sickness), reduced reflexes and impaired vision, among others. Horses exhibiting mild symptoms usually recover; the acute cases die.

There isn't much a veterinarian can do once a horse contracts the disease, other than provide supportive treatment. In mild cases, the horse generally will recover after several weeks of complete rest. Since the mosquito is the prime vector of transmission, the horseowner should implement a program of insect eradication during the late spring months. And, like so many other diseases still prevalent, there are vaccines which can guarantee immunity from infection — if the horseowner has them given. There is a combination vaccine, given initially in two doses one week to ten days apart, which is highly effective. After initial

Bob Morris, Serology Laboratory manager at University of California, Davis, holds blood checked for brood stock. USDA veterinarian Lloyd C. Weldon takes blood sample from colt suspected of infection with VEE during late 1971.

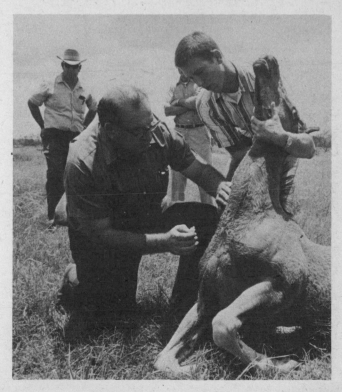

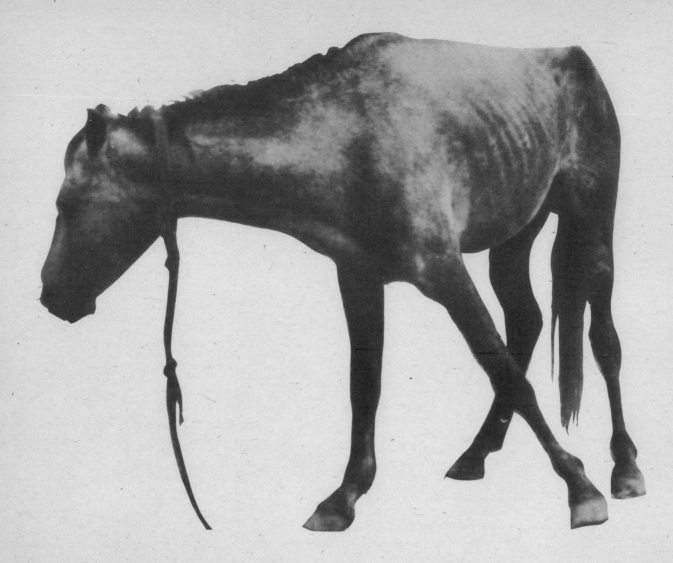

This is classic example of horse suffering from EEE (above). Check the text for symptoms of the disease.

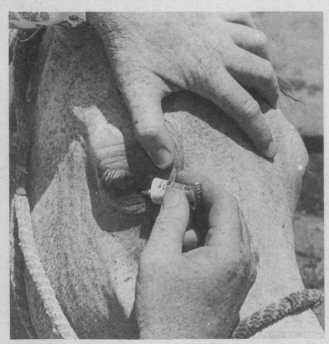

Leptospirosis usually is not serious on its own, but can lead to periodic ophthalmia, main cause of blindness. A veterinarian may prescribe use of eye drops (left).

application, the horses need only annual boosters to ensure their protection.

LEPTOSPIROSIS

"Lepto" in horses generally is not a serious disease. Some horses will suffer fever, depression, loss of appetite, lethargy or jaundice, while others will exhibit none of these. It can cause pregnant mares to abort or lead to periodic ophthalmia, the most common cause of blindness in horses.

The ailment is caused by spiral-shaped bacteria known as spirochetes, of which more than fifty strains have been detected, broken into nonpathogenic and pathogenic categories; the latter cause the problems mentioned earlier. It is transmitted to susceptible horses through contact with secretions or excretions from infected animals and the bacteria can live for many days in damp or saturated soil. The bacteria is rather fragile and cannot survive on dry soil or in direct sunlight. It can survive up to a month in a warm, stagnant pond.

Most horses are able to fight lepto on their own, but it

Leptospirosis is caused by spiral-shaped bacteria and cattle are also susceptible. It can reduce a working ranch horse into a helpless animal.

can lead to abortion or blindness. A vaccine is available to guarantee protection, which should be administered as necessary.

Periodic ophthalmia, often erroneously called moon blindness, is a serious matter. The first symptoms are watering of one or both eyes. The pupil constricts, the eye is sensitive to light and the eye membrane may be inflamed. The cornea may become cloudy and the horse may keep his eye closed during attacks, which are recurrent in history. Each attack, which occurs at regular intervals, further dam-

ages the eye and blindness is the result unless carefully treated.

A horse suffering the aforementioned symptoms should be placed in a dark barn or stall until the attack subsides to rest the eye and help relieve pain caused by bright sunlight. A veterinarian will prescribe a treatment schedule that should be followed rigorously.

TETANUS

Tetanus, often called lockjaw, is a disease to which both horse and horseman are susceptible. It is caused by a bac-

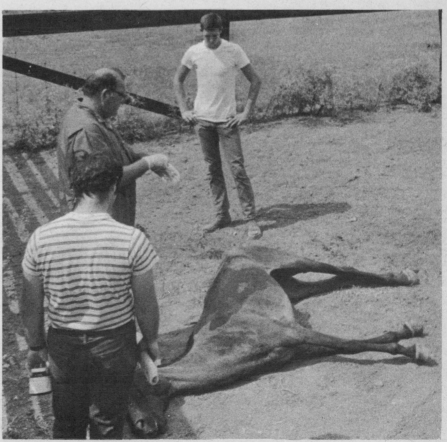

The cause of tetanus is found nearly in all soil, just waiting to be introduced to a horse by some type of wound. The result, as shown here can be fatal.

teria called *Clostridium tetani*. This bacteria, which survives without oxygen, is found in the soil and the feces of horses. Deep punctures from nails or slivers is usually how the bacteria enters the skin, where it begins to grow and multiply, producing a poison that affects the motor nerves or central nervous system.

Anywhere from a week to four months after infection, the symptoms begin to appear. This usually will first be a stiffness of the area surrounding the puncture, or perhaps stiffness of the hind legs. About a day later, the horse may begin having tonic spasms, where he continually contracts his muscles involuntarily. It's the tonic spasm of the head muscles, which makes opening the mouth difficult, that leads to the "lockjaw" term.

As the disease progresses, movement of the limbs becomes difficult, due to muscular contraction. The involuntary muscles — those that work independently, like the heart, liver, kidneys, etc. — are upset by this behavior and often work at increased rates, especially in fatal cases, accompanied by a fever that sometimes hits 110 degrees. In mild cases of tetanus, both pulse and temperature may remain nearly normal.

If a horse has received a deep wound with the possibility of tetanus high, a veterinarian usually will inject tetanus antitoxin into the animal to be safe. If the animal is exhibiting signs of the disease, the veterinarian will administer a massive dose of the antitoxin, along with tranquilizers, which have proved effective in the past. He then will clean and thoroughly disinfect the wound site and, if the horse is going to survive, it will recover fully after some six weeks of supportive treatment. During that time, the horse should be placed in a quiet, darkened box stall since, when infected, sudden movements send the animal into panic. A constant source of feed and water should be available and high enough that the animal suffers no discomfort when trying to take either.

As in man's case, there is a vaccine which can be administered to prevent tetanus. Annual vaccination with tetanus toxoid is widely done and recommended.

Horseowners should take great care to remove sharp objects which horses can contact. Periodic inspection of all stalls, paddocks, fences, mangers and water troughs — or any other possible source of injury — with appropriate corrective action taken will reduce the chances of lockjaw visiting your spread.

MALIGNANT EDEMA

Clostridium septicum, the cause of malignant edema, is a cousin of the tetanus producer. And like its cousin, *C. septicum* grows in an oxygen-free environment, usually entering

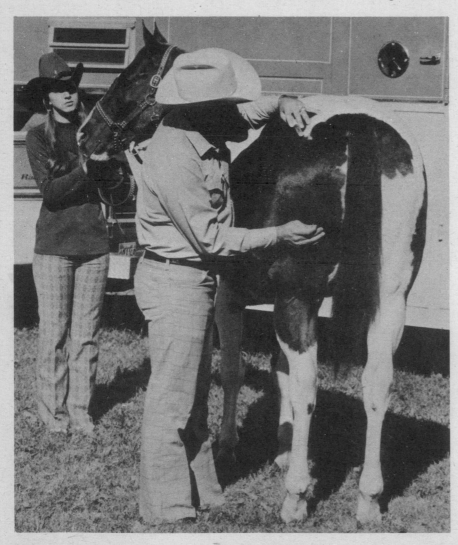

After initial inoculation, only annual boosters are required to protect against tetanus. It's foolish to forego shots!

160

the body through a puncture or similar injury and is found in most pasture soil. It's as deadly as *Clostridium tetani*, if not more so.

Usually within hours after picking up the bacteria, a horse's temperature starts rising and there is swelling directly around the puncture site. The skin is hot and touching the wound causes great pain. The horse also goes off his feed, is depressed and exhibits signs of respiratory difficulty. From the wound site a thin, reddish secretion will run and, as the disease progresses, the horse will suffer convulsions.

If caught early enough, there may be something the veterinarian can do in the way of administering antibiotics such as penicillin. But once the disease gets a firm hold on the animal, death is inevitable.

When the symptoms become noticed, isolate the horse from others and, because the horseman is susceptible to infection, only handle the horse when suitably protected with rubber gloves. After the horse has expired or been put down by the veterinarian, either cremate the carcass or bury it deeply; the causative spores will live on after the host has died and this will prevent the possible spread to other mounts.

There is a vaccine available which protects horses from malignant edema and this should be included in any regular inoculation program. It's better to pay now than later.

PIROPLASMOSIS

Equine piroplasmosis, also known as *babesiasis*, is common in most tropical countries and was introduced into the United States over a decade ago. Now restricted to southern Florida, piroplasmosis is transmitted by tropical horse ticks only. The disease manifests itself as a blood disorder following initial sickness accompanied by fever and anemia. It can be treated by a veterinarian and rarely results in death.

CHRONIC PULMONARY EMPHYSEMA

More usually called heaves or broken-wind, this is a seri-ous respiratory ailment, the specific cause of which is unknown, that reduces a horse into a useless boarder.

Heaves occurs principally in stables and scientists feel it is contracted through ingestion of dusty, moldy hay, which causes bronchitis that leads to this strange disorder, although the cause of chronic pulmonary emphysema is unknown. The first symptoms, which are usually overlooked, include a shortness of breath after moderate working. As the disease progresses, however, the symptoms become readily apparent: Respiratory rate is increased and, upon expiration, the abdominal muscles contract in an extra expiratory effort. Try it a couple of times and the painful effect of this disease is readily apparent.

After a short period, a horse with heaves develops a barrel chest and a "heave line" behind the rib cage. A chronic cough may develop, along with a nasal discharge. He begins losing weight.

If the disorder is a by-product of bronchitis, a change of diet to pasture grass or pelleted feeds sometimes brings about normal respiratory function. This diet change can be supplemented with medication to treat the bronchial condition. But if the disease is caused by chronic pulmonary emphysema, no known cure is available. Sometimes the diet change will provide relief.

Since scientists feel the bronchitis condition which often causes heaves comes from eating moldy or dusty hay, the horseowner should take pains to avoid feeding this to the animal. If the feed is merely dusty, it should be wetted prior to feeding, which cuts down the dust. The stable also should be adequately ventilated, since perhaps the mixture of stable dust with that from the roughage may help bring on the disorder.

COLITIS X

Colitis X is a noncontagious, usually fatal disease affecting the intestinal tract that is brought about mostly through exposing a horse to stress too soon after having been sick with some infection, such as a racehorse being put into a

Veterinarians are equipped with about everything except an operating room. The diseases and injuries to which a horse can fall victim are enormous.

race before he has completely recovered from a bout with the flu. Because of the suspected cause, it sometimes is called exhaustion shock.

The symptoms of the disease progress rapidly and the first to appear usually is severe diarrhea or flatulent colic (explained later in this chapter). The horse begins breathing rapidly, breaks out in patchy sweating, dehydrates, the pulse may be weak and he may exhibit colic-like pain. Death usually occurs within three to twenty-four hours after onset of the symptoms.

Veterinarians can and do save many cases if they get to them early. Large quantities of fluids and electrolytes are given both intravenously and by stomach tube. The solutions must be given before the case gets well advanced,

hence the need for the owner to be observant and call his veterinarian at once. Time is of the essence.

NEONATAL PYOSEPTICEMIA

Better known as Navel-Ill, this disease is caused by any of several bacterial strains, usually with the same result: death. In fact, the mortality rate is up around ninety percent.

This disease can be passed to the foal either prenatally or after foaling, in the former through the umbilical cord. The stump of the umbilical cord also can be the entrance after foaling, although researchers feel it is more often picked up through other means, principally ingestion or inhalation.

Symptoms vary according to age of the foal, but general-

A foal suffering from neonatal pyosepticemia has swollen, painful joints, accompanied by swelling and discharge from the umbilical cord stump. It can be contracted prenatally, also through umbilical cord after birth.

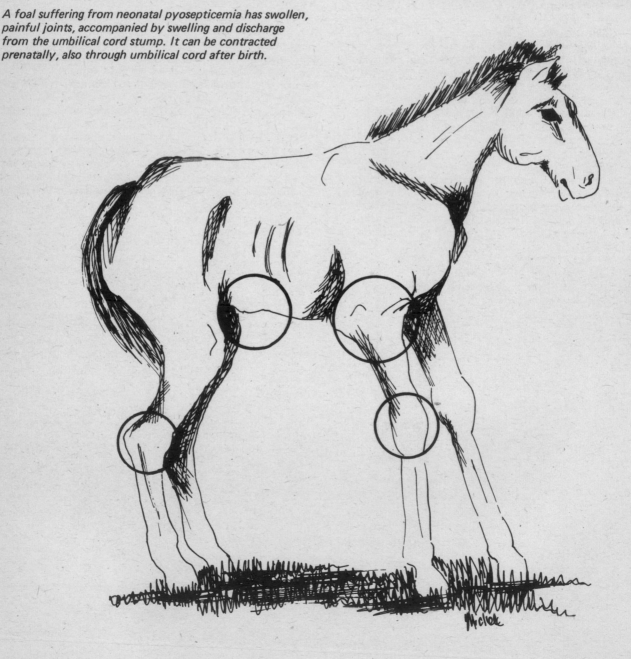

ly the horse's temperature will be high, he suffers lack of appetite, is generally depressed and the joints will become swollen and sore. There often is swelling and discharge at the umbilical cord stump.

The survival rate of the foal is in direct proportion to his age: the older he is, the better his chances. When infected prenatally, death usually comes between one to three days after foaling and there's nothing the veterinarian can do. If the foal is a couple of weeks old when symptoms develop, the veterinarian will treat the animal and the chances of recovery are good.

If the foal already has the disease through prenatal infection, there is little the horseowner can do at foaling time. However, he should always paint the stump of the umbilical cord with iodine as quickly as possible.

VISCOSUM INFECTION

This foal disease is generally fatal if not discovered and quickly treated. It has been known by horsemen for years as the "sleeper" or "dummy" foal and is caused by *Actinobacillus equuli*, not by *Shigella equirulis* as was previously thought.

This illness, rarely prenatally contracted, is characterized by a listlessness, he's dull and little concerned with his surroundings. Temperature, pulse and respiration rates increase dramatically and, as the disease progresses, the foal becomes weaker until finally it cannot stand at all. During this course, the foal will not nurse. There is a mortality rate of approximately thirty percent within twenty-four hours of the first symptom's appearance.

As quickly as possible after detection, the veterinarian will begin administration of dihydrostreptomycin, following this with proper supportive treatment. If caught in time, the foal's chances of survival increase fifty percent.

NEONATAL ISOERYTHROLYSIS

Usually called Hemolytic disease or the jaundiced foal syndrome, this condition is not a disease in the communicable, virus or bacterial-caused sense. Rather, it is a problem which occurs because of differences in the blood of a foal and his dam and, if not properly handled, it leads to certain death for the foal.

During fetal development, the jaundiced foal's blood develops a genetic incompatibility with the mare's and her blood begins building antibodies against the foal's. Upon birth, these antibodies are collected in the colostrum found in mother's milk. Consequently, upon nursing the foal takes in antibodies against his own blood which destroys the red blood cells and causes death.

The jaundiced foal's mucous membranes take on a yellowish color and, should this be noted during foaling, the new arrival should be muzzled to prevent him from nursing. He should be bottle-fed for the next forty-eight hours and, at the same time, the mare should be milked until the potentially dangerous antibodies have disappeared. The foal then can begin nursing.

While there are many other communicable diseases a horse can suffer, these are the bulk the American horseman may expect to contact. As mentioned, most can be avoided by simple vaccinations, usually just once a year. When the cost of the shot is measured against the expense incurred with a sick horse, it's easy to see that it doesn't pay to be "penny-wise and pound-foolish."

This is the life a foal is supposed to lead: carefree, happy, inquisitive. Exposure to one of these diseases can change all that, so prevent them!

B: INTERNAL DISORDERS

Using tractor tires as feed troughs for rental horses appeared a fine idea, until horses began dying from colic at this stable in California. Autopsy disclosed intestinal blockage with rubber as cause of death — horses had been cribbing on the tires.

There are internal disorders a horse may suffer which comprise a separate classification in our look at the complex world of veterinary medicine. The most common are: azoturia (paralytic myoglobinuria); colic (flatulent, spasmodic and impaction); exhaustion; fractures; roaring (laryngeal hemiplegia); sprains (sore shins, carpitis, bog spavin, capped hock, capped elbow and tendinitis); sunstroke (heatstroke, heat cramps and heat exhaustion); teeth problems; thumps; and tying up (myositis).

As with the segment on diseases, consult professional advice immediately if your horse exhibits any of the ailment symptoms outlined in the following section. Pay strict attention to the therapy recommended by your veterinarian.

AZOTURIA

The scientific name, paralytic myoglobinuria — which basically means paralysis accompanied by iron-containing, muscle-protein pigment in the urine — is much more fitting in describing this serious ailment than azoturia, which translated roughly means nitrogen in the urine.

While the scientific reason of *why* it happens is unknown, researchers have discovered *how* azoturia develops. A horse has been working hard and his owner has been feeding him accordingly. Then the horse will get a few days' rest, still being fed the increased ration. When the horse-owner attempts to put the horse back into service, problems arise.

Usually within a few moments, often within sight of the barn, the horse begins to sweat profusely and stiffness in one or both back legs begins; rarely are all four legs involved. Unless halted, the horse becomes extremely nervous, stiffness continues until he cannot extend his legs fully, respiratory and pulse rate increase and the horse usually goes down. The muscles of the croup and hindquarters are swollen and rock-hard. If the horse urinates, it usually is a dark red or even coffee color, caused by the myoglobin in the urine.

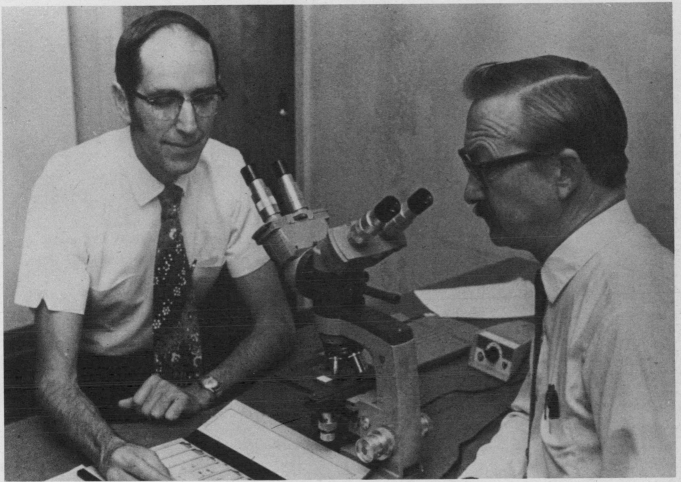

It's in the laboratory where such noted veterinarians as Dr. Albert E. McChesney (left) and Dr. Jerry L. Adcock hunt for cures, that knowledge relative to internal disorders is gathered. Much has yet to be learned of equine inner workings.

If the horse is stopped upon first indication of stiffness and sweating, usually he will remain standing and, if not moved for several hours, the attack usually subsides to the point that he can be returned to the barn. He then should be given complete rest for up to two weeks and brought back to work gradually.

If the animal goes down his chances of recovery aren't as good, unless he remains relatively calm. If nervous, the veterinarian can administer tranquilizers and, after a twenty-four-hour period, the horse usually recovers control of the muscles and can be moved to the barn. During the time he's down, the veterinarian may change his position to avoid bedsores and remove the urine with a catheter, if muscle stiffness precludes normal bodily function. During recovery, mild laxatives often are given and horses appear to respond favorably to vitamin E and selenium therapy.

The simplest way to avoid this disorder is through sound animal management. If the horse is rested several days, his feed — especially grain — should be cut back accordingly.

Daily exercise, even if of relatively short duration, is better than none.

COLIC

One of the most common yet serious maladies to befall horses, colic is divided into two basic categories: true and false. True colic can be categorized even further, into flatulent, spasmodic and impaction colic. None are any fun, either for horse or horseman.

Looking first at false colic, this is a term given for colic-like symptoms that aren't caused by colic in its true form. Rather, false colic sometimes is caused by inflammation of the intestinal organs. When discussing spasmodic colic, the distinguishing characteristics will be noted for accurate preliminary diagnosis by the horseman.

Generally, colic is believed caused by eating feed spoiled through mold or containing indigestible elements like oat husks; by rapid consumption of feed; overeating; sudden changes in feed; poor chewing; feeding or watering when extremely fatigued; watering too soon after working; using the horse for hard work too soon after feeding; irregular feeding schedules; fermentation of feed in the stomach; windsucking (inhaling great quantities of air); and the presence of foreign matter like dirt or sand in the stomach.

There recently has been another theory advanced for the cause of colic: parasitism; specifically, infestation by *Strongylus vulgaris* – the bloodworm. A group of researchers estimate that ninety percent of all colic cases result from damage done by bloodworm larvae migrations in the horse's bloodstream. A respected authority, Dr. James Rooney, performed autopsies on over ten thousand horses and claims eighty-five to ninety percent of those cases diagnosed as colic were directly or indirectly caused by the bloodworm.

To understand why the bloodworm is so dangerous and how he does his damage, one must understand his life cycle and how he lives. We have long known that the adult worm attaches to the inside wall of the horse's intestine where it lives and produces eggs which pass out with the droppings. In a few days larvae emerge from these eggs on the ground, attach to blades of grass and are ready to be consumed by a horse.

Eggs may lay dormant on the ground for months. The adult egg-laying worm may live in the intestine for many months where it does very little damage. From the time a larvae is swallowed, it may be eight to nine months before it ceases migrating in the body tissues and matures in the intestines.

In an attempt to determine the migrating route of *Strongylus vulgaris* larvae, Dr. J.L. Duncan in Scotland infected each of nine work-free pony foals with a pure culture of 750 infective larvae (such as a horse might consume in an infected pasture). Ponies then were killed and examined at intervals over a period of nine months. Results clearly showed that the larvae penetrate the intestine wall within a few days where they moult. They then penetrate the very small arteries which supply the intestine and migrate up the lumina of these vessels to the anterior mesenteric site in about fourteen days (this is the site where mass thromboses and damage is most commonly found).

In this site — or other site of choice — the larvae further develop for three to four months and, after a fourth moult is completed, the young adults migrate back down the arteries, penetrate the wall and enter the inside of the intestines where they mature. The total migration within the horse's body is complete within six or seven months after infection. Other research workers have confirmed this damaging migratory pattern of the bloodworm.

It is these larvae migrations that cause the damage to blood vessels — inflammation, swelling, debris, stoppage. Mass migrations produce sufficient damage to cause a horse to die in shock. The cause is obvious when it happens.

Less obvious and much more common are problems that result later from the damage left behind by the larvae. Blood vessels are restricted, clogged, damaged, scarred so that an adequate blood supply cannot reach various portions of the intestine. Thus, areas of the digestive tract are weakened to where only a minor stress causes it to improperly function — and the resultant colic.

These stresses or insults to the system in most instances are the immediate triggering cause of the colic. However, the real cause may be a deficient blood supply to some portions of the intestine due to previous damage done by the bloodworm which makes it unable to function normally and withstand stress.

Looking first at flatulent colic and keeping in mind the bloodworm theory, this results usually from the fermentation of spoiled feed in the stomach, which gives off large quantities of gas but can result from windsucking or ingestion of large amounts of green feed at one time. There is no mistaking flatulent colic for other intestinal disorders, for the stomach is bloated and distended. Tapped with a finger, it gives off a resonant sound not unlike tapping a drum.

As the amount of gas builds, it puts pressure on the internal organs, causing pain and leading to respiratory difficulty; internal organs pressing upon the lungs makes breaths short and rapid. He may sweat profusely, paw the ground, kick at his stomach or lie down and, if the pressure isn't relieved, death is probable through ruptured intestines, twisted bowels or shock.

When the veterinarian arrives, he will attempt to rid the gas without resorting to work inside. But under threat of imminent death, the veterinarian will puncture the bowel or colon, freeing the gas.

In cases of spasmodic colic, the horse suddenly shows signs of abdominal pain through groaning, anxious facial expression, straining to urinate or defecate, kicking at the belly (which isn't distended as in flatulent colic), turning the muzzle to look at the stomach, pawing the ground, sweating, rolling and may even throw himself down as if

Dr. Willard D. Ommert removed these concretements from small colon of 8-year-old gelding. Similar to gallstones, these form in small intestine. They fitted so tightly together they blocked intestine, causing colic.

pole-axed. Then, just as suddenly, the pain diminishes and the horse acts normally by eating or drinking until the next and usually stronger spasm begins. These will increase in intensity until the animal dies or gradually decrease in intensity, thus effecting recovery.

The difference between flatulent colic and inflammation of the inner organs is readily apparent through distention of the belly in the former. But accurately diagnosing spasmodic colic is somewhat more difficult and takes a sharp eye on behalf of the horseowner.

Probably the biggest difference is that inflammation affords no periods of relief, as does spasmodic colic; the pain in the former is continuous. Also, horses suffering from spasmodic colic generally have a normal temperature and pulse rate, unlike inflammation which causes increases in both. Another important difference is that inflammation usually leads to tautness of the belly, which causes pain when touched. This same procedure seems to cause relief when the horse suffers from spasmodic colic.

Impaction colic is still another serious category of this malady, a blockage of the intestines which, if not removed, causes death. This is the result of ingestion of foreign matter like sand or dirt from eating roughage thrown on the ground, but also can be caused by insufficient mastication of feed, overeating or bad feed, among others outlined earlier.

A horse suffering from impaction colic, often called simply impaction, usually resembles a horse with spasmodic colic except that feces will be passed for a time before the animal becomes constipated. If mild, the horse will recover upon passage of the obstacle. If severe, death through ruptured intestines may be the result.

When the veterinarian arrives, he will try administering enemas or other purgatives to break the blockage and, if he begins within the first day of the condition, results usually are satisfactory.

The proper way to handle all types of colic is through prevention, which is only sound stable management. Feed only what the horse needs relative to his service and make sure the hays and grains are of good quality, free from spoilage or dust. Don't offer forage that is highly fermentable or grains that can combine in lumpy masses. Make any

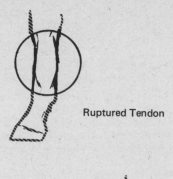

Ruptured Tendon

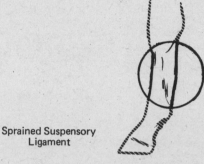

Sprained Suspensory Ligament

Ruptured tendons and sprained suspensory ligaments can cause lay-up at best, lameness at worst. See comments under sprains for treatment routine.

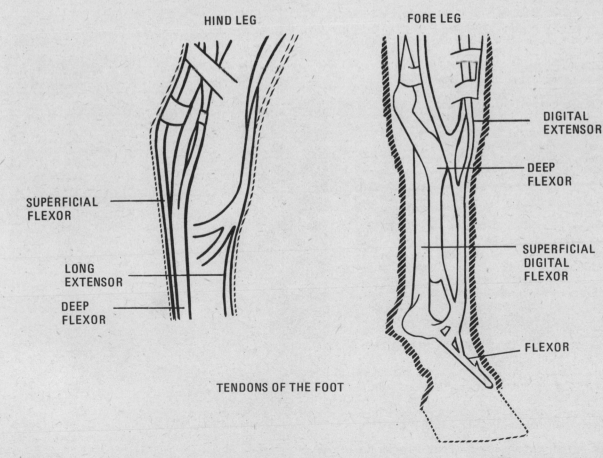

HIND LEG

SUPERFICIAL FLEXOR

LONG EXTENSOR

DEEP FLEXOR

TENDONS OF THE FOOT

FORE LEG

DIGITAL EXTENSOR

DEEP FLEXOR

SUPERFICIAL DIGITAL FLEXOR

FLEXOR

It behooves each horseman to know the physical makeup of his horse. This aids in proper early diagnosis of ailments which can save having the condition turn into a permanent disability. A horse provides indications when injured, so watch for them.

ration changes slowly and keep the horse on a regular feeding schedule. Remember, horses are used to eating more than one meal per day so two or more feedings are best. This keeps the level of bacteria in the intestines — which break down the ingested feeds — high enough to preclude problems. Use a feeder box or a manger; never feed on the ground.

Keep the horse fit through adequate exercise and never work the horse immediately after eating. Assure that fresh water is available at all times. Have the horse's teeth checked regularly and floated as necessary. Teeth problems will be covered later in this chapter. Initiate a regular program of parasite control. This also will be covered later in this chapter.

EXHAUSTION

Exhaustion or extreme fatigue usually is brought about through overwork or strenuous working of an out-of-condition horse. The horse will be visibly tired upon arrival back at the barn, then may shun any food offerings made, even grain. At the same time, the animal will be extraordinarily thirsty and may lie down between waterings.

The best treatment is to cover the horse with a cooler to prevent chilling and the legs should be massaged vigorously to increase circulation. Small amounts of water should be given frequently and, if rested completely for two or three days, the horse should be fine.

Horseowners should take pains to keep their horses in condition, not overly fat or thin. The work schedule should revolve around the horse's condition and environmental factors. Don't try accomplishing too much work in one day, as you may end up losing the animal's services for several.

There is a great difference in severity between simple exhaustion and sunstroke, which is covered later in this section. It behooves the horseowner to recognize the differences and know how to treat accordingly.

FRACTURES

Fractures are divided into two categories, simple and compound, and neither is good news for the horse. Simple fractures denote a clean separation of a bone, while compound means a bone broken in more than one place, shattered, or with part of the bone sticking through the surface of the skin.

During the time when cowboys rode the range, it was the normal and unwelcome practice to put down any horse which broke a leg. This is the usual prognosis for the average horse today. Nearly the only exceptions are expensive racehorses with impressive records; while their racing careers may be over, they still can make money in the stud.

Until 1971, fractures of the legs were, after being set, encased in plaster casts for the healing period. Plaster casts are heavy, break fairly easily and preclude much free movement of a horse. Most fractures still are treated in this manner, although a new fiberglass cast seems to be finding favor with top orthopedic veterinarians around the world.

It's termed the Lightcast and lives up to its name, being light of weight, much more resistant to breakage than plaster, is thinner, lasts longer and sheds moisture. It is responsible for the continued existence of such top-name racehorses as England's Mill Reef and America's Gaelic Dancer, Hoist the Flag and Sham, among others.

After the affected area of the limb is protected with a cushioning gauze, a web-like wrap is applied, then a fiberglass tape. After the tape is bound around the protective

Wrapping the injured limb of a horse is an art in itself: too tight and circulation is impaired; too loose and no good will result. The wraps shown, with Velcro backing, are made by 3M Company and can aid in immobilizing an injured joint.

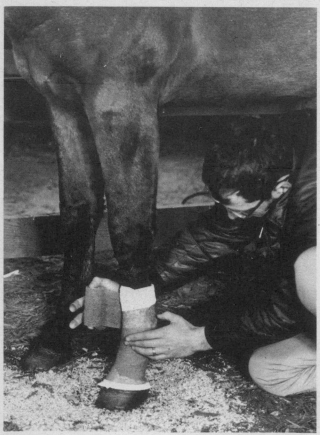
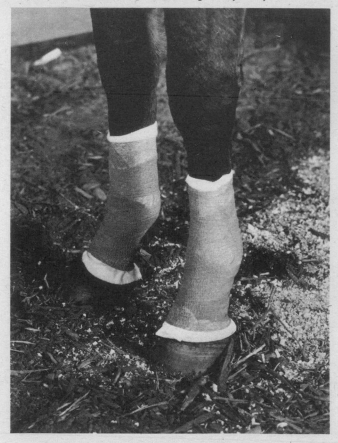

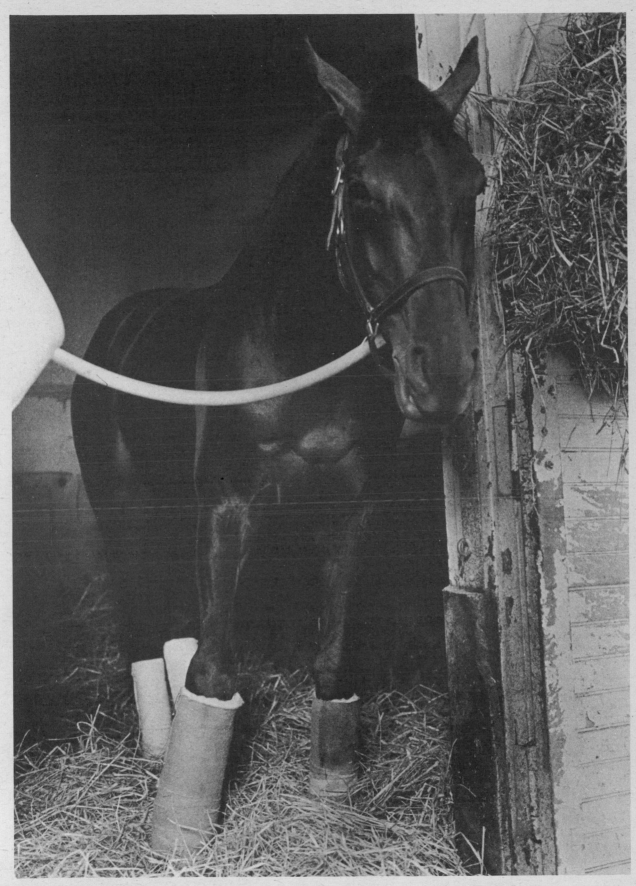

Sham, the famous 3-year-old that so gallantly raced in Secretariat's shadow, broke a bone in his foreleg during his last race and was fitted with a Lightcast II fiberglass cast following surgery and implantation of screws in the right foreleg. Much lighter in weight, much better at shedding moisture — and much more expensive — than plaster, it saved his life.

plastic wraps, a "black light" is used to harden the cast, which takes three minutes. There is no heat and it's the light's energy that cures the cast. Another advantage is that it's possible to take X-rays through the cast.

The main disadvantages to the Lightcast are that not many veterinarians are yet able to apply it, local anesthetic needs to be used for roughly one and one-half hours (compared to one-half hour for plaster casts), it's around twice as expensive as plaster and immediate veterinary attention is needed to confine animal movement.

Because of the disadvantages of cost, inexperienced practitioners and immediate attention needs, the Lightcast treatment isn't used often. In fact, the prognosis for a horse with a broken leg receiving any kind of treatment isn't good. Consider, too, that even if the bone is set, most horses' active usefulness will be over after recovery. This is

the horse grunts, there is reason to believe it has laryngeal hemiplegia.

Roaring robs a horse of its usefulness and about the only correction comes from surgery on the larynx. Some seventy percent of the horses going under the veterinary surgeon's knife are restored to usefulness.

As there is speculation that roaring can be hereditary, it is wise to refrain from using such animals in the stud or brood mare band, at least until a causative element has been isolated.

SPRAINS

Technically, a sprain is a wrenching or twisting of a joint or muscle that results in torn or stretched ligaments, without breaking the overlying skin. There is soreness, swelling and heat at the location.

Horse (above) is suffering from heat exhaustion, a condition brought about through continued exposure to hot, muggy temperatures. The heat causes blood vessels to dilate and, if blood volume doesn't likewise increase, veins may collapse. A capped elbow is depicted at right, a swelling caused by horse bumping his elbow with a rear foot. See text for remedy.

why most pleasure horses with broken legs are put down even today.

Other bones break occasionally. A horse's fondness for rolling in the dirt sometimes results in a fractured point of the hip. When so incapacitated, a horse will show visible signs of lameness on that leg and the point of the hip may be tender and swollen. This malady usually will heal, if the horse is given complete rest for a month to six weeks or until a veterinarian deems him sound again.

Broken leg bones usually are the result of either a blow from another horse or by stepping into a prairie dog's burrow. Nearly all a horseman can do to prevent this occurrence is to watch his animals and separate warring horses, and institute a good rodent control program. Pay attention when riding and avoid areas that can result in animal injury.

ROARING

Roaring, or laryngeal hemiplegia, is characterized by audible inspiration of each breath and, when so afflicted, there is little that may be done to correct the problem.

While scientists aren't definitely certain, there seems evidence to believe roaring is caused by an irritation of the larynx — the voice box — or as a result of another disease, an overextension of the head, or it may even be hereditary. In nearly all cases, the laryngeal nerves on the left side of the larynx become paralyzed, which leads to the roaring sound. The sound usually is evident during or immediately after exercise. A test which can often give indication of a roarer is a quick jab in the ribs of an unsuspecting horse. If

Before understanding the treatment for sprains and strains, one first must comprehend the anatomical processes which occur in sequence immediately following injury. The first thing that happens is the animal feels pain, which serves two vital purposes: it keeps the horse from manipulating and perhaps further injuring the muscle/joint, and increases the amount of blood flowing to the affected area.

Blood flows to the injury faster than it leaves, resulting in a surplus that builds, producing two other recognizable signs: heat and swelling. If the sprain is minor, often these natural processes of forced rest, heat and increased circulation — bringing white blood cells to the site — will cure the injury after a few days. There are steps a horseman can take, however, to make the horse's convalescence more tolerable.

The first of these is to reduce the flow of blood to the injury. This requires constriction of the blood vessels, brought about through application of cold. If out on the trail when the sprain occurs, bathe the affected area in a stream or cool pond. If back at the barn, run cold water over the area from a hose, or apply ice wrapped in a towel or other cloth material. This action, by reducing the blood flow, keeps swelling down and relieves pain.

After an appropriate period of cold therapy, it's wise to take the opposite tack: applying heat and massage to the area. Heat, in the form of liniment, will open the blood vessels and allow more blood to reach the affected part. Massage aids in increasing circulation, thus speeding flow of the blood's necessary ingredients to and from the site. Make sure the three to five-minute massage isn't too vigorous; the horse will react adversely from pain!

Sometimes bandaging helps to immobilize the joint further. Most horsemen use two long strips of absorbent cotton wadding, applied separately, followed by bedsheet strips or one of the commercially available bandages. Apply the first layer of cotton loosely, the second with just light pressure, then the outer bandage just snugly. Don't tighten too much or not enough blood will reach the site to promote rapid healing.

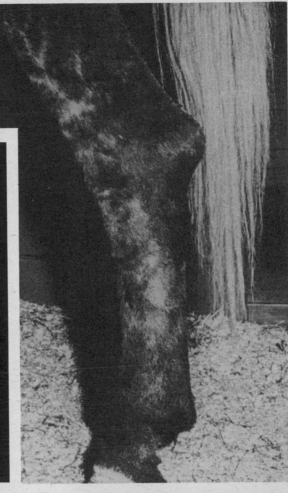

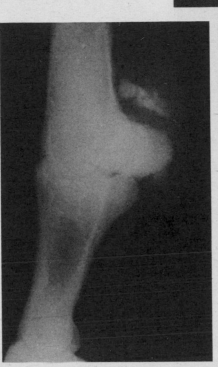

Fractured sesamoid, shown clearly in X-ray photo, much resembles the capped hock at far right. The proper diagnosis is of utmost importance.

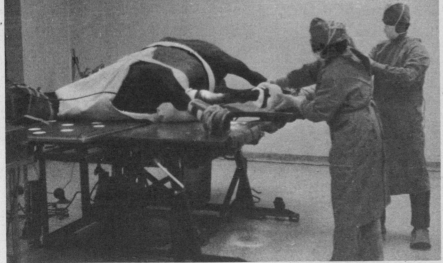

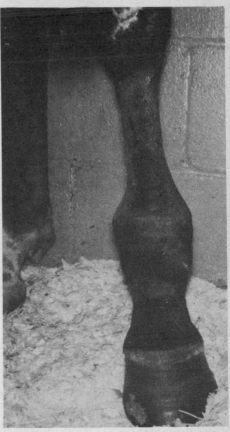

Surgery to repair fracture is expensive and usually limited to horses of great value (above). Following surgical repair, most are limited to work in the stud or brood mare band. Enlargement of fetlock denotes trouble, here osselets (right).

In extreme cases, a plaster or fiberglass cast may be required to totally immobilize the joint or muscle. Application of such a cast requires skills normally beyond the casual horseman and are best left to a veterinary surgeon.

The types of strains or sprains to be discussed herewith include sore shins (bucked shins), carpitis (sore or popped knee), bog spavin, capped hock, capped elbow and tendinitis. It will be helpful to refer to the sketches showing internal configurations of bones and muscles making up the horse's legs.

Looking first at sore shins, this malady doesn't often befall pleasure or work horses used for Western equitation, striking mostly young thoroughbred or quarter horses used for racing.

Most common in the front legs, sore or bucked shins is an inflammation of the connective tissue at the front of the large metacarpal (cannon) bone, marked by swelling, pain and lameness. It is caused by concussion of leg striking the ground in racing, although the connective tissue, called the periosteum, can be stretched or torn by other strenuous activity not confined to the flat tracks.

When a horse shows the signs of sore shins, there is no recourse but to remove him from training or work. Application of cold packs may reduce the swelling and relieve pain. The horse should remain laid up until all signs of lameness have disappeared, then be brought back to work gradually. The rest period, depending upon severity of the condition, may sometimes last several months.

Carpitis, better known as sore or popped knee, is a common physical ailment around racetracks. It takes the form of an acute or chronic inflammation of the joint capsule of the knee and, in old cases, there sometimes is a spur or bony outgrowth present.

The cause appears to be concussion during hard training and horses not in peak condition sometimes break down with the malady. The horse will exhibit immediate signs of lameness and the knee swells. A veterinarian has to check for fractures in the knee, as often the symptoms are identical.

Rest is essential for a horse with carpitis. Like football players who develop water on the knee, removal of excess fluids in the joint may reduce the pain and this generally is followed by injection of cortisone or phenylbutazone, both procedures best left to a veterinary surgeon. He can't undo all the damage, however, and the knee never will be totally sound again.

Bog spavins are found on the hocks of a horse, being caused by faulty conformation, rickets or strain. It is characterized by distention of the capsule at the front of the hock joint, although the sides of the joint may also be involved. Unless the bones of the hock are affected, there usually is no hindrance on performance, although the bump remains visible. A veterinarian, depending upon the size of the spavin and its effect on the hock, may aspirate the accumulated fluids and inject muscle relaxants into the joint.

A capped hock is another injury-caused disability, affecting the rear of the horse's hock and characterized by a bulbous protrusion which normally is the result of reclining on hard floors, a kick, bumping the tailgate of a horse trailer, or a fall. It rarely causes lameness. If untreated, the bump may become fibrous and hard, to remain forever as a blemish which would detract from sale value.

Treatment of a capped hock is comprised of applications of a paint or liniment, which a veterinarian will prescribe. It's far better to remove the cause of capped hocks, though, through proper bedding, separation of horses showing physical dislike for one another, assuring adequate distance between the rump chain in a trailer and the tailgate, and removing obstacles which could lead to a fall in the barn area.

A capped elbow is much the same as a capped hock, the distinguishing feature being the area involved. Often called a shoe boil because it resembles a boil and is caused sometimes by brushing the elbow with a horseshoe when the horse is reclining, a capped elbow has a bulbous swelling which is more unsightly than serious. In fact, many veterinarians prefer not to treat a capped elbow, since the majority heal themselves in time.

Other causes of capped elbow are the horse assuming an unnatural position while resting in a stall, caused by the stall being too narrow, or having let the heels grow too long. A deep bed is the best prevention for capped elbow. Other corrective measures should be undertaken.

If a horse develops tendinitis, or bowed tendons, the horseowner has just lost a riding companion for about a year. Tendinitis is caused by exceptionally hard work on muddy, rough or hard ground, by beginning work too early with an immature horse, poor shoeing or, in some cases, conformation defects.

Tendinitis is an inflammation of the flexor tendons, the suspensory ligament or the check ligament, usually occurring in the foreleg, which generally shows up during hard work. The horse will be severely lame and stand pointing his toe to relieve pressure on the affected tendons. The affected area will be hot, swells rapidly and be painful to the touch. If caught in time, the ailment can be treated with good results before the tendon becomes fibrous or thick — the true bowed tendon.

The first step of treatment is to give the horse absolute rest and the inflammation should be treated with ice packs to reduce the swelling and pain. The affected tendons may be injected with a pain killer and the veterinary surgeon may opt to cast the limb in plaster or fiberglass.

When the cast is removed, bandages are applied for another month. When removed, the horse is rested for at least a year, after which time he is brought back to work with the utmost care. If the injury tends to be chronic in nature, it's doubtful the horse ever will be useful for hard work again.

The best prevention method is removal of the cause, that of working a horse too hard under adverse conditions or starting a horse working at too early an age. Naturally, if bowed tendons are apparent upon inspection of a horse prior to purchase, the animal should be overlooked.

SUNSTROKE

Actually, sunstroke is broken down into three separate categories including heatstroke, heat exhaustion and heat cramps, all of which are serious to the welfare of the horse. Similar to the afflictions of man, all three disrupt the heat-regulating mechanism inside the body.

Heatstroke is probably the most serious of the three and requires fast action to stave off death. Symptoms are abnormally rapid or deep breathing, the eyes may become glassy and staring, the rectal temperature hits nearly 110 degrees and the horse may collapse.

The best treatment is to immediately attempt to bring body temperature down, although not too fast. Cold water should be applied to the body, cold water enemas may be given and ice packs may be used around the brain. Temperature at the rectum should be taken at least once every five minutes and, if the temperature is dropping quickly, suspend ice pack and cold water therapy temporarily, then resume. If treatment isn't begun immediately, death results quickly.

Heat exhaustion, often called heat prostration, generally occurs following long periods of exposure to extremely hot, humid conditions, which causes the blood vessels to dilate or expand. Unless this dilation is followed by an appropriate increase in the volume of blood passing through the veins, the veins may collapse. Activity only aggravates this already serious condition.

Signs of heat exhaustion are characterized by rapid pulse, increased respiratory rate and/or deep breathing, muscular tremors and weakness. The horse doesn't usually have an increased body temperature at the outset, but it will rise if treatment isn't begun.

Just as with human heat-exhaustion victims, a horse should be moved to a shady spot and cold water should be given, if the horse will take it, in small amounts frequently offered. If a veterinarian is close-by, he may attempt intravenous introduction of a physiological saline solution. Because the circulatory system already is functioning abnormally or is impaired, he may opt to forego this procedure, however.

Heat cramps usually are the result of extended working periods in hot weather, which cause an electrolyte imbalance from the loss of too much salt through perspiration.

Generally the first sign of something amiss is the horse will stop sweating. He may then suffer muscle spasms. The horseman should immediately stop working, remove tack from the animal and try to replace the lost salt through offerings of cool water mixed with salt. It sometimes is given via stomach tube and, unless salt loss is overt, the horse usually will recover with rest.

As a horseman can't as yet control the environmental conditions of humidity and heat — unless he invests in an air-conditioned barn — there is little he can do to prevent heat exhaustion. As heatstroke seems partially tied to ventilation, he should assure the latter is adequate for his stable. Heat cramps can be avoided by using common sense when working in extremely hot, muggy weather; frequent rest stops are in order, as is the offering of salt and limited amounts of water during such breaks.

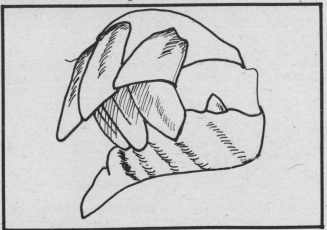

A parrot-mouthed horse should be avoided whenever possible, since it's a serious defect. They have great difficulty in grazing, nutrition problems, too.

TEETH CARE

It's not surprising that a horse's teeth play an important part in his overall health and his teeth should be examined at least once per year for abnormalities and/or corrective dentistry.

Except under rare circumstances, horses don't suffer from cavities, although they may have toothaches. In such cases, the tooth generally is extracted. But a much more common malady comes from sharp protrusions forming on the teeth through regular chewing which requires "floating" the teeth.

As a horse chews, or masticates, he gradually wears the surface of his teeth away. Unless the teeth grate perfectly atop one another during this process, not all of the teeth surfaces will be worn down uniformly, resulting in ridges on the inside portions of the teeth, next to the tongue. This causes discomfort and even injury to the tongue or gums, which can make a horse go off his feed or bolt it without thorough mastication, sometimes leading to impaction colic.

Teeth problems can be suspected when a horse will shun hard grain or, when munching grain, tends to open his mouth and let the granules drop out. While it also can be indicative of a greedy eater, horses with teeth problems sometimes bolt their grain, which will show by examination of the droppings. Too, if he eats exceptionally slowly he may suffer from teeth problems that need correction.

When eating roughage, horses needing dental attention sometimes will "quid" their feed, or partially masticate it then let it fall to the ground. Other horses sometimes will pack it in the side of the mouth instead of swallowing.

Floating a horse's teeth is an easy procedure for a veterinarian, who uses a special rasp and files down the protrusions. If a tooth is bad, it usually is pulled.

Teeth problems of a more serious nature are caused by conformation defects, two of which are parrot or salmon-mouthed horses. In the former, the upper jaw doesn't align with the lower in front — the horse has an overbite — which makes grazing difficult if not impossible. In the case of the salmon-mouthed horse, the lower jaw protrudes beyond the upper, resulting in underbite. As these defects can be inherited, it's wise to refrain from breeding animals with such defects.

THUMPS

Thumps are characterized by spasms of the diaphragm, which are regarded as the equine form of hiccoughs by some horsemen. Sometimes a distinct thumping sound will be heard, hence the name, and thumps are caused by strenuous exertion by unfit horses during hot weather.

If a horse develops thumps, the best treatment is through immediate rest. The horseman can sponge the body with cool water and, when the thumping subsides, the horse is returned to the barn. Water should be offered frequently, given in small amounts to avoid the possibility of founder, until all thumping ceases.

The best way to avoid thumps is to have a horse in proper condition before subjecting him to strenuous exercise. Also, use common sense when working under extreme temperatures: Horses don't like hard work in the hot sun anymore than does the horseman.

TYING UP

Myositis in horses often is confused with azoturia because many of the symptoms are the same. However, this muscular disorder generally strikes horses that are in service every day, without the rest period/full feeding which causes azoturia.

The initial signs of myositis are the same as for azoturia: increased respiratory rate, sweating, dark-colored urine and muscle stiffness in the hindquarters. But unlike azoturia, it is recommended to keep the animal moving, even if pain is apparent. Converse to azoturia, in which continued movement results in the horse going down, forced movement when afflicted by myositis seems to clear the condition. He should be removed to the barn and rested. Administration of vitamin E and selenium seems to produce favorable results. Bring the horse back to work cautiously.

There are other internal disorders a horse can suffer, but this has been an attempt to cover some of the most frequently encountered ailments. As outlined at the beginning of this section and elsewhere, always structure therapy around the instructions of your veterinarian. He is familiar with specific conditions as they exist relative to your horse, which can lead to a different diagnosis and necessitate treatment alteration.

C: EXTERNAL DISORDERS

On the average, more damage occurs to the outside of a horse than the inside and in this section we will describe various physical maladies incurred externally by horses. As mentioned at the outset of this chapter, there is much cross-over of disorders into more than one category and, with this in mind, this section will deal with fistula of the withers; poll evil; allergies (photosensitization, nettle rash); wounds; acne (pyoderma); hidebound; dandruff; burns; saddle sores; and warts.

SADDLE SORES

Saddle sores can lead to a myriad of serious problems, including internal tissue destruction, unless treated early.

Saddle sores are caused by an ill-fitting saddle, which irritates one or both sides of the backbone. Unless the ailment is treated and the cause of injury removed, saddle sores progress in severity and finally require lay-up of the horse for an extended period.

Prospective saddle sores should be detected when grooming after a ride. The site is tender and the horse usually will exhibit signs of pain when the region is brushed or massaged. The hair follicles may be inflamed, although this is difficult to observe on most horses.

If a saddle sore is noticed early, applications of ice and later warm packs usually will relieve the irritation, provided the horse is rested during the process. If the sore is ignored, it will worsen and become a "gall" — a raw, open lesion. If the sore isn't treated at this stage, oftentimes hemorrhage occurs beneath the skin, causing swelling, heat and obvious pain. The skin sometimes will rupture and fluids will drain, which leaves the horse open to secondary infection. Untreated, the tissue may begin to die beneath the area or a

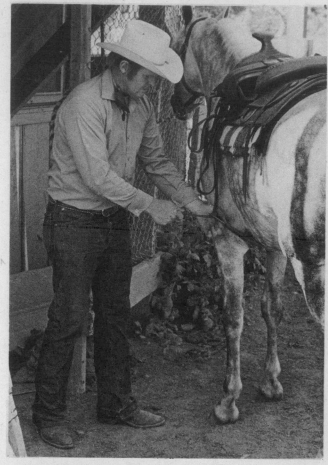

Saddle sores, as noted in the text, are caused usually by an ill-fitting saddle and should be detected upon after-ride grooming. When noticed, begin treatment outlined.

There is some feeling that fistula and brucellosis syndromes/may be related, the latter striking cattle. Horses should be segregated from cattle with disease.

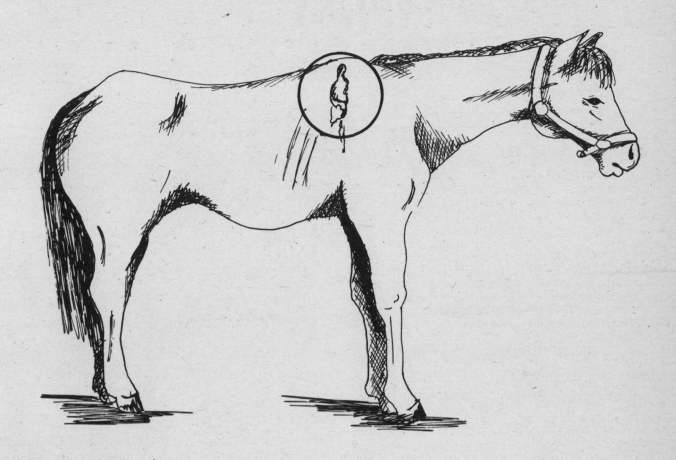

Fistula of the withers results from a variety of causes, most of which horsemen can remove. The wither area swells and later ruptures, then drains as tissues die.

scar will develop. And if the wound becomes infected, the condition could terminate in death through tetanus or other bacteria.

There is no excuse for failing to notice a saddle sore, as the horse will give all the clues necessary. He will exhibit pain when the horseman touches the sore, even if not yet visible. As the condition worsens the horse will perform erratically when ridden, because of the pain. The lesion then will become hairless and can't be overlooked.

Treatment calls for complete rest, daily applications of antiseptic ointment following cleansing of the wound with physiological saline solution. If the sore is a gall, daily treatment with saline solution will aid in hardening the surface. Keep insects away from the horse during recovery.

It is essential that each horseman match his tack to the animal to avoid this problem and others yet to be discussed. Only by so doing can be expect the maximum performance from his mount and the pleasurable experience horseback riding is supposed to be.

FISTULA OF THE WITHERS

This serious condition incapacitates a horse for extended periods, sometimes causing death. Its origin is disputable; some veterinary surgeons feel it arises from a bump or bite

at the withers, while others are exploring the possibility it might be caused by bacteria or an internal parasite.

Let's first examine the plausible explanation that fistulous withers is caused through a bump, bite or fall. It's understandable that the withers are affected more than any other part of the body because of its unique structure. It's here where the vertebrae of the spine reach their highest level, forming a hump that can contact a low roof, corral fence or rocks when the horse rolls.

Fistula of the withers begins when the tissue bruises, causing inflammation. Because the tissue is of relatively low order on the healing scale, it sometimes breaks down and a hollow cavity filled with pus forms. Swelling occurs on both sides of the withers and, in rapidly developing cases, the withers will be hot and cause the horse pain when touched.

Eventually, this swelling terminates in an eruption at the withers, whereupon pus or other exudate drains. The destruction process continues, involving other interior areas, with tendon sheaths or membranes acting as "pipes" for the transfer of fluids to the surface for draining. This arrangement of pipes is where fistula gets its name: defined, fistula means an abnormal passage, hollow like a reed or pipe, from one abscess or hollow organ to the body surface.

The skeletal structure of the horse clearly shows how easily bone and spinal cord becomes involved in fistula cases. The result of fistulous condition usually is death.

As the situation deteriorates, bone may become affected in the destructive process with death as a consequence. Blood poisoning also causes its share of deaths in these cases, as does paralysis if the tissue and bone destruction reaches the spinal cord. Horses deeply involved generally are put down humanely by the veterinarian.

A theory advanced by other veterinary scholars is that fistulous withers may be caused by a bacteria, *Brucella abortus,* or an internal parasite, *Actinomyces bovis.* This theory is based upon the positive reactions to brucellosis agglutination tests of horses with fistulous withers, and isolation of *Br. abortus* in fluid aspirated from the withers prior to rupture. Also, *A. bovis* has been regularly discovered in the infected connective-tissue wall. In tests, injection of only one member of this team has failed to produce the

fistulous symptoms, although simultaneous injection of both has resulted in the characteristic signs.

Adding strength to the theory of bacterial or parasitic passage of fistula are findings that cattle infections both with *Br. abortus* and *A. bovis* occurred concurrently with the condition in horses, and outbreaks of brucellosis in cattle followed contact with horses having open fistulous lesions.

However it is contracted, it's not good news for horse or horseman. If noticed early in development, the horseowner can cool the withers with water or ice packs three times daily, which tends to reduce the swelling and heat. If this fails to check continuation, the only hope is surgery; remission is virtually nil.

Several days before operating, the veterinary surgeon

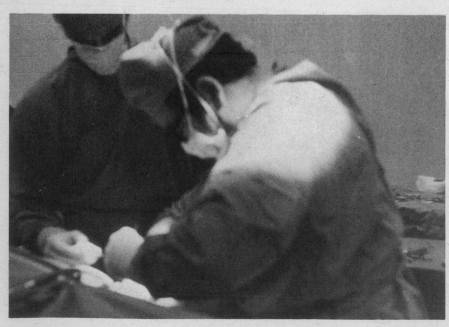

Surgery to remove any dead bone and necrotic tissue can be disappointing. It's much sounder to remove the cause!

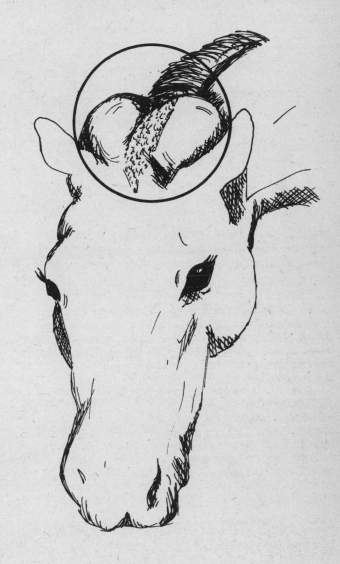

Poll evil differs from fistula of the withers only in how fast a horse dies; closer proximity to brain and the spinal cord speeds the conclusion of the disorder.

will begin antibiotic therapy with streptomycin or the like. On the operating table, he will remove all dead and diseased tissue and bone, then continue treating the area with sulfa-based drugs. If lucky, the destruction will be halted.

One big problem with treating fistula of the withers is expense: Even if caught early, the veterinary attention required over the long course will exceed the horse's value. Too, results of surgery can be disappointing; such a horse generally has little further working value.

POLL EVIL

The poll is the second region most often affected by fistula, perhaps caused by a blow, bacteria/internal parasite, or a tight-fitting halter. The only great distinguishing feature between poll evil and fistula of the withers is that the former usually leads to a quicker termination in death through close proximity to the brain and spinal cord.

If the true cause of this fistulous syndrome is an internal parasite or bacteria, only sound stable management can prevent it. This includes keeping the horse away from cattle suffering from either infection. If the cause is a blow of some type, eliminate all likely causes of such. This should be extended to horses, also. One particular animal in the herd may be biting others on the withers or poll.

Remove all likely structures which could result in a blow to the withers or poll, and assure proper halter fit. It can save a great deal in the long run.

ALLERGIES

Horses seem more fortunate than other four-legged critters in that they aren't affected too often by allergies. The most frequently reported type — which isn't seen often — is a condition called photosensitization: allergy to sunlight.

This condition isn't a natural phenomenon. Rather, it affects horses that have impaired liver function, perhaps caused by the ingestion of plants like St. John's wart or buckwheat. It generally affects only nonpigmented areas of the body and at first resembles sunburn. If the horse remains in sunlight, the white areas of the body will swell,

then become cracked and dry. Continued exposure to the sun's rays will lead to necrosis of the tissues involved; these will be sloughed off.

If the condition is noted early, the nonpigmented areas should be cleaned and a salve administered. The horse should be kept out of the sunlight. A veterinarian will treat advanced cases with antihistamines, which seem to clear the liver condition and the horse will recover, if kept in the shade. Once total recovery is effected, keep horses off pasture containing St. John's wart or buckwheat and chance of recurrence is slight.

Nettle rash or hives, scientifically tagged as urticaria, is an allergy caused by a substance to which the horse is allergic, or perhaps by insect bites. It is characterized by welts or plateau-shaped swellings measuring from one-half to as large as eight inches in diameter, appearing on the neck, flanks, back, legs and eyelids. They appear suddenly,

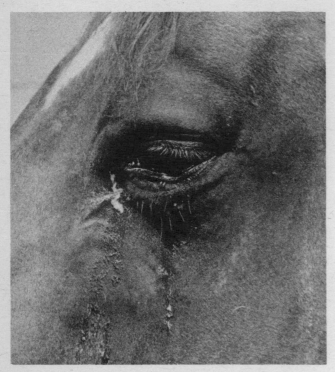

A horse's eyes can tell so much about what's happening on the inside that every horseman should be able to "read" them. In this case, the eye clearly denotes a sick animal.

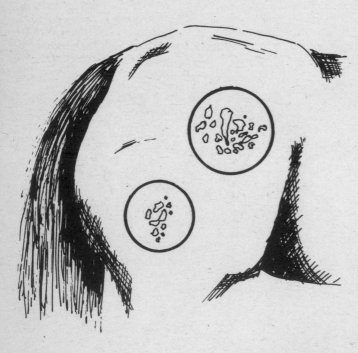

Symptoms of allergic reaction to the environment or parts thereof take differing shapes, such as nettle rash (above). Photosensitization generally affects unpigmented areas.

accompanied by lack of appetite, listlessness and temperature slightly above normal.

After several minutes or hours, the welts disappear just as suddenly as they appeared. Usually no treatment is needed, unless the horse literally is covered with the rash, whereupon antihistamines or the like are given. The symptoms will recur if the cause of this reaction isn't isolated and removed, and there is no simple way of doing this. Just as with a child too young to talk showing an allergic reaction, the horseman must begin a systematic elimination of all items with which the horse came in contact. Start with anything new around the stable which could have led to onset of the symptoms. Initiate a good program of insect control.

WOUNDS

Wounds can be divided into five different categories, depending upon severity: bruise, abrasion, incised, laceration and puncture.

A veterinarian follows a regular course of action when treating a wound, which is sound practice for individual horseowners. This sequence, from beginning to end, is: control the bleeding; relieve pain; prevent shock; control infection; control the patient; and provide supportive care.

A bruise is caused by a bump, fall, kick or other contact that doesn't break the skin. In humans, a bruise is easily recognized by discoloration of the skin, caused by excess accumulation of blood. Many times the bruise is indistinguishable in horses because of his coat or coloration.

If a bruise is minor in scope, no treatment is necessary; the excess blood will be reabsorbed into the surrounding tissues in time. If the horse has a bad bruise that has resulted in the formation of a blood blister, recovery often is slower. In fact, many times a veterinarian will puncture the blister and let the excess blood drain off. The horse then recovers with no ill effects, providing some type of germ-killing agent has been added to the lanced spot.

The second least-serious wound is an abrasion. This occurs when a horse scrapes against a rough surface, usually causing slight bleeding from the capillaries and it's painful. Because the skin has been opened, it should be cleaned gently with a mild disinfectant like physiological saline solution or soap and some type of antiseptic ointment applied. If infection develops, a veterinarian should be consulted as soon as possible.

An incised wound is more serious than either a bruise or abrasion because it constitutes a clean cut into the tissue. The first concern is bleeding, since severing a major artery could cause death if bleeding isn't stopped.

The best way to treat an incised wound bleeding slightly is through application of direct pressure to the wound site. If back at the barn where the first-aid kit is kept, a pressure bandage is best used for this task, pressed firmly over the wound until all bleeding ceases; this takes several minutes. If in the country, the palm of the hand will suffice, applied in the same manner as a pressure bandage.

If a major artery is severed by an incised wound, the situation is more grim. Such occurrence is easily recognized by blood squirting from the wound each time the heart beats. If the blood is bright red, an artery carrying blood from the heart has been cut; if dark red a vein carrying blood back to the heart has been severed.

In either case, immediate attention is required to keep the animal from bleeding to death. Dr. Wayne O. Kester, executive director of the American Association of Equine

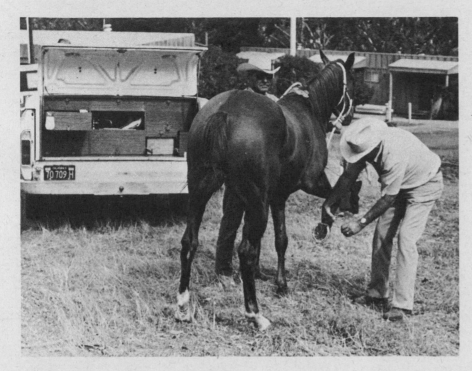

The frog is particularly susceptible to puncture wounds from glass, nails, wire and the like. Here, a veterinarian examines a foot of horse showing signs of lameness in his right foreleg.

Practitioners and one of the most respected veterinary surgeons in the world, never recommends use of a tourniquet in these cases. "There are several reasons for this," says Dr. Kester. "First, the arteries are so placed in a horse's leg that it is difficult to constrict them without extreme pressure. Second, damage to the tendons, ligaments and other underlying tissue is unavoidable, even if the tourniquet is released every five to ten minutes. And third, a tourniquet is painful and a horse will fight it, thus stimulating circulation.

"The best procedure is to place an absorbent patch or wad of gauze, cotton, a bath towel — even a dirty shirt — over the wound and bind it down snugly with some kind of bandage over the wound," continues this eminent authority. "Any absorbent pack bound firmly over the wound and around the leg soon will saturate and cause the blood to clot and back up into the wound for rather prompt control of bleeding. It can be removed in an hour or so and the wound treated properly."

After bleeding has stopped, the injured area should be bandaged properly. Old sheets torn into strips work well, but in emergency any material can be used.

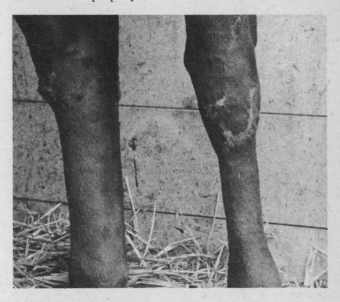

This horse's back legs have been so scarred he no longer can be used in show classes or performance events. The equine nemesis, barbed wire, did the damage here.

*Friday Jacobs and Sal Llamas examine a blunt pipe
that injured horse shown on these two pages. The pipe
entered right at the throatlatch in freak accident, cutting
a jagged hole in horse's windpipe, almost killing him.*

When the bleeding has stopped, the wound site should
be cleaned if dirty, foreign matter removed if present and
an antiseptic ointment daubbed generously on the wound.
A bandage then can be used to keep it clean if in a tenable
position.

The major difference between incised wounds and lacerations is the nature of the cut; the latter is jagged, a tearing
of the tissues rather than sharp separation. The chance for
permanent scarring — development of proud flesh — is
greater with lacerations, which makes proper treatment important.

The first step is to control the bleeding, using the same
practices for incised wounds. The wound then should be
cleaned thoroughly and rinsed with a saline solution, then a
mild antiseptic ointment is applied. The hair surrounding
the wound should be shaved and coated with a substance
like petroleum jelly, which keeps draining fluids from sticking to the hair, irritating the skin. Reapply ointment as
needed, which will repel insects and keep germs from penetrating. If the laceration is severe, consult professional advice. He may decide to stitch the wound closed.

The last category of wounds is punctures, most often
caused by a nail or stiff splinter penetrating the body surface or the foot. A veterinarian should be called immediately and he will administer a tetanus antitoxin to guard
against the growth of *Clostridium tetani* bacteria. He will
shave the site and enlarge the opening to promote better
drainage during recovery.

*Dr. Bob Hunt gives Windy's King a
tetanus injection after suturing the
wound closed. Upon closure, because
of clogged nasal cavity, horse began
suffocating and required tracheotomy.*

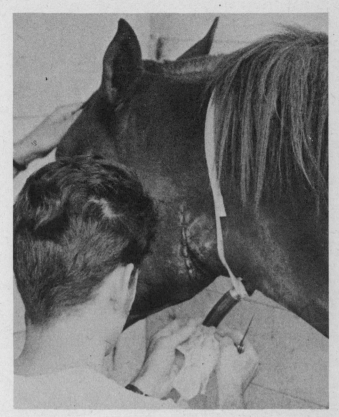

The end of the makeshift tracheotomy tube is covered with a gauze wrapping, to keep the horse from inhaling insects or dirt directly into the lungs for more trouble.

Terri Lester gently comforts the injured horse, which required twenty-eight stitches. One jugular vein was severed but the horse is mending. Note the garden hose used for emergency tracheotomy that's taped to neck.

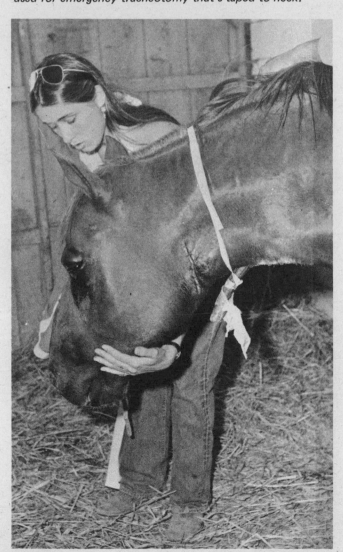

Puncture wounds of the feet can lead to lameness. The nail or splinter shouldn't be removed until the hole can easily be seen. This wound then is packed with iodine or an antiseptic paste, following a thorough cleaning with a disinfectant like hydrogen peroxide to kill existing germs. The affected foot then should be bandaged to keep foreign matter from the wound and a veterinarian will administer a tetanus antitoxin. Other steps may be necessary to prevent lameness, depending upon depth of the puncture.

ACNE

More accurately called pyoderma, this skin disorder usually is caused by the entry of *Staphylococcus aureus, Staphylococcus epidermidis* or *Streptococcus* into the skin, seen initially as inflammation of the hair follicles.

Most often seen around the saddle area of the back, pyoderma manifests itself initially as swelling and extreme sensitivity, followed by the appearance of what look like pimples (hence the colloquial term acne). These pimples may fill with pus and after two or three days rupture and become small cysts, or they may merge into raised welts. If untreated, this condition can worsen until nearly all of the surface skin is involved or underlying tissues become inflamed.

Sometimes, however, this condition will disappear spontaneously after several weeks. If it doesn't and leads to inflammation of other skin layers, treatment is difficult and best left to a veterinarian, who should have been called upon first notice of the disorder.

HIDEBOUND

When healthy, it is possible to pull a horse's skin and it will stretch, as with a dog. When a horse is hidebound, the skin is taut.

A hidebound condition usually is the result of improper feeding, lack of nutrients, a digestive disorder or lack of condition, characterized by tightly drawn skin over all portions of the body. The ribs usually will be visible because fatty tissue between bone and skin isn't present.

The first course of action is determination of the cause. Once isolated and corrected, the horse will return to normal, aided through addition of high protein supplements to his feed.

DANDRUFF

This condition usually is the result of improper grooming or poor diet, but also can indicate high parasite load or digestive upset. It is characterized by flaky, scaly skin, similar to the human condition.

The best treatment for dandruff, which is more unsightly than serious, is through elimination of the cause. Proper diet, good grooming and efficient parasite control are important. Clearing the condition can be hastened through addition of generous amounts of linseed meal to the feed.

BURNS

Though infrequent, horses do suffer from burns and these command the attention of a veterinarian. They can be caused by chemicals, steam, flames or contact with hot

When riding through brushy terrain, keep on the lookout for partially hidden obstacles like downed logs or sharp tree limbs (below left). The horse could stumble and fall or receive a nasty wound, the last thing desired when away from the barn! Upon completion of the ride, the horse is groomed thoroughly (below right). At this time, check for sores or any injuries.

 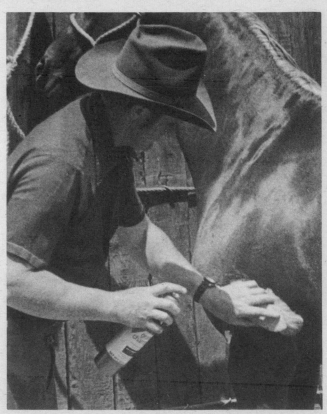

surfaces and the prognosis depends upon severity of the burns.

Since there is constantly changing thought on the part of veterinary surgeons regarding treatment of even minor burns, we won't offer suggestions which could be outdated as new treatment practices become known. Rather, we suggest contacting a veterinarian at the earliest opportunity and leaving the burn alone. More damage can be done by people with good intentions than had they done nothing. Simply attempt to keep the horse quiet and free from insects until the vet's arrival.

WARTS

These unsightly blemishes, which generally show on the face and nose of the horse, don't usually cause trouble unless they appear at a spot over which tack fits, causing irritation. They are caused by a virus and can spread through a herd in short order.

As with humans, horses sometimes rid themselves of warts in time. If there is more than one horse present, the horse with warts should be isolated to prevent spread. A veterinarian can treat warts, sometimes with good success, with vaccines or external medications.

It's true that horses sometimes suffer from other external disorders not outlined here. In such cases, it is the common and advised practice to call a veterinarian, which should be done when the disorder first is noticed. Oftentimes this can preclude advancement of a minor ailment into a serious, expensive problem.

Besides being a cribber's delight, this wooden barrier poses still another possible source of injury. Like, what happens if something spooks this horse right now? He could possibly slam his chin or jaw on the wood!

Horses, just like humans, are susceptible to warts. In nearly all cases, they disappear on their own. Isolate affected horse to prevent spread of warts.

D: PARASITISM

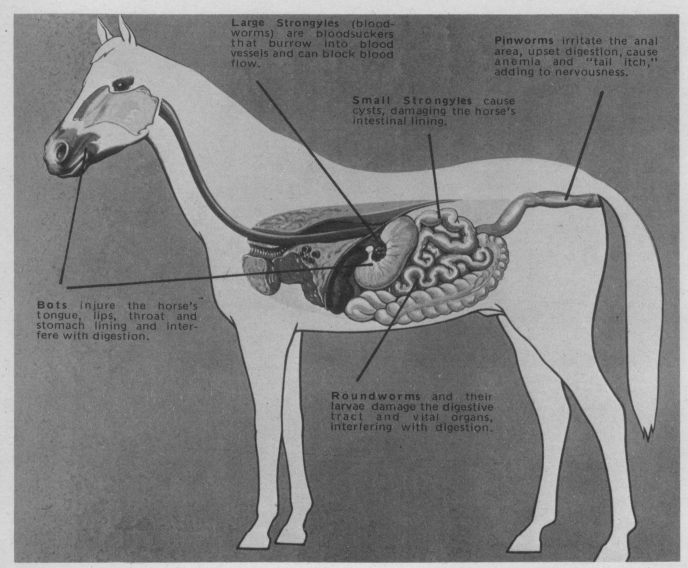

Large Strongyles (bloodworms) are bloodsuckers that burrow into blood vessels and can block blood flow.

Pinworms irritate the anal area, upset digestion, cause anemia and "tail itch," adding to nervousness.

Small Strongyles cause cysts, damaging the horse's intestinal lining.

Bots injure the horse's tongue, lips, throat and stomach lining and interfere with digestion.

Roundworms and their larvae damage the digestive tract and vital organs, interfering with digestion.

The five most common types of internal parasites found in horses, and the area inside the body they favor, are shown in the illustration above. All cause problems, though some of a less severe nature than others, but none are beneficial.

Parasites, by their very natures, are freeloaders. They depend upon a host — in this case, the horse — for survival, but contribute nothing to the horse's welfare. Indeed, the more than 150 different types of parasites which can infect horses do nothing but cause problems, varying in scope from mild annoyance to death.

For ease of classification, parasites are divided into either external or internal types, dependent upon their specific area of involvement. External parasites usually are easier to spot. In fact, many times a horse will appear normal when carrying a high load of the internal "bad names."

Some of the symptoms which can denote internal parasitism are: colic; tail rubbing; anemia; rough coat; lameness; weakness; wasting feed; enlarged, distended abdomen; cough; and emaciation. Since these symptoms also can be indicative of other ailments, a veterinarian will examine feces samples under a microscope, although many internal parasites will be plainly visible in the droppings.

Of the 150-plus parasites which can infect horses, only a handful are seen with any degree of regularity. Internally, these are bots, pinworms, ascarids, large and small strongyles, large and small stomach worms, and tapeworms. Externally, the pests include mites, fleas, mosquitos, lice, gnats, ticks, ringworm, houseflies, stable flies, horseflies and blowflies. Treatment procedures for both will be covered at the end of each respective section.

Internal

LARGE STRONGYLES

As outlined in the section dealing with colic, strongyles are perhaps the most serious of all internal parasites — they can cause death of the host. Often called bloodworms or redworms, there are three major groupings of strongyles: *Strongylus vulgaris, Strongylus edentatus* and *Strongylus equinus. S. vulgaris* is the most troublesome.

To recap the history of this parasite which grows from one-half to two inches long at maturity, a host defecates manure containing eggs in a pasture. Under favorable conditions, the eggs hatch some seven days later and the worms feed on the manure. If the surrounding grass is wet, the worms slither up blades of grass and gain entry to the horse's digestive system as the horse grazes on the contaminated pasture.

Inside, the immature worms migrate extensively throughout the horse's system, to the lungs, heart, liver and pancreas, among others, causing severe damage by burrowing into the wall of the small arteries, or disrupting the flow of blood through large arteries to the intestines. When nearing maturity the worms migrate back to the large intestine, cecum or colon, where the female lays thousands of eggs. These are passed with the feces and the life cycle begins anew.

It's safe to suspect large strongyle infestation if a horse is anemic, performs poorly, is weak or emaciated and has diarrhea. Strongyle infestation can set up a horse for colic, due to impaired blood flow to the intestinal area. If sufficient blockage of arterial blood flow to the intestines or other organs is attained, a horse can die quickly from shock. Heavy infestation in a young horse can lead to stunted growth. Lameness has been encountered through interference of the circulatory system.

SMALL STRONGYLES

Small strongyles, of which there are many types, don't provoke the problems of their larger relative, apparently because they don't migrate but collect in the colon and cecum after maturing in the intestine. They don't suck blood, but one species, *Triodontophorus tenuicollis,* can produce severe ulcers in the colon wall.

PINWORMS

Oxyuris equi causes severe discomfort, more than serious damage. These are small, whitish-colored worms that concentrate in the colon, cecum and rectum of a horse. The females lay eggs that are passed with the feces, but sometimes crawl out of the anus and deposit their eggs near the rectum. The latter causes intense itching, which a horse tries to relieve by rubbing on fence posts or the like. The eggs fall to the ground whereupon they again are ingested

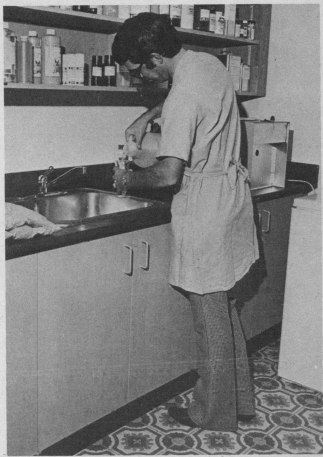

Research and development in the laboratory have given us the tools to fight internal parasites, though none are one hundred percent effective. Use them as directed.

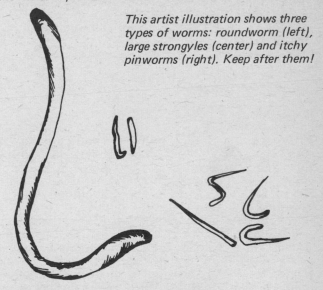

This artist illustration shows three types of worms: roundworm (left), large strongyles (center) and itchy pinworms (right). Keep after them!

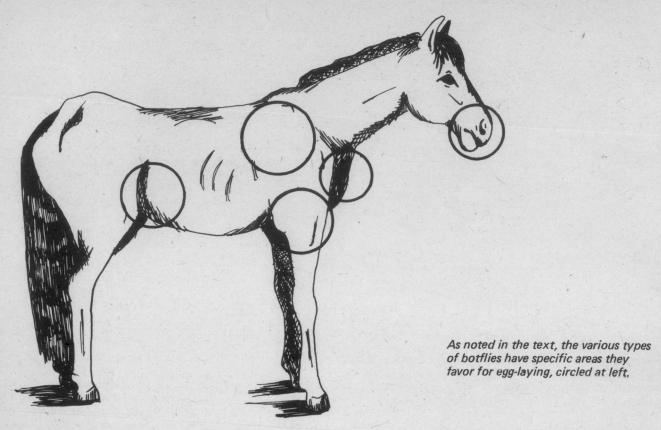

As noted in the text, the various types of botflies have specific areas they favor for egg-laying, circled at left.

by the horse before they hatch and the cycle starts over again.

Pinworms often can be seen in the droppings of a horse heavily infested, but more often the signs are constant rubbing of the buttocks on stationary objects. This leads to poor hair growth or, if rubbing is frequent, secondary infection may develop. There are medications which can control pinworms which will be discussed later.

ASCARIDS

Parascaris equorum has a gruesome-sounding life cycle, affecting young horses from foal age to nearly 4 or 5 years of age. A young horse ingests the roundworm eggs, which can survive for several months on contaminated soil, whereupon the eggs hatch in the small intestine. Roundworms, which measure up to fifteen inches at maturity, nearly half an inch thick, then penetrate the intestinal wall and migrate to the liver, heart, then the lungs.

They remain at this location for a week or so, whereupon they migrate in the bloodstream to the windpipe. They either crawl or are coughed up the esophagus to the pharnyx, then are reswallowed. They develop to maturity in the small intestine, where the female lays eggs that are passed with feces, completing the cycle and starting it again.

Migration of these large worms can cause damage to the liver, heart and lungs, even impairing circulation or causing impaction of a foal's small intestine. They can be suspected in young horses showing respiratory difficulty, lack of energy, digestive disturbance or unthriftiness.

BOTS

Bots are not worms, but are the larvae of the botfly. There are three types of bots to which the horse is susceptible: *Gasterophilus intestinalis,* the common bot; *Gasterophilus nasalis,* the throat bot; and *Gasterophilus haemorrhoidalis,* the nose or lip bot.

Rotational pasture system is beneficial in reducing quantity of parasites in a horse's system. This kills eggs, larvae.

The botfly much resembles a bee (above) and is most persistent in laying eggs. Since they don't feed, usage of poison baits or repellents generally is ineffective.

After the eggs hatch and make way into horse's mouth, the bot larvae remain until passing to the stomach and attaching to intestinal wall (above). Pits lead to infection.

The botfly is a specialized critter that exists solely for reproduction, dying when nutrients carried over from the larval stage are exhausted, usually in about two weeks. During that two-week flight period, the botfly lays numerous eggs on the hairs of a horse. The common bot glues its eggs primarily to the hairs of the forelegs and shoulders, where they will hatch in about a week if stimulated by the horse's licking or rubbing. The nose or lip bot glues its eggs to the hairs of the lips. After a couple of days, the larvae hatch without stimulation and crawl into the mouth. The throat bot glues its eggs to the hairs beneath the muzzle, which hatch a week later with no stimulation. They crawl up the hairs and into the mouth.

Once the larvae enter the mouth, they attach to the mucous membranes or around the molars and remain for about a month. They then are swallowed and attach to the stomach lining where they remain for eight to ten months before passing out in the feces. They pupate in the soil for approximately a month and emerge as the botfly to start the whole procedure again.

Botflies are most prevalent during late Summer or early Fall in most areas of the country before the first frost kills the flies. In some arid regions, botfly activity subsides during hot summer months, appearing in early Spring and again in the Fall.

While the botfly doesn't sting a horse when laying eggs, the perennial buzzing has been known to cause horses to run blindly in an effort to escape the pests. Internally, bots create digestive disturbance, robbing a horse of nutritional value and scar or pit the lining of the stomach. This pitting can lead to bacterial invasion, creating other problems.

LARGE STOMACH WORMS

This *Habronema* family of worms can cause both internal and external damage. The three main types which infect a horse internally are *Habronema muscae, Habronema microstoma* and *Draschia megastoma,* the latter causing the most severe problems, including swelling of the stomach wall and colic.

Eggs are passed in the manure of an infected horse, which then are ingested by stable or houseflies feeding on the feces. The eggs then are passed to horses when the flies feed on the horse's lips, or from ingestion of an unwary fly by the horse. They then hatch and attack the mucous mem-

branes of the intestines or, as noted, the stomach wall. Reaching maturity, females lay eggs which are passed in the feces and here we go again!

When the worms have hatched, their affection for mucosal linings leads to inflammation which causes digestive upset and even colic. The *Draschia megastoma* worm infects the stomach wall and tumor-like enlargements, filled with worms and dead tissue, result. This naturally leads to digestive upset.

The *D. megastoma* culprit also is guilty of causing external trouble, often called summer sores. A horse has some type of skin abrasion or cut. Stable or houseflies which have ingested large stomach worm eggs while feeding on contaminated manure feed at the wound site, in the process re-depositing the worm eggs. When the eggs hatch, the larvae burrow into the open sore, irritating the wound and protracting healing. Small, round granules appear in the

One species of large stomach worm infests open sores and causes condition known as summer sores. This can lead to more servere problems so cover all open sores.

A foal wormer such as this offering from Top Form can be effective in controlling ascarids and other parasites. Use only as directed, or the poison could kill the foal.

wound, which resemble scar tissue. Treatment to date has not been too effective; granulations usually require cauterization following surgery for removal.

SMALL STOMACH WORMS

Not much study has yet been devoted to this *Trichostrongylus axei* worm, or to the damage it does. However, enough is known to recommend that horses don't get them!

The small stomach worm causes a chronic inflammation of the intestinal mucous membranes which leads to digestive upset, pain and lack of condition. It can cause congestion of the stomach, as the afflicted mucous membranes exude a variable amount of mucus.

TAPEWORM

Scientists know that three different types of tapeworms affect horses, but little else about them. The guilty species are *Anoplocephala magna, Anoplocephala perfoliata* and *Paranoplocephala mamillana. A. perfoliata* usually is found in the cecum and only occasionally in the small intestine, home of the other two parasites.

If infestation with tapeworms is light, the horseowner may not even suspect anything is out of whack. But if the horse is heavily infested, there can be digestive disturbance, anemia and even emaciation as the worms rob the horse of needed nutrients.

This is about the extent of knowledge of tapeworms in horses, but research is continuing. Hopefully, treatment methods will be isolated that prove totally effective in dealing with this parasite.

TREATMENT

Since man has so long equated solutions to problems in terms of what it will cost in dollars and cents, it's a wonder there still are internal parasites to hinder horses. Destroying worms through the methods to be outlined here, everywhere in the world, at first glance seems monetarily and logistically impossible. However, when the cost of this global effort is measured against what the average horseowner spends for veterinary treatment, dollar loss through waste of food, purchase of worming compounds, dollar loss through worm-caused equine fatalities, and cost of compounds for post-worming treatment, it would be cheaper in the long run. A world-wide effort of this nature shouldn't meet opposition from pharmaceutical houses. While their long-range business would be gone, they would make enough money during the course of the program to make even the Arabian oil sheiks look like paupers!

However, a program of this nature never will be contemplated, let alone initiated, so it will remain the horseman's chore to control his horses' individual worm problems. Toward that end, researchers have developed compounds

Wormers designed for addition to horse's feed must be tasty or the animal won't eat it. Apple-flavored wormer has had good equine results.

which kill internal parasites and these are called anthelmintics. The better-known compounds are piperazine, dichlorvos, trichlorfon, phenothiazine, thiabendazole, carbon disulfide, pyrantel tartrate and combinations of these.

The term, "broad spectrum," often is associated with various brands of horse wormers, which means the ingredients are active against more than one species of parasite. This saves time and money for the horseman, not having to purchase several wormers to administer at different times.

There are several ways of administering anthelmintics and it is imperative the horseowner follow manufacturer's directions explicitly. One of the most effective ways of worming a horse is through use of a stomach tube, a long, rubber, hose-like implement that is inserted into the throat through the nasal cavity, where the solution is deposited. This ensures all of the medicine reaching the stomach at one time, which leads to improved efficacy.

Another popular administration method is a dose syringe, which usually is filled with the proper amount of worming compound to doctor a horse needing attention. This is placed in the corner of the horse's mouth and the contents are discharged on the animals' tongue, which he swallows (hopefully!). This method demands that the compound be palatable to horses, usually through some type of molasses-flavored base. It's safe and effective, providing the proper amount is administered.

Sometimes capsules, called tabs or boluses, are used for worming. These resemble large pills which are inserted into the horse's mouth and passed to the stomach by swallowing. The bolus has a pre-measured dose of anthelmintic which gets right down to work.

The final worming method is perhaps the easiest, but also requires a great deal of care. This entails sprinkling the worming compound on the feed, which the horse ingests when eating. Using packaged wormers of this type is by far the easiest and cleanest method of administration, but a wormer of this type has possible flaws: It must taste good or the horse isn't going to eat it. Too, it must have a wide safety margin in the event a horse takes in too much of the compound.

Which brings us back to label directions: Worming compounds contain some type of poison which, if taken in great quantities, can kill the horse along with the worms! Most are administered according to body weight; the heavier a horse, the more wormer he's given.

In addition to describing how much of the compound to use, package instructions will also inform the horseowner under what conditions he should not use that product. For example, many anthelmintic manufacturers flatly state a wormer shouldn't be administered if a horse is suffering from diarrhea, severe constipation, shows symptoms of colic, shows symptoms of heaves or other respiratory ailments, has blood poisoning, has an infectious disease of some type, is severely debilitated or under veterinary treatment with tranquilizers, muscle relaxants, medications for the central nervous system or insecticides. Take time to thoroughly read and understand all label directions, then follow them!

Looking at the parasites involved, we will list the individual compounds which have proven effective in killing them. Therefore, when a horseman has determined the types of parasites infecting his horse, he should check for the appropriate compounds within the wormers on a dealer's shelf.

Large and small strongyles are knocked by thiabenda-zole, pyrantel tartrate, dichlorvos, phenothiazine (when combined with other drugs), dyrex, neguvon, dizan and parvex plus. Because of the migrating habit of strongyles, the horse should be wormed every two months.

Pinworms, the itch in the rear, meet their demise through use of dyrex, pyrantel tartrate, trichlorfon, dichlorvos, thiabendazole, dizan and piperazine/phenothiazine combinations. As horses can be reinfected with pinworms at any time, constant vigilance, accompanied by further anthelmintic administration, may be required to keep the parasite in check.

Ascarids, better known as roundworms, usually are found only in immature horses. Once a horse hits 4 or 5 years of age, he develops some type of immunity to the damaging parasite and rarely requires treatment.

Young horses which contract ascarids are treated with trichlorfon, dichlorvos, dyrex, dizan, parvex, piperazine/phenothiazine combinations, piperazine and pyrantel tartrate. Interestingly, thiabendazole therapy nets poor results against roundworms. Because of the migrating nature of ascarids, it is necessary to worm infected horses regularly, starting at two and one-half to three months of age.

Bots, the larvae of the botfly, aren't wiped out by the majority of anthelmintics heretofore mentioned. A combination of carbon disulfide and piperazine is effective, as is trichlorfon, dyrex and dichlorvos.

As noted in the treatment section on these and following pages, trichlorfon is effective in controlling pesky bots. Since no horse is ever free of worms, repeat as needed.

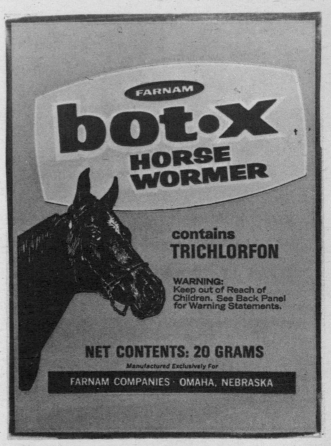

FARNAM
bot·x
HORSE WORMER

contains
TRICHLORFON

WARNING:
Keep out of Reach of
Children. See Back Panel
for Warning Statements.

NET CONTENTS: 20 GRAMS
Manufactured Exclusively For
FARNAM COMPANIES · OMAHA, NEBRASKA

Most veterinarians feel young horses should be wormed at least quarterly for bots and older horses a minimum of twice per year. Because cold weather kills botflies, the horses should be wormed after the first killing frost. Larvae passed in the feces won't pupate and the anthelmintic gets most of the remaining number in the stomach. The worming routine should be repeated at least two months following the fall worming, which will kill the bots migrating from mouth to intestines. The horse then is virtually bot-free during Winter.

An additional word about bots: During peak botfly activity, a horseman should pay particular attention to grooming. Frequent and thorough grooming will remove many of the yellowish-colored eggs which are glued to body hairs. Bots can be artificially hatched by rubbing warm soap suds or warm mineral oil and water (over 105 degrees Fahrenheit) on the affected areas. Thus exposed to the environment, they die before reaching the horse's mouth and sanctuary.

And it's virtually impossible to prevent botflies from attacking horses, if botfly activity is present. Since botflies don't eat, they can't be attracted to poison baits. Insecticide works poorly at repelling the stubborn, bee-like insects.

As stated earlier, no reliable treatment has been found for either large or small stomach worms. Anthelmintics have virtually no effect, perhaps caused by the protection afforded through mucosal secretions. Hopefully, research

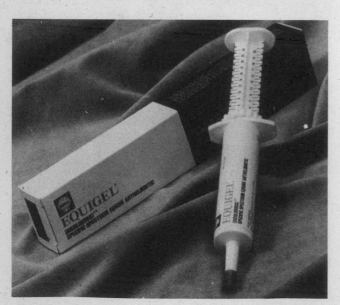

Some wormers, like Equigel in paste form, are dispensed via a syringe-like arrangement. The paste is squirted on the horse's tongue and swallowed. Dichlorvos works well.

being conducted into the behavioral patterns of these parasites will result in a therapy scheme.

While little is known about the tapeworm in horses, science has developed a compound that apparently kills it. The name is teinatol and this may have to be administered separately from commercial worming compounds since it may not be found in many.

Administration of anthelmintics is sound animal management for a horse infected with internal parasites, as nearly all are. But this is only one part of a parasite control program.

Horsemen should utilize a pasture rotation system, which entails moving horses from one pasture to another at regular intervals and running other species of livestock, primarily cattle or sheep, on the pasture formerly grazed by horses. Most equine parasites can't survive inside the body of another host species.

If it is impossible to graze another type of livestock on the pasture, that section should be clipped. This action not only promotes grass growth, but also exposes eggs and larvae to environmental conditions which kill them. If the pasture is severely contaminated, horses shouldn't be grazed on it for several months.

Many horsemen favor usage of temporary seeded pasture. Every three to five years this pasture is plowed and reseeded, which keeps concentrations of parasites from building to high levels. Before turning horses out on such a pasture, ensure they've been adequately wormed.

Since foals are born virtually parasite-free, every effort should be made to run them on uncontaminated pastures. Move them to other clean pastures at regular intervals, which will keep the parasite load at a low level.

If horses are kept in stalls or small paddocks, more work is required of the horseman. Manure should be removed daily and stored in an insulated pit for at least two weeks. Manure so stored generates heat which kills eggs and larvae. Even after a safe storage period, it is not recommended that the manure be spread on pastures; contact local residents who desire free fertilizer, or have it hauled away.

When feeding horses, never throw rations on the ground — they may become contaminated through contact with eggs or larvae in the feces. Use a manger or feedbox of some type.

Use care in the selection of bedding material. Don't use hay for bedding, since horses may eat it, including any eggs or worm larvae present. Always take a stall down completely once per week, replacing all bedding. If the stall floor is of clay or regular dirt, it should be dug up annually to a depth of six inches or so, then new flooring material deposited. This will remove all eggs or parasitic larvae existing in the soil.

Parasite eggs have the nasty habit of surviving in water. Therefore, if near a pond into which pasture drainage is possible, restrain a horse from drinking. He may imbibe parasite eggs which will hatch in his stomach.

Parasitism is a dirty subject, but one that too often is ignored. This lack of attention will manifest itself in dull-looking and performing horses. Worm him as needed.

External

Just as man is bedeviled by external parasites, so is the horse. While man has at his disposal many chemicals and equipments to aid in his fight against "bugs," the horse only is equipped with an equine version of the flyswatter: his tail. He also has control of muscles underlying the skin which he will use in an effort to shake insects or parasites from the hide. Even so, he isn't a match for the pests attacking him externally.

The types of external parasites which will be discussed here are: mites, fleas, mosquitos, lice, gnats, ticks, ringworm, houseflies, stable flies, horseflies and blowflies. As with the section on internal parasites, treatment programs will be presented at the end of this classification.

MITES

So tiny they are invisible to the naked eye, results of mite infestation fall into four categories of contagious skin diseases: Sarcoptic mange, Chorioptic mange, Psoroptic mange and Demodectic mange.

Sarcoptic mange is perhaps the worst of the lot, usually chronic in nature once contracted. All four produce similar skin disorders, distinguished mainly by locations they prefer. After burrowing into the skin, the small mites produce lesions which exude a watery fluid that dries, forming scaly crusts. The hair falls out and the skin thickens. This process causes extreme itching and, in an effort to relieve it, a horse literally will rub the skin raw at infected locations.

Psoroptic mange usually affects areas protected by long hair — forelock, root of the tail and the mane — but spreads rapidly over the body. Sarcoptic mange doesn't favor areas covered with long hair, first becoming visible on the head, neck and shoulder regions. Chorioptic mange oftentimes is called leg mange, since the mites prefer the lower parts of the hind legs. In severe cases of involvement, the disorder spreads rapidly to the flanks, shoulders and neck. Demodectic mange, seldom seen in horses, generally confines its involvement to hair follicles and the sebaceous glands, particularly around the eyes and on the forehead. If unchecked, the entire body may become involved.

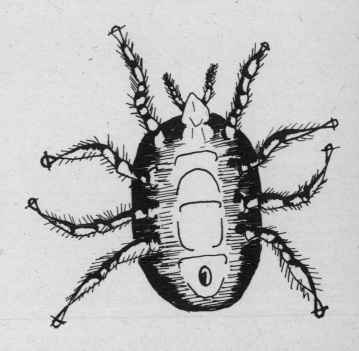

Mites are the cause of mange in horses and can be stubborn to treat. The itching they cause can lead to lost hair coat or such rubbing the skin is broken, leading to infection.

FLEAS

Tiny, dark brown or black critters, fleas bother dogs and cats more than horses. But a great many horsemen keep dogs or felines around their stables, so transferral of fleas from canine to equine occasionally occurs.

Fleas are bloodsuckers that cause intense itching and irritation for a horse. In his efforts to quell this itch, a horse will bite or rub the location of the flea activity, often to the point the spot becomes raw or sore. This behavior gives the horseowner indication of flea infestation.

The adult flea spends nearly its entire life on a horse, often laying its eggs on the coat. More frequently, however, the flea will disembark at egg-laying time and deposit eggs in a horse's bedding. After about five days of incubation, the young fleas emerge from the larval stage and jump onto the waiting host; thus, the life cycle begins anew.

Specific treatment, which will be given at the end of this section, can control fleas.

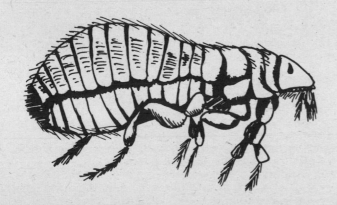

While fleas bother dogs and cats more than horses, occasionally the latter contract them. Like mites, fleas cause intense itching and can lead to problems.

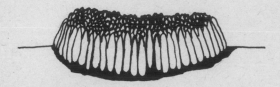

The life cycle of the mosquito is shown on this page, beginning with a raft of eggs laid on the surface of a quiet water source. Up to 400 eggs are laid at once.

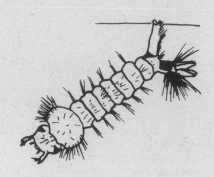

In the first of its larval stages, the mosquito breathes through a tube at the rear of the body. After moulting four times, the adult begins to take shape, seen below.

MOSQUITOS

Mosquitos are not only irritating, they are potentially dangerous to the health of a horse. Of the more than 140 species found in the United States, several are capable of transmitting debilitating or deadly diseases.

The life cycle of the mosquito begins when a female lays from one to four hundred eggs atop or near a water source. Common mosquitos lay their eggs directly on the water surface in a mass called a raft and the eggs hatch in a day or two.

In the larval stage, the mosquito comes to the surface and breathes through a tube called a siphon on the rear of its body. It moults or sheds its skin four times during rapid development to the pupal stage.

As a pupating mosquito, the insects cannot eat and only breathe through tubes on their backs. After about two days of development, the pupae breaks through its protective skin as a full-grown insect. It rests on the water surface until strong enough to fly away in search of a meal. The entire process can be accomplished in as little as seven days during warm weather.

Interestingly, only the female mosquito uses her proboscis for sucking blood from birds or mammals; the male exists solely on plant juices. Females can live up to three weeks during the Summer, laying rafts of eggs every second day of her adult life. She also survives quite well during Winter, laying her eggs again after the spring thaw.

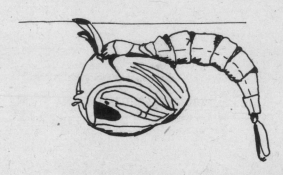

About two days after hatching, the mosquito pupates, breaking through its larval skin. It does not eat during pupation and breathes through tubes connected to back.

Diseases are transmitted when the one of several species of mosquito bites an infected animal or human, itself becoming infected in the process. When it bites other mammals or birds, it then spreads the infective bacteria to the new animal, and so on. It therefore is possible to have quick and widespread outbreaks of diseases over entire states or countries, like the Venezuelan equine encephalomyelitis epizootic of late 1971. The outbreak began in Central America and was carried via the mosquito through Mexico and into the Southwest.

It takes lots of work to protect against this flying trash-can, which will be outlined later.

LICE

There are two types of lice which affect horses, usually during winter months. These are the common biting louse and the sucking louse. The former causes great itching as it bites the horse, as does the second when sucking. Both types seem to constantly be scurrying around and, if severe-

After shedding larval skin, the full-grown mosquito emerges and sits atop the water resting, until strong enough to fly off. Only female mosquitos suck blood.

Lice, active during the cooler months of the year, can drive a horse to distraction. The constant itching leads to rubbing against stationary objects with hair loss.

ly infested, a horse literally will be at wit's end, not knowing which spot to bite or rub next. He will appear restless and anxious, as would his owner if likewise infested.

As stated earlier, lice activity usually is present only through the winter months, subsiding with the arrival of Spring. Probably this is because more thorough grooming is possible during the warmer seasons.

It is possible to detect lice by separating the hairs and examining the skin at the roots under strong light. Sometimes lice will be found sucking or attached to the hair at the skin juncture. Lice can spread through a whole herd of horses in short order, passed from one to another. It is possible for eggs and larvae which have dropped to the ground to survive for up to three weeks in warm weather, simply waiting for a horse to amble by.

GNATS

Small in size but large in numbers and appetite for blood, gnats have been responsible for the death of vast herds of horses and cattle each year, primarily in the South and Midwest sections of the country. After spending the larval portions of their lives in swift-running streams or irrigation canals, innumerable numbers become airborne at once and resemble black clouds buzzing around livestock.

They exist by sucking blood from livestock, at the same time injecting a toxic material into the skin. In severe cases, this toxic substance builds to a level that causes death through hemorrhage. In cases of mild attack, horses usually will be restless, have poor coat condition, may be anemic, lose weight and go off their feed.

Preventing gnats is a costly, time-consuming and potentially dangerous chore. It behooves horsemen in areas of the country sustaining periodic attacks by gnats to review the treatment section following listing of parasites.

TICKS

A great deal is known about ticks and the damage they can do to livestock and man. There are two families of ticks in the United States, both of which act as disease carriers or can lead to secondary infection as the horse attempts to rid himself of the parasites: *Ixodidae,* or "hard" ticks, and *Argasidae,* or "soft" ticks.

Ticks have an interesting life cycle, either dependent upon a single host throughout its lifetime or three separate hosts, and all are bloodsuckers. Most "hard," three-host ticks mate on one host, which stimulates the female to faster feeding. About a week after mating, when her abdomen is engorged with blood, she drops from the host and spends another week feasting on the blood she has stored. Eggs then are laid under surface debris or in the soil.

If the weather is warm, eggs hatch in approximately two weeks and six-legged ticks emerge. These babies crawl up foliage and wait for passing horses for as long as eight months if conditions are suitable. When a to-be host contacts the tick-infested plant, the six-legged parasite transfers and crawls to a suitable spot, then begins to feed. It usually takes several days to become engorged with blood, whereupon the tick drops to the ground and moults, becoming a four-legged nymph. The new nymph crawls on vegetation and repeats the process of waiting for a host to pass by.

The successful nymphs that find hosts then spend a week or so filling up their self-contained tanks, then drop to the ground. After moulting for the last time, the nymphs emerge as adults and repeat the crawling-up/lying-in-wait procedure a last time.

The difference between three and one-host ticks naturally lies in the number of times a tick leaves the host. A one-host tick doesn't drop to the ground and go through the moulting stages; it's entire life is spent attached to one host.

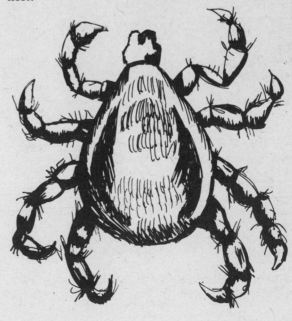

Ticks have an interesting life cycle and many types can hurt horses. Besides sucking blood, the ticks pass all manner of diseases to horses, some resulting in death.

Should a horse's ear hair be clipped, some type of insect repellent should be used to protect the ear canal (left).

The "hard" ticks of importance, which will be discussed here, are the Lone Star tick, Gulf Coast tick, Rocky Mountain wood tick, American dog tick, Brown dog tick and the Winter tick. Some aren't often found on equines, thankfully.

The Lone Star tick is not named after the fair state of Texas, but derives it's name from a silvery-white spot resembling a star on the female's body. It is found mostly on a line from Oklahoma to Virginia and all states to the south, most active during early Spring, Summer and late Fall. A three-host tick, it is capable of transmitting Rocky Mountain spotted fever.

The Gulf Coast tick extends inward from the Mexican border in Texas some two hundred miles, then east to the Atlantic Ocean. A three-host tick, it affects cattle more than horses, primarily during late Summer or early Fall.

The Rocky Mountain wood tick, understandably, is found primarily in the Northwestern regions of the country. A three-host tick, it has a life cycle lasting as long as two years from egg to adult stages. Adult Rocky Mountain wood ticks are seen mostly during Spring and early Summer, attaching usually around the head and ears of a horse.

The American dog tick, also three-host in cycle, is almost totally confined to the Central and Eastern sections of the country and doesn't affect only dogs. Rather, it is the vector (scientific term for disease carrier that infects others) for most outbreaks of Rocky Mountain spotted fever in the East.

The Brown dog tick much favors a host of the canine species, only rarely attaching to livestock. With dogs around horses, transfer from canine to equine is a possibility and bears watching.

The Winter tick is a serious parasite of horses in open ranges from the Gulf Coast states to Canada. A one-host tick, it usually attacks horses during winter months or in the early Spring, making it unique from other tick species which winter on the ground.

On a host, ticks mate and the female spends the next several days gorging on blood. When to the bursting point, she drops from her host and spends the Winter on the ground. Eggs are laid in the Spring and young ticks emerge in three to six weeks. They remain clustered together throughout the Summer, becoming active in Fall's cool temperatures. They then attach to horses and, after about a month on the host, are adults. They then mate and the cycle continues.

The only "soft" tick of any importance to horsemen is the spinose ear tick, a member of *Argasidae* band. When larvae hatch from eggs deposited on the ground, they crawl

Mosquito-transmitted Venezuelan equine encephalomyelitis struck down this new foal. Erradicate mosquitos!

While caused by a fungus, not an external parasite proper, ringworm is itchy and leads to hair loss, specifically around the eyes. The disorder can be treated effectively.

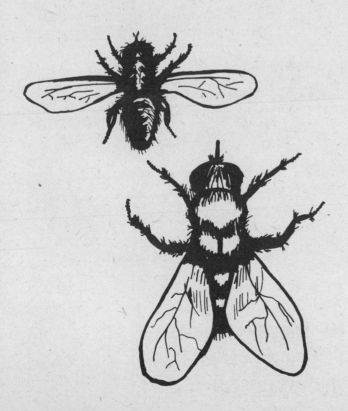

The housefly is a dwarf compared to the insidious stable fly (left). Houseflies can transmit parasitic eggs, while stable flies can cause anemia along with severe anxiety.

onto vegetation and await the close passing of a horse or other livestock, then attach to the host and make their way to the ears, crawling deeply inside and remaining there for one to seven months. After developing through the nymphal stages, the ticks drop out and, after finding a spot with some type of shelter, moult to adults. They then mate and the female deposits her eggs to start the cycle again.

Horses infested with spinose ear ticks show marked pain through anxious expression and restlessness. He may cock his head to the side and, if infestation is severe, may be slightly deaf in that ear. He usually will be hard to bridle and will rub his ear, trying to dislodge the parasites. Permanent hearing loss can result if treatment isn't effected soon.

RINGWORM

Ringworm is a disorder caused by a fungus rather than specific parasite, but is logically included in this classification. Extremely contagious, the fungus lives in damp, warm soil and usually appears as a circular lesion with scaly exterior. Little hair grows at the site and it usually appears on the head, neck, croup, base of the tail, shoulders or breast, but can strike anywhere. It spreads rapidly from small, half-dollar-sized rings to huge lesions, or many small rings that are yellow or gray in color. They may itch and a horse will rub the spot to relieve irritation, often spreading the fungi spores to other parts of the body.

HOUSEFLIES

There are many types of *Musca domestica,* the common housefly, which irritate horses and can lead to serious problems. The housefly loves nothing better than manure, on which it feeds and breeds. In the act of feeding, it can ingest the microscopic eggs of the roundworm or large stomach worm. When it then feeds on the body secretions of a horse, particularly around the eyes or at the muzzle, it re-deposits these roundworm eggs in its feces and the horse gets ascarid infestation. When feeding on blood from bites by stable flies, it deposits large stomach worm eggs which can lead to summer sores, noted earlier in this section. They also are suspected of transmitting various eye diseases, which makes their control of importance to the horseman.

STABLE FLIES

These insects seem to favor the legs of horses and their bites are the most painful of all biting flies. Eggs are laid in damp or fermenting vegetation, not necessarily manure, and timespan from egg to adult is as short as three weeks.

When they appear in large concentrations, they can seriously affect the overall health of a horse or other livestock. He is naturally restless and anxious, continually flicking or biting at the insects as they land on him. He may go off his feed, losing as much as ten to fifteen percent body weight. Severe attack can lead to an anemic condition through blood loss. As noted in the section on houseflies, blood left from the stable fly's bite is attractive to the former, which can lead to introduction of large stomach worm eggs or secondary infection.

HORSEFLIES

These pests can literally drive a horse berserk. When present in fairly large numbers, they stimulate activity on the horse's part in his effort to escape from the buzzing clouds. By so doing, he spends less time feeding and consequently loses weight which, if coupled with numerous bites over a short period, can lead to anemia or death through blood loss, though death is rare.

More often, death comes through diseases the horsefly introduces. The most prevalent are equine infectious anemia or equine encephalomyelitis, which the horsefly passes through his biting behavior. It's possible for a whole herd to be infected with either of these diseases in a short period of heavy fly attack.

Like the stable fly, horseflies aren't overly fond of manure as an egg-laying spot. Rather, most horseflies lay their eggs in clusters near or projecting above a water source, which hatch in five to ten days. The larvae fall into the water and crawl ashore on a muddy bank where they feed on minute organisms. When ready to pupate, the larvae crawl to higher ground where they won't be submerged for extended periods, then emerge as winged insects after a short period. They then mate, the female lays her eggs and the cycle begins again.

Because of scattered egg-laying sites, it's difficult to control this insect. More will be said on this under the treatment segment.

BLOWFLIES

These insects have a fondness for laying eggs in carrion, manure and open wounds of horses. When the larvae deposited on a wound, called screwworms, hatch, they burrow into the wound and exist on the juices collecting at the site. The distinguishing difference between the screwworm fly and blowfly is that the former lays its eggs only in the wound of a living, warm-blooded host, while the blowfly will lay its eggs on a dead animal or in manure, etc.

In severe infestations, animal death has been reported. The blowfly larvae cause irritation. Blowflies bother horses when feeding on their blood and a good insect control program is necessary to control them.

TREATMENT

A mange condition in horses, and treatment of same, is dependent to a large degree on the time of year and environmental conditions present. Therapy calls for a warm, lime-sulfur "dip" — liberally applying a solution to the hair coat some four to six times at ten to twelve-day intervals. In cold parts of the country, care should be taken to assure the horse doesn't chill, which could lead to respiratory ailments.

Another solution which has proved effective in killing the parasites is a nicotine sulfate dip, used only once. But it sometimes is difficult to eradicate both Sarcoptic and Demodectic mange with killing agents, resulting in a chronic infestation. A veterinarian will prescribe the solution to use and rely on his judgment. At the same time, he will prescribe treatment for any sore spots caused by the horse's rubbing in attempt to rid himself of the itchy bugs; usually an antiseptic ointment application following thorough cleaning and disinfecting.

Treating fleas requires attention not only to the horse, but also his bedding. As noted in the segment dealing with fleas, adults lay their eggs on bits of debris in the stall, so treatment of the horse alone won't solve the problem; it's just a matter of time until the young reinfest the animal.

Commercially available powders and sprays containing

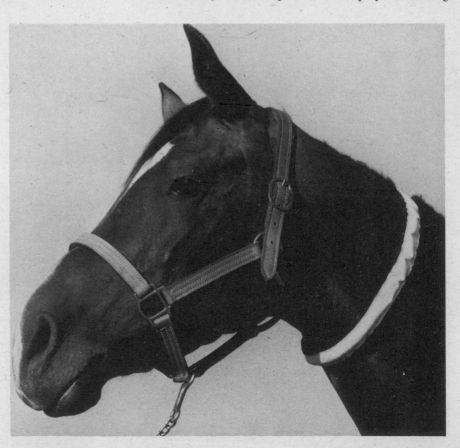

Some folks have been experimenting with the possibility of using fly collar for horses, similar to dog's flea collar.

During winter months, when lice become most active, it's usually impossible to shampoo a horse. This dry Top Form shampoo has helped in such circumstances.

pyrethrum, rotenone, lindane or malathion — used according to the manufacturer's recommendations — are effective in killing fleas on the horse. His bedding should be removed and burned, and before putting new bedding in a stall, the area should be dusted or sprayed with the compounds listed. DDT also is effective in killing larvae and adults, but many horseowners shy away from it...it also can kill horses!

When fleas have been removed, attention should be paid to any sores the horse might have acquired while trying to rid himself of the fleas. Disinfect the area and apply an antiseptic ointment. This will keep flies from the sore and lessen the chance of secondary infection — which could prove fatal.

Treatment of mites and fleas is within the grasp of the horseman, but most aren't equipped to do battle on a large scale against the mosquito. Each horseman can greatly reduce the mosquito population on his property through simple procedures, though.

Since relatively little water is needed for egg-laying, females often deposit rafts in water troughs, ornamental ponds, plastic wading pools, stock tanks, in scattered junk like tin cans, jars, bottles, tubs, barrels and old tires which have collected rainwater, and even under homes with leaky plumbing.

Because of this, horseowner should remove the trash on his property and store all buckets or barrels upside-down when not in use. Water troughs and wading pools should be cleaned at least weekly and faulty plumbing repaired.

Larger bodies of water or ornamental ponds call for the introduction of *Gambusia affinis,* better-known as the mosquito fish. This species has a positively voracious appetite for mosquito larvae, snapping them up as fast as they hatch. The two-inch fish require no care or supplemental feeding and perhaps can be secured free of charge from the nearest mosquito abatement office.

Draining swamps, spraying with DDT and other insecticides is best left to professionals or government agencies charged with direct responsibility. DDT is pretty tricky and will kill fish in streams or other life forms if not used properly.

Also, the horseowner can install fine-mesh screening on his stalls and barns, which cuts down considerably the number of mosquitos entering. Fogging the area with commercially available preparations will afford some protection, but must be repeated with regularity.

If horses are kept in pastures where screening or fogging is impossible, little can be done to protect a horse from mosquitos. Unfortunately, insect repellents don't afford lasting protection and usually must be reapplied every eight to twelve hours.

Since most lice infestation occurs during the winter months, treatment at those times is restricted usually to dusting with a commercially prepared lice powder containing rotenone, ronnel, Ciodrin, pyrethrins, malathion, lindane or similar compounds. Dipping at cold times could cause respiratory problems.

During the summer months, it's the usual practice to shampoo a horse vigorously, then spray, dip or dust the following day with one of the aforementioned chemicals in a lice powder. Once the horse has been treated, he should be moved to another stall for up to three weeks and his old stall thoroughly disinfected, the bedding burned. This protects against reinfestation, since eggs will hatch two to three weeks after being laid.

Efficient control of gnats, which mass in blood-sucking black hordes, is similar to the mosquito in scope and requirements. Since water again is involved, eradication is best left to authorities with experience in the matter.

The individual horseowner can, however, take certain measures to guard his horses from continual attack. Though temporary, some relief is available through combination of pyrethrum, synergist and repellent sprays. Cattlemen have long used smudge pots during times of heavy invasion and this also can work for the horseman. Cattle soon learned to crowd around the smudge for protection. If using this type

Using foggers like this from London is one of the most effective ways of checking insect numbers when used with regularity around stables during hot times of year.

197

Diseases like fistula of the withers — which may be caused by a parasite — have been discovered following outbreaks of bovine brucellosis, and vice versa. Therefore, keep close watch on herds of cattle and horses, segregating as necessary.

of arrangement, make sure no open flame is present or horses could be burned.

Careful attention should be given to the hair coat of the horse following attack by gnats. The small punctures are ideal entry spots for bacteria or other germs that could lead to bigger problems. Watch for eggs of the blowflies or screwworm flies, which will be removed with normal grooming that should be carried out daily.

Tick infestation requires attention to both horse and premises. If ticks are few in number, spray with a tick bomb or other tick killer. It is not advisable to pluck ticks from the skin, since often the heads or mouthparts break off and remain embedded, leading to infection or ulceration.

If tick infestation is severe, it is wise to dip the horse in lindane, toxaphene, malathion, ronnel or coumaphos. Dips or squirt-can application of these compounds into the ear is more effective than attempting to pick spinose ear ticks from the cavity. Follow directions listed on the package or can explicitly; these poisons could kill the horse if used in

too strong concentrations. If the compounds are not pre-mixed, use a fresh batch with each application to assure efficacy.

Tick eradication in large pastures or open ranges is virtually impossible. Steps can be taken around the barn, however, using sprays or dusts of chlordane, diazinon, dichlorvos, dieldrin, lindane or malathion. These should be used only on limited areas and utensils, feeders, waterers or feed proper should not be treated. The horse should be kept isolated from the site until the chemicals have dried thoroughly. Remember: most of these compounds are poisonous to man, so use them with care at a veterinarian's direction.

Studies have shown that horses deficient in vitamin A tend to be more susceptible to ringworm than others, which means a good, balanced diet is a primary requirement in controlling this fungus disease. Washes and dips will effectively fight the condition, which a veterinarian will prescribe. As contaminated equipment can transfer the disease, disinfect all tack and grooming equipment coming in contact with the horse. His stall also should be cleaned and disinfected. Use rubber gloves when treating ringworm, since many types are contagious to man, also.

Treatment for houseflies rests with good stable management. They feed and breed in manure, so it should be collected daily and stored well away from the barn in a pit. Screened stalls will keep most houseflies out. An open-sided shelter with a roof for shade will allow breeze to enter and this keeps some flies away. Fly repellents also afford some relief but, because the housefly feeds on secretions from the mouth, nose and eyes, care needs to be taken when applying repellent to these areas. Follow label directions.

Stable flies only bother a horse at their dinnertime, which hampers effective treatment. Repellents are of little value in killing more than a few flies. Spraying the exterior of barns does provide some relief, as does fogging with synergized pyrethrum or dichlorvos.

Keeping horses in screened enclosures will give the best protection, turning them out at night when fly activity is at ebb. The horse gets enough exercise from this procedure to make it worth the time and effort on the horseman's part.

Horseflies are one of the most difficult insects to control and nearly any solution isn't fast-acting enough to keep flies from biting. The best results come from heavily wetting a horse's coat with synergized pyrethrins, which last for approximately three days, whereupon the procedure needs to be repeated.

Since water plays an important role in the development of this fly, control can be facilitated by professionals with

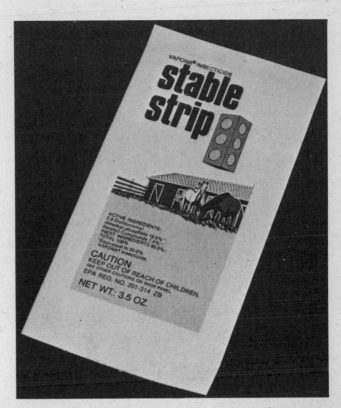

Shell Chemical Company has developed an off-shoot of their No-Pest Strips for home use, the Stable Strip. Charged with Vapona insecticide, it kills the bugs.

Probably the most effective way of keeping insects away from horses is spraying with repellents on the market.

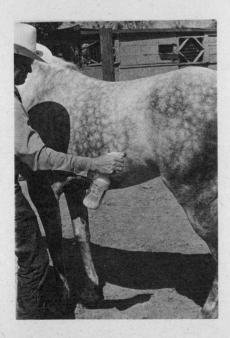

spraying equipment. A horseman can examine his irrigation system and, if it can be straightened or the water flow-rate increased, he should take these steps.

During a period of heavy fly activity, the wise horseowner watches his horses closely and grooms them regularly. This will remove eggs and lessen the possibility of bacterial invasion from fly-caused punctures.

Blowflies are tough customers that sometimes are repelled by such compounds as pine oil, but also respond well to poison baits. Since they lay eggs in manure, open wounds and carcasses of dead animals, the wise horseowner will store manure in a pit well away from the barn; treat all injuries and open lesions with disinfectants and antiseptic ointments to repel bacteria and flies; and deeply bury or burn all dead animals. These procedures will reduce the number of blowflies present and more protection can be had by stalling a horse in a screened enclosure. He may be turned out at night.

Parasitism is one of the most overlooked areas of equine health. Not all is yet known of the effects of parasitic involvement and a veterinarian will first get the word on new developments. Therefore, follow his recommendations and do your part to eliminate these freeloaders.

E: POISONING

THOUGH IT MAY SEEM hard to believe, U.S. Department of Agriculture officials estimate that between three and five percent of all livestock on America's ranges succumb to poisons annually. This doesn't mean solely cattle and sheep: horses figure in the statistics, too.

The sad part, besides the loss itself, is that the horseman is to blame in most cases of poisoning. The main cause, as established by controlled studies, is lack of normal forage; hungry horses look elsewhere for their food. Conversely, horses that aren't watered regularly are particularly susceptible to grazing on poisonous plants.

Horses run on pasture when poisonous plants are at peak danger also is a frequent cause of poisoning, as is driving horses to different ranges through stands of poisonous plants.

Four preventive measures to poisoning already have been established: provide suitable feed always, water regularly, keep horses off infested pastures during peak plant danger periods and direct herd movement away from dangerous spots. There are other steps a horseman can take to protect his livestock, however.

One of these is learning to identify the flora growing on his range, distinguishing between harmless and potentially dangerous species. This should be followed by close inspection of the property prior to turning any animals loose, with eradication of poisonous species through a manner recommended by local agriculture extension service personnel. Keep the horses off pastures treated with chemicals for at least two weeks; seeds present on the ground could begin growing or the horse could ingest the plant's seeds, many times the most toxic part of the plant.

Before pasturing horses in the Spring, assure there's sufficient graze available and seed the area to good forage if necessary. Don't let the animals overgraze; in their quest for food, they often will eat the poisonous plants previously untouched.

Should a horse on pasture begin exhibiting the symptoms of poisoning outlined in this segment, immediately move the animal to a stall or barn and contact the local veterinarian as soon as possible. In cases of poisoning, timing is of the essence since many poisons are fast-acting. A delay could cost the horse's life.

Since many of the poisonous plants to be discussed also grow in cultivated fields, it's the wise horseman who inspects his hay prior to feeding. Many plant parts remain toxic even after being cut and dried. Consequently, it ranks first and foremost in a horseman's mind to procure the best-quality, uncontaminated hays he can find. This falls into the category of sound stable management.

For ease of classification and reportage, we shall divide the poisonous plants to be discussed into geographical prevalence either East or West of the Mississippi River, with a separate category devoted to those plants found nationwide. They further will be broken down into times of the year they are most dangerous to livestock, with a short description of the plant and symptoms of poisoning. Charts on accompanying pages can be used for quick reference.

POISONOUS PLANTS — EAST

Throughout the Eastern half of the country, several plant species retain the potential for death during all seasons. These include silverling, crotalaria, Jimson weed, yellow jessamine, laurel, common oleander, laurel cherry,

castor bean and sorghum.

Silverling, often called Baccharis after its botanical family bearing the same name, usually is found in open, moist coastal plains from Massachusetts southward. A member of the sunflower family, it's a woody plant with whitish flowers that contain a toxic agent causing paralysis that leads to death shortly after ingestion. In cases "lucky" enough to survive, the horse is chronically depressed and weak, virtually useless as a work or show animal.

Crotalaria

Jimson Weed

POISONOUS PLANTS — EAST

Dangerous Season	Plant Name	Description	Symptoms
All Seasons (especially Fall)	Silverling	Woody plant with whitish flowers	Paralysis, death in terminal cases. Weakness, depression in chronic cases.
	Crotalaria	Annual blooming legume with yellow flowers and small pods	Diarrhea, stupor, walking in circles, temporary remission followed by death
	Jimson weed	Wavy leaves, four-inch flowers, spiny pods	Thirst, nausea, vertigo, dilated pupils, convulsions, rapid death
	Yellow jessamine	Green vine, with yellow tubular flowers	Rigidity, lowered temperature and respiration, weakness, convulsions, death
(especially Winter and Spring)	Laurel	Woody plant with glossy evergreen leaves	Nasal and salivary discharges, paralysis, death
	Common oleander	Evergreen, ornamental shrub, leaves growing equidistantly around stem	Depression, nausea, increased pulse rate, dilation of pupils, bloody diarrhea, weak and irregular heartbeat, death
Spring & Summer	Buckeye	Small tree or shrub with palm-like leaves, seeds glossy brown with scar	Depression, incoordination, paralysis, twitching, inflammation of mucous membranes
	Fly-poison	Bulbous, blossoming herb surviving year-round	Salivation, rapid and irregular respiration, weakness, death through respiratory failure
	Lantana	Ornamental shrub with fruiting stalks	Watery lesions, sloughing of skin, stomach pains, bloody, watery feces, sensitivity to light
	Bracken fern	Triangular-shaped fronds, black, horizontal root-stalks, height 2-4 feet	Loss of weight and condition, progressive incoordination, depression, twitching muscles, weakness, crouched stance with back arched and legs apart, weak, fast pulse, prostration, convulsions, death
	Chokecherry	Shrub about 4 feet high, or tree reaching 20 feet, white flowers in long clusters, glossy green leaves, small cherries in black or dark purple	Salivation, nervousness, increased respiration rate, rapid, weak pulse, trembling muscles, convulsions, rapid death through respiratory failure
	Oak	Trees of varying height, with four leathery leaves at end of each twig, bears acorn fruit	Weakness, emaciation, constipation often followed by profuse diarrhea with blood and mucus, frequent urination, thin, rapid pulse, prostration
Summer	Corn cockle	Green year-round, with fine hairs on underside of leaves, purple flowers, black seeds	Irritation of mucosal linings, vertigo, diarrhea
	White snakeroot	Herb with leaves tapering to a point, numerous small white flowers	Trembling, labored respiration, depression, death
	Nightshade	Tomato-like plant with yellow, red or black fruit when ripe	Nausea, constipation or diarrhea, trembling, death
	Bladder pod	Tall plant with flat, tapered pods bearing two seeds	Severe intestinal inflammation, yellowish diarrhea, frequent urination, short, rapid breathing, death
	Johnson grass	Coarse weed grass with white line up blades	Excess salivation, pulse and respiration rates increase, convulsions, death
Fall & Winter	Rattlebush	Shrub with orange blossoms, four-angled pods	Rapid pulse, weak respiration, diarrhea, death
All Seasons (especially Winter and Spring)	Laurel cherry	Shrub with evergreen, leathery, shiny leaves, broken twigs smell of cherry bark	Excess salivation, pulse and respiration rates increase, convulsions, death
	Castor bean	Cultivated plant with palm-like leaves, beans	Nausea, diarrhea, thirst, goes off feed, death
	Sorghum	Cultivated plant that may reach height of 8 feet at terminal flower	Excess salivation, pulse and respiration rates increase, convulsions, death

Crotalaria favors fields and roadsides from Virginia westward to Missouri and all states southward. It is an annual-blooming legume having yellow flowers and small pods, all of which contain an alkaloid toxic to horses.

After ingestion of crotalaria, a horse suffers from diarrhea and walks in circles, apparently in a stupor. The condition then will seem to clear, only to be repeated. There is no known cure and death is the result.

Jimson weed is another year-round danger found in fields or other unused land with rich soil. It has wavy leaves, flowers some four inches long upon maturity and a spiny pod. The alkaloid causes rapid death upon ingestion, which follows the symptoms of thirst, nausea, vertigo, dilated pupils and convulsions. Because death is rapid, a veterinary surgeon needs to be called upon first notice.

Yellow Jessamine

Yellow jessamine, of the species *Gelsemium,* favors the open woods and thickets of Pennsylvania, Michigan, Iowa and points to the south. It grows like a vine with leaves retaining green coloration throughout the year, and yellow tubular flowers. This plant also contains an alkaloid which causes the extremities to become rigid, respiration rate and temperature drop, the horse becomes weak and may suffer convulsions. If a veterinarian doesn't arrive quickly to administer sedatives and the like, the horse usually dies.

Laurel, also called ivybush or lambkill, favors soil with high acid content and rocky hillsides. Especially dangerous during Winter and Spring, this woody plant's evergreen, glossy leaves attract most grazing animals, especially sheep (hence the name, lambkill). After it reaches the stomach, it causes both nasal and salivary discharges, paralysis and, ultimately, death. A veterinarian will administer laxatives and nerve stimulants, which sometimes combat the toxoid sufficiently to bring about recovery.

The common oleander is a pretty, evergreen shrub that many Southern residents plant around their homes. Its aesthetic beauty is enhanced by leaves growing concentrically from the stalk. This shrub can likewise be appealing to horses and, upon ingestion, causes depression accompanied by nausea, increased pulse rate, dilation of the pupils and bloody diarrhea. A weak and irregular heartbeat occurs as the poisoning progresses, terminating in death. There is no known treatment.

If common oleander is recognized on one's land and he wishes to dispose of the shrub, it should be hauled to the dump, not burned. Man can be similarly affected through inhalation of the poison-bearing smoke. If there are any exposed cuts on the hands, wear rubber gloves; absorption of the poison through an open wound is possible.

Laurel

Oleander (leaf)

Spring and Summer are the times to watch for buckeye, fly-poison, lantana, bracken fern, chokecherry and oak.

Buckeyes, found in the woods and thickets of Pennsylvania, Michigan, Iowa and states southward, grow as small trees or shrubs with palm-like leaves. Its young shoots and seeds are the most poisonous parts of the plant. Seeds can easily be recognized, being large and glossy brown, with a visible scar.

Ingestion of the buckeye causes depression, incoordination, paralysis, twitching and inflammation of the mucous membranes. A veterinarian will administer stimulants and purgatives to clear the intestines of the poison-bearing plants and effect recovery.

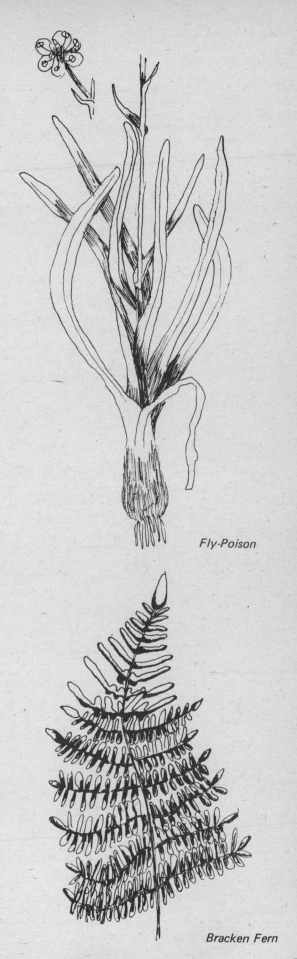

Buckeye

Fly-Poison

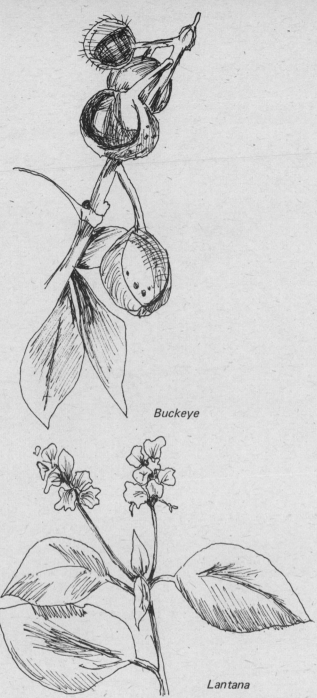

Lantana

Lantana, of the genus bearing the same name, is another ornamental shrub found around homes for aesthetic appeal. What happens upon eating the leaves, however, isn't appealing: the horse breaks out in watery lesions and the skin at these spots later sloughs off. The horse suffers stomach pains and usually passes a bloody, watery feces. Call a veterinarian immediately. Moving the horse into a darkened box stall seems to give relief, as the eyes seem to become extremely sensitive.

It's uncertain exactly how fly-poison got its name and this year-round, blossoming herb accounts for livestock losses each year. Found in open woods or around acid bogs north to Missouri, Pennsylvania and Long Island, fly-poison contains an alkaloid that causes salivation, rapid and irregular respiration, weakness and death, termination usually coming from respiratory failure. There isn't any known cure, so prevention is the way to avoid this killer.

Bracken Fern

Bracken fern has triangular-shaped fronds which grow from stout, black horizontal rootstalks and often reaches two to four feet in height. It is capable of growing just about anywhere, beginning in early Spring. It remains an attractive green until the leaves are killed by the first frost, whereupon the leaves assume a brownish coloration.

Bracken fern poisoning generally is seen only where forage is scarce, since horses will forego the fern for other fodder and researchers have found it takes between two to four weeks of feeding on the plant before a horse exhibits symptoms of the disorder. These symptoms are progressive loss of weight and condition, accompanied by progressive incoordination, marked depression, muscle twitching, prostration and convulsions. Horses detected early in the syndrome can be treated satisfactorily with intravenous introduction of thiamine hydrochloride. If unnoticed, a horse can be chronically affected or dies.

Chokecherry
(blossoms)

Oak

The chokecherry grows as a large shrub or tree, bearing long fingers of white flowers and small cherries, the latter ranging in color from purple to black when ripe. Found throughout the East, it sprouts most frequently in vacant lots, along fence rows, in deep woods and orchards. Horses prone to snacking on wind-fall apples in an orchard containing chokecherry can be poisoned through ingestion of the leaves, although a lethal dose must be consumed in a relatively short time — less than an hour.

A horse that's eaten enough of the plant to become poisoned usually will salivate excessively, have an increased respiration rate, a rapid, weak pulse, may have convulsions and dies. Death generally is the result of respiratory failure.

The poisoning resulting from ingestion of oak leaves is not to be confused with poison oak, of which many horsemen have rueful remembrances. Rather, oak poisoning is

brought about when a horse eats the leaves of this tree, generally found in most stands of deciduous trees, but not restricted to those, however.

The leaves contain a tannic acid that causes passage of black, pelleted feces prior to total constipation, which then is followed by diarrhea with blood and mucus, frequent urination, dry muzzle and a thin, rapid pulse. Call the veterinarian who will prescribe moving the horse from contact with oak leaves, among other supportive care.

There are several plants which bear watching during the summer months, including corn cockle, nightshade, bladder pod, Johnson grass, rattlebush and white snakeroot.

Corn Cockle

The seeds of corn cockle — the most dangerous part of this plant — sometimes turn up in harvested grain since the plant has a fondness for growing in grain fields. The plant proper stays green in Winter with fine, white hairs on the underside of its leaves. Its flowers are purple, the dangerous seeds, black. Upon ingestion, the seeds irritate the mucosal linings, often leading to diarrhea and vertigo. A veterinarian will administer heart stimulants and other medications.

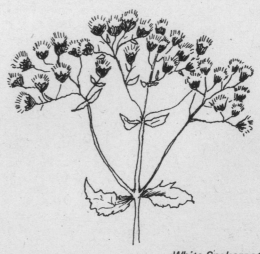
White Snakeroot

White snakeroot, scientifically tagged *Eupatorium rugosum,* is a year-round herb with many small, white flowers. It generally favors rich soils that are slightly moist, as sometimes found in forests or cleared lands. The results of eating white snakeroot are trembling, labored respiration, depression and death. Call the veterinarian at once, who sometimes can pull an afflicted horse through.

Bladder pod is a relatively tall plant with flat, tapered pods bearing two poisonous seeds. Favoring low ground all along the coastal plains of the Southern states, ingestion causes severe inflammation of the intestines with yellowish diarrhea, frequent urination, short, rapid breathing and death. Naturally, prevention rests with removal of the causative element. But ensure horses remain off the pasture for several weeks to avoid ingestion of seed pods already on the ground.

Nightshade

Nightshades, also called nettles or Jerusalem cherries depending upon the locale, somewhat resemble the tomato plant with yellow, red or black fruit when ripe. Found mostly on unworked land, along fence rows and in hay and grain fields, nightshade causes nausea, constipation or diarrhea, trembling and death if the horse eats the leaves, shoots or berries, any of which may contain the toxic agent. Quick action by the veterinarian is required and the chances of recovery are dependent upon this factor.

Johnson Grass

Bladder Pod

Johnson grass is a coarse weed grass with a white line splitting the blades in the center. Found primarily in fields throughout the South, it does dot the countryside as far north as New York, clean across to Iowa. When stunted by dry weather or when in its second growth, the plant is at its danger peak.

Johnson grass yields prussic acid upon digestion, which causes excess salivation, an increase both in pulse and respiration rates, convulsions and death. Speed of treatment is of vital importance. A veterinarian will administer sodium nitrate intravenously, often concurrently with sodium thiosulfate. The two compounds have proved effective in combatting absorption of the toxic agent into the system, which causes death.

Rattlebush

Castor Bean

Rattlebush causes most problems during the Fall and Winter along the coastal plains of the Southern states. A shrub with orange blossoms and pods which have four sharp angles, ingestion of the seeds results in a rapid pulse, weak respiration, diarrhea and death if not handled promptly. The veterinary surgeon will administer some type of laxative to rid the system of the offending seeds, then introduce stimulants and gentle feeds to speed recovery.

Laurel Cherry

Laurel cherry, castor bean and sorghum grow throughout the year, but are most dangerous during Winter and Spring.

Laurel cherry is easily distinguished as it grows in woods, along fence rows and in other uncultivated areas, by its shiny, leathery, evergreen leaves. Broken twigs give off the aroma of cherry bark and the wilted leaves cause prussic acid poisoning when eaten.

The symptoms of poisoning are the same as Johnson grass poisoning, as is the treatment scheme. Here again, speed is vital but secondary to preventing the condition initially.

The by-product of the castor bean is familiar to many horsemen as the hated castor oil. Horses don't share the trepidation horsemen associate with this plant, which is cultivated throughout the South, the oil going into the making of many popular lubricants.

Upon eating the beans, a horse becomes nauseous, has diarrhea, is thirsty, goes off his feed and oftentimes dies. A veterinarian will administer sedatives and heat, along with washing the intestines through an introduced solution. Sometimes he's successful.

Sorghum is known by a variety of names, some of them being Sudan grass, Kafir, milo, broomcorn, schrock and durra. No matter the name, the result's the same: death, if not treated promptly.

Sorghum is cultivated widely in the South, a coarse grass with a flower that reaches nearly eight feet in height. Ingestion of sorghum — especially the most dangerous second growth or stunted plant — results in the prussic acid syndrome associated with Johnson grass and laurel cherry; the treatment scheme is identical, too, and the best course is in prevention rather than after-the-fact attention.

POISONOUS PLANTS — WEST

The Western half of the U.S. has its share of poisonous plants, many having been committed to legendary tales of the Old West. A prime example is locoweed; there aren't many horsemen — or ordinary citizens, for that matter — unfamiliar with the name or the crazy antics it causes.

Looking first at plants which pose potential danger throughout the year, locoweed, chokeberry, groundsel, arrowgrass, milkweed and rayless goldenrod will be discussed.

Locoweed, also called poison vetch, is found virtually anywhere throughout the Western half of the nation, but usually goes uneaten unless other forage is scarce. Once a horse has gotten a taste of the purple, white, blue, or yellow-flowered plant, however, he favors it over anything — a condition which leads to his demise.

A horse generally must eat great amounts of the highly

POISONOUS PLANTS — WEST

Dangerous Season	Plant Name	Description	Symptoms
All Seasons	Locoweed	Low-growing weed with purple, white, blue or yellow flowers resembling sweetpeas	Loss of flesh and sense of direction, irregular gait, weakness, withdrawal, loss of muscular control, nervousness, unpredictability, death or chronic affliction
	Chokeberries	Large shrub with white flowers and small cherries	Nervousness, respiratory difficulty, convulsions, death
	Groundsel	Herb growing year-round with yellow flowers	Staggering, depression, aimless walking, running into obstacles, cirrhosis of the liver
	Arrowgrass	Grass-like, with thick leaves, fruit	Nervousness, trembling or jerking muscles, either shallow, rapid respiration or slow, deep breathing, convulsions, death
	Milkweed	Weed growing 1-3 feet high with greenish-white flowers, fruit, and plant exudes white sap when broken	Bloated, distended stomach, loss of muscular control, weak, rapid pulse, respiratory difficulty, convulsions, death through respiratory failure
(especially Fall and Winter)	Rayless goldenrod	Bushy, 2-4 feet tall with many yellow flowers	Trembling, depression, impaired respiration, death
Spring	Death camas	Bulbous root, similar to green onion with flat leaves	Drooling, staggering, weakness prostration, coma, death through cardiac/respiratory failure
(also Summer and Fall)	Yellow star thistle	Leaves bear dense coating of cottony hair, bright yellow flowers	Twitching of mouth, flicking of tongue, holding mouth open, death through starvation or thirst
(also Summer)	Lupine	Shiny green leaves, flowers of blue, white, pink, yellow or blue and white	Nervousness, convulsions
	Timber milkvetch	Low-growing weed with paired green leaves extending from stalks at base, flowers varying from white to violet resemble sweetpeas	Nervousness, cracking of hoofs, lameness, stiffness of joints, dullness, lack of vitality, emaciation, hair loss, "blind staggers"
(also Summer)	Indian hemp	Grows to 5 feet, leaves turn bright yellow in Fall, hollow stalks exude sticky, white sap when broken	Dilated pupils, blue coloration of mouth/nostril linings, temperature/pulse rate increase, weakness, staggering, coma, labored respiration near termination in death

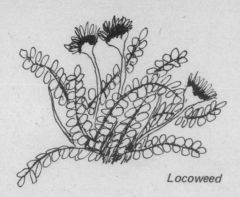

Locoweed

Groundsel

toxic weed over a period of two to five straight weeks, whereupon the toxic agents build to a level which causes death. Even if removed from contact, a horse having eaten of the weed seldom recovers normal behavior completely, making him virtually useless as a saddle, pack or show animal. Too, a horse once affected is prone to repeated poisoning upon subsequent contact with the plant.

The typical symptoms of a horse suffering locoweed poisoning are loss of flesh, loss of sense of direction, irregular gait, weakness, withdrawal from other animals, loss of muscle control, nervousness and he's prone to violent, unpredictable actions when disturbed or frightened. There's no known treatment regimen for locoweed poisoning, so it's up to the horseman to remove his animals from infested pasture or range lands.

Groundsel is another plant to be watchful for throughout the year. Found primarily in grassy areas and plains, the yellow-flowered herb causes these symptoms: slight staggering, lack of interest in his surroundings, aimless walking, running into fences and other obstacles, and cirrhosis of the liver, among others. About the only treatment routine is removal of the horse from infested pasture, with supplemental feed given. Naturally, the herb should be eradicated where found.

Chokeberry

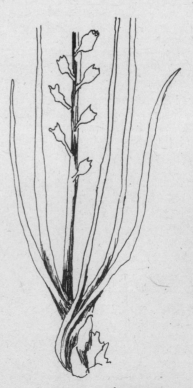

Arrowgrass

Chokeberry, also called wild cherry, is found on prairies and dry slopes throughout the West, growing into large shrubs adorned with white flowers and cherries. Interestingly, it's not the cherry fruit which causes the problem, but the leaves. Upon ingestion, the leaves result in the formation of prussic acid. This causes nervousness, difficult breathing, convulsions and, ultimately, death. Similar to the treatment scheme for Johnson grass and sorghum, prompt administration of sodium nitrate and sodium thiosulfate intravenously can effect recovery.

Arrowgrass contributes to the three to five-percent loss of range livestock per year and its history is interesting. Found on a line from Montana to New Mexico and states west, it grows mostly in marshy pastures or around some water source. So long as the plant receives adequate moisture, it doesn't cause poisoning. But should its growth be stunted by drought or a sudden frost, this grasslike plant assumes the poisonous trait.

The amount of arrowgrass required for death depends upon the relative toxicity of the plant. And the horse must ingest the fatal amount at one feeding; the poison isn't cumulative and therefore is dissipated. But when sufficient amounts have been eaten, the horse will appear nervous, have trembling or jerking muscles, may either have shallow, rapid respiration or slow, deep breathing, and convulsions which terminate in death. Sodium nitrate and sodium thiosulfate therapy has proved beneficial in some cases, providing they are treated rapidly.

Rayless Goldenrod

Milkweed

Ground Level

Death Camas
(root & blossoms)

While cattle and sheep are affected more often than horses, equine cases of milkweed poisoning crop up occasionally. Distribution ranges throughout the Western states, with the exception of Montana, Wyoming, southern Idaho, North and South Dakota, much of eastern Nevada, a hunk of northwest Utah, and eastern Kansas and Oklahoma.

The plant, which derives its name from the sticky, milk-white sap that exudes from any broken part, favors uncultivated land like roadsides, ditches, vacant lots, et al., but can creep into land under cultivation. Growing from one to three feet high, festooned with greenish-white flowers and fruit often concurrently, its life cycle begins in early Spring and it's dangerous all year. As with other poisonous plants, horses will leave it alone unless extremely hungry and can munch their last meal in a short period.

Afflicted horses will have bloated, distended stomachs, lose all muscular control, stagger or fall repeatedly, have a weak, rapid pulse and respiratory difficulty, and may suffer convulsions. Death usually results from respiratory paralysis. Time from onset of symptoms to termination in death ranges from several hours to several days. There is no known treatment for milkweed poisoning.

Rayless goldenrod is a year-round plant that's most dangerous during Fall and Winter. A bushy plant some two to four feet tall with numerous yellow flowers, it dots the grasslands, banks of irrigation canals, dry plains and open woodlands of the West, showing its adaptability to differing soil conditions.

Upon ingestion, the plant produces trembling, depression, impaired respiration and death. A veterinarian can't do much upon arrival, so responsibility for eradication of the source rests with the horseman.

Poisonous plants to be on guard against during Spring are death camas, yellow star thistle, lupine and timber milkvetch.

Death camas claims the lives of numerous range animals during the early spring months, since it's one of the first to emerge from the sandy plains and foothills. Horses will readily eat the bulbous-rooted plant, which resembles a green onion with flat leaves, if other forage is scarce, often the case early in the year. Generally in April or May, the yellow or white flowers appear in clusters atop the stalk, which measures from four to eighteen inches in height.

Death camas affects the central nervous system, leading

possible the plant will take root in cultivated haying pastures. The plant, even when cut, retains its toxicity so the wise horseman will examine the feeds given to his animals.

Another plant that's dangerous in the Spring — but also during summer and fall months — is the yellow star thistle. During late Summer and early autumn, this perennial poisoner blooms with bright yellow flowers, rising above leaves that bear a dense, cottony covering of hair. Found primarily in waste or uncultivated areas, although it can thrive in pastures, yellow star thistle causes twitching of a horse's mouth muscles, accompanied by constant flicking of the tongue, both symptoms seemingly involuntary. In latter stages, the horse generally will keep the mouth open and dies either from starvation or thirst. While the condition should be instantly reported to a veterinarian, don't hope for miracles; there's no known treatment regimen for a horse so poisoned.

Lupine

Yellow Star Thistle

to abnormal function of the heart and respiratory systems. The horse will drool, stagger, become too weak to stand and slips into a coma followed by death. Some horses that eat slight amounts may recover, although individuals consuming great quantities of the highly poisonous plant generally die.

Since death camas grows throughout the year, it's

Lupine, while dangerous from the time it begins growing in the Spring until killed by autumn's first frost, is deadliest during Summer when in its seed stage.

Growing in most dry to slightly moist soils in the foothills and mountains of the Western states, lupine has shiny green leaves crested with an attractive clutch of blossoms in blue, white, pink, yellow or blue-and-white coloration. The plant generally is shunned by horses when good forage is available, but will be consumed readily if such is lacking.

Since the poison isn't cumulative, a horse can ingest varying amounts of the feed without expiring, depending upon the time of year and toxicity of the plant. If a horse has eaten several pounds in one sitting, expect him to exhibit signs of nervousness and convulsions. If caught in time, a veterinarian will administer purgatives to rid the intestines of the plant, perhaps giving sedatives to calm the horse and ease the convulsions.

Timber milkvetch, which infrequently affects horses, is found from the Rocky Mountains westward, with isolated stands in South Dakota, usually at altitudes between six and eleven thousand feet. These areas are beneficial to the development of selenium in the foliage, which causes the problems when ingested in large quantities over short periods.

stumbling over obstacles in his path, although there needn't be any deviation of other bodily functions like respiration or pulse. The condition worsens until the horse dies through respiratory failure, often some two to three months after eating the poisonous plant. And once the horse begins manifesting symptoms of selenium poisoning, there's nothing that can be done; there's no known cure for selenium poisoning.

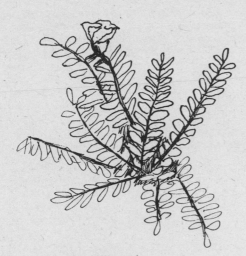

Timber Milkvetch

The horse suffering from selenium poisoning, as the condition is called, often has cracking hoofs, lameness, stiffness of the joints, dullness and lack of vitality, emaciation and a condition known as the "blind staggers." The first signs of selenium poisoning are loss of long hair from the mane and tail. Shortly thereafter, the hoofs crack at the coronary bands, resulting from an interruption of horn growth. When hoof growth is resumed, the dead horn is pushed downward where it is sloughed off.

If a horse has the "blind staggers," he usually begins

Indian Hemp

Indian hemp, also known as dogbane, grows to altitudes of about 7000 feet, from Montana to New Mexico and all

POISONOUS PLANTS — NATIONWIDE

Dangerous Season	Plant Name	Description	Symptoms
All Seasons	Poison hemlock	Purple-spotted, hollow stem, leaves resemble parsley with small clusters of white flowers, odor of parsnip when crushed	Bloating, salivation, loss of appetite, feeble, rapid pulse, trembling, incoordination, dilation of pupils, coma, death from respiratory paralysis
(East, Spring; West, All Seasons)	Water hemlock	Hollow stem, tuberous roots, white flowers	Salivation, convulsions, diaphragm contractions, dilation of pupils, pain, death
(East, Spring; West, All Seasons)	Larkspur	Commercially grown, height from 12 inches to 3-4 feet	Repeated falling, nausea, rapid pulse/respiration, straddled stance, constipation, bloating, death
(East, Spring and occasionally Fall; West, Spring, Summer and Fall)	Cocklebur	Low-growing weed, fruit is covered by spikes	Nausea, depression, weak pulse, prostration, spasms, death; chronic cases have slow recovery

states west. A sturdy plant that begins growth during late Spring or early Summer, Indian hemp grows to a height of nearly five feet and is easily recognized during the Fall because its leaves turn a bright yellow color.

Normally, horses will avoid the plant, which has a bitter, sticky white juice in the hollow stalks. However, when exceedingly hungry or when being driven to summer ranges through concentrations of Indian hemp, the odd horse may nibble; it doesn't take much to cause death, either. In fact, researchers feel that only one-half to three-fourths ounce of leaves per one hundred pounds of body weight is all that's required for death.

A horse stricken with Indian hemp poisoning usually will have dilated pupils with a blue coloration in the linings of the mouth and nostrils. Too, temperature and pulse rate increase and the horse exhibits signs of weakness within six to twelve hours after ingesting the plant. The horse may stagger and, as the condition worsens, drop into a coma with accompanying convulsions. Just before death, his respiration will be labored.

There isn't much a veterinarian can do and the speed of progression makes treatment difficult. There aren't any known drugs that combat the poison, but introducing mineral oil to coat the stomach — followed by drenching to avoid dehydration — has proved beneficial in some instances.

Poison Hemlock

Poison hemlock is a relatively attractive plant with a purple-spotted, hollow stem. The leaves resemble parsley and, upon being ground between the fingers, give off a smell not unlike the parsnip vegetable. It proliferates along roadside ditches and in damp waste areas.

The alkaloid poison, which is strongest in the seeds, causes bloating, salivation, loss of appetite and the horse has a feeble pulse. Contact a veterinarian as soon as any of these symptoms become apparent.

Spring is the most dangerous period for water hemlock, larkspur and cocklebur. The water hemlock, akin to its name, favors moist or wet ground in open clearings. A hollow-stemmed plant, it has tuberous roots and white flowers.

After eating the leaves, flowers or stems, the horse begins to drool, followed by convulsions, diaphragm contractions, dilation of the pupils and the horse appears in obvious pain. Death terminates the condition if a veterinarian doesn't arrive quickly. He may try sedatives to control the convulsions and heart spasms, along with laxatives and astringents.

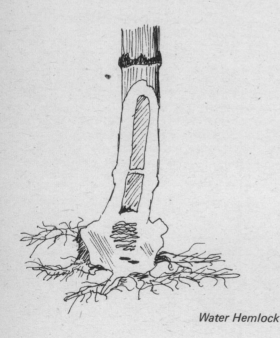

Water Hemlock

POISONOUS PLANTS — NATIONWIDE

There are some poisonous plants that don't respect the boundary formed by the Mississippi River, being found on both sides with consistency. There are water hemlock, poison hemlock, larkspur and cocklebur.

Larkspur

212

Larkspur is a member of the *Delphinium* species that is present throughout the year and most dangerous during Spring. In some areas, it's grown commercially and frequently is found growing wild in clearings. It contains an alkaloid that causes repeated falling, nausea, rapid pulse and respiration, a straddled stance, constipation and bloating. Upon arrival, a veterinarian will administer injections of physostigmine salicylate and pilocarpine hydrochloride. These often will clear the condition.

Cocklebur

Cocklebur is found growing throughout the country. The fruit of the plant is armed with spikes, hence its name, and ingestion causes depression, prostration and a weak pulse. Recovery is slow in chronic cases, even with supportive care prescribed by a veterinary surgeon.

There may be other poisonous plants indigenous to specific areas of the country. Since they don't exact much of a toll on the equine population, reportage isn't possible. Horsemen aware of such dangers in their communities — as with the plants listed here — should keep their animals out of contact that could lead to their death or loss for all practical purposes.

As stressed earlier, the wise horseman inspects his feeds carefully and refrains from feeding any contaminated with foreign material of questionable origin. But the horseowner also should watch for spoilage in his horse feeds, as this can lead to poisoning.

Sweet clover poisoning occurs infrequently and it usually takes several weeks or even months of continuous feeding before a mature animal exhibits symptoms that something is awry. Usually, the first symptoms are stiffness and lameness, often with swelling caused by hemorrhaging beneath the skin surface. The horse may pass blood-tinged feces and appear anemic. Concurrently, pulse and respiration rates increase. This syndrome often terminates in death.

About the only way a horseman can be assured of

avoiding sweet clover poisoning is through not feeding this roughage. If sweet clover is well-cured, however, there is no danger. But if there are visible signs of spoilage, get rid of it.

At times, a horseman won't detect other-than-usual appearance of feeds, but they can be contaminated nonetheless. There are specific types of fungus or bacteria that can be absorbed into or attach to the feeds which are invisible to the naked eye. For this reason, if a horse begins exhibiting any symptoms compatible with the poisons outlined heretofore, contact a veterinarian immediately.

Equine poisoning isn't confined solely to ingestion of plant matter, however. Snakes account for a respectable percentage each year and, in snake-infested areas, it's unusual for a veterinarian not to see cases of snakebite.

There are four species of poisonous snakes indigenous to the United States, though horsemen need be concerned only with three: rattlesnake, copperhead and cottonmouth moccasin. The fourth reptile, the coral snake, is the most poisonous of the lot. His mouth is not equipped with fangs like the other pit vipers, his poison being introduced through a chewing motion. This fact, coupled with his relatively small mouth, makes the coral snake more of a danger to horseman than horse.

There are at least twenty-six different kinds of rattlesnakes in the contiguous forty-eight states, most prevalent being the diamondback. This pit viper is a swift striker and is capable of injecting large amounts of venom quickly.

Contrary to popular belief, a rattler doesn't always rattle before striking. Many times the rattling will attract a curious horse, resulting in a bite on the head. The legs are the second target most often hit by fangs.

Unless the horseman is present when the bite occurs, he may not recognize the animal's problem; the hair coat conceals fang puncture marks. Careful examination should be made at the site of any swelling, usually the first reaction to the bite. Scientists feel this swelling is nature's way of counteracting the poison, slowing its absorption into the bloodstream.

If the horse is bitten on the head, it swells grotesquely. If on the leg, swelling generally causes lameness. There may be intense pain throughout the body and the horse may be weak, have impaired vision, be nauseous, suffer paralysis and the skin may slough off at the bite site.

Treatment requires clipping the hair from around the site of fang entry and, if on a leg, a tourniquet should be applied just above the wound. The fang marks then should be cut with a sharp razor blade in the form of a cross, with suction being applied through suction cups furnished with each snakebite kit.

Many equine practitioners feel that the time involved with the tourniquet and incision procedures is better spent getting the horse to a veterinarian. Horses rarely die from snake-bite and, in those odd fatal cases, death is the result of suffocation caused by the nose swelling shut.

Most veterinarians, when treating a horse with a snakebite on the nose or face, promptly pass a stomach tube or hose up the nose, into the trachea if necessary, to get above the area affected or that may be affected by swelling. The end of the tube then is fastened to the exterior of the halter and left in place until the swelling subsides.

Some deaths connected with snakebite are the result of secondary infection. Because of this, a veterinarian will administer antibiotics to guard against this problem, along with other symptomatic treatment as indicated.

As stated at the beginning of this segment, poisoning takes the lives of nearly five percent of all range livestock, a toll which could be avoided. We hope this segment aids toward that end.

Chapter 10

FOCUSING ON FEET

A Fact-Finding Expedition Inside The Hoof Details Its Complexities!

BASIC UNDERSTANDING of anatomy is important whether your interest in the animal is strictly for pleasure or eventually, a combination of profit and pleasure. Although medical science has advanced tremendously the past few years, enabling the veterinarian to control illness more proficiently, proper care of the horse is preventive medicine no horseowner should ignore.

The old saying, "No hoof, no horse," isn't an old wives' tale; it actually is a fact. Knowing the parts comprising the lower leg which includes the hoof along with their specific function, helps you practice proper leg and foot care just a little better. Once the question, "why" is answered, it will be easier to recognize the difference between proper care, adequate care or carelessness. The results of the care given will be quite apparent after a little time and experience.

Few potential horse purchasers bother to consult a veterinarian or horseshoer for advice concerning a horse they consider buying. Any unsoundness in the animal would be brought to their immediate attention and just might possibly affect the purchase. The present consideration is that a lame horse is more often than not a poor selection as a riding horse.

The horse with a perfect hoof need not have even wear on them. A competent horseshoer, through trimming and special shoeing if required, keeps each leg and hoof in proper position so the internal parts are functioning properly. When the hoof is neglected, the lower leg becomes involved in short time. There are many cases of the horseshoer being confronted with different hoof conditions on the same animal.

In the natural state, horses travel barefoot and nature seems most often to supply what is required to keep a healthy hoof. Unless man uses him on surfaces detrimental to hoof soundness, or the horse develops problems requiring corrective shoes, the great majority of horseshoers will tell you the shoe is not required or suggested.

Since there is little difference between the front and hind lower leg and hoof they are cared for in the same way. Each is composed of bones, tendons, and ligaments. The horse carries more weight on his front end than the rear, therefore the front hoof is slightly larger.

Bones of the lower leg are shown in the accompanying illustration. The cannon bone extends from the knee (or hock) to the fetlock. Although this bone is exposed to all sorts of injury, it rarely is broken because of its strength.

On each side, toward the rear of the cannon bone, there are two splint bones extending about three-quarters the length of the cannon. At the lower end of the splints, support and attachment to the cannon is by means of a strong ligament. Any excessive strain in this lower area results in damage referred to as splints.

Sesamoids are two triangular bones forming a part of each fetlock joint. They are covered with ligaments and cartilage, moving in conjunction with the action of the rear area of the cannon bone.

The navicular bone (distal sesamoid) is located in an opening to the rear of the coffin bone and moves with the action of the short pastern bone.

The two sesamoids and navicular bone have the deep flexor tendon toward the rear and covering the lower portion of the navicular bone. It is in this area that navicular problems are found.

Each end of the bones mentioned are parts of a moving joint and attached to each other by means of ligaments. Ligaments are strong, slightly elastic bands of connective tissue. The ends of the bones are covered with a smooth, protective covering called cartilage, and contained within a sac producing the liquid synovia for the lubrication of the joint. Synovia is produced as it is needed by the joint and when damage occurs to the joint, synovia production is increased.

An injury to a joint may result in an opening within the joint, thus increasing the normal production of synovia, which in turn seeps through the opening. The healing process is retarded considerably, subjects the area to infection, and last but by no means least, is painful to the horse. The result of this damage could be permanent disability.

In the upper leg, muscles are present that continue from the knee or hock as tendons. The common digital extensor muscle of the upper foreleg acts as an extensor to all joints below the elbow but flexes the elbow as well. Knee action is controlled by this extensor, which is located to the front of the knee and down to its attachment on the upper end of the cannon bone.

The superficial digital flexor is a muscle, continuing from the back of the knee as a tendon, and divides into two branches at the fetlock joint. The ends of these two branches continue on, attaching into each side of the short pastern bone upper end. It is located to the rear of the deep flexor tendon and performs the function which its name implies, that of flexing the knee, fetlock and pastern joints.

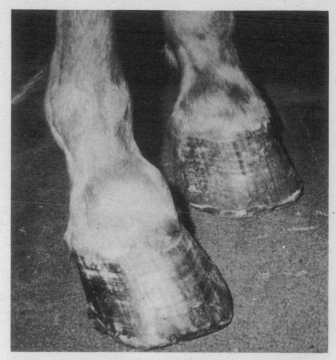

A key to hoof problems lies in formation of odd shapes, like this right front foot. The cause here was ringbone. Other hoof/leg ailments are outlined in accompanying text.

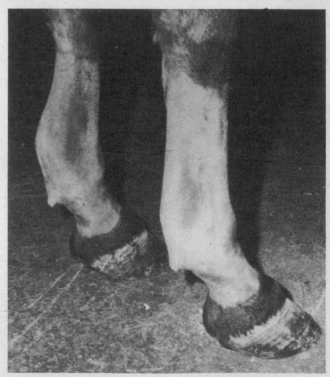

The classic example of a bowed tendon is shown on this left foreleg. The right foreleg, while almost normal, shows signs of having been bowed tendon victim, too. Horses with this condition require protracted vet care.

The deep flexor tendon is located to the front of the superficial flexor tendon, beginning in the upper leg as the deep digital flexor muscle. This tendon is the strongest in the lower leg and ends on the bottom of the coffin bone. These muscles and tendons act as shock absorbers for the leg as well as providing joint mobility.

Tendons in the foreleg, especially the cannon area, are subject to injury and strain far more often than the tendons in the hind leg. The deep flexor tendon is most often injured and inflamed, resulting in the impairment called bowed tendons or tendinitis.

If you visualize the tendons and ligaments as strong, heavy-duty rubber bands holding each of the bones in the proper place and relationship to each other, it is easier to understand just how much elasticity is required of them, and any damage done is extremely difficult to correct and impossible to replace. As good horsemen, the only recourse is to avoid damage or injury whenever and wherever we can.

The horse's foot consists of more than the hoof. It is comprised of the long pastern bone, short pastern bone, coffin bone, navicular bone, hoof, elastic parts, sensitive parts, and horny parts.

Hoof growth, being a continual process, varies slightly among different horses. All growth is in a downward and forward direction. Conditions under which the horse is kept must be taken into consideration when discussing hoof growth rates. Of the many practices involving horse maintenance, correct feeding, regular trimming and proper hoof moisture content are important to overall well-being. Surprising as it may seem, hoof growth definitely is affected by them. Dry, hot climates or surroundings will produce a hard, dry hoof; moist climates or surroundings will produce a soft, moist hoof.

Each condition mentioned requires the horseman to balance the situation correctively. Hoofs require a specific amount of moisture to remain healthy and if moisture does not come from the surrounding areas, it must be applied manually in the form of hoof dressings. When these dressings are applied, it is to the coronet (coronary band) area since this is the origin of all hoof growth. Many horsemen prefer using the wet soaking boots rather than the commercially prepared dressing compounds. How you accomplish the task of maintaining proper moisture in the hoof is not as important as being certain it is present.

Generally speaking, most hoof problems stem from improper care and some effects cannot be totally corrected. A prime example is a contracted heel developing from lack of proper moisture content. Once this condition is established, corrective shoes can help, but never will eliminate the actual problem.

The foot is a skillfully designed piece of living machinery performing many more functions than flexible support. You could compare the foot acting as shock absorbers to springs on a car. Can you imagine how uncomfortable it would be to ride in a car on uneven surfaces for long periods of time? Could you begin to estimate the extensive wear and tear on related automotive parts without these shock absorbers?

A great deal of pressure is exerted on the leg when the horse is in motion. As the horse travels faster, the pressure impact increases proportionally. Because of this pressure, the healthy hoof will expand to cushion the tremendous impact.

The frog is a V-shaped spongy, though horny, part first receiving the impact. Under pressure, it spreads out, forcing the bars outward. At the same time, the digital (plantar) cushion spreads and forces the lateral cartilages outward. The digital cushion is a wedge-shaped pliant cushion; the large lateral cartilages are between the upper wings of the coffin bone and the upper coronet. These are the highly elastic parts within the foot structure.

This is the main reason most horseshoers will advise against shoeing a horse unless it is absolutely required. The shoe is

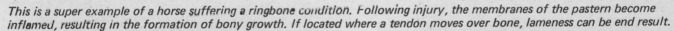

This is a super example of a horse suffering a ringbone condition. Following injury, the membranes of the pastern become inflamed, resulting in the formation of bony growth. If located where a tendon moves over bone, lameness can be end result.

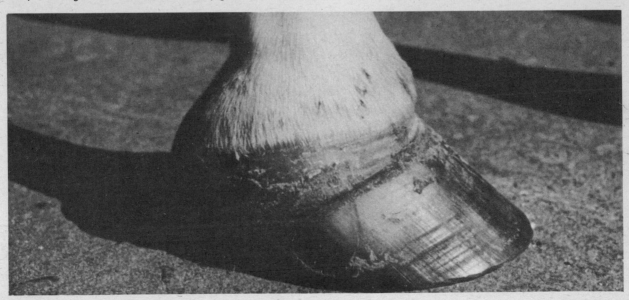

metal and will not contract and expand with the hoof as it was designed, to cushion the pressure exerted upon it in motion.

Sensitive parts of the leg contain numerous veins, the healthy spongy frog contains proper moisture. When the horse is in motion, the natural expansion and contraction of the foot parts stimulate internal blood circulation.

As noted previously, all hoof growth originates in the sensitive parts of the foot. One sensitive part, the corium, covers the bones and elastic parts of the foot. The coronary band (coronet) circles the top of the hoof from one bulb to the other. It is a strong piece of flesh, approximately an inch wide, and contained in the coronary groove along the upper interior surface of the wall. From the papillae covering the surface of the coronary band, growth of the horny wall takes place. A thin band of flesh above the coronary band, the perioplic ring, produces the periople which is the glossy surface of the hoof wall retarding moisture evaporation.

In addition to the sensitive parts mentioned, there are sensitive coverings on the surfaces of the coffin bone and lateral cartilages. This develops into the horny laminae of the inside hoof wall. The sensitive sole covers the bottom surface of the coffin bone and develops, through papillae, into the horny sole. The sensitive frog covers the lower surface of the digital cushion and its papillae develop into the horny frog.

Because of wear upon the bearing surfaces of the hoof itself, nature has provided it with continual growth, as man has

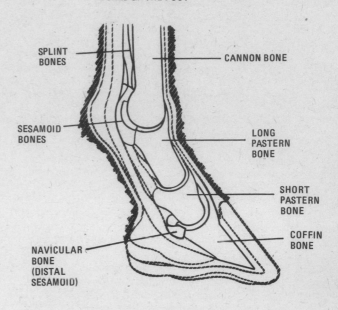

As noted in the text, a horse's foot is a complex piece of animal engineering. This view shows hoof components.

The bones of a horse's foot are highly complex and the accompanying text outlines some of the possible ailments.

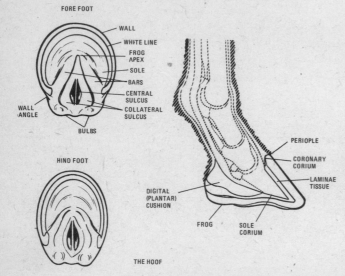

fingernail growth. The hoof composition is tough and durable to withstand most hard use within reason. Hoof parts are the wall, the sole, and the frog. The wall is a sturdy protective wall for the sensitive portions within the hoof itself and is support for the animal's weight. At the front, or toe, the wall thickness is greater than it is at the back, or heel, since the heel area expands when weight is present. The top portion of the hoof is the corona and it is from this portion that the wall covers the entire outer surface of the hoof. The area falling halfway between the toe and heel is referred to as the quarters, and directly behind are the bars, which act as weight bearing sur-

faces and control hoof expansion.

The frog function has been discussed, but it is good to remember that although it is a tough, spongy part, it is located near tender portions above it and punctures or diseases of the frog can spread to them, causing infections and possible permanent disability through injury.

Enough horse leg anatomy has been covered to keep anyone but the anatomy-avid reader switching from text to illustration and back to text. It will require little memorization on your part to perceive that when an unknowing or careless horseman abuses the functions of the leg, he is asking for trouble. Each part of the leg was placed in specific relationship to another and the functions of each is clearly defined. When undue stress, strain, injury, lack of care are present, faults or impairment will be the result you have to live with.

It is certain that you know at least one "cowboy," no relation to the good old Western horseman by any loose definition. This guy or gal just gets on a horse and puts him through all the hot and fast motions he can think of, whether the horse is in balance for the move or not, whether the animal is trained for the maneuver or not. Another common failing in the would-be horseman is apparent when you see him pounding his mount on frozen ground. Then there is the poor horse who doesn't know how to pivot and is repeatedly abused in the leg area because the rider doesn't know how to train him to pivot properly.

The reason for pointing out faults in horsemen is for no other purpose than to restate a thoroughly sound practice when purchasing a trained and mature animal. If at all possible, consult your veterinarian and horseshoer prior to horse purchase if you are not as qualified as they are in spotting problem legs. Remember, once you purchase the unsound animal as a pleasure horse, the pleasure may end abruptly. Not one of us would expect the novice driver or one who doesn't drive at all, to purchase a used car without mechanical inspection first, so why not be as reasonable when buying a horse? Some horsemen have no idea how the horse was taken care of, or possibly abused, any more than the non-mechanic does about a "good buy used car" from Friendly Sam's lot number three!

One problem with the leg is extremely difficult to illustrate clearly and is primarily the product of unsanitary barns. It is a disease of the frog known as thrush. To anyone with half a nostril, the odor is unappetizingly overwhelming. Needless to say, with cleaning the hoof daily and sanitary stable practices, the disease should not be found in your barn. If the frog is extremely moist and infectious, with an fetid odor, call your horseshoer or vet; he'll tell you immediately what medication to use as a remedy for the problem.

A few of the more common areas to examine when trying to spot poor legs or poor conformation faults are shown in the accompanying illustrations with brief descriptions. No one is expected or encouraged to become a specialist overnight in the subject, but a more knowledgeable horseman can make it easier for the professional when called on a visit.

Sesamoiditis: The sesamoid bones — a part of the fetlock joint, are injured through concussion or joint abuse. A visual swelling is present and is hard to the touch. In this laming condition, new bone may be formed in an area where it interferes with ligaments and joint action.

Ringbone: Ringbone occurs in the bones of the pastern through injury or abuse. The membranes covering the bone/bones may become seriously inflamed, resulting in a production of bony growth. If the growth is located where a tendon moves over bone, lameness is the final effect.

Sidebone: Sidebones is a condition where the cartilage on either wing of the coffin bone becomes ossified. Since the cartilage is part of the leg shock absorbing system, heavy and repeated concussion causes them to lose resiliency. Lameness in the usual meaning of impaired motion is not a permanent effect.

Contracted Heel: In this condition, normal expansion and contraction of the heel does not take place. It is not a disease nor does it initially cause lameness. Many causes of this condition can be and are eliminated through correctly regulated hoof trimming by a qualified horseshoer. However, two causes of contracted heel can fall within the confines of good horse care — in that neglect of the owner to have the hoof properly trimmed at all times, and allowing the hoof to dry out excessively and remain in this condition. When the hoof reaches this radical stage of contracted heel, the horseshoer must resort to a corrective shoe, and the owner must make every effort to return moisture to the heel. In many radical cases, the heel is never returned to a normal condition, and the heel remains in a limited degree of contraction and expansion.

Sprained Tendons and Ligaments: Tendons, a portion of a muscle, are composed of strong strands of fiber but are far less able to contract and expand as the upper muscle tissues do. This limitation makes them subject to injurious sprains, the

Splints sometimes are hard to detect at the outset and, when seen plainly, usually indicate advanced condition. They aren't necessarily bothersome, but they can hamper performance.

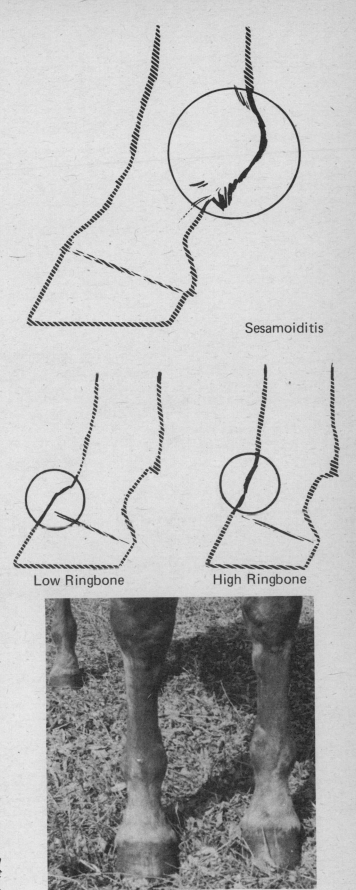

Sesamoiditis

Low Ringbone

High Ringbone

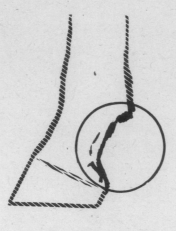

Sidebone   Contracted Heel

This is a sad example of how bad founder can become, the Shetland pony's feet having grown so long the horn is curving upward. Owner neglect was the cause.

cause of which are varied and numerous. Ligaments are similar to tendons in basic structure, but they are not a portion of elastic muscle. Their function is to hold one or more bones together or support joints. When the superficial tendon is slightly strained, a minor swelling may be seen and heat is generated. Although no apparent lameness is seen, the horse will flinch when slight pressure is applied to the affected tendon. In severe strains, the tendon fibers may rupture, causing a great degree of swelling along the entire tendon. The effect will be lameness and severe pain results when the area is touched. The suspensory ligament is attached to the top of the cannon bone, just behind the knee. It continues down the back of the cannon bone between the two splint bones to the sesamoid bones, where it divides into four strands. Two front strands wrap around the fetlock joint and merge with the extensor tendon, located to the front of the pastern bone; the rear two strands attach to the sesamoid bones. This ligament suspends the fetlock joint in its correct position and also acts as a tendon support. Generally, this ligament is not affected by strains unless a tendon ruptures as a result of hard, fast, and regular punishment from work on hard surfaces. When this condition occurs, the cause or area of trouble is difficult to

This out-of-condition horse may suffer leg ailments!

diagnose correctly at times due to the great amount of swelling present. If the leg is carefully examined, no "bow" will be present in a ruptured suspensory ligament as there will be in severe cases of ruptured tendons.

Founder: Founder is the common name given to laminitis, a serious disorder that causes excruciating pain to the afflicted horse. Essentially, it starts with inflammation of the interior of a horse's hoof. Since the hoof wall prohibits expansion, pressure on the nerves builds within the foot, causing pain.

Founder is caused by having the feet trimmed too closely, although more often through allowing a hot, sweating horse all the cold water he wants. Too, founder can be caused by ingestion of large amount of grain in one feeding, or eating too much grass at one time. A horse can be foundered, also, by working on hard ground, and mares have been foundered by retention of some afterbirth materials. Laminitis also has been linked to uterine infection in mares, or the strenous working of an out-of-condition horse. Usually only the forefeet are affected, but cases in which all four extremities were involved have been recorded.

Horses once foundered are prone to the condition in the future. Chronic cases are characterized by a dropped sole, the bone of the third phalanx extended downward farther than normal. Hoof growth will be speeded, resulting in telltale rings of growth. In extreme cases, the toe actually curves upward like a ram's horn.

Navicular Disease: The navicular bone is small, smooth and round, located at the rear of the cannon bone. Sometimes this bone may be fractured or drained of its lubricating fluid through a puncture of the frog, causing pain when the tendons controlling hoof movement slide over it. A horse with this incurable condition generally places weight on the toe of the affected foot, resulting in stumbling and making him unsafe for riding. It's difficult condition for a veterinarian to diagnose and an X-ray is the only sure method.

Thrush: This frog infection, characterized by dead sole and foul odor, is guaranteed to clear a horseman's sinuses! Caused by unsanitary conditions or failure to clean the horse's feet, it can involve the sensitive tissues of the foot and cause lameness. Sometimes an extremely thrush-riddled frog will be shed completely, a new frog growing in its place.

"No hoof, no horse" is valid, providing more is included in the old saying than hoof alone. The lower leg is the part of the horse referred to in the old axiom, the hoof being one part of the intricate system of animal engineering.

B: Shoeing The Normal Foot

NOT ALL HORSES are blessed with perfect feet and legs. Sometimes, due to poor conformation or accident, a horse may have a defect. The seriousness of the abnormality will depend upon the degree to which the horse's gaits are affected. If the horse paddles slightly, his gait may be unsightly but he still can be a useful, dependable animal. But if the faulty foot conformation is such that the horse strikes himself or is not surefooted, his usefulness and even his safety as a riding animal may be limited. The horse is an athlete and his greatest usefulness is in being able to move with speed, agility, balance and safety. If he is limited in these aspects because of abnormal feet and legs, his value is drastically reduced.

Some abnormalities can be corrected or at least improved with proper trimming and shoeing of the horse's feet. Ideally, corrective trimming should begin shortly after foaling. Regular and frequent trimmings can help to straighten feet and legs as the young horse grows, often completely correcting minor faults and greatly improving ones more serious. Some faults never can be fully corrected, but proper trimming and shoeing can help to the extent that the horse still can be useful and sound.

Corrective work on a horse's feet always should be done gradually and with care. The object is to make the shape, level and the angle of the foot as nearly normal as possible so the horse will have a normal gait. Trimming never should be too drastic, because you may put strain on the bones of the leg. You cannot really change the bone structure once the horse is mature and to attempt it usually will make the horse lame and sore, or create problems worse than what you started with.

Faulty gaits in a mature horse cannot be totally corrected because any permanent changes in the conformation of the horse's feet and legs can't be made. But corrective trimming and shoeing can modify the horse's gait and way of going to improve it and perhaps make the horse more functionally agile in his traveling. Remember that this improvement is only temporary — the correction must be repeated with each trimming and shoeing.

Before describing in detail corrective trimming and shoeing, attention should be given to trimming and shoeing the normal foot. One always should have a good knowledge of a horse's feet, legs and gait — and horseshoeing in general — before attempting corrective trimming and shoeing.

FRONT SHOE — Parts of a shoe
Heel
Crease or Fullering
Quarter
Branch
Nail-holes
Web
Toe

Hind feet are smaller and narrower — more pointed. Front feet are rounder.

HIND SHOE

Plain "Plate" Shoes

A. B. C.

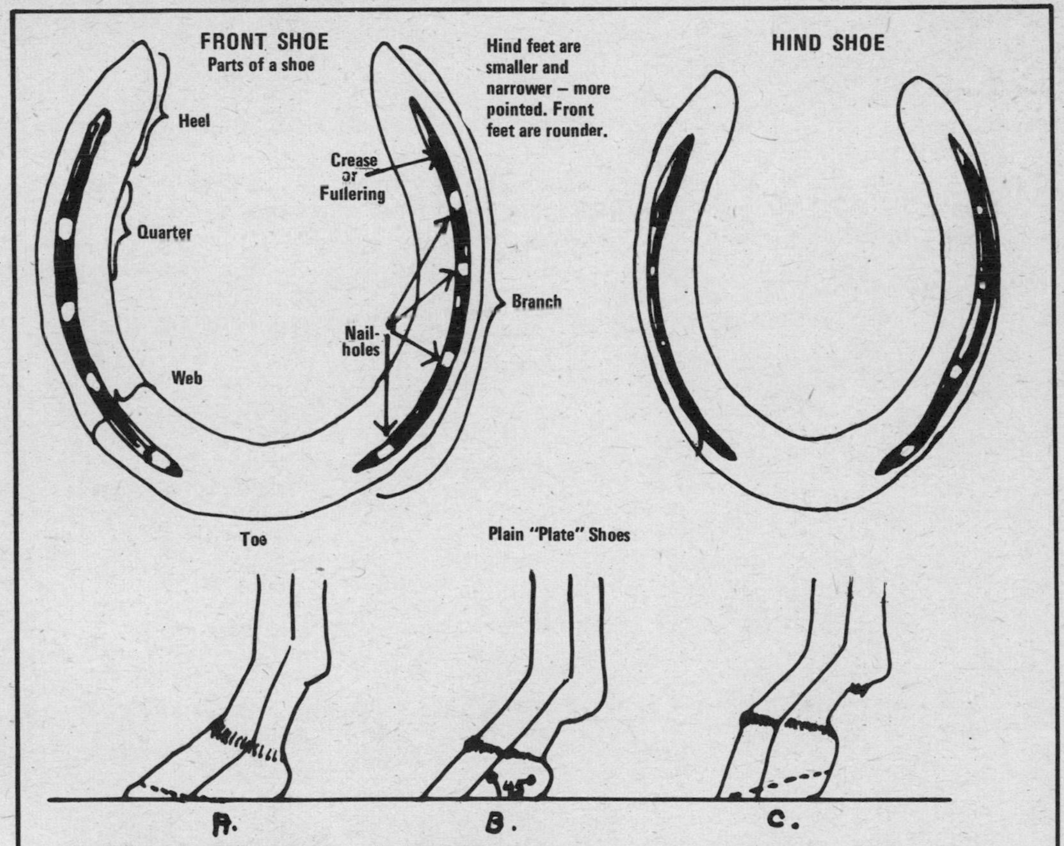

A. Toe too long — foot and pastern angle broken backward. Dotted line shows how foot should be trimmed to straighten the foot angle.

B. Normal, balanced foot.

C. Stumpy foot with heels too long — angle broken foreward. Heels and quarters should be trimmed.

The horseshoe has come a long way since the first attempts using leather, et al. Plates today are of steel or aluminum, which are changed every four to six weeks.

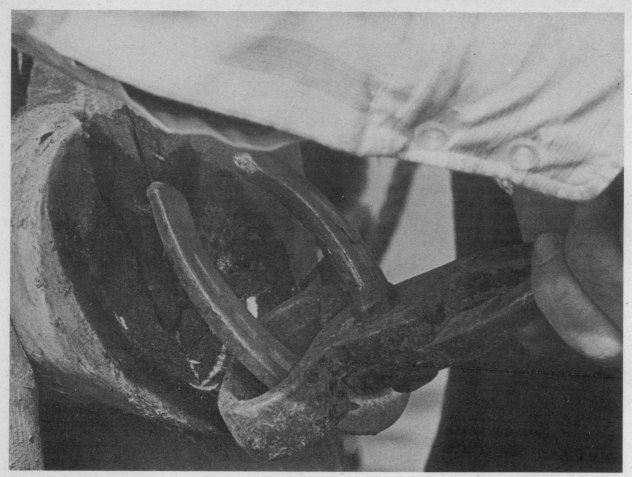

The first step for the farrier is to cut or straighten clinches and remove old shoe (above). A horseowner should not have applied hoof dressing, as this collects dirt on farrier's hands, apron, which isn't needed. With the shoe removed, frog is trimmed and shaped. The excess hoof wall then is nippered away. An owner need not express concern for the safety of his horse; the entire process is painless and farrier knows his job. He won't remove more than necessary.

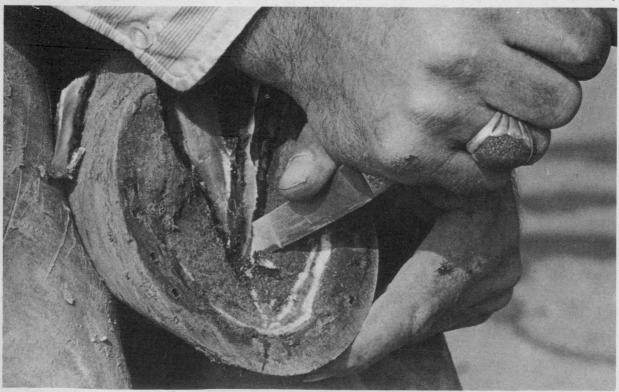

Once trimmed with nippers, hoof bottom is leveled and smoothed with rasp. Too much rasping weakens hoof.

The horse's foot is a unique structure with an outside horny covering which grows continuously and protects the inner parts. In the natural state of running wild, the horse wore down his feet about as fast as they grew, thus his feet never were too long nor worn too short. The true wild horse seems to have been almost free of serious foot problems, but with domestication, confinement and use by man, trouble started. The horse was brought from soft ground and grassy prairies to hard roads; from light exercise to hard work; and from healthy, sanitary grasslands to confined and dirty housing in some cases. Today's domesticated horse sometimes is put in situations where his feet grow too long from lack of exercise, or is worked so regularly and steadily that the feet wear down faster than they grow.

If feet grow too long, they put a strain on the structures of the horse's legs — bones, tendons, ligaments and joints — and make the feet more subject to breaking and splitting. Besides lameness, long feet also can throw feet and legs out of balance by uneven wear on broken hoofs. This can result in strained joints, crooked legs or even a permanently crippled horse. At the other extreme — if feet wear down too far from excessive use, the horse loses the protective, insensitive outer covering, becoming lame and tenderfooted from walking on the sensitive tissues of his feet.

A domestic horse usually does much more traveling than a horse running wild and, unless the horse has unusually tough feet or is always traveling on soft ground like grassy sod, he needs some protection for his feet. Man discovered this fact quite early in his association with horses.

Several thousand years ago, horsemen tried to protect the feet of their horses using everything from socks to sandals attached with straps or thongs. The procedure of nailing iron shoes to the hoof wasn't introduced until about the Second Century B.C., and wasn't a common practice until the end of the Fifth Century A.D.

Once the new shoe has been shaped to conform with the horse's foot, it is tacked to the hoof. Horseshoe nails have beveled edge to aid the farrier in identifying placement, as text notes. Nails, after being started, are driven sharply to cause curve.

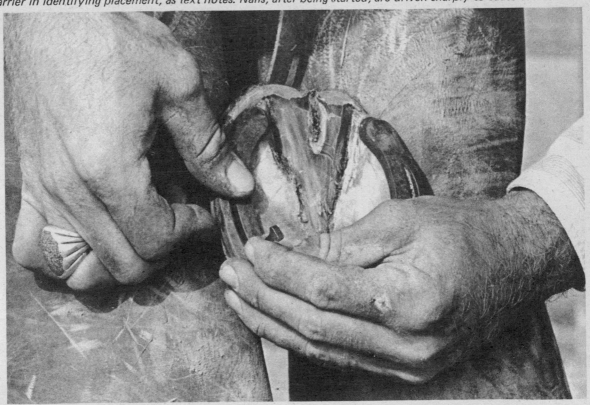

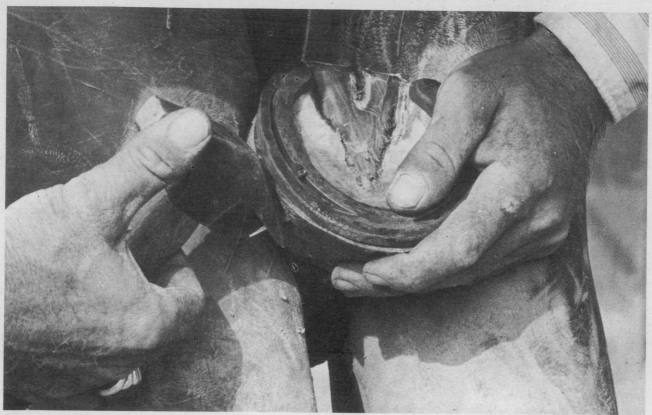

With the nail driven through hoof wall, excess is wrung off close to wall, for obvious reasons (above). The owner should attempt to keep horse calm, avoiding farrier injury. Once tips have been removed, a clinching block is used to tighten the shoe and turn the clinches. All that's left is rasping smooth the rough edges of the nails protruding from the hoof wall.

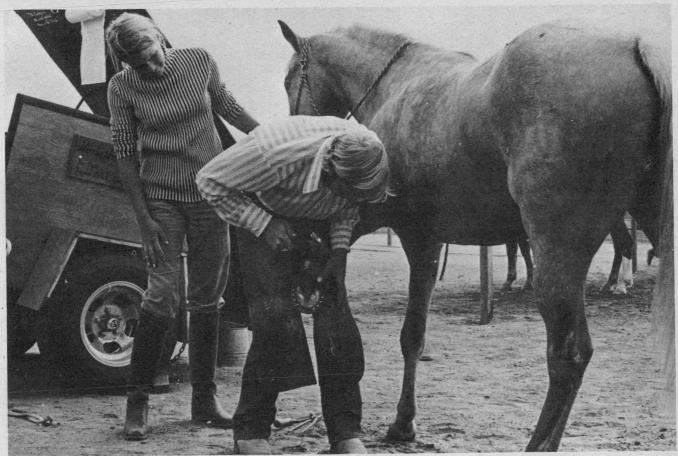

The task of a farrier is simplified greatly by owners cognizant of the problems facing the shoer, and attempting to keep them from happening. A horseowner should remain on the same side as the shoer and focus his attention on the animal, not man.

PARTS OF THE FOOT

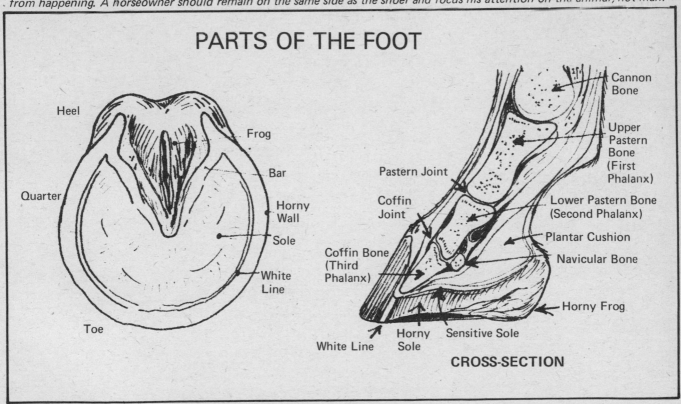

Heel
Frog
Bar
Quarter
Horny Wall
Sole
White Line
Toe

Cannon Bone
Upper Pastern Bone (First Phalanx)
Pastern Joint
Coffin Joint
Lower Pastern Bone (Second Phalanx)
Plantar Cushion
Navicular Bone
Coffin Bone (Third Phalanx)
Horny Frog
White Line
Horny Sole
Sensitive Sole

CROSS-SECTION

As can be seen in the two illustrations above, the foot of a horse is a complex structure that belies its outward appearance. Aspiring farriers require a sound, knowledge of the hoof's internal components and gaits, and here's a place to start!

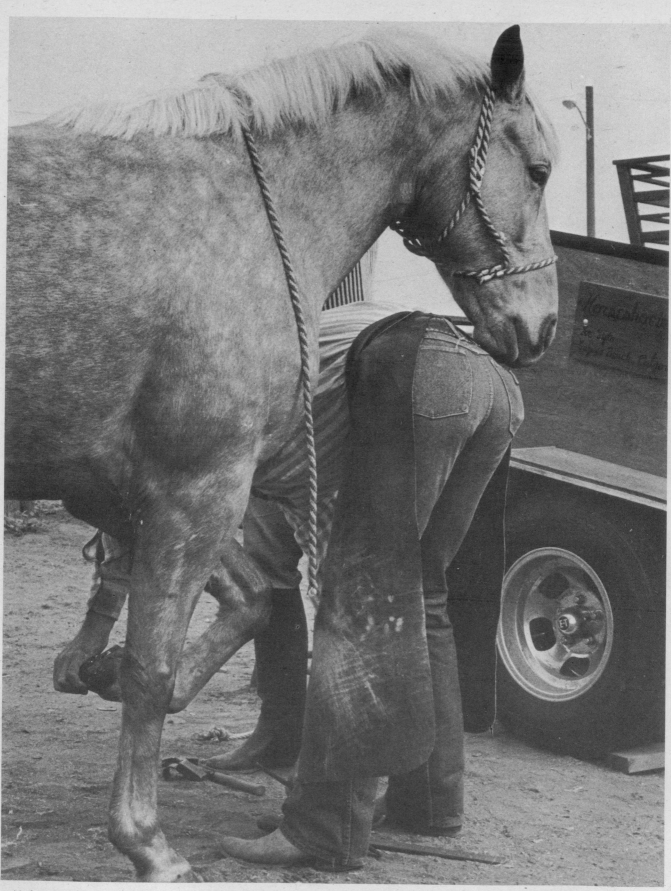

Unfortunately, not all horses faced by the farrier are as docile as this palomino. For this reason, it is imperative that the owner advise the shoer of behavioral quirks that could result in injury. Farriers aren't trainers; don't expect them to be.

WELL-SHOD HOOF

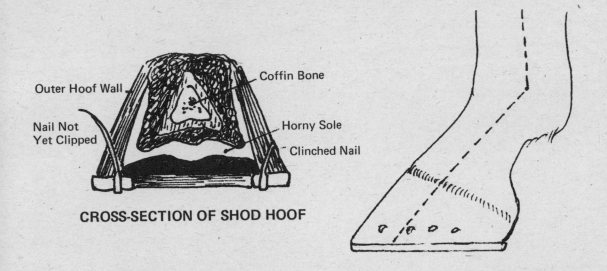

Outer Hoof Wall

Nail Not
Yet Clipped

Coffin Bone

Horny Sole

Clinched Nail

CROSS-SECTION OF SHOD HOOF

These two views show well-shod hoof the farrier strives for. The angle formed by the slope of the hoof's leading surface is complemented by attention to the bottom of the foot. The cross-section shows nail placement in wall.

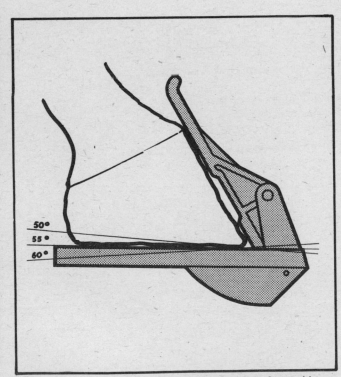

50°
55°
60°

To aid farriers in determining the exact angle formed by bottom and face of hoof is this hoof gauge from Diamond Tool and Horseshoe. Like others on the market, it takes the guesswork out of most important angle determination.

The first step in any shoeing job is to carefully observe the position of the feet and legs when the horse is standing squarely and then observe him in action, at the walk and trot, to see the normal angles of his feet and to tell how he handles his feet — whether there is any paddling, winging or deviation from straightforward movement. Notice the point at which the foot breaks over and leaves the ground — whether the break-over point is at the toe where it should be, or off to one side. Uneven wear of the feet shows that the horse is not traveling straight but is breaking over crookedly and landing on one side of the foot instead of squarely. A horse that travels straight on sound, straight feet and legs will wear down the shoe evenly, with slightly more wear at the center of the toe.

When the horse is standing squarely there should be about a forty-five-degree angle in the slope of the hoof and pastern. Individual horses may vary somewhat from this; some have more sloping hoofs and pasterns, while others are more upright. Trimming never should be too drastic in an attempt to give the feet a perfect angle, because each horse has his own normal angle and radical changes may cause problems.

The foot always should be trimmed so that the pastern and hoof are of the same angle, forming an unbroken line. If you try to make a forty-five-degree angle on a horse that normally has less or more angle than forty-five degrees, you will be working against nature and the way the horse was put together; you'll be straining parts of the horse's legs.

The important thing is to trim the foot so that pastern and hoof are the same angle. If the horse's toes have grown too long, this angle line will be broken, putting strain on

229

The proper method of picking up a horse's front hoof is shown by noted equestrienne Heather Smith Thomas. In left photo, the right hand is run down the leg to the fetlock, while left hand pushes against the horse's shoulder, causing him to shift his weight off that leg. It then is picked up and cradled between the legs with the shoer's knees. If horse pulls, it comes away.

the legs. If the heel and hind parts of the hoof are too long, the angle line will be broken in the other direction. You will have to study the feet when the horse is standing squarely in order to judge how much hoof to remove to make the foot level at the proper angle. Some farriers use a special protractor to measure hoof angle and this can be helpful.

When you begin trimming the foot, first clean it thoroughly. A hoof pick or the blunt edge of a hoof knife is the best instrument for cleaning the dirt out of the hoof. Never use a sharp or pointed object for this cleaning; you could injure yourself or the horse if he happened to jerk his foot at the wrong time. When all dirt and debris are removed, trim any dead sole tissue with a hoof knife. All loose material should be scraped away, but don't trim much deeper — unless the horse has an abnormal buildup of dead material — for the horse needs this horny sole as protection for the inner tissues of his foot. After the frog is trimmed of loose tags, the outer hoof wall can be trimmed level with the sole, except at the quarters, with hoof cutters.

Trimming should be done from heel to toe or in a complete circle from heel to heel for a smooth, consistent cut. The hoof cutters should be held in such a way that they make a flat, level cut, to make a level seat for the shoe. In order to make a flat surface when trimming the hoof wall you must leave extra wall at the quarters, as the sole at the quarters is concave and slightly lower than at the heel or toe; if you cut this area level with the sole, you will have cut too much away and the wall won't meet the shoe in this place. If the bars need trimming, trim them level with the hoof wall at the heels.

After the excess horn of the foot is removed with hoof cutters, the trimmed hoof wall should be rasped smooth to make a level seat for the shoe. The rasp always should be held flat and level so that one side of the wall is not accidentally made lower than the other.

If the horse is to go barefoot, you should leave about one-fourth-inch of hoof wall projecting below the sole when trimming; don't remove all the extra hoof wall or he soon will become tenderfooted or sole-bruised from walking on the sole.

The outside edges of the wall, for a barefoot horse, should be smoothed and rounded with the rasp — leaving a sharp edge will make the hoof prone to split, crack or chip away. Rounding the edges also prevents injury to other horses in his pasture; wounds on lower legs can result from being stepped on or by running into the sharp snags of other horses' untrimmed hoofs.

If the horse is to be shod, trim the hoof wall level with the sole at the toe and as low as necessary at the heel to establish the proper foot angle. The shoe should be shaped to fit the foot, not vice versa, unless for the purpose of correction of some defect in gait. The shoe should fit evenly on the foot — the bottom of the hoof wall should rest flat down against the shoe. The heels of the shoe should not stick out excessively beyond the heel of the foot, especially on the front feet, or the horse may step on his front shoes when he travels. The shoe should fit the foot so that the outer edge of the shoe closely follows the outline of the trimmed hoof at the toe and around to the quarters. But at the quarters and heels the shoe should always be slightly wider than the hoof — except, again, in some instances of corrective shoeing for interference — and should extend slightly beyond the heels of the horse.

The heels and quarters of the horse's foot must rest on the shoe and have a little extra shoe width to allow for hoof expansion when weight is placed on the foot. If the shoe is too short or doesn't properly fit at the quarters and heel, it may cut into the foot as the hoof wall grows (the hoof may grow down around the outside of the shoe) or cause corns or other lameness. If the shoe is too narrow and short, the hoof tends to expand out over the shoe when weight is placed on it and the narrow shoe limits proper hoof expansion.

The shoe should be properly centered on the foot. For horses with good conformation and normal feet, the shoe can be centered by using the point of the frog as a guide, the frog dividing the bottom of the hoof into equal halves and pointing toward the toe. But in horses that are pigeon-toed or splay-footed, the frog usually points offcenter and cannot be used as a guide.

If a hoof is worn excessively on one side because of poor conformation or faulty gait, or if part of the hoof wall has been chipped, cracked or broken away, it might be impossible to make the foot level by trimming unless too much is removed on the opposite side. If one side of the foot is broken or exceptionally low, the branch of the shoe on the worn side can be shimmed with leather so that the foot will be level when the shoe is on.

When the shoe has been shaped properly to fit the trimmed foot, nails can be driven. Nails should be of the proper size for the hoof and the shoe, having heads that protrude slightly after they are driven. A nailhead that sinks too deeply into the crease of the shoe is too small and won't hold properly; the shoe may eventually work loose.

The nails should enter the hoof at the white line, the

Hind feet are held diagonally across the farrier's knees instead of between the legs. Should the horse pull on the leg, it is freed without damage to farrier's inside thigh.

The ball peen hammer and anvil still are the stock-in-trade of a farrier. Roger Erichsen, one of the first to work with the Nature Plate, here shapes a new shoe.

area where the hoof wall and sole unite. In nailing on the shoe, hold the nail with thumb and index finger, resting your hand on the shoe to keep it in the proper position as you drive the nail. The location of the first nail doesn't matter greatly, as long as the shoe is properly centered and stays in position during the nailing. After the first two nails are driven, one on each side of the shoe, it will stay in place for the remaining nails.

Horseshoe nails are made with both straight and beveled sides so they will curve when driven. The beveled side of the nail point always should be toward the inside of the foot so that the nail will be directed outward as it is driven. The beveled side can easily be determined by the rough side of the nailhead; the bevel and rough side both are on the inside of the nail, thus the rule for horseshoe nails: Rough side inside. The rough edge being on one side, it's easy to tell which way to set the nail by feeling the head.

The nail should be held straight and aimed at the spot where it should emerge from the hoof wall. The nail should come out about three-quarters of an inch above the shoe, or about one-third or less of the way up the hoof wall. The actual distance will depend, of course, on size of the horse. A draft horse has much bigger feet than an Arabian, for instance; larger nails will be used in his shoes and the nails will come out higher in the hoof wall.

If a nail comes out too high or low, it should be pulled and redriven. If the nail is bent, use a new one. A high nail may press on the sensitive tissues inside the foot and make the horse lame. A low nail may break out of the hoof, not holding the shoe. Nails driven to a uniform height give the shod hoof a pleasing appearance, but if the nails come out somewhere near the proper position it is best to leave them; a nail pulled and redriven may weaken the hoof wall with the second perforation and eventually cause the shoe to loosen.

Because the foot — especially at the heel — should expand when weight is placed on it, nails never are driven into the hoof too far to the rear. The last nailhole of the shoe shouldn't be farther back than the bend of the quarter, or expansion of the hoof at the heel and quarters will be greatly limited.

Nails should be driven in the same direction as the hoof fibers, parallel with them, to minimize the cutting of these fibers and resultant weakening of the hoof wall. The fibers of the hoof grow parallel to each other and perpendicular to the coronary band. The driven nails should go into the outer portion of the hoof wall, never inside the white line that separates the wall from the sole, or they will puncture the sensitive part of the hoof.

A high nail is more apt to prick sensitive tissues or put pressure on them if it bends inward inside the hoof. If a horse ever flinches during the driving of a nail, the sensitive tissues may have been pricked or punctured. If this ever happens, the nail should be pulled out and iodine poured into the nail hole to prevent infection.

If you use light hammer taps when driving the nail, the point of the nail will travel parallel to the horny fibers of the hoof wall and won't sever them. Use light taps until the nail is about two-thirds the required distance, then strike one sharp blow to force the nail through the wall and finish its journey. The bevel on the nail point makes it curve outward and curves most when the nail is driven sharply and rapidly through the horny fibers.

Once a nail is driven and the head sunk into the shoe crease, twist off the sharp point with the hammer claws or cut off the end with nail cutters. The sharp nail tips should be cut off immediately: if the horse moves or tries to pull his foot away, the sharp tip could cut your leg. Keep track of those nail tips and discard them properly, so they won't cause a flat tire.

After all the nails have been driven and the tips cut off close to the hoof wall, cut a small notch underneath with the rasp. This notch will help keep the hoof wall from splitting when the nail end is turned over and clinched, and also will provide a place for the clinch. The nail end, when clinched, will be sunk into this little notch and leaves a smooth surface on the hoof wall. A clinch that is short and fairly well sunk into the hoof wall isn't apt to get knocked loose when the horse travels through rocks.

To clinch the nails, pound each nailhead tightly into the shoe crease while holding a piece of iron against the tip end, which bends the tip over into the notch you cut as it comes farther out of the hoof wall. Nails should be clinched alternately from one side to the other (two toe nails first, or the two heel nails, then working back or forward), rather than clinching all the nails on one side before nails on the other. Clinching alternately from one side to the other gives a more uniform seating of the shoe.

Nails should be clinched firmly, but not so tightly that the horse's foot becomes sore and nail-bound. If you clinch the nails too tightly, the horse may be lame for several days. Finish the clinch by bending the nails with the hammer, pounding the tips flat against the hoof wall into the notch cut. A short clinch holds better than a long one and looks nicer. A long clinch can be knocked and unbent in rocks or rough country and will work loose faster.

Nails always should take a short, thick hold on the hoof wall and should not be too high. Thus, they damage the least amount of hoof horn and the old nail holes can be removed with the natural growth of the hoof the next time the horse is shod. This is especially important if the horse is used steadily and will be wearing shoes out regularly, as when he is used as a ranch horse, in mountainous terrain, in training for endurance rides, etc. If the horse must be shod often, you'll want room in the hoof wall for the new nails for each succeeding set of shoes.

With the rasp, smooth the outside edge of the hoof where it meets the shoe, but be careful not to rasp the hoof wall too much. This horny wall is made up of tiny tubes — the horn fibers — and excessive rasping cuts and leaves them open, letting the hoof dry out. If the shoe was properly fitted and nailed on with no slipping, little or no rasping will be needed to smooth the hoof wall to the shoe.

After the horse is shod, have someone lead him for you at both the walk and the trot so you can observe the new shoes and the horse's feet in action, to determine if the shoes are set properly, aiding and not hindering his gait, and to be sure the horse is not lame or "ouchy" in any way from the shoes.

Shoes should always be as light as possible, taking into consideration the wear demanded of them, to interfere as little as possible with the normal flight of the horse's foot. The ground surface of the shoe is best plain, unless the horse needs extra traction. A plain plate will hinder and interfere least with his way of going. Toe and heel calks are not necessary, except for horses traveling in rocky or steep terrain, on ice, for draft horses that need extra traction for pulling, or for other special conditions when a certain amount and kind of traction is needed. Calks also are used on some corrective shoes in certain situations.

If a horse is used often and wears out many shoes, a hard-surfaced material like borium can be welded to the wearing surface of the shoe to make it last longer. Borium is the trade name for a material that comes as a steel tube impregnated with crystals of tungsten carbide that are very sharp and nearly as hard as diamonds. When this material is welded to an ordinary horseshoe, the steel melts and forms a bond with the shoe, while the tungsten carbide crystals retain their sharp edges. The rough surface that results will give good traction on rocks, concrete, ice, frozen ground, etc., and, with spots of borium added to toe and heels, may last many times longer than an ordinary shoe. This borium shoe will have to be reset periodically to allow for the growth of the horse's feet, but it will not wear out before the horse needs a reset, as some ordinary horseshoes do when a horse is used often.

Borium also can be added to shoes for a corrective effect, reinforcing wear points where a horse breaks over incorrectly and wears away the shoe on one side. Because the borium does not wear away, the shoe retains its original shape and keeps its corrective effect longer, helping the horse break-over more toward the center of the toe.

A horse's feet should be trimmed, or shoes reset or replaced every four to six weeks, depending on the individual horse's rate of hoof growth and the amount of wear on the feet if he is barefoot. A barefoot horse that gets some wear on his feet may not need to be trimmed this often.

All too often, shoes are left on a horse too long. Some people actually leave a horse's shoes on until they fall off of their own accord! A horse whose feet have grown too long because his shoes were left on may suffer leg wounds from striking himself with his long hoofs, strained legs, contracted feet, corns, or the like. Since the hoof wall grows perpendicular to the coronary band, the horse's base of support actually grows out from under him if his shoes are left on too long.

The farrier's tools are largely unchanged; they fit the bill, so why bother? Nippers, shown trimming away excess hoof wall, have been around for many decades.

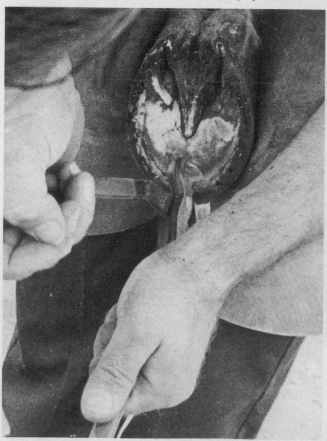

To remove a horseshoe, cut the clinched nails on the hoof wall with a clinch cutter or unbend them with old hoof nippers, then pick up the foot and use pulling pincers or old hoof nippers to pull the shoe. It is better to pull the shoe nail by nail than simply cut the nails, for cutting leaves nail pieces in the horse's hoof which will have to be removed after the shoe is off. Pulling nail pieces out is not easy and is more likely to break or crack the horse's hoof than removing the shoe properly with pulling pincers.

The pincers should be placed under the shoe, starting at one heel branch. Close the handle and push away from yourself to loosen the heel branch, pushing slightly toward the middle line of the foot. After that heel is loosened, the opposite heel should be. Each nail can be removed individually as it is loosened. As you pull the shoe, hold the foot securely and never twist the pincers or pull crookedly, and you will not injure the fetlock joint. Continue working down both branches alternately until the entire shoe is loosened.

This is the goal of every farrier: a well-shod hoof. If there are doubts about the ability of your shoer, bring in another who will give honest testimony about job done.

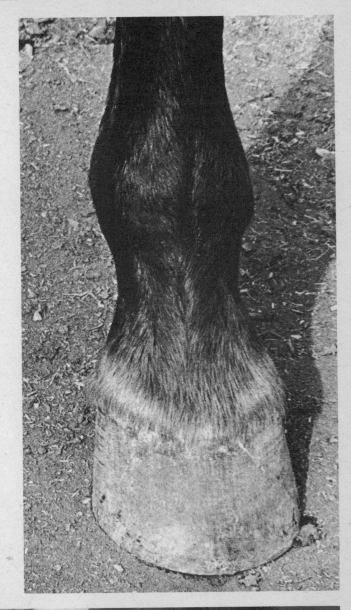

Shoeing a horse is not a casual task to be undertaken lightly by individual horsemen. It takes know-how in determining the proper amount of frog to pare away (below) and amount to be removed with a rasp. Unless you plan to do it right, don't bother. Leave feet alone.

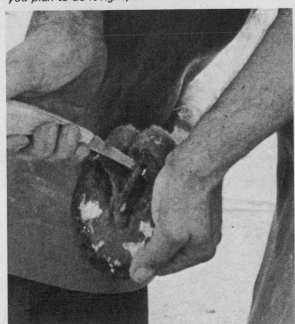
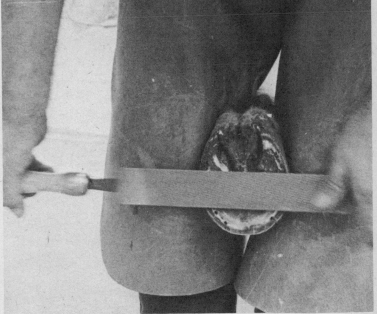

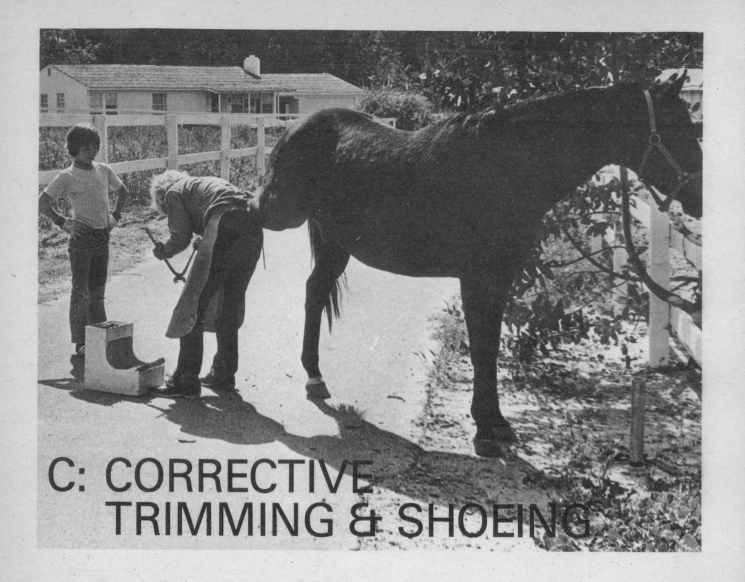

C: CORRECTIVE TRIMMING & SHOEING

Corrective shoeing is done to improve or correct faults in the horse's gait that result from inherited conformation faults or injury, and also to relieve pain and encourage healing of certain diseases or injuries to the legs and feet.

There are many kinds of shoes used to correct foot problems in a horse. These new shoes can be made by a farrier or by welding additional pieces to, or cutting from, an ordinary horseshoe.

Many corrective shoes were designed in the days of the draft horse and were useful because they transformed a serious lameness into a mild lameness, allowing a horse still to be useful for work. But for today's horse, used under saddle, even a slight lameness or foot problem is too much. A shoe that reduces lameness isn't good enough, because the horse only is improved, not cured. Thus, a great number of the special shoes used in the past aren't satisfactory today.

A basic concept of horseshoeing is that weight in the form of horseshoes always reduces speed and decreases agility, no matter how it is added to the foot. Corrective shoes always should be as light as possible. The normal flight of the foot is a straightforward line. Any deviation from normal flight takes the form of an arc, either to the outside or the inside.

Adding weight through horseshoes will increase the arc because of the additional centrifugal force. Consequently,

ordinary shoeing often will accentuate or increase a horse's defect in gait, the reason many horses overreach or interfere only when shod. A horse that interferes — strikes one front limb against the other, or one hind limb against the other — or forges — strike a front foot with a hind foot — will do so even worse when shod. The added weight of the shoes makes his strides longer and arcs of foot-flight more pronounced.

Therefore, he must be correctively shod when he wears shoes, to prevent these problems if possible.

When attempting to correct a faulty gait, one must try to balance the foot both on the ground and during its flight through the air, producing a straighter way of going. One must fully understand the structures of a horse's feet and legs, and how a horse moves. Every horse must be considered individually when determining how best to correct his way of traveling, for no two horses move exactly alike. Though several may have the same fault or similar conformation that suggests a certain type of correction, it may require different shoeing methods to correct them.

A horse may indicate he needs one type of shoe when actually another will be better. For example, a horse that stands splay-footed, toes-out, usually will land on the inside of the hoof when he travels, wearing down the inside wall more than the outside. Occasionally, though, a horse will be splay-footed yet do just the opposite, wearing down the outside wall. One must study the horse carefully while standing and traveling to determine his way of going and shoe required.

After trying a corrective shoe, carefully observe the horse's movement again for improvement. Sometimes two or three methods must be tried before the best is found.

As a general rule, always try the least drastic method first, using a correction that will alter a horse's foot least. If this won't correct the gait enough to solve the horse's problems, more drastic methods may be needed. But remember: drastic changes can cause other problems.

Most horses need corrective trimming and shoeing to some degree because of faulty conformation. Few horses are blessed with perfectly straight feet and legs. Because of this, the hoofs wear unevenly. Since the foot is worn unevenly, it tends to grow unevenly and the problem can only get worse. The misshapen foot will continue forcing the horse's leg out of line even more, aggravating the problem.

When trimming uneven feet, the main objective is merely to trim away the areas that have grown too long due to uneven wear. The idea is to trim the foot more nearly level, so the horse will both pick it up and put it down straighter.

If the horse toes-in — pigeon-toed — the outside walls of his feet usually are worn down too much. When trimming, take off the excess hoof on the inside wall, from toe to heel, to help level the foot. Horses that toe-in or out usually don't break-over the center of the foot when it's picked up, but break-over to one side, causing more wear.

To help a horse pick his feet up straight, the toe can be squared somewhat, making the horse break-over the center.

If one side is flared out, he probably has a conformation fault in the leg, putting uneven distribution of weight on the foot as he travels. The cause may only be minor but the problem gets worse in time, making a weak hoof wall which breaks easily. By trimming and rasping the flared side of the hoof wall, one can help the foot regain its normal shape over a period of time.

Other problems can be helped by corrective trimming and shoeing. Consider the horse that toes-out, called splay-footed. In serious cases, the horse strikes himself as he

C.J. "Calamity Jane" Desrosiers, one of the few female farriers, shows proper hold for working on a front hoof (below). Gaits which can be corrected with trimming and shoeing outlined herein are pigeon-toed and splay-footed.

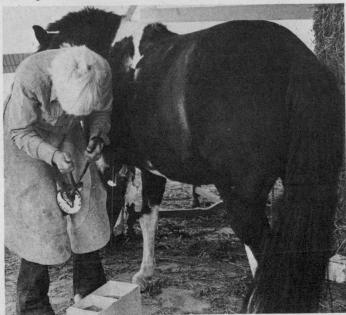

travels because the foot swings inward as it flies through the air.

When a horse toes-out, his foot is not level because he wears down the inside wall. The foot breaks over the inside of the toe and lands on the inside toe and wall after an inward arc through the air. These feet should have the outside wall trimmed to help level the foot. If to be shod, special shoes can be used to help level the foot properly, made from ordinary shoes by cutting or welding additional pieces of iron to them.

If the foot is worn down exceptionally, a piece of leather can be used on that side between shoe and foot to level it.

Several corrective shoes can help a splay-footed horse. The purpose of them all is two-fold: to raise the inside wall to where the foot is more level, and to make the foot break-over the center of the toe.

A half-rim shoe has a rim on the outside edge of the side which will go on the inside wall of the foot. When this shoe is on the horse's foot, placed upon the ground, the shoe raises the inside of the foot. This interferes with the foot's breaking over the inside of the toe, forcing it to break-over more at the center.

A half-rim can be made from an ordinary shoe by welding a small rod to the edge of the shoe, from heel to the toe nailhole. A shoe of this type also can be used on a pigeon-toed horse, in the opposite manner, to raise the outside wall. This shoe is used to raise the low side of the foot and helps the horse break-over at the center.

Another shoe that can be used either for splay-footed or pigeon-toed horses has high inside rims and an open toe. This shoe is made by welding a rod about one-quarter-inch in diameter to the inside of the branches, leaving the toe

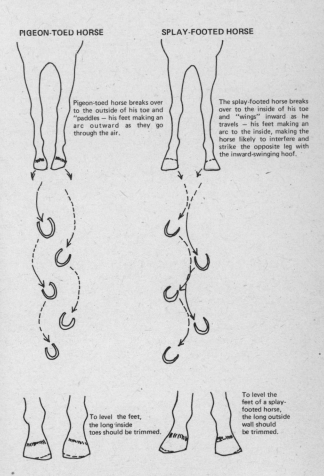

PIGEON-TOED HORSE

Pigeon-toed horse breaks over to the outside of his toe and "paddles — his feet making an arc outward as they go through the air.

To level the feet, the long inside toes should be trimmed.

SPLAY-FOOTED HORSE

The splay-footed horse breaks over to the inside of his toe and "wings" inward as he travels — his feet making an arc to the inside, making the horse likely to interfere and strike the opposite leg with the inward-swinging hoof.

To level the feet of a splay-footed horse, the long outside wall should be trimmed.

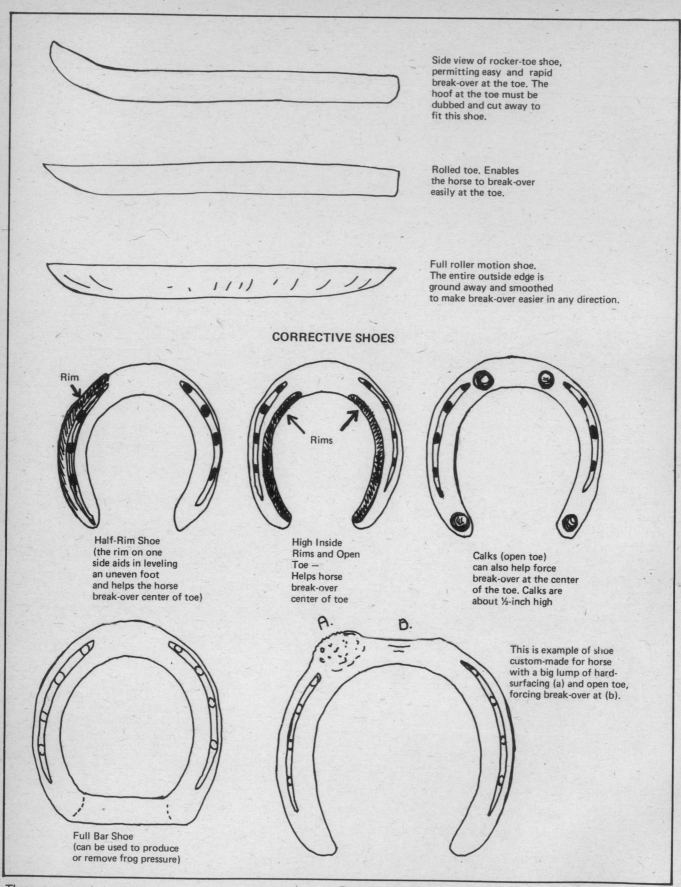

Side view of rocker-toe shoe, permitting easy and rapid break-over at the toe. The hoof at the toe must be dubbed and cut away to fit this shoe.

Rolled toe. Enables the horse to break-over easily at the toe.

Full roller motion shoe. The entire outside edge is ground away and smoothed to make break-over easier in any direction.

CORRECTIVE SHOES

Rim

Half-Rim Shoe (the rim on one side aids in leveling an uneven foot and helps the horse break-over center of toe)

Rims

High Inside Rims and Open Toe — Helps horse break-over center of toe

Calks (open toe) can also help force break-over at the center of the toe. Calks are about ½-inch high

Full Bar Shoe (can be used to produce or remove frog pressure)

A.   B.

This is example of shoe custom-made for horse with a big lump of hard-surfacing (a) and open toe, forcing break-over at (b).

These are several examples of corrective shoes most frequently used by the skilled farrier. As noted in text, make all corrections gradually and employ the least severe first. More hoof can be removed if needed, but there's trouble if too much is removed initially. Corrective trimming and shoeing won't cure the gait defect, but it can restore usefulness.

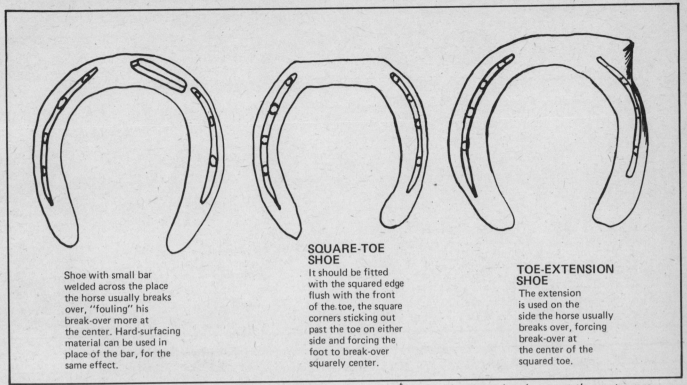

SQUARE-TOE SHOE
It should be fitted with the squared edge flush with the front of the toe, the square corners sticking out past the toe on either side and forcing the foot to break-over squarely center.

Shoe with small bar welded across the place the horse usually breaks over, "fouling" his break-over more at the center. Hard-surfacing material can be used in place of the bar, for the same effect.

TOE-EXTENSION SHOE
The extension is used on the side the horse usually breaks over, forcing break-over at the center of the squared toe.

Three examples of corrective shoes that help correct improper break-over, forcing the toe to break-over at the center, are illustrated above. A horseman first must discover the true nature of the gait defect, then apply the proper corrective shoe.

undisturbed. The rods on each side help make the horse break-over the center of the open toe. A shoe of this sort can be used if the foot is trimmed quite level initially.

Shoe calks sometimes can be used to create the same effect as the welded rod. The calks should be about one-half-inch high and are welded to the heels and to either side of the toe at the first nail position. Like the high inside rims, these calks help force break-over at the center of the toe.

Many mild cases of toe-in or toe-out are corrected by using square-toed shoes. The square toe makes the foot break-over straight. The foot should be trimmed level and the shoe placed so the toe of the foot is even with the toe of the shoe, the square portion sticking out on either side. Don't dub off the horse's toe.

A toe extension on the shoe serves the same purpose even more effectively. This shoe is made by welding an extension to the toe of the shoe, on the side over which the horse breaks. This extension thus interferes with the crooked break-over and helps the horse break-over straight.

Interference can be a serious problem. Sometimes it's only mild, if the horse merely brushes one leg against the other or does so only when tired or excited. But interference becomes serious if the horse does it consistently or forcefully enough to cause injury. Interference is most common in the hind legs and the fetlock joint is the most common site of injury. Trotters and pacers tend to interfere in front, striking the opposite knee.

Severe interference usually can be corrected by squaring the toe — or using a toe-extension shoe which forces the foot to break-over squarely at the center of the toe — then altering the shape of the hoof and shoe so it won't strike the opposite leg. This can be done by carefully determining the part of the foot or shoe doing the striking. This is done by using chalk or some other coloring substance, coating the opposite leg in the area the horse strikes, then observing where the telltale coloring is brushed onto the hoof or shoe

that does the striking. That portion of the hoof is then rasped and the shoe altered to fit. The offending foot then will not quite reach the opposite leg. Corrective shoes for a horse that interferes always should be extra-light.

Other problems that can occur when the horse travels are forging and cross-firing. Forging is a fairly common defect in which the toe of the hind foot or shoe strikes the heel or sole of the front foot on the same side and occurs

This is the appearance of a hoof that was surgically removed from a dead horse, with inside components removed. Note the thick edge at the coronary band.

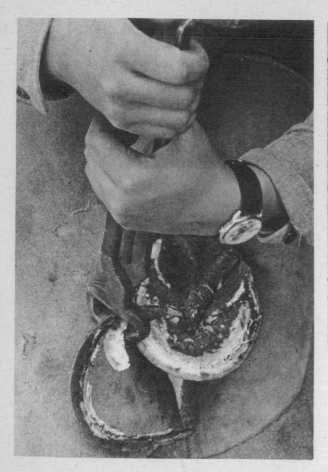

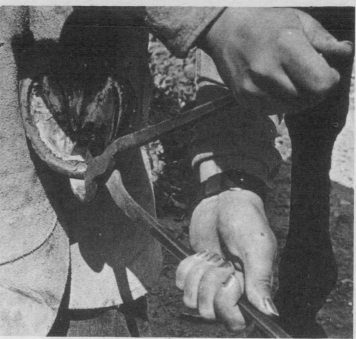

Removing shoe and trimming (left and above), Calamity Jane uses nippers. These are first two shoeing steps.

A heavy rasp then is employed to level hoof (left). When smooth, white line is easily distinguished (below). Nail inward no farther.

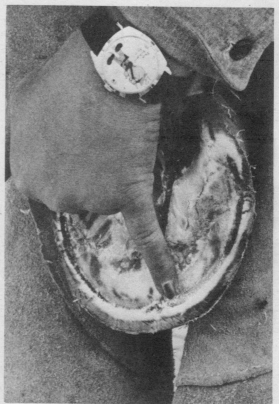

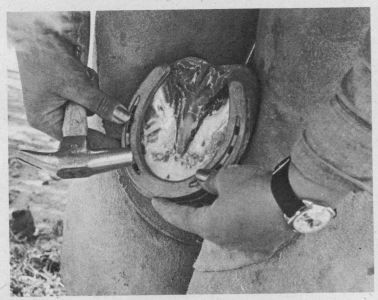

A farrier will shape a shoe to fit the hoof, not vice versa (right), as feet often don't comform exactly to shoe shape.

During shaping, the shoe continually is matched against the foot (above), until conforming perfectly. If necessary, a leather pad is cut from a large blank, then tacked on. This is common with horses used for endurance riding.

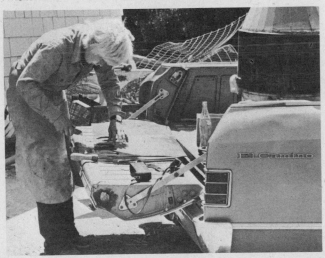

most commonly at the trot. Forging can be due to poor conformation: a horse that has hind legs too far underneath his body; sickle-hocked; from having a short back and long legs; or long hind legs and short front legs. It also can be caused by leaving too much heel on the front shoe.

In severe cases of forging, there is damage to the front foot from the continual striking, or the horse periodically pulls a front shoe by stepping on it with his hind foot, perhaps tripping in the process. In more common, milder forms of forging, the trot is simply a noisy gait because the front and hind shoes clack together.

To correct forging, keep in mind that the front foot must be encouraged to break-over and be lifted from the ground more quickly to get out of the way of the approaching hind feet. Too, the hind foot must take a slightly shorter stride so that it won't quite reach the front feet.

The horse should be ridden at the walk and trot as his leg action is observed to determine the rate of speed at which the forging is worst. Also, check the horse's conformation to see if the feet are properly balanced. If the horse is wearing shoes, check if they are properly fitted and of proper weight; a heavy shoe will aggravate the problem.

When shoeing a horse that forges, the heel of the front shoes and the toes of the hind shoes should be shortened so they will be less likely to meet. Lightweight shoes should be used, for weight increases the length of the horse's stride. A rocker or roller toe — or dubbing the front toes a little shorter — can be used on the front feet to encourage faster break-over and to come off the ground sooner. The hind feet should be left a little longer than normal so they won't break-over as quickly and shod with very light shoes. Shortening the toe of the hind foot too much in an attempt to keep it from hitting the front foot will usually make the problem worse, because the short toe will cause the foot to come off the ground faster. This makes it more apt to reach the front foot before it's moved out of the way.

The hind shoes can have slightly turned-out heels that extend one-half to three-fourths of an inch beyond the hoof, the extra heel tending to stop the hind foot as it is being put down, or can be shod with heel calks and a rocker toe to increase hock action, making the horse pick his foot up higher instead of swinging it so far forward. The heel calks tend to stop the hind foot before it hits the front foot.

Cross-firing is about the same as forging except it usually only occurs in pacers. The toe of the hind foot strikes the heel of the diagonal front foot. This problem is most likely to occur in a pacer that is splay-footed in front and pigeon-toed behind. The splay-footed front hoof moves inward during the first part of its stride and the pigeon-toed hind

239

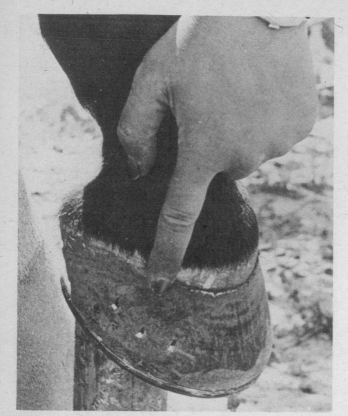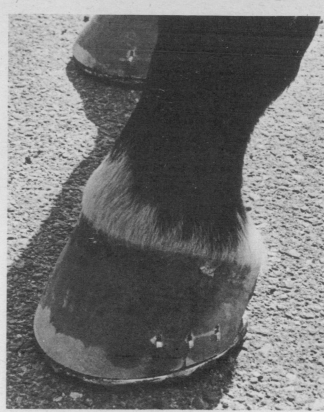

After the shoe has been nailed to hoof and the nail tips wrung off, they must be rasped to avoid horse cutting himself (left). The finished hoof, seen at right, is quite different than prior to shoeing. Farrier's attention is required again in a month.

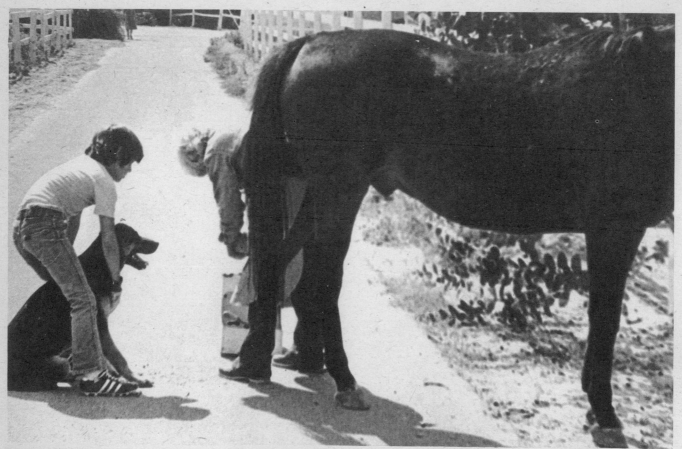

Spectators of all types gather when the farrier plies the trade. Unfortunately, not all horseowners know how to best ease the farrier's job and this is covered in following section of this chapter. Shoeing is dangerous, so learn the proper routine!

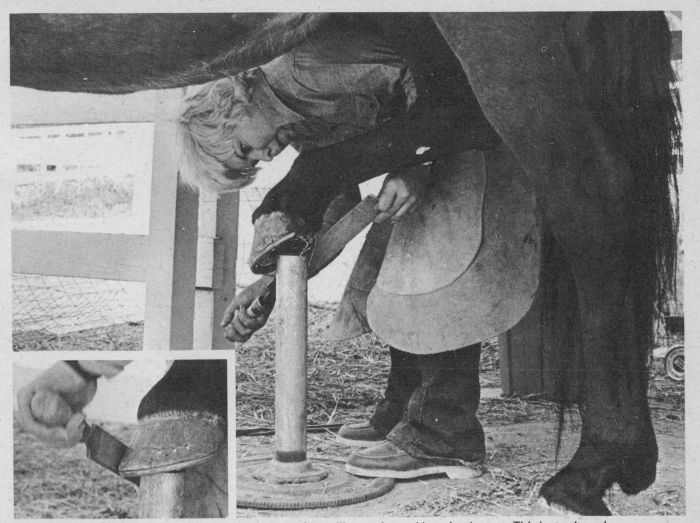

During the rasping part of shoeing routine, Ms. Desrosiers utilizes a pipe and base implement. This is sturdy and a horse isn't likely to knock it over — especially when she stands on it! The inset photo shows the final rasping of the hoof.

foot moves inward during the last part of its stride, so diagonal feet meet. To correct this, both the fronts and hinds should be encouraged to move forward in straighter lines. The best way to accomplish this is to make the feet break-over the center of the toe and thus begin the stride in the proper direction — straight ahead.

Corrective shoeing also can be beneficial in treating certain types of injuries and abnormalities in the foot, such as flexor tendinitis, lameness from corns, chronic laminitis, contracted heels, ringbone, sidebone, cracked hoofs and wire cuts in the coronary band.

When shoeing a horse with contracted heels, remember that the frog must have pressure to help establish the normal functions of the foot and gradually spread the heels again. If possible, the horse should be allowed to go barefoot, since shoes tend to hinder normal expansion of the foot. If the horse can go barefoot, with his feet trimmed often, frog pressure and foot expansion will help correct the contracted condition.

If the horse must be shod, a tip shoe which just covers the toe area can be used if he isn't ridden much or in rocky areas. The tip shoe protects the toe from excessive wear but leaves the heel area unshod for greater frog pressure. A full-bar, half-bar or "T" shoe induces more frog pressure, the bar or "T" putting pressure on the frog when the horse puts weight on the foot. A slipper shoe lets the heels of the foot slide outward when weight is applied.

A contracted foot also can be helped by thinning the hoof wall at the quarters with a rasp. This thinning should start about half an inch below the coronary band in the area of the quarters and heels, gradually decreasing until the hoof wall at the ground surface is of normal thickness. This thinning helps the hoof wall expand when the horse puts weight on the foot. If the foot is thinned, it should also be shod with a pressure bar shoe which increases frog pressure and treated with hoof dressing daily to keep the thinned wall from cracking.

Corrective shoeing for a horse with ringbone calls for shortening the toe and putting on a full roller motion shoe. This shoe helps transfer action from the pastern and coffin joints to the bottom of the foot, the roller motion shoe making the foot break-over quickly and easily. The same type of shoe can help a horse with sidebones.

A horse with corns should go barefoot if possible. If he must be shod, the hoof wall and bar in the corn area should be cut away so there will be no pressure on the sole. A half or full-bar shoe can be used, fitted so the frog absorbs most of the concussion.

Cracks in the hoof wall sometimes require corrective shoeing. A shoe often will help keep the split hoof wall from cracking farther.

The foot should be trimmed so there will be no direct pressure on the split; in other words, that area of the hoof wall must not bear weight. This will allow the hoof wall to

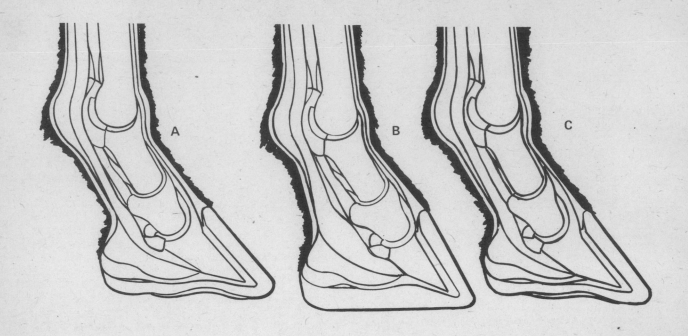

(A) The author's impression of the normal foot and lower leg of the horse. Note conformation of bones.

(B) In this instance, the hoof is not trimmed properly at the heel; internal parts are repositioned.

(C) This hoof has been improperly trimmed at the toe, rearranging the internal parts. Damage can result.

The above illustration shows the need for hoof knowledge. At left is normal foot, center is hoof with heel too long, and right is improperly trimmed toe. This shifts stress points within the foot and can cause serious lameness.

begin growing out without further widening of the crack.

The progress of the crack should be halted, if possible, by rasping a groove at the farthest point of the crack. If the crack penetrates into the sensitive tissues of the hoof, the horse will be lame because of infection. If this is the case, the crack should be thoroughly cleaned and disinfected with iodine, and the horse should be given a tetanus shot.

If the horse is left barefoot, the crack should be grooved and the bearing surface of the hoof wall in that area should be cut away so it doesn't bear weight and expand the crack. For a toe crack, the toe should be trimmed on either side of the crack. For a quarter crack, the hoof wall at the heel should be trimmed, from the crack on back, so the heel area will not take weight and spread the crack. Heel cracks are treated identically.

When shoeing a horse with a hoof crack, the foot is trimmed so the area around the crack does not touch the shoe and bear weight. Sometimes a clip on each side of the crack is helpful to keep the hoof wall from expanding, helping to support the hoof in that area. A half-bar shoe

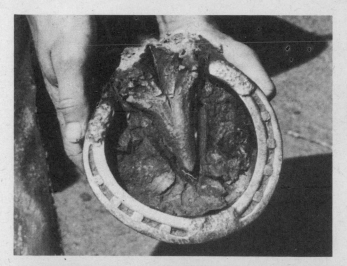

Borium is added to shoe (above right) to aid traction on slippery surfaces. Leather pads control loss of a hoof's moisture, necessary for healthy, normal frog (right).

sometimes is helpful for a quarter crack, producing frog pressure by allowing the frog to bear some of the weight that ordinarily would be borne by the hoof wall that has been trimmed away from the crack.

Part of the secret of growing out a hoof crack is to trim the foot often, so there will be little expansion pressure on the crack. If the hoof wall grows too long, the crack will tend to split farther. Careful grooving of the top of the crack and frequent trimming or corrective shoeing eventually will clear up a hoof crack that begins at the ground surface of the hoof wall.

If the crack is kept from widening or progressing, the normal hoof growth will eventually grow it out. But a hoof crack that originates in the coronary band from injury will be a more difficult and persistent problem. Corrective shoeing may be necessary for the rest of the horse's life, for a defect in the coronary band causes distorted and defective growth of the hoof in that area. The hoof wall in that place may have to be rasped every two weeks to keep the horn growth as nearly normal as possible, and the coronary band rubbed daily with olive oil or some other suitable softening agent if hard and dry.

Sometimes a severe hoof crack can be repaired with a strong glue. We saw this several years ago on a bad quarter crack in a 20-year-old mare's right front foot. She had a stubborn crack originating at the ground surface of the hoof, made worse by scar tissue at the coronary band above it, weakening the hoof wall in that place. Because of the weak strip in the hoof wall, this quarter crack spread upward rapidly in spite of conventional methods used to halt its progress. A strong, fast-drying glue was used to help hold the cracked area together and prevent further splitting as the hoof wall grew out. A glue used for this purpose must be strong or it won't hold the hoof wall solidly together when weight is placed upon it, expanding the hoof. The hoof wall must not expand in the area of the crack.

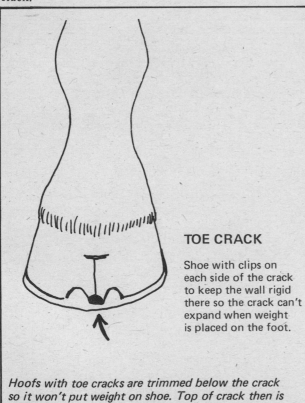

TOE CRACK

Shoe with clips on each side of the crack to keep the wall rigid there so the crack can't expand when weight is placed on the foot.

Hoofs with toe cracks are trimmed below the crack so it won't put weight on shoe. Top of crack then is rasped to help keep it from extending upwards farther.

First, the ground surface of the hoof wall was trimmed so the cracked area would not bear weight, then thoroughly cleaned to ensure there would be no dirt or foreign material to interfere with the adhesion of the glue to the hoof wall. A strip of strong fiberglass mesh was put over the crack area to add strength and the glue applied, thoroughly filling the crack. Her foot was held for twenty minutes so that the glue would have time to set before she placed weight on the foot. She was patient, even though the glue used produced some heat during its drying. After drying, it was solid enough to hold the crack and keep the area solid and unexpanding.

If done carefully and adequately, this is a procedure we would highly recommend for holding a stubborn hoof crack as the foot grows out. The foot still must be trimmed often, or the corrective shoes reset, and the glue may have to be replaced periodically until the crack has grown out sufficiently.

When shoeing a horse with flat feet, the sole should not be trimmed much, if any, and the frog shouldn't be trimmed. The wall should be trimmed only a little, enough to smooth it for the shoe. The shoe should cover the wall and white line and just barely touch upon the sole. If the shoe is seated merely on the hoof wall, the sole will tend to drop farther as the hoof wall grows and pushes outward. If the shoe is seated in such a way that there is too much bearing upon the sole — if the web of the shoe is too wide sole pressure may cause bruising and lameness.

If a horse has chronic laminitis or founder, he sometimes can be helped by corrective trimming and shoeing. The foundered foot should be trimmed as closely as possible, more often than for a normal horse. Wide-webbed shoes may keep the sole from dropping farther. The heel can be trimmed as much as possible without making the horse tender to help correct and counteract the downward rotation of the third phalanx or coffin bone. The toe of the hoof wall can be trimmed and rasped back to a more nearly normal shape. The edge of the hoof wall at the toe should be shortened slightly so it doesn't bear on the shoe. The toe of the shoe should be rolled to help the foot break-over easily when in motion.

In a foundered horse, the pain is mostly in the toe area of the sole. Therefore, the best type of shoe for founder is designed to remove all pressure from the painful sole and transfer it to the wall and frog which are less sensitive. A wide-webbed shoe should have a concave upper surface so that when the horse bears weight on the foot, all pressure is upon the hoof wall and none upon the sole. The wide web is there to help keep the sole from dropping. It may also be necessary to protect the sole by using a rubber or leather pad under the shoe, or even a metal plate.

Corrective trimming and shoeing cannot always completely correct a fault or defect in a horse's way of going, or completely cure an injured or diseased foot. But corrective trimming and shoeing, carefully and conscientiously done, usually can help the problem to some degree, often making the horse more useful, or alleviating his pain so he can move more normally.

Corrective trimming and shoeing cannot produce miracles; in many cases an unsound horse will always be an unsound horse. But if the horse's feet or gaits are helped in any degree, it may lengthen the life of that particular animal as a pleasure horse or breeding animal, or enable him to fill whatever other role he may be used in.

In a very real sense, every farrier should be able to trim and shoe correctly, for few horses are perfect and most can be helped by proper trimming and shoeing methods that take even the minor defects into consideration.

While it doesn't yet fall into the classification of normal corrective shoeing operations, use of acrylics and plastics is finding wider application in the restoration to normal of injured or diseased feet. To a great degree, experimentation on new fronts regarding foot ailments is done at racetracks. Presumably, this is because racehorses have more value than ordinary pleasure horses and owners have more money to spend on trial-and-error solutions that might bring their animals into the winner's circle again.

Dr. Daniel Farwick, a veterinarian around racetracks for many years, has played a role in restoring usefulness to horses with quarter cracks, founder and other disorders. When teamed with Mike Woebkenberg, a professional shoer since age 16, the results can be superb, working with acrylic resin.

Patching quarter cracks and partial reconstruction of horse's feet has been done for a decade or so and Dr. Farwick's experience with this type of work goes back almost that far. When he made his first attempts at patching feet, he employed a material used to line dentures, at the old Florence Raceway in Kentucky.

The denture liner set quickly and was easy to work with, but it never got much harder than a firm rubber ball.

"We called it the bubble gum patch, due to its lovely pink color," Dr. Farwick says. "These patches would last about two races, then we would have to peel them out and apply more of the material. It worked rather well on horses that weren't being put to hard use over hard surfaces, but it didn't stand up too well under stress of racing. It was rather embarrassing when your patch blew out fifty feet from the wire and hit the driver in the face!"

It was clear that something better was needed to advance the state of the art. The next step up was to an epoxy-type bonding material. It, too, had faults.

The epoxy primarily was the type used in sealing the cooling units of refrigerators and it was rather temperamental. The mixtures of resin and hardener had to be correct or it wouldn't harden. Also, the temperature had to remain within the sixty-five to eighty-degree range for the cast to harden, which took about twenty-four hours.

The next advancement came with acrylic resin, a substance similar in function to conventional epoxy, but much easier to work with. It's easy to work with at most temperatures and sets up in about ten to fifteen minutes. The material can be worked into the foot defect one day, rasped smooth the next and, as soon as the rough edges have been taken off, the horse can be back in service.

Reconstructing a portion of the foot led to reconstruction of a whole foot. Then, in the Summer of 1972, the blacksmith and veterinarian did their first work on a horse with laminitis, or founder.

Discussing founder, Dr. Farwick refers to the four feet of a horse as pumping stations. "In a sense, a horse has five hearts," he explains. "In founder, the blood vessels swell

Dr. Dan Farwick (foreground) and Mike Woebkenberg inspect sole of front foot for extent of bone rotation and infection (left) while owner looks on. Infection must be cleared before Woebkenberg can begin cutting back foot (right). This is done slowly.

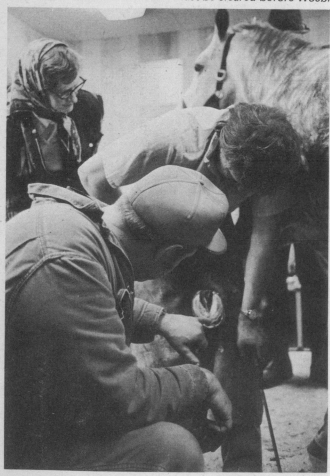

and there is no give in the horny wall. What follows is that the bottom bone rotates and drops, and the sole follows it down. This is painful, so a horse puts more weight on the back legs or lays down.

"In the old days, we used to gouge holes and let the blood escape, but that wasn't too successful. To reduce the swelling is the reason behind using cold water and ice."

The first foundered horse the team attended — and still are working on — was Shakers Firelight, a registered Morgan gelding. Just before the 1972 Gold Cup National, a large Morgan show at Columbus, Ohio, the horse started breathing hard and limping.

Infection settled in the feet and the horse couldn't bear

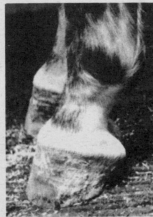

Foundered foot (left) shows weight carried on heels to relieve pain in front foot. After being cut almost to stump (right), angle of foot is raised, forcing animal off his heel.

to lie down because he was covered with bed sores, and he couldn't stand up because of his feet hurting.

Mike Woebkenberg recalls that he could stick a knife through the foot without any reaction. Mud and water would go through a hole in the sole and out through a hole at the coronet band. After the veterinarian/farrier team got through, the horse had a slight difference in the angle of his front feet, but the dead portion of the hoof has grown out and the team then started working on their second case history, a foundered horse named Clearcreek Carissa, a half-Arabian show mare.

Only four or five points away from qualifying for a Legion of Merit, the 5-year-old mare had been entered in the nationals to be held in Oklahoma City during August, 1973. Early that month, the mare went lame from what at first was thought to be a flare-up of a previous but slight founder condition suffered as a 2-year-old. However, it turned out that gravel was the cause of lameness.

Infection from the gravel in her foot got into her bloodstream and went throughout the mare's body. Three different bacterial strains grew in blood samples taken and, for months, the only goal was to keep her alive. After treating the horse with antibiotics and other medications with little success, acupuncture was tried.

"I can give her new feet if I can just keep her alive," Dr. Farwick said.

Finally, with her blood chemistries and blood count within normal range, work on reconstructing her feet and correcting the founder, which had become quite bad during her illness, was begun.

How does the acrylic system work? The first thing that needs to be done, after all infection has been cleared, is to cut the affected feet as far back as possible, until they are nearly bloody stumps. The foot is cut back slowly and carefully, much of the work being done with a rasp. Cutting

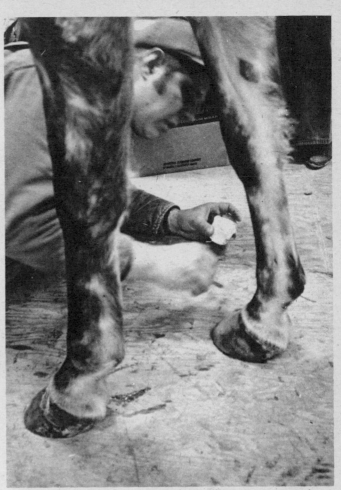

Dr. Farwick applies acrylic resin to fill out area created by shoe extending forward of what's left of rasped wall, as shown on following two pages. Resin hardens fast.

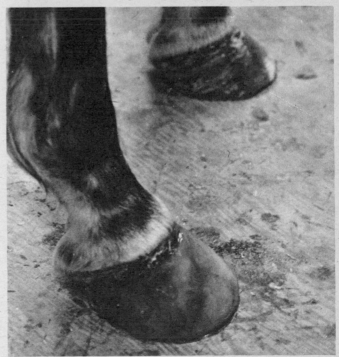

Foundered foot takes on normal appearance after the resin has been applied. It must be removed and reapplied often, which allows the foot to grow back nearly to former angle.

A plastic shock absorber, shown at left in above photo, must be cut and attached to the shoe as shown at right, which forms a toe wedge that lifts foot angle and gets horse off his heels. The front foot and toe have been cut to blood line and shoe with attached toe lift nailed on (below). Note the resulting toe defect, which later is covered with acrylic resin to restore looks.

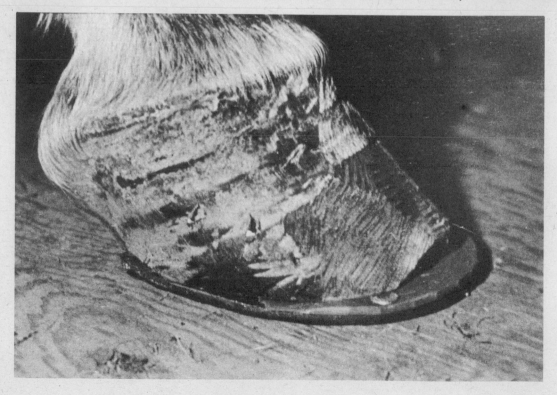

A bottom view of corrected foot illustrates how pad is used with the shoe. Sole of horse's foot now is concave.

the foot almost to the blood line allows the blood vessels to shrink, so more of the hoof can be cut later.

"You need a blacksmith with an artistic knack," states Dr. Farwick, who has worked with Mike Woebkenberg on this procedure in the past. "The first session is the most difficult. The heels are cut down as far as possible and all the dead horn in the toe and walls is cut away. In most cases, this will leave a large toe defect and there may be little or no area left for nails. In that case, shoes with perforated clips can be used without nails."

The foundered Clearcreek Carissa had front feet with angles of fifty-nine degrees before the shoes were pulled and the cutting begun. After cutting and with the toe snipped back, the angle was fifty degrees. Forty-eight to fifty is normal, feels Woebkenberg.

After cutting to fifty degrees, a regular racing shoe was taken and a plastic shock absorber was cut to make a toe wedge. The plastic won't absorb moisture and won't dry out. They took what normally would be a heel wedge and put it in front.

The shoe and wedge attached to the toe allowed the mare's front feet to be reduced another degree, to forty-nine. "We go lower than this to rotate the bone, then go back up," adds the farrier, whose first association with Dr. Farwick was a quarter horse colt with a club foot, that he drew out to normal. "By changing the angle, we're using the weight of the body to force the bone up and create movement. The bone will return to approximately ninety-five percent of its original position and, unless someone is aware that the horse has been foundered, the signs are so slight that no one else would be able to tell."

When fitted onto the foot, the shoe extends forward of what was left of the rasped wall. This is the area filled with the acrylic resin after the foot first is cleaned with ether to remove all moisture.

Woebkenberg refers to the use of acrylics in reconstructing the feet of a foundered horse as a "walking cast. It's a walking cast which is changed about every three to five weeks," he says. "It's about the same as a cast on a broken bone."

Dr. Farwick continually stresses the elimination of all infection before attempting acrylic repair of any kind. "It may take up to two weeks to get the foot in shape to repair," he advises. "In working with quarter cracks, we've often cut a little too deep on a non-infected foot and caused some hemorrhage. There usually follows some bad language under the shed, but the only thing to do is fold your kit, pack the defect in alcohol, and wait until the next day."

Make no mistake, this process is expensive. Not only does it take plenty of time, but the repeated application of acrylic by the veterinarian/farrier team adds to the bill. And, no actual reconstruction can begin until all signs of infection have disappeared. But the time factor probably is the main reason why this operation isn't undertaken with more frequency.

Experimentation in reconstructing feet of a foundered horse and rotating the third phalanx back into position has been done and documented as far back as 1963. Yet, in a recently published equine veterinarian textbook, only one paragraph is devoted to the use of acrylics in founder. However, the knowledge Dr. Daniel Farwick and Mike Woebkenberg have accumulated might just add a chapter or two to future textbooks!

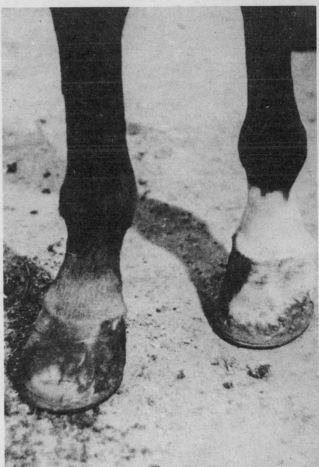

Some 1½ years after team began working on this case, feet are close to normal although some dead wall has yet to grow out on right foot. The left was the worst.

D: OWNER ETIQUETTE FOR FARRIERS!

DOESN'T YOUR BACK ever hurt?"

"Mmmm mmm."

"Come on, Pumpkin, don't step on the tools. You aren't cutting off too much, are you?"

"Mmmm mmm."

"She would probably stand better if you would take the apron off. She was mistreated by a man and she hasn't liked them since. Oh, my God, what did you do to her. There's blood on your apron! Oh, you just cut your finger on a nail! I thought for a minute that you had hurt her.

"Oh, there's Thelma. I'll be right back — I'm sure she'll stand good for you."

"All right, your mama isn't here now, so if you don't kick me, I won't kick you and if you don't bite me, I won't twist your ear."

Whack. Thump. Whack. Thump. Whack. Thump.

"Oh, you're all finished! How was she?"

"Just fine."

"She looks nice. Thank you. Oh, I forgot my money, I'll have to catch you later. Come on, Pumpkin, mama has a carrot for you."

This was a typical conversation with a horseowner and her shoer. The "Mmmm mmm" answers usually are emitted by a shoer during the nailing portion of his work. Some people feel slighted by this type of answer. But it's difficult to give a detailed, clearly pronounced answer when you are concentrating on proper expansion, angle of nails versus angle of hoof wall, considering thickness of white line, variation in intensity of hammer blows, movements and counter-movements with the horse so that she remains most comfortable, keeping your fingers out of the sharp nail points as the horse suddenly jerks — and not getting under her if she jerks her leg free. Besides this, it is hard to talk with both hands and legs occupied and a mouth full of slippery horseshoe nails.

There are a few basic duties that the horseowner can perform that not only will help the shoer, but also the horse.

These basic duties also will be most appreciated by your veterinarian.

When holding your horse for shoeing, it is good practice to stand on the same side as the shoer. If a horse acts up, this enables you to immediately see when the horse kicks and by pulling his head toward the shoer, you will move his rear-end away.

If your horse is fidgety, it will often help to shake his head slowly and steadily and talk to him firmly but softly. This will relax a nervous horse and give him something else to think about. Always avoid loud, fast or sudden movements.

Avoid the use of hoof dressing prior to shoeing. A farrier's hands, apron and tools pick up plenty of foreign material as it is, without the base coat of grease.

Be kind to your horse, but for both of your sakes, discipline him when he is wrong. There is nothing more nerve-racking to a shoer than the owner who baby talks a horse that is intentionally trying to kick a man's head off. A sharp whack with a blunt instrument is to a horse what a smack on the bottom is to a youngster. Remember to take into consideration the difference of toughness between a horse's hide and a youngster's hide and you will have a guide as to how hard to smack.

Above all, don't tell your shoer how to shoe your horse. Acquaint him with any problems the horse has, but let him determine the corrections. If you are more qualified to shoe than he, either you have done a lot of professional shoeing, or you have a pretty sorry shoer.

It is inconceivable for anyone who has not been a professional horseshoer or a large animal veterinarian to imagine the scope of questions that are asked by horseowners. We will touch upon the most commonly asked questions and give you the answers.

No answer given can be absolute, unless the specific horse is known. Horses are like people in that they are all individuals. What works fine on most horses will have a different effect on other horses. This is a basic law practiced by successful horsemen.

For those who do not possess the knowledge obtained by

years of close experience with horses, a word of advice: Ask questions of only professional horsemen. Beware of advice given by the pseudo-expert. Bad advice from the unqualified is the reason for the large number of soured and/or mistreated horses that have flooded the country.

Owning a horse doesn't make one any more an authority on horses than owning an automobile makes one an authority on engines. The ratio of automobile owners to mechanics is higher than the horseowners to the professional horseman. Seek your advice from the horseman whose ability with horses you respect.

What is thrush and what can be done about it?

Thrush is an anaerobic bacteria that forms in the bottom of a horses' hoof, especially in the area of the frog. It is readily recognizable by its foul odor and cheesy texture. Most horses carry a little thrush with no bad effects. It is not a serious problem, unless it gets out of hand. Proper trimming by a competent shoer, regular cleaning of the hooves and dry bedding are good preventatives.

Thrush is treated by thorough cleaning of the bottom of the hoof with special attention to the frog area. As much actual thrush as possible should be removed, followed by a liberal application of seven-percent iodine, regular laundry bleach, or a commercial thrush destroyer. In extreme cases, your veterinarian should be consulted.

How often should a horse's feet be trimmed?

Every horse grows hoof differently. Not only does a horse's individuality determine hoof growth, but weather, feed, exercise, and stabling conditions also enter into the picture. As a general rule, horses should be trimmed at six to eight-week intervals. If you have a regular shoer, ask him about how long your horse should go before he needs trimming again.

Should my horse have shoes or just be trimmed?

Shoeing is a necessary evil. If a horse's feet break up without shoes, it is the lesser of two evils to shoe him. If he has good feet and no major leg problems, it is much healthier for the foot not to have a shoe on it. No matter how well a shoe is fitted, it will limit hoof expansion to some extent. Expansion is important as a shock absorber to the horse's legs. Ask your farrier which your horse needs and follow his advice. It is his job to know and do what is best for your horse — so leave the decision up to him.

What can I do for dry feet?

Proper use of any hoof dressing will help. I have had the best results by soaking a horse's feet prior to application. After soaking the feet, clean them thoroughly and apply dressing to the bottom of the foot. In extreme cases and, if it is practical, you can overflow your waterer. This will cause the horse to soak his own feet every time he gets a drink. If this method is used, it is wise to be alert for a thrush problem.

Can the size of a horse's hoof be made smaller?

Yes, but it is seldom a good practice. It is normal to remove any prominent flares on the side of a hoof; however, excess rasping of the hoof wall weakens the hoof. If your horse wears a number six shoe, you will no more change his hoof size by putting on a number five shoe than you would your own by wearing a size smaller shoe.

What is the lump on the elbow of a horse's leg?

It can be a shoe boil caused by irritation to the elbow by the heel of the hoof when a horse lies down. This problem usually arises when a horse's hooves are too long or the heels of the shoe extend too far to the rear. Proper trimming and shoe fitting should eliminate this problem. If a shoe boil is large and persistent, it is wise to consult your veterinarian to see if lancing is required.

Is hot shoeing better than cold shoeing?

With the various sized shoes being produced today, it is no longer necessary to cut the heels on shoes. This eliminates the need for a forge other than for drawing chips, turning heels or other extreme corrective measures. The old method of seating a hot shoe onto a horse's hoof is not a good practice. Not only does it draw moisture out of the foot, but it sears many of the pores in the bottom of the hoof, interfering with normal moisture intake.

The only bad effect of cold shoeing is that it makes it easier for incompetent fly-by-nights to get into the shoeing business. Whether or not a farrier hot shoes is not an indication of his ability. Only the products of his efforts determine this — the finished foot.

How do you know how deep to go when trimming a hoof?

The usual guideline for depth is the white line. This is the yellow band separating the hoof wall from the sole. When a glossy material is reached and it holds the imprint of your thumbnail, the depth is almost correct. The most important guideline is the shoer's experience. This is a knowledge developed through years of working with various types of hooves.

Will my horse be sore after shoeing?

It is unusual for a horse to be sore after normal shoeing. It is, however, common for a horse to be a little sore after trimming, especially if he was abnormally long on wearing shoes. A freshly trimmed horse that is a little tender is the mark of an honest shoer and is much more desirable than leaving a horse too long.

Most professional horsemen want their horses trimmed close. It is a common practice among Western trainers to trim a young horse short in front and shoe him behind to start him working more on his hindquarters. It doesn't hurt a horse to be trimmed close any more than it hurts beach-goers to go barefoot in the Summer. The feet of both soon callous. On the other hand, a horse left too long will have a greater tendency to crack up, will be more apt to pick up flares, will pick up thrush, and will be due for work sooner.

Try to find a shoer who is honest and dependable. A man who is conscientious about his appointments is usually conscientious about his work. Try to use a man who is a full-time shoer, not someone who uses it as a part-time job. Above all, beware of the man who shoes for less than the going rate. There is usually a reason other than the goodness of his heart.

Things to look for in a finished foot include:

1. Angle: The angle at the front of the hoof from cornet band to shoe should be about the same as the angle at the front of the short pastern.

2. Levelness: The bottom of the hoof should be flat with the shoe fitting tightly at the heels and toe.

3. Expansion: The shoe should extend slightly outside of the hoof edge between the quarter and the heel. This allows for the expansion and contraction of the hoof as it hits and leaves the ground.

4. Excess rasping of the hoof wall: As stated earlier, rasping of the hoof wall should be kept to a minimum. The practice of rasping off a large degree of hoof to make a shoe fit is unprofessional. Rasping should be kept on the bottom third of the hoof and used only to remove flares or irregularities.

5. Clinches: Clinches should be turned, tightened and slightly rasped to remove roughness. Nails should be driven deep enough to hold the shoe securely, but no deeper than necessary — usually about three-fourths-inch.

6. Frog: The dead and loose parts of the frog should be as close to level with the bottom of the hoof as possible. The cracks on each side of the frog should be opened to allow air penetration.

7. If a hoof is not shod, the edges should be rounded to prevent breaking up of the hoof wall.

A horse is only as good as his feet and legs. Don't neglect the most critical part of your horse by infrequent or incompetent shoeing or trimming.

Chapter 11
PRACTICAL HORSE FEEDING

This Is A Complicated Subject, But One The Horseman Should Understand!

Feeding horses seems a mysterious art, of which only nutrition experts have a sound knowledge. It needn't be this way; in fact, any horseman can learn the rudiments of equine nutrition, without learning to pronounce all the fourteen-syllable terms!

A horse has nutrition needs like any mammal, including man. These include vitamins, minerals, protein and energy. The horse receives these from his feed and water in most cases, or from compounds supplemented because the feed is lacking of those compounds.

Each horse has different nutritional requirements, due to weight, age, usage and individualism. Therefore, one diet cannot be outlined for, say, all roping horses. It's up to the individual horseman to prescribe the feed rations for his horses, a trial and error process. If the horses appear thin, their rations should be increased; if they look fat, cut back the feeds. The horse should receive only enough feed to keep him healthy and fit, neither skinny nor hog-fat.

The tables which follow can be used to set up a feeding program for individual horses without much fuss or bother. The keys to any formula are: the horse's requirements, the amount of essential nutrients in the hay being fed and the nutrients in the grain added to the feed.

Table 1 gives the required nutrients of growing horses, while Table 2 gives the same information for mature horses according to their usage and weight. These simply list some of the chemicals the horse needs for continued good health. Table 3 lists the nutritive components found in hay, while Table 4 lists the nutritive compounds found in grain. Table 5 does the same for pasture grasses and Table 6 lists components of supplements.

What the horseman does, therefore, is first determine the nutritional needs of his horse, dependent upon his usage and weight. He then checks to see which of those compounds, and the amounts, are found in the hay he's feeding. In most cases, the hay alone won't provide all the nutritional elements needed in the proper amounts, the reason grain is fed. The horseman then checks the nutritive components of the grain he's feeding to determine if the grain, when added to the nutritive components of the hay, provide all the needed elements. If it does, that's the ration his horse requires for good health.

If the combination of grain and hay does not provide all the needed compounds, he then must supplement with commercially prepared products that have the elements his horse's diet is lacking. Most horses can receive all the nutritive elements they need through hay and grain.

There is another course open to horseowners, aside from purchasing supplements. This is in the feeding of different hays or grains. Not all hays and grains have the same nutritive content, so by switching to a different hay/grain combination, the horseman might then provide all the requirements needed without supplementing.

Economics enters the picture at this point. Many horsemen have adopted the attitude that one specific type of hay or grain is best, the others suitable only for feeding to goats. In direct relation to the law of supply and demand, the price for this type of hay or grain has risen substantially, while less-popular hays and grains are considerably cheaper.

This attitude, according to internationally known nutritionist Dr. William K. Tyznik, is foolish. He advocates feeding the grains that are cheapest in the horseman's part of the country, meeting the nutritive requirements through other mineral supplements. He feels people should quit buying exotic supplements and additives to a great degree, using the money saved to purchase the best-quality hay affordable.

Rather than stoke the fires of controversy, we'll just say that the horse's nutritional needs must be met. Any of the methods outlined herein will work toward that end.

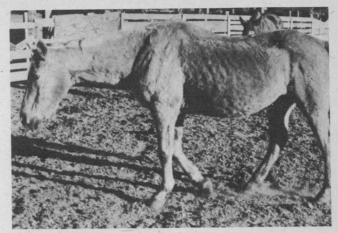

This is a sad example of owner negligence through insuficient quantity, compounded by inadequate types of feed. This horse was returned to health and strength.

QUANTITATIVE NUTRIENT REQUIREMENTS OF GROWING HORSES
(Daily Nutrients Per Animal)

EQUINE GROWING TO 450 POUNDS MATURE WEIGHT:

Body Weight (lbs.)	Daily Gain (lbs.)	Dig. Energy (calories)	Dig. Protein (lbs.)	Calcium (lbs.)	Phosphorus (lbs.)
100	1½	7400	.8426	.0383	.0240
200	1	8530	.6930	.0365	.0229
300	½	7950	.4532	.0264	.0165
350	¼	8080	.3082	.0220	.0143
450	0	8240	.3520	.0176	.0132

EQUINE GROWING TO 900 POUNDS MATURE WEIGHT:

Body Weight (lbs.)	Daily Gain (lbs.)	Dig. Energy (calories)	Dig. Protein (lbs.)	Calcium (lbs.)	Phosphorus (lbs.)
200	2¼	10,440	1.2166	.0574	.0361
400	1½	12,410	.9460	.0770	.0482
550	1	13,630	.8140	.0484	.0326
725	½	14,100	.7458	.0418	.0304
900	0	13,860	.5896	.0352	.0264

EQUINE GROWING TO 1100 POUNDS MATURE WEIGHT:

Body Weight (lbs.)	Daily Gain (lbs.)	Dig. Energy (calories)	Dig. Protein (lbs.)	Calcium (lbs.)	Phosphorus (lbs.)
250	2½	12,070	1.3596	.0671	.0420
500	1¾	15,400	1.1792	.1012	.0632
725	1¼	16,810	1.0384	.0572	.0383
900	¾	17,160	.9196	.0506	.0354
1100	0	16,390	.6974	.0440	.0330

EQUINE GROWING TO 1325 POUNDS MATURE WEIGHT:

Body Weight (lbs.)	Daily Gain (lbs.)	Dig. Energy (calories)	Dig. Protein (lbs.)	Calcium (lbs.)	Phosphorus (lbs.)
300	2¾	14,150	1.5510	.1144	.0708
600	2	17,210	1.2804	.1126	.0704
850	1¼	18,860	1.1528	.0724	.0453
1050	¾	19,200	1.0076	.0689	.0431
1325	0	18,790	.8008	.0528	.0396

TABLE 1
(Derived from "Nutrient Requirements of Horses," compiled and published by National Research Council, 1973.)

QUANTITATIVE NUTRIENT REQUIREMENTS OF MATURE HORSES
(Daily Nutrients Per Animal)

MATURE HORSE, IDLE

Body Weight (lbs.)	Dig. Energy (calories)	Dig. Protein (lbs.)	Calcium (lbs.)	Phosphorus (lbs.)
450	8240	.3520	.0176	.0132
900	13,860	.5896	.0352	.0264
1100	16,390	.6974	.0440	.0330
1325	18,790	.8008	.0528	.0396

MATURE HORSE, LIGHT WORK (2 hours per day):

Body Weight (lbs.)	Dig. Energy (calories)	Dig. Protein (lbs.)	Calcium (lbs.)	Phosphorus (lbs.)
450	10,440	.4444	.0176	.0132
900	18,360	.7810	.0352	.0264
1100	21,890	.9328	.0440	.0330
1325	25,390	1.0802	.0528	.0396

MATURE HORSE, MEDIUM WORK (2 hours per day):

Body Weight (lbs.)	Dig. Energy (calories)	Dig. Protein (lbs.)	Calcium (lbs.)	Phosphorus (lbs.)
450	13,160	.5610	.0202	.0154
900	23,800	1.0120	.0378	.0286
1100	28,690	1.2166	.0466	.0352
1325	33,550	1.4278	.0625	.0418

MARE, LAST 90 DAYS OF PREGNANCY:

Body Weight (lbs.)	Dig. Energy (calories)	Dig. Protein (lbs.)	Calcium (lbs.)	Phosphorus (lbs.)
450	8700	.4752	.0229	.0716
900	14,880	.8250	.0429	.0330
1100	17,350	.9548	.0528	.0396
1325	19,950	1.1044	.0616	.0462

MARE, PEAK OF LACTATION:

Body Weight (lbs.)	Dig. Energy (calories)	Dig. Protein (lbs.)	Calcium (lbs.)	Phosphorus (lbs.)
450	15,240	1.0560	.0748	.0515
900	24,390	1.6456	.0924	.0783
1100	27,620	1.8238	.1034	.0849
1325	30,020	1.9272	.1122	.0858

TABLE 2
(Derived from "Nutrient Requirements of Horses," compiled and published by National Research Council, 1973.)

NUTRIENTS IN COMMON HORSE FEEDS: HAY (ONE POUND)

TYPE	Dig. Protein (lbs.)	Dig. Energy (calories/lb.)	Calcium (lbs.)	Phosphorus (lbs.)
Alfalfa:				
Early Bloom	.1110	951	.0112	.0021
Mid-Bloom	.0981	911	.0120	.0020
Full Bloom	.0868	836	.0112	.0018
Mature	.0702	803	.0065	.0015
Dehydrated	.1470	1025	.0152	.0026
Timothy:				
Pre-Bloom	.0585	940	.0058	.0030
Mid-Bloom	.0318	778	.0036	.0017
Late Bloom	.0317	759	.0033	.0016
Clover:				
Alsike	unk	881	.0115	.0022
Crimson	unk	864	.0124	.0016
Ladino	.1351	unk	.0153	.0029
Red	.0748	883	.0131	.0021
Native	.3900	687	.0053	.0016
Oat	.3800	784	.0023	.0021

TABLE 3

(Derived from "Nutrient Requirements of Horses," compiled and published by National Research Council, 1973.)

NUTRIENTS IN COMMON HORSE FEEDS: CONCENTRATES (ONE POUND)

Grain	Dig. Protein (lbs.)	Dig. Energy (calories/lb.)	Calcium (lbs.)	Phosphorus (lbs.)
Barley	.0730	1477	.0006	.0049
Corn (yellow dent)	.0470	1618	.0002	.0027
Cottonseed meal	.3510	1374	.0016	.0120
Linseed meal	.2967	1473	.0044	.0089
Molasses:				
Beet	.0380	1369	.0017	.0003
Cane	.1356	74.1	.0041	.0004
Oats:				
Rolled	.1252	unk	.0008	.0043
34 lb./bushel	.0760	1275	.0008	.0030
Skim milk	.3350	1616	.0126	.0103
Soybean meal	.3980	1425	.0032	.0067
Wheat bran	.1148	1037	.0014	.0117
Yeast, brewers	.3841	1304	.0013	.0143

TABLE 4

(Derived from "Nutrient Requirements of Horses," compiled and published by National Research Council, 1973.)

NUTRIENTS IN COMMON HORSE FEEDS: PASTURE (ONE POUND)

Type	Dig. Protein (lbs.)	Dig. Energy (calories/lb.)	Calcium (lbs.)	Phosphorus (lbs.)
Bluegrass:				
Immature	.0370	337	.0017	.0014
Milk Stage	.0240	346	.0007	.0009
Brome	.0530	347	.0020	.0018
Fescue, Meadow	.0469	787	.0044	.0032
Orchardgrass:				
Immature	.0310	255	.0014	.0013
Mid-Bloom	.0130	282	unk	unk
Milk Stage	.0010	261	.0007	.0007
Prairie Hay	.0264	unk	.0032	.0013
Sudangrass	.0520	unk	.0036	.0027
Wheatgrass, Crested:				
Immature	.0540	330	.0014	.0011
Full Bloom	.0240	420	.0019	.0014
Overripe	0	566	.0022	.0006

TABLE 5

(Derived from "Nutrient Requirements of Horses," compiled and published by National Research Council, 1973.)

NUTRIENTS IN COMMON SUPPLEMENTS: (ONE POUND)

Type	Calcium (lbs.)	Phosphorus (lbs.)
Dicalcium Phosphate	.0222	.0178
Oyster Shells	.0385	0
High Calcium Limestone	.0330	0
Defluorinated Phosphate	.0330	.0180
Monosodium Phosphate	0	.0217
Sodium Tripolyphosphate	0	.0216
Steamed Bone Meal	.0290	.0136

TABLE 6

(Derived from "Nutrient Requirements of Horses," compiled and published by National Research Council, 1973.)

POSSIBLE DAILY FEED RATIONS (POUNDS)

HORSE	Legume hay*	Grass hay+	Oats	Barley	Wheat bran	Corn	Salt, Calcium, Vitamin Suppl.
400-pound weanling	3.5	3.5	3	2	1	0	Yes
	3.5	3.5	4	0	2	0	Yes
	3.5	3.5	5	0	1	0	Yes
1200-pound pleasure/show horse	0	14.0	5	0	0	0	Yes
	0	14.0	4	0	0	1	Yes
	0	14.0	4	1	0	0	Yes
1200-pound average work	0	14	11	0	0	0	Yes
	0	14	9	0	0	2	Yes
	0	14	8	0	0	3	Yes
1200-pound strenuous work	0	14	16	0	0	0	Yes
	0	14	11	2	0	3	Yes
	0	14	10	6	0	0	Yes
1200-pound brood mare or service stallion	4	9	8	0	2	0	Yes
	4	9	4	0	3	3	Yes
	4	9	11	0	0	0	Yes
1200-pound mare with foal at side	6	8	14	0	2	0	Yes
	6	8	9	4	3	0	Yes
	6	8	15	0	1	0	Yes

*alfalfa, clover hays
+timothy, prairie, brome, bermuda, Kentucky, orchard hays

TABLE 7

VITAMINS

NAME	SOURCE	BENEFIT
A	Green leaf plants, manufactured bodily through most normal feed or supplements	Body metabolism growth, reproduction; necessary for reproductive, digestive and respiratory systems
D	Sunlight, supplements	Sound bones and teeth; assists assimilation of nutrient calcium and phosphorus
E	Prime hay, green leaf plants, supplements	Increased reproductive ability
B Complex	Green leafy feed, fresh or dry	Body metabolism

TABLE 8

MINERALS		
NAME	SOURCE	BENEFIT
Calcium	Supplements; basic feed	Development of bones; body metabolism
Cobalt	Basic feed	Necessary bacterial action of the digestive system
Copper	See Iron	See Iron
Iodine	Supplements — rarely in proper amounts in basic feed	Body metabolism
Iron	Supplements; basic feed	Oxygenation of circulatory system; required by the digestive system
Manganese	See Sulfur	See Sulfur
Magnesium	See Sulfur	See Sulfur
Phosphorus	See Calcium	See Calcium
Potassium	See Sulfur	See Sulfur
Salt	Supplement	Assimilation of nutrients in body metabolism; aids in elimination of waste materials
Sulfur	Basic feed	Body metabolism

TABLE 9

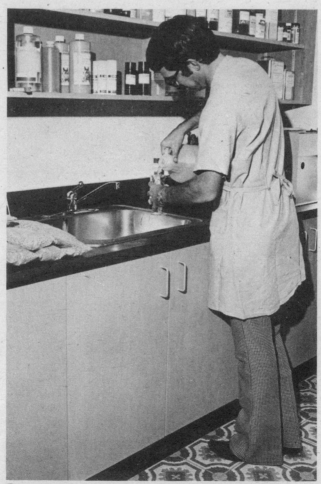

Many talented researchers are employed by horse feed companies that spend thousands annually in the search for the proper nutrients horses require, among others.

Proper exercise daily is compatible with a sound feeding program, to avoid some of the health hazards outlined in Chapter 9. A healthy horse is a happy individual.

Using these charts, it's easy to figure the horse's diet. As an example, suppose you own a mature horse weighing 900 pounds that is used at medium work for two hours per day (Table 2). This horse requires 23,800 calories, 1.0120 pounds of protein, .0378 pounds of calcuim and .0286 pounds of phosphorus per day.

He is being fed thirteen total pounds of hay, seven of early-bloom alfalfa, with six pounds of pre-bloom timothy (Table 3). In addition, he receives eight total pounds of grain, four each of corn and oats, the latter weighing 34 pounds per bushel (Table 4). He receives these nutrients total: digestible energy (calories), 23,864; digestible protein (pounds), 1.6200; calcium (pounds), .0472 and phosphorus (pounds), .0555. The formula for calculation of this ration is:

DIGESTIBLE ENERGY (CALORIES)
7 lbs. Early-Bloom Alfalfa @ 951 calories/lb. = 6657 cal
6 lbs. Pre-Bloom Timothy @ 940 calories/lb. = 5640 "
4 lbs. Corn @ 1618 calories/lb. = 6427 "
4 lbs. Oats (34 lb./bushel) @ 1275 calories/lb. = 5100 "
    Total Digestive Energy = 23,864 cal

DIGESTIBLE PROTEIN (POUNDS)
7 lbs. Early-Bloom Alfalfa @ .1110/lb. = .7770 pounds
6 lbs. Pre-Bloom Timothy @ .0585/lb. = .3510 "
4 lbs. Corn @ .0470/lb. = .1880 "
4 lbs. Oats (34 lb./bushel) @ .0760/lb. = .3040 "
    Total Digestible Protein = 1.6200 pounds

CALCIUM (POUNDS)
7 lbs. Early-Bloom Alfalfa @ .0112/lb. = .0084 pounds
6 lbs. Pre-Bloom Timothy @ .0058/lb. = .0348 "
4 lbs. Corn @ .0002/lb. = .0008 "
4 lbs. Oats (34 lb./bushel) @ .0008/lb. = .0032 "
    Total Calcium = .0472 pounds

PHOSPHORUS (POUNDS)
7 lbs. Early-Bloom Alfalfa @ .0021/lb. = .0147 pounds
6 lbs. Pre-Bloom Timothy @ .0030/lb. = .0180 "
4 lbs. Corn @ .0027/lb. = .0108 "
4 lbs. Oats (34 lb./bushel) @ .0030/lb. = .0120 "
    Total Phosphorus = .0555 pounds

Of course, a ration is only as good as the feed used. If the horse is fed the best-quality hays and grains affordable, he will receive nearly all of the nutrients vital to his subsistance. A salt/mineral block can be put in his paddock or stall and he will take in the other minerals and compounds as needed.

Various feed facts have been provided throughout this book and they will be capsulated at this point:

Make any ration changes slowly, since the horse doesn't seem well-suited to rapid diet changes. These have led to many internal problems, among them colic.

The horse is able to better utilize nutrients in his feed if fed more than once per day. These feedings should be at the same times each day and always feed hay prior to grain. Since the grain is higher in nutrients, feeding it after the hay allows it to remain in the stomach longer before passing in the feces, leading to better utilization of the nutrients.

If the horse has a tendency to bolt his grain without thorough chewing, which leads to faster passage from the intestines, feed small amounts of grain often. Another solution is to put some smooth, flat stones in the grain bucket or manger, forcing the horse to eat more slowly and carefully.

Always buy the best-quality hay that's affordable, since there's more nutritive benefit in quality over quantity. Assure the feeds aren't moldy, dusty or spoiled and feed only what the horse requires to keep fit.

Provide cool, clean water at all times, even during the dead of Winter, since the horse derives nutrients from it. Never water a hot horse and don't water the horse after feeding grain. The bulk of the water will force passage of the grain before all the nutrients are utilized.

Keep a salt/mineral block available to the horse at all times. This free-choice aspect of supplementing allows the horse to take the minerals he requires when needed, and studies have shown the horse will use the salt/mineral block when needed.

Regular exercise is compatible with proper equine nutrition. As noted in Chapter 9, lack of exercise can lead to such problems as azoturia or tying-up.

Feed him right, exercise regularly and your horse will be serviceable for many years.

SUCCESSFUL BREEDING PRACTICES

Chapter 12

THERE ARE SOME eight million horses in the United States today and the number is steadily growing.

All kinds of people raise horses: ranchers, businessmen, movie stars, kids with 4-H projects, families with a horse or two in the backyard, professional horsemen. Raising horses is a hobby for some, a business for others. But no matter what the reasons for raising horses, the goals should be the same — to raise the best ones possible. To breed and raise inferior animals is bad for the breed, bad for the person who ends up with the horse, bad for the industry in general.

Anyone seriously going into the horse business to raise horses to sell rather than horses for their own personal use will want to raise purebreds. There are many good grade horses and some are champions in their fields, but there is a limited market for grade horses. Too, you are limited in the

price you can get for them unless they are highly trained, and the breeder often doesn't have the time to raise, train and sell mature horses; most prefer to raise stock they can sell as weanlings or yearlings. They'll have less valuable time and feed in them.

So unless you have a specific purpose in mind, like raising and training specialized horses to sell (roping horses, barrel horses, etc.) you'd best raise purebreds. But when selecting breeding stock, remember that just because a horse is purebred with papers doesn't necessarily mean he's a good horse. There are good and poor horses in every breed, and you need to be very selective, choosing the best you can afford.

When buying fillies and mares, one finds a great variation in prices, partly dependent on the breed. Individuals in a

Goals, Stallion And Brood Mare Management, Foaling And Foal Care Are Covered In This Chapter!

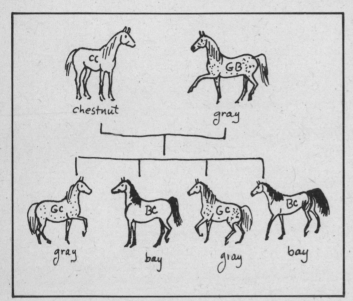 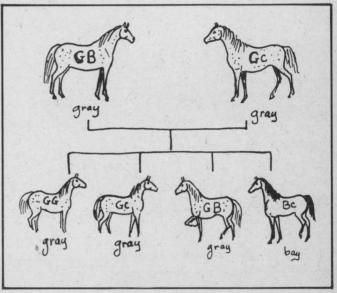

(Left): A chestnut bred to impure gray carrying bay gene will produce all impure foals, 50 percent gray with recessive chestnut, 50 percent bay with recessive chestnut. (Right): Impure grays, one with bay, the other with recessive chestnut, produce these colors in group of four: one pure gray, one gray with chestnut, one gray with bay, one bay with chestnut.

breed with limited numbers usually will cost more than horses of a breed with numerous horses. It may be harder and take longer to get into a higher-priced breed if you haven't much money, but your foals will be worth more when sold.

It costs more to buy a national champion, the son or daughter of a national champion, or a popular bloodline. Here again, foals from popular or championship bloodlines may be worth more. But don't get caught in a "fad" that may not last and don't spend more than a horse actually is worth. Never sacrifice conformation, action, quality, disposition and so on for name alone. A few of the "top" horses got to the top partly because their owners had lots of money for publicity. Some of these "top" horses don't always produce "top" offspring. There are many other horses running around that are equally as good but not as well-known and therefore won't cost as much.

When buying breeding stock, look at plenty of horses before selecting, buy the best you can afford, and try to improve upon it by careful and selective breeding. If you breed good horses consistently, there always will be a market for them.

The highest-priced female stock usually is the young

stock with good or famous parentage, and the producing young and middle-aged brood mares that already have produced good foals. The most economical age groups are the very young (unproven) and the older matrons. You sometimes can buy a good-quality, older mare reasonably, often from someone cutting down his herd numbers or making room for younger stock. With luck, you'll raise a few more fillies from her to add to your brood band.

When buying an older mare, you're gambling that she will keep producing for a few more years. If she is healthy, sound and has a record of being a good producer, it may be a gamble worth taking. But beware of buying an older mare that hasn't produced a foal for several years. Older mares can become infertile or sterile from old age. A mare that consistently has produced foals for the last few years will be more likely to keep producing than an old mare that hasn't.

Above all, in selecting mares, try to get good conformation. Conformation is so important in a horse, whether for show or pleasure, ranch work or racing, because everything he does is linked with how well or how poorly he is put together. We are trying to breed riding animals — athletes — and this never should be forgotten.

The breeder who never rides his animals or who concentrates primarily on "halter prospects" tends sometimes to overlook the important points of conformation that determine how well a horse can move and how well he can hold up under steady riding. The horse with good conformation will move better, be more pleasant to ride, have nicer action, stay sounder longer and be a safer mount than the horse with poor conformation. You're trying to breed the best, so don't settle for anything less; eventually you'll have trouble selling the offspring. Besides, we want to improve and upgrade our particular breed, rather than tear it down. Breeding horses with poor conformation really hurts the breed.

Often overlooked when talking about brood mares and breeding stock is trying to select mares (or fillies from mares) that are good mothers. A good brood mare should be feminine and maternal, just as a good stallion should be masculine; you'll have less problems. Too many mares are selected for their masculine characteristics — speed, power, strength, etc. — and as a result, some aren't very feminine, very fertile or very good mothers if they do produce foals. Keep this in mind when looking at prospective brood mares.

When buying a stallion, buy the best affordable, for it's the stallion you rely upon to upgrade your breeding stock. He will produce many foals, whereas a mare only will produce a dozen or so in her lifetime. If the stallion is very good, you may be lucky enough to raise foals better than their mothers.

It is foolish to breed a good mare to a stallion that isn't as good as she; if you breed her to one that's as good or

As discussed later, leaving mare and foal to walk behind horseman free of restraint is improper and leads to host of problems. If necessary, leave mare free, but not foal!

better, you begin to upgrade your herd. If you are fortunate enough to breed horses that complement each other, you actually may produce a foal that is better than either of his parents. This is the big challenge and what the selective breeding game is all about — trying to improve upon what you already have.

You may want to buy a good-looking weanling colt as a stallion prospect, then raise and train him. This perhaps is the cheapest way to buy a stallion, but also is risky: you can't always tell how the weanling or yearling will turn out as a stallion.

Judge him closely. If you still like what you see, look at his parents (and half-siblings, full brothers and sisters, if he has any) to get a glimpse of what he might look like when mature.

Whenever you buy breeding stock, try to see as many of the horse's relatives as possible. If there are poor ones in the family, you'll have to realize your horse may carry genetic possibilities for poor offspring, too. But if the relatives of your stallion prospect are of consistently good quality, go ahead and gamble. If there are inconsistencies and characteristics you don't like in some of his close relatives, look a little longer somewhere else.

A 2 to 4-year-old stud will cost more than the weanling or yearling, if he's good. The stallion is starting to mature, you can see what he may look like, and he probably has some training put into him.

When judging a young stallion, don't expect yearlings and 2-year-olds to look mature. If they do, they may be too large, coarse or heavy when mature. A 2-year-old stallion should still have something to look forward to, using the words of one good horse judge. Also keep in mind that some breeds mature more slowly than others. The quarter horse probably is the fastest in reaching his size. Don't expect the 2 or 3-year-old Arabian stallion to look as mature as the 2 or 3-year-old quarter horse.

The mature stallion of 5 or 6 to about 12 or 15 will probably be the most expensive, if he's good. He's at his peak, is easily judged, you can see what kind of offspring he produces and can easily determine what kind of sire he is. It's always advantageous to see a horse's offspring, as you have a better guess of what he can do for your mares. Not all good-looking horses are the best sires and some of the plainer ones may surprise you with exceptional foals. Though usually "like begets like," it's best to see what a stallion produces; his offspring are his proof. If a stallion is of breeding age but never sired a foal, be cautious. He may not be fertile.

The older stallion may be somewhat cheaper than the stallion still in his prime, but an older stallion with a good show record or famous offspring still may command a high price. If you feel you cannot afford a good stallion at first, you might breed your best mare to a good stallion — with a stud fee you still can afford — in hopes of raising a colt that might work as your first stallion. You also might lease a stallion for a year, hoping to get a good colt or two from your mares that might make future stallion prospects.

When selecting a mare or stallion, check conformation, disposition and pedigree. Bloodlines are important because ancestors produce the horse. But pedigree alone means nothing; a horse must be a good individual, too.

Try to see as many of the individuals in the horse's pedigree as possible — sire, dam, grandparents, etc. — at least in pictures if not available in the flesh. The first fourteen ancestors — sire, dam, grandparents and great-grandparents — are the most important to consider. Ancestors farther back aren't likely to have as much influence in the characteristics of the horse, though occasionally it does happen. If the individuals close-up in a horse's pedigree are

Mating a pure gray with a bay will result in all gray offspring, yet all retain recessive bay gene (right). This could be passed to offspring, perhaps coloring them bay.

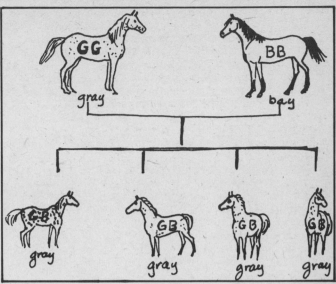

Two impure bays, each having recessive chestnut genes (below), can produce the following colors in a group of four foals: one pure bay, two impure bay, one chestnut.

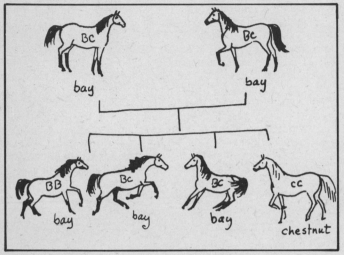

A pure gray mated with a chestnut — also pure — will produce only gray foals, all being impure with chestnut gene (right). Thus, chestnut can be passed to their foals.

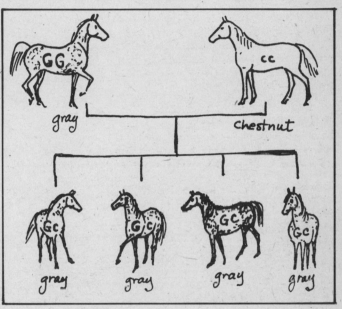

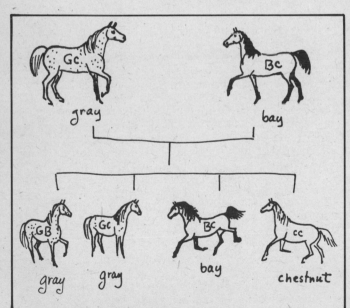

An impure gray with a chestnut gene, mated to an impure bay also carrying chestnut, can produce in a group of four foals: one gray/bay, one gray/chestnut, one bay/chestnut and one pure chestnut (above). Genetics are confusing!

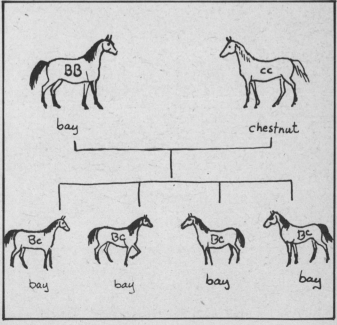

A pure bay mated with a chestnut, which is genetically pure for that color, produces solid bay foals, each being genetically impure with the recessive chestnut gene (right).

259

A frisky, sound, well-built foal of good parentage is the desired result of a breeder's conscientious program. Before breeding, have a sound knowledge of horses you own.

consistently good, that horse likely will produce good-quality foals when mated to an equally good horse.

Inbreeding and linebreeding should be mentioned. If a horse is bred to another in its immediate family such as sister to brother or half-brother, mother or father to son or daughter, it's called inbreeding. This sometimes is done deliberately with outstanding individuals.

Inbreeding always is risky because it doubles up many characteristics and recessive traits can emerge that were hidden in both parents. You can get a really poor foal this way. But if a horse carries only good genetic characteristics and is bred to a close relative that carries the same, the offspring has a good chance of inheriting only good qualities and being truly outstanding, particularly in the genetics he then passes to his offspring.

With luck, an inbreeding product from good parents only will carry these doubled-up good qualities in his genetic make-up (he will be genetically "pure" for these characteristics, carrying no others) and he may truly be outstanding as a sire or dam, passing on consistent, good qualities to his foals. But inbreeding always should be done with care, with horses that aren't known to carry any undesirable traits. If the inbreeding produces a doubling up of undesirable characteristics or recessive weaknesses that weren't obvious in the parents, it can be harmful rather than beneficial.

Linebreeding is a form of inbreeding, but in a more cautious manner. Linebreeding is when related horses like uncle to niece, grandsire to granddaughter or great-grand-daughter, etc., are bred. Not as close in relation, there are more unrelated horses in the pedigree, supplying different genetic possibilities and somewhat lessening the chances of doubling up something bad.

Careful linebreeding is done by many breeders of horses and other livestock to improve the breed, concentrating on certain desirable family traits. It can produce outstanding animals by doubling up good qualities and concentrating on certain desirable characteristics in families of horses, but isn't quite so risky as inbreeding.

An outcross is when a horse of one family strain is bred to a horse of another family strain that isn't related. In other words, if the two sides of the horse's pedigree are not the same — none of the horses on his sire's side are the same as any of the horses on his dam's side — he is the result of an outcross.

A horse that is the product of an outcross may be an outstanding individual, but his genetic makeup will be more varied than the inbred or linebred individual and there may be more variance among his offspring; no two may be quite alike.

Crossbreeding between two different breeds gives the same results. The individual produced usually is exceptional — if the parents were of good quality — but there likely will be a great variety of traits within the horse's genetic makeup and that horse's offspring may be quite varied. They all may be good individuals, but won't look alike. Some will inherit traits from the breed of one grandparent and some will inherit traits from the breed of the other grandparent.

On the subject of genetics, a few facts about color should be mentioned. Some colors are recessive and others are dominant. The more common horse colors are chestnut, bay and gray.

Chestnut always is recessive. This color does not show up unless a horse inherits two recessive genes, one from each parent. In other words, a horse must get two chestnut genes in order to be chestnut. If he inherits a dominant gene, he will not be chestnut; he'll be the color of the dominant gene.

A chestnut horse has no other color genes so all he can pass on to his offspring is chestnut, even though it may be overshadowed in the offspring by the genes passed from the other parent, if a dominant gene such as bay or gray. So a chestnut bred to a chestnut always will produce a chestnut foal.

Bay is dominant over chestnut. If two bay horses are bred, they may or may not produce a bay foal, depending on whether the bay parents were genetically pure for this color. A bay horse may carry a recessive chestnut gene as well as bay, but because bay is dominant the horse himself will be bay. However, if he is mated with another bay that carries a recessive chestnut gene, there is one chance in four that the foal will inherit a chestnut gene from each parent and be chestnut instead of bay. But a genetically pure bay, carrying only bay genes, always produces bay unless he is mated with a gray.

The graying gene seems to be dominant over all others. A bay mated with a gray will produce a gray, unless the gray parent carries a recessive gene. A pure gray with no other color genes always will produce a gray foal, for the graying gene is dominant.

To be gray, a horse must have a gray parent, for gray cannot skip a generation as can the recessive chestnut gene. If a horse receives a gray gene, he will be gray. He also may receive a recessive gene that he might pass to his own offspring. A horse inheriting a gray gene will be gray, though he may be born another color and turn gray as he ages to 2 or 3 years old and upwards. But a horse can receive a recessive gene from his gray parent and be another color; he then will have no gray gene to pass on.

Brown and black can be considered as related to bay color in equine color genetics. They are merely darker varieties. White markings on horses usually are dominant. If a horse has white markings — star, blaze, etc., on his face, or white on his legs — he usually passes them to his offspring.

Unless you are raising a color breed like Appaloosa, pinto, palomino, paint, etc., color should be the last worry when breeding horses. A good horse is a good horse, regardless of color, and beautiful color won't really improve a poor one. You can't ride color. Even in the color breeds, the color should just be the "frosting on the cake," for a poor horse, regardless of color, is a detriment to the breed. Work toward ideal conformation and good disposition first, then concentrate on color.

To be a good horse breeder, you must be a good judge of horseflesh. There are no perfect horses. If your horse has faults, mate it with a horse that is strong where yours is weak. Mating two horses with the same faults is a sure way to go downhill in a hurry, which is why a horse breeder must be able to recognize and evaluate the faults of his horses.

Many horsemen see faults in other people's horses but are unable to see the faults in their own. This can be detrimental to their breeding program. To be a successful horse breeder, you must be able to critically judge your own horses.

Remember that disposition, conformation, action, soundness, fertility, masculinity and femininity, good milking ability and mothering ability are greatly heritable. If a mare hasn't quite got perfect straightness of action, she should be mated with a stallion that is perfectly straight in his way of going. If a mare has a poor disposition, she should be mated with a stallion that has a good disposition. Lameness or unsoundness that is due to injury or accident can be overlooked in a breeding animal because it isn't hereditary. But if a lameness or unsoundness problem is partly due to faulty conformation, the horse will not be a good animal to use as breeding stock.

Breeding good horses is a time-consuming job that involves much work and expense. But it costs no more to keep a good brood mare than it does to keep and feed a poor one, so every effort should be made to try to buy or raise the best breeding stock possible.

A stallion's breeding fee should be reasonable, especially if he is young or not yet well known. You can always raise it later, but if you start out with the fee too high and later want to lower it, it can be an embarrassing matter.

If the fee is reasonable, there will be more people able to afford your stallion; if the fee is too high, you might get better mares (if the stallion is really that good), but there won't be many and the stallion will have less offspring to represent him, to show what kind of foals he can produce. His offspring are the final proof of his value as a sire, and if he can consistently produce good-quality foals out of a variety of mares, more people will want to breed their mares to him.

If you truly are conscientious about your role as a breeder of good horses, you won't let money or fads overrule your judgment in what is best for the breed and for the horse industry in general. You don't have to be rich or have the most popular bloodlines to raise good horses. If you are consistent in your goals and your goals are set high, there always will be a market for your horses.

No matter the desired coat color, a breeder never should sacrifice conformation for that color. To do otherwise does damage to the industry, to the breed and to the horse (left).

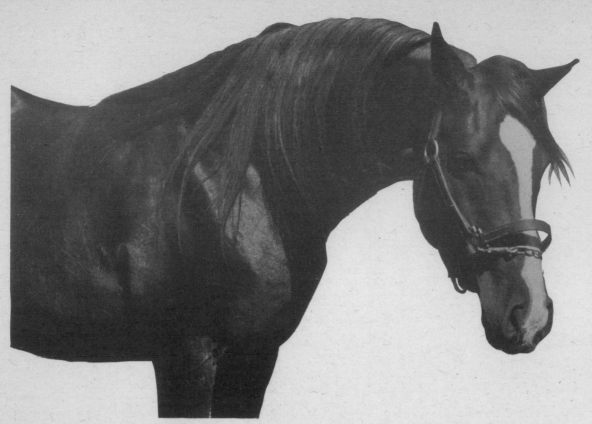

STALLION MANAGEMENT

There's much paperwork involved with any breeding operation and, at Claiborne Farm, this falls on the shoulders of Mildred Downing. It's a tedious job!

With the goals of a sound breeding program already outlined, it's time to examine the mechanical aspects of a breeding operation. While some breeders of Western-type horses have large operations, the most well-known of the horse breeders are found in the bluegrass country of Kentucky.

While Kentucky is thoroughbred country, it is widely recognized that breeders of racehorses are leaders in the field; they've been doing it much longer and have a great deal more at stake in most cases.

For this reason, we've chosen to examine the stallion and brood mare operations of separate, reputable farms in the bluegrass country: Claiborne Farm, Spendthrift Farm and Plum Lane Farm.

While we first will examine stallion operations on Claiborne Farms, it should be considered that many of these techniques apply to all stallions. As the late Claiborne owner, A.B. "Bull" Hancock, Jr., was fond of saying, "Horses are horses, no matter whether they run, trot, jump, pull big loads or just have to look pretty."

A popular misconception among many horse-owners is that stallions are vicious, untrustworthy and difficult to handle. Because of the hot-blooded nature of the thoroughbred, it is generally acknowledged that, as a group, thoroughbred stallions are the most difficult to handle.

Yet, at Claiborne Farm in Paris, Kentucky, they stand twenty-six thoroughbred stallions and every stallion at the farm has nearly impeccable manners. What does Claiborne do with their stallions to achieve this outstanding record? According to farm manager Bill Taylor, nothing special. He says the secret to good manageable stallions is having good stallion men. His techniques are applicable outside thoroughbred circles, too.

"We have an exceptional stallion foreman here in Lawrence Robinson," Taylor reports. "He and the men who work for him all are very quiet around the stallions. They never get rough with one, unless the horse deserves it. But, when he acts up, they get on him immediately and make it clear to the horse that the kind of behavior he is exhibiting is unacceptable. This is, I think, the secret to handling any stallion, no matter what breed he is. Treat them kindly, with gentleness, but be firm with them and never let them get out of hand."

According to Robinson, the secret of handling stallions is in knowing their idiosyncrasies. He feels that each horse has his own personality and you have to know what he likes and dislikes.

"The stallions are a lot like people, really. You can talk to some people a little rougher than you can talk to others. It is the same with the horses. For example, Forli, an Argentine horse we have here, won't stand much punishment before he'll start to fight back. We had a horse that stood here — a really great old horse named Nasrullah, who led the American Thoroughbred General Sire List for five years and sired Bold Ruler, who led it for seven consecutive years — and you couldn't hit him at all. If you did, he wouldn't do anything. He'd just get mad and go off and sulk. He wouldn't cover the mare or do anything.

"A horse like Nasrullah simply had to be conned into doing whatever you wanted him to do. You had to make him think that what you wanted him to do and the way you wanted it done was his idea.

"When he stood in Ireland, before he came here, they called him a maneater. I expect that it was because he wouldn't take any punishment. He'd sulk, then when they kept after him, he would eventually retaliate. But we never had a bit of trouble with the horse. He behaved beautifully once we figured out his ways. This old horse simply had a mind of his own.

"But, I'll say this for Nasrullah: For all his obstinacy, he never once got out of hand with us. And I attribute that to the fact that the man who handled him was able to anticipate his moods and had figured out how to handle him."

After a stallion has been selected and brought to the farm, the real work begins for Lawrence Robinson and the stallion men.

"When we get a new stallion in here — a young horse just entering the stud or even one like Le Fabuleux, that stood in France for several years — we have to actually break him to be a stallion," Robinson says. "They have to be taught how to cover a mare.

"We, of course, do all of our breeding with the horse in hand. These stallions are too valuable to risk in pasture breeding. In my opinion, there is no excuse for a stallion to be unmanageable in the breeding shed. If he is, it is a sign that he has been improperly trained.

"For example, when we got Le Fabuleux, he always wanted to run at the mare. This is the way he was allowed to do it in France. Secondly, he wasn't at all accustomed to the methods we use here. We back our stallions up in a corner and wash them before we breed them. This is to help eliminate the chance of infection. When the stallion covers a different mare every day, there is a chance that he can

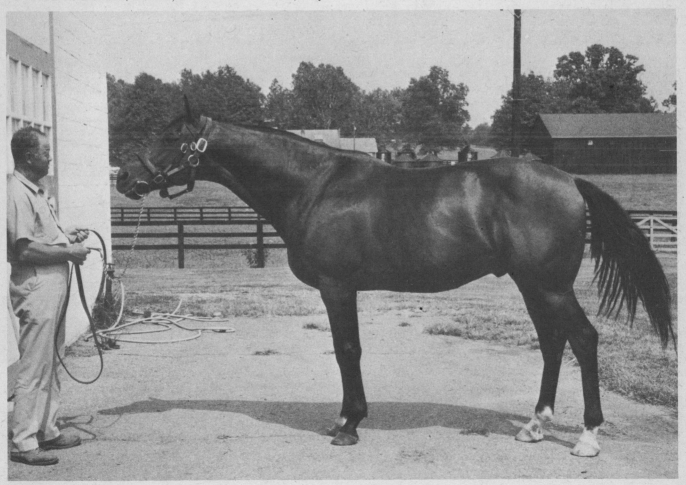

Ready for the breeding shed, Nijinsky II wears a halter and stallion bridle consisting of a heavy bridle without reins, but with a straight bar snaffle bit. The chain of the lead shank is run through the rings of the stallion's bridle for control.

Most breeders like to turn new foals out on the first day of their lives and, with a week-old youngster, it's standard routine. Exceptions are due to weather.

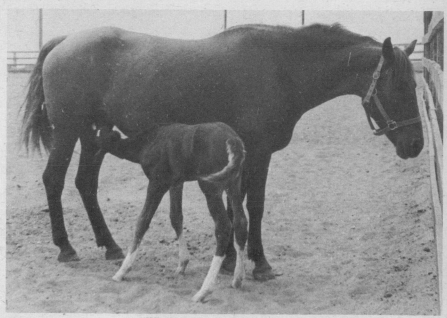

Don't overlook the femininity of a mare when selecting brood stock. Some aren't good mothers and you can have a real hassle in that case.

carry an infection from one mare to the other, if he isn't properly cleaned up before every breeding. We wash them with warm water with a mild soap solution in it, so that we can get him completely cleaned up. The horses that we have had here for awhile know what is coming and they don't fuss.

"Le Fabuleux, when he came here, apparently had never had this done to him and he wasn't just terribly thrilled about the whole thing. It took him awhile to get used to it. A horse that hasn't been in the stud before is much easier to break, because he doesn't have any bad habits or preconceived notions to change.

"Another thing about imported stallions like Le Fabuleux is that they don't understand English. I guess that is sort of a funny thing to say about a horse, but they are accustomed to hearing commands and corrections in French, Italian or Spanish and, when you tell them in English to quit or stand up here, they haven't the faintest idea what you want. I'll say this about Le Fabuleux, though: It didn't take him long to catch on."

Robinson says that, with a maiden horse, it is a little different. They just never let the young horse get bad habits. As an example, he used champion Buckpasser.

"When we got Buckpasser in here, he had just been syndicated for several million dollars. Well, he got the idea that he should stand on his hind legs in the breeding shed; that he should rear and rush at the mare. I had to straighten out his thinking on the subject with force. I don't care how valuable a horse is, he is going to be a gentleman in the breeding shed. These stallions are much bigger and heavier than I am and they can get a lot meaner. So it is just as well to quash any ideas about exercising this muscle before it really gets under way."

Robinson and his men are generally quiet around the horses and gentle with them. But, Robinson says that, when the horse needs correction, he gets it immediately. He also states that, after the stallions are washed, they are walked up to the mare and all of them stand there until the personnel in the breeding shed are ready for the stud to mount the mare.

"Our stallions more or less mount on command," Robinson says. "That's the best way to have them. If you teach them like this, you have no problem. We use no more restraint on our stallions in the breeding shed than a stud bridle, which is just a straight bar snaffle bit."

What about day-to-day routine of stallion care? During

the breeding season, which starts in February and goes until the end of June, the routine is necessarily different than it is during the off-season. At Claiborne, they start breeding at 8 a.m. and breed both morning and afternoon. As each mare is bred in the morning, the stallion is taken to his paddock and turned out. In the afternoon, the stallions are brought up about 2 and, around 3:30, the handlers start taking them to the breeding shed. The stallions are fed when they come in in the afternoon. During much of the off-season, the stallions are turned out all night and are in the barn during the heat of the day from about 7 a.m. until about 3 in the afternoon. This is to keep the stallions out of the hot sun, which bleaches the coat, and also to keep them away from the worst of the flies.

"Many people who are prospective breeders to our stallions come to look at them during the Summer," Bill Taylor, the farm manager, says. "The stallions are the show-pieces of the farm. We want them to look their best, no matter what time of the year it is. If their coats are all bleached or they are all thin from worrying about the flies or are all fly-bitten, they don't make as good an impression as we would like.

"Breeders, rightly or wrongly, sometimes judge your whole operation by the appearance of the stallions. This is why it is important that the stallions always look their very best."

At Claiborne, the stallions are fed plain oats along with vitamin supplements. During the off-season, the stallions eat about two-thirds as much as during the breeding season. All of the stallions at Claiborne get their rations increased during the breeding season because of the increased work, although there is always an exception.

Taylor cites the case of one stallion that actually had his rations cut during the breeding seasons, because he was getting hog fat.

In addition to the oats during the breeding season, the horses are fed a vitamin B compound. They also get mixed hay that is sixty to seventy percent clover. They get hay year around but in lesser amounts in the Summer, when the grass is thick in the paddocks.

Taylor says, "We have been feeding our horses this type of ration for thirty years, I guess. We just do things the old-fashioned way around here. Actually, we don't have to feed a lot of supplements, because the grass here is quite high in both protein and mineral content. During the Winter, we feed the weanlings and the yearlings along with the 2-year-olds that aren't in training some corn for the heat. Aside from that, we do things pretty simply."

At Claiborne, the stallions are permitted to exercise at their own rate. The paddocks are two or three acres in size. Lawrence Robinson says, "We used to ride some of the stallions every day — those that retired sound. But, Mr. Hancock didn't see any great benefit in this. When we turned them out, they seemed to be as quiet and easy to manage as when they were being ridden, then turned out. Our stallions seem to settle right down after the breeding season. I think that having the older horses around helps the young stallions. The old studs seem to know when the season is over and when they quiet down, the young horses do, too.

"We keep our stallions quite close to each other in the paddocks. There is only about four feet between fences. We try to arrange the horses so that the young horses always have an old horse near them. For example, Round Table is about 20 now and we have two young stallions in paddocks next to him — Hoist the Flag, who just entered the stud in 1972, and Sir Ivor, also a very young horse. Round Table seems to have some sort of stabilizing influence on these two young stallions."

Two of Claiborne Farm's stallions head for their individual paddocks. Round Table (left) wears muzzle because of an odd personal quirk — he bites himself! Drone, the other sire, has no such problems. Note their well-behaved natures!

There is no special fencing on the paddocks at Claiborne for the stallions. Most paddocks are just three-board fences, but are double-fenced so stallions in adjacent paddocks can't get at each other. The only paddock that isn't just a simple three-board fence is Le Fabuleux's. His is a rather strange configuration of boards, dictated by the needs of the horses who occupied the paddock before him. Robinson says, "The five fairly solid boards on the bottom were put there for Nasrullah. When people used to come and see him, he'd get mad and kick at the boards of his paddock. Mr. Hancock was afraid that he would manage to kick through the boards and get his leg caught, so the extra boards were added.

"The top three boards were put on the paddock for Bold Ruler. He had a cancer that interfered with his breathing, so the veterinarians performed a tracheotomy on him. They had to leave the tube in him so he could breathe and Mr. Hancock was concerned that he would get his head over the fence and pull out the tube. The top three boards were added so he wouldn't get his head over the fence.

"If we can get oak, that is the kind of board we use for our fences. But, since it is usually so hard to get, we often

Personal idiosyncrasies of the stallions are humored, if within reason. Herbager, a French-bred stud, seems to favor taking his feed in his paddock, so that's what's done.

substitute pine. We use a type of creosote on the fences. This preserves the wood and really discourages chewing on the fences. You know, a nice soft, untreated pine board is the finest thing in the world to chew on, so a horse thinks. They like those things better than hay."

According to Robinson, young horses coming to the farm usually are given some preparation at the track for the life of leisure unless they have been hurt.

"The horse entering the stud always is let down pretty well at the track before being shipped here. They gallop him at the track until he gets unwound from being a race horse, then they come here. When we get them, they have already made the main adjustment to being retired from competition.

"Horses that are injured are a different story. They can't be let down. You just have to hope that the horse is intel-

ligent enough to settle down by himself. Many times, with a severely injured horse, this ability to adjust means the difference between life and death. Sir Gaylord came here right off the track with a cracked sesamoid. He settled right down and just stood around in his stall waiting for it to heal. He seemed to know that he had to behave himself in order to survive.

"The same was true of Hoist the Flag. He practically shattered his hind leg in a workout in preparation for a major race. If you could see the X-ray of the fracture, you would marvel that the horse is able to walk at all. It took several hours of surgery to repair him. At any rate, he stood in his stall at Belmont for months in a cast and virtually didn't move.

"When he came here, we had to walk the horse for two months. He was walking badly on his toe on the injured leg, so we hand-walked him every day for two months, then finally turned him out. After he was turned out, he started walking flat-footed and has been walking flat-footed ever since, except he has a limp — always will have, I suppose.

"In addition to being a horse psychologist, a stallion man sometimes has to be sort of a physical therapist, too."

One other aspect of stallion management involves keeping of the stallion's book; the actual paperwork of any successful breeding farm.

At Claiborne, this is the bailiwick of Mildred Downing, who has been handling the book work for a multiple stallion operation since 1950. "Each stallion has a certain number of seasons available," she explains. "With thoroughbreds, this is usually between thirty and forty per year. This means that the stud will cover between thirty and forty mares each year.

"You begin organizing the book by listing all the people who have breeding rights to the stallion each year. The way we do it is to take each stallion and, in his file, we list each owner who is breeding to the stallion that year, along with the name of the mare or mares the owner is breeding to that particular stallion. When the number of mares booked to the stallion reaches the number of seasons he has available, the stallion's book is filled and no more mares can be booked to him, unless somebody cancels a season.

"There is another part to the book of a stallion. If the mare is boarded off our farm, as most are, when she is ready to be bred, we try to arrange for her to come to the breeding shed then. It gets a little tight if two mares are ready the same day. When this happens, one of them has to come on their second choice time. We also use a form sheet that lists every stallion and every breeding, morning and night. For each day and each breeding, we enter the name of the mare and her owner in the stallion's box on the form. A copy of this stays in the office and a copy goes to the breeding shed. In this way, we avoid breeding the mare to the wrong stallion.

"It happens occasionally that someone will make a mistake and the mare gets bred to the wrong stallion, but we take every possible precaution to make sure it is a rare happening."

This is how stallions are managed in one multiple stallion operation. The basic principles of stallion management at Claiborne would seem to apply to any stallion operation, no matter what breed or what size. There is one point of stallion management that both Lawrence Robinson and Bill Taylor emphasize over and over, though. No matter how gentle and well-behaved a stallion seems to be, never turn your back on him.

According to Robinson, the smartest move one can make in handling stallions is to watch them all the time.

That way, trouble can be stopped before it gets started and it is less traumatic for both the man and the horse.

BROOD MARE CARE

The science of brood mare management has been the subject of considerable research in the last two decades, spearheaded by efforts on farms specializing in thoroughbreds. When yearlings can sell for more than $500,000, it's easy to see why!

For this reason, we endeavored to discover the intricacies of brood mare management from a man regarded as one of the best: Harry Schmidt, who's been at Spendthrift Farm near Lexington, Kentucky, for twenty-plus years. Harry Schmidt is responsible for the two hundred-plus brood mares in residence at the farm, as well as the outside mares that come to be bred to the farm's thirty stallions.

"With the tremendous increase in the prices being paid for horses these days, the importance of good brood mare management is pretty apparent. If you have a mare that is producing foals that are selling in the fifty to hundred thousand dollar range, you can't really afford to let her go barren for too many years," he says.

According to Schmidt, there are really three areas that require special consideration when discussing brood mares — managing barren mares, maiden mares and pregnant mares.

According to Schmidt, the problem with barren mares is to make sure they are in good condition and have established a normal estrus (heat) cycle. He says, "We start breeding the barren mares about the fifteenth of February, so we start teasing them in October and November. At this time,

we also culture the mare to make sure she isn't infected. If she is, we have the time necessary to clean up the infection before it is time for her to be bred.

"We also start bringing the mares up to the sheds that are in their fields about four in the afternoon and locking them in. We turn the lights on in the sheds so that the mares are in light for at least twelve hours a day. The length of time that the lights stay on varies, of course, with the time of the year. The lights are set so that they go off automatically, then the night watchman turns the mares out.

"It has been shown in research here at the University of Kentucky that using lights can move a mare's cycle up about thirty days. This means she can be bred thirty days sooner, if she is kept under the lights, than if she were allowed to establish her own pattern by the normal sun patterns. Essentially, we are altering the mare's biological clock."

Occasionally the mare refuses to show to the teaser. When this happens and it gets along toward March with no normal heat pattern established, the mare is brought up and examined by the veterinarian with a speculum. With this instrument the veterinarian determines when the mare is cycling and when she ovulates. When the veterinarian says the egg is in the best spot for conception — determined by ovarian palpation — the mare is bred.

Why won't a mare show to the teaser? According to

Harry Schmidt prefers to segregate his brood mares into times at which they're expected to foal, then putting them in relative distance to foaling barn. These mares are due to foal soon, so are kept closest to barn, visible in background.

Nashua, the first stallion in the U.S. to be syndicated for over $1 million, stands in breeding shed at Spendthrift. Note padding on doorway and wall, ventilation, light.

Schmidt, there are usually two basic reasons — the most important usually is psychological. The other reason would be some physiological condition that keeps her from cycling. Schmidt says, "The psychological problems, usually the reason why mares won't show to the teaser, often are the result of going too fast with a maiden mare.

"If the mare's first trip to the breeding shed is a painful and traumatic experience, she may be turned off of stallions forever. So, we take it very slow with the maiden mares. We do a hymenectomy on all our maiden mares far enough in advance of when she will be bred so that she is all healed by that time. Then, we get her used to the idea of being teased and bred by putting her with some older mares who know what's going on and we bring the teaser up to the fence. When the maiden mare has accepted the teaser over the fence, we gradually bring her up into the teasing chute.

"Something I should add here is that a noisy but gentlemanly teaser is worth his weight in gold when you are dealing with maiden mares. When we get the maiden into the teasing chute, we gradually let the teaser come on until he has done his whole act and the mare is mentally ready to be bred. A maiden mare's first sight of a stallion can be a little scary anyway, so we take it slow and use gentleness with these mares, so that they associate only pleasant things with the breeding shed. We don't just grab the mare out of the field, drag her to the breeding shed, slap a twitch on her and let the stallion at her."

Mares coming into the stud right off the track present another kind of problem for Schmidt.

"When we get a mare off the track — and I suspect that the same must be true of highly tuned mares coming out of the show ring — we like to let the mare have four or five months to let down before she is bred. When they come off the track or out of training they are fit, their muscles are tight and their reproductive organs are all crammed into a small space. When they relax and get out of condition, the reproductive system has an easier time stretching to make room for the larger foal. I think that this is where the majority of the first foals come from — the small, weak foal that is the stereotype of the first foal — the mare who has come right off the track or right out of training with no chance to relax and let down."

Sometimes, though, this waiting period is not possible. The mare might have broken down in May and it isn't economically feasible to wait until the next breeding season. When this happens, Schmidt says, you have to go ahead and breed her while she is still tight and fit. If you have to do this, you have the best chance of conception in her first heat after she comes home. According to Schmidt, with each succeeding heat until three or four months have passed and her adjustment to the new, quieter environment is complete, you'll have diminishing chances of catching her. If it is at all possible, the mare should have the time to adjust to her new environment.

"Time after time, when the mare does have this chance, we've seen that her first foal does not look like the typical first foal."

With pregnant mares, you can expect a whole new set of problems and these mares are the ones that require the most time, energy and patience for the brood mare manager. At Spendthrift, after weaning, the lactating mares are turned out on the grass. Their feed is tapered off gradually two weeks before weaning and the mares live in fields with no sheds and are given no feed or hay until the time comes for the pregnant mares to be separated from the barren mares.

Schmidt reports that "We wean about the middle of September and we separate the mares in October. We separate the pregnant mares even further because we group them by foaling date. We put the ones with the earliest foaling dates in the fields closest to the foaling barn and so on down the line, until the mares with the latest foaling dates are in the fields farthest from the foaling barn.

"We turn the mares out after weaning, because we want the mares to run around and worry. We do this for two reasons. One, the action of her legs helps massage her udder. Two, the exercise tends to relax her and the milk then can drain out of her bag. This keeps the bag soft and enables her to dry up more rapidly. We simply do not milk our mares after we wean. The more milk you take from a mare, the more she will keep producing. Also, the bag will get sore from the milking and she will start fighting you. In the twenty years I've been here, the only cases of mastitis I've ever seen were two — one in a barren mare and one in a nursing mare. We never have had a case of mastitis after weaning."

At Spendthrift, the in-foal mares are fed a ration of approximately seven parts oats, one part cracked, shelled corn, rolled barley, wheat bran, loose salt and a pellet made of soybean grass and alfalfa. According to Schmidt, the percentages in the ration vary according to the season; the corn goes up in the cold months and down during the warmer months. The barren mares are fed no grain, Schmidt says; just the best hay they can buy, along with the grass that remains in the fields.

"We feed the pregnant mares just a maintenance amount of grain until foaling time. Of course, a thin mare would get more feed or an older mare that needs more grain to keep her up in flesh would get more.

"After she foals, the mare gets all the feed she will eat. The only exception to this are those mares who are so piggish that they eat and eat until they get too fat. These mares are converting the grain ration to fat instead of milk for the foal. After the foal is 9 days old, we start supple-

268

menting pellets in the ration. What we are after here is the approximately twenty-five percent lactose or milk sugar in these pellets. We want the foal to start eating the pellets. The lactose is not utilized by the mature animal," Schmidt states.

According to the brood mare manager, the mares are turned out every day, regardless of weather, until they foal. When the mare shows signs of getting ready to foal, they start putting her in the paddock next to the foaling barn where the men in that barn can keep an eye on her all day.

"We look for the obvious signs — the milk in the bag and the mental signs that most mares exhibit. They go off by themselves in the field or will be difficult to get up to the gate at night. When the mare starts to act like she wants to be alone, it is usually a pretty good indication she is getting close to foaling.

"Usually, if she starts to foal outside, we bring her in although if the weather is warm, I don't mind the mare foaling on the grass as long as she is alone. I don't want the other mares around hassling her while she is foaling," Schmidt says.

He adds that most foals seem to be born at a certain time of the day. "We have examined the records for times of foaling for seven years and we found that most of the foals are born at eleven at night. The curve starts up sharply at 7 p.m. and increases until 11 p.m., when it drops off sharply. Few foals are born after 1 a.m.

"In our foaling barn, we have lights down the middle of the shed but we keep the lights off in the stalls. There is just enough light that spills into the stalls for the foaling man to see what the mare is doing. When she really starts to foal, the lights in the mare's stall are turned on. I keep strange people out of my foaling barn, because I don't want the mares disturbed by the presence of different activity or different people.

"The reason a mare foals at night in the first place is because she is alone, she's quiet and she feels safe. As long as everything is peaceful and quiet in the foaling barn, things seem to go along normally. We also keep the mare in the foaling barn for awhile before she foals so that she is accustomed to the people who are in the barn all the time. The mare always goes in the foaling barn a week before she foals. Sometimes she goes in there two or three weeks before foaling."

After the mare has foaled safely, if she foals at night, the first thing the day man does is put a halter on the foal. He also checks for any yellow coloring around the eye membranes. If this jaundice condition occurs, the foal is not compatible with his mother and must be muzzled so he won't nurse. Assuming everything is normal, the foal is turned out, except in the most extreme bad weather, every day of his life, even if it is only for ten or fifteen minutes at a time. The guide as to when a foal has been out long enough being that he is left out as long as he will stand up, run around and play. When he lies down or stands in a corner and shivers, he comes in.

When the weather warms up, the foals are turned out all day and can sleep on the grass. But, the really important part of the immediate turnout is that it gives the mare a chance to cast off any residue left from foaling, helps improve the muscle tone of her uterus and helps her clean up so that she will be breedable in foal heat, which occurs about the ninth day after foaling.

Occasionally, a mare will not have enough milk for her foal, will refuse to accept her foal or a foal is orphaned. When this happens, a nurse mare must be provided. In Lexington, these mares are leased from a man who is in the business of supplying nurse mares.

"When we get these mares," Schmidt says, "we put them

This is desired result of good brood mare management: healthy foals with now-pregnant mothers in the pasture.

in the stall in a set of stocks with the mare against the wall with a board in front, behind and along her outside. Then her head is tied so she can't reach down and smell the foal.

"We put a hay rack up where she can reach it to keep her occupied. The board on the outside of the mare has a hole cut in it that is about two by two feet — just big enough for the foal to put his head through and nurse. We also smear the foal with oil of peppermint or oil of wintergreen along his back and we put the same oil on the mare's nose, so she won't recognize the foal as not being her own. Some mares are so motherly that they will just accept any foal you give them, but they are pretty rare. After about twenty-four hours of being together, most of the nurse mares have started to accept the foal. But most mares will not accept the foal while they are still standing in the stocks. Thus, it is necessary to turn her loose in the stall with the foal.

"When we turn the mare loose, we stand there and watch her until she seems to have completely accepted the foal. Most mares, if they are picking on the foal, will quit when you holler at them, but we keep the door open in case we have to run in. Occasionally a mare will not offer to hurt the foal but she keeps walking around in the stall so he can't nurse. Then we have to tie the mare up. There are some mares that will not accept certain foals. They might work fine one year and the next year with a different foal absolutely refuse to accept it. Just because these nurse mares are cold-blooded mares doesn't automatically mean they will accept just any foal you give them.

"It also is true that it is difficult to get an older foal to accept a nurse mare. Sometimes, if the foal is orphaned at, say, three or four months, we'll just wean him and buy a companion for him that is about the same age. Then we feed them out of a bucket. Also, nurse mares are reluctant to accept a foal that is much younger or much older than her own foal. The first week, the foal doesn't really know who his mother is. He'll follow any mare. To him, a mother is a mother. This is the time when it is easiest to get him to accept a substitute mother. After that, the identity of his real mother is sort of imprinted on him.

"We also take the foal away from his real mother when it's necessary about three or four hours before we bring in the nurse mare so that, when the nurse mare becomes available, the foal is good and hungry. All these things make it easier for the mare to accept the foal and vice versa."

Foals are halter broken at Spendthrift right away — the first day of their life usually.

"I insist that the foal has to be led to the field and caught, and led back to the barn every night. I'd rather see the mare go along by herself than the foal. We never let the foal follow along behind the mare by himself except in emergencies," Schmidt reports.

The mares and foals go out during the day until sometime around the first of June. Then the schedule is altered and they go out at night and come up during the day. This is to avoid the heat of the day and the worst flies. Schmidt wants the foals to be out in the fields as many hours each day as possible. The only reason he wants them to be brought up to the barn is to be fed or handled.

"When we start keeping the mares and foals in during the day, we keep them in from 8 a.m. to 3 p.m. The only reason we keep them in this long is so that we can get two feedings in them a day. During this time, after the foals have eaten, we handle them. We brush them with a soft brush and after they get older, we start picking up their feet. Each man has his own mares and foals that he cares for."

After the mares have foaled safely, along about the seventh or eighth day after foaling, the veterinarian checks each mare with a speculum. If she is not bruised from foaling and is ovulating normally, she is bred in foal heat.

Schmidt said that they breed fifty to sixty percent of their mares in foal heat and they have found that about twenty-five percent of these mares get in foal.

"We like to get as many early foals as we can. This is especially important in a commercial breeding operation like this. We'd like to have all January foals, if we could get them. What sells a yearling for a high price is maturity. The highest-priced yearlings I've ever seen have looked like 2 or 3-year-olds. They are big, mature-looking individuals. Therefore, we want to breed as early as possible.

"But if the mare isn't ready on the ninth day, we don't force it. We really get serious about breeding the mare on the twenty-seventh day. The decision on the ninth-day breeding is left to the veterinarian. Actually, the term ninth day is a misnomer because we breed as many mares on the eighth and tenth days as the ninth. The time that a mare should be bred is determined by ovarian palpation."

That Schmidt's brood mare management policies have been successful goes without saying. Spendthrift has consigned more yearlings to the prestigious Keeneland Summer Sale that have sold in excess of $100,000 than any other commercial breeder in the country.

Henry White, manager of nearby Plum Lane Farm in Lexington, elaborates further on after-foaling procedures. For instance, if the delivery is normal, White attempts to get the foal to the mare's head as quickly as possible. He believes that this helps keep the mare down, until she really should get up. Often when a mare can't see her foal, she gets up too quickly to look for it. This is particularly true, White says, of maiden mares.

"If she can see the foal and nuzzle it, she'll stay down longer. We just catch these little wet foals by the front feet and pull them like a wheelbarrow. You should never pick up a foal by grabbing him under the chest and lifting.

"The bones of these babies are soft and not set, so it is easy to fracture a rib. If you pull the foal by his front feet, you can't hurt him. As soon as the umbillicus breaks, we use navel iodine on the stump. We observe the navel stump closely for about seventy-two hours after the foal is born and, after that, we just watch it. If the navel should start to fill on a foal, the first thing we do is increase the dose of combiotic."

White notes they routinely give the foal 5ccs of combiotic within the first two hours after it is born. After that, the foal gets 3ccs of combiotic twice a day for five days.

"We never hurry a foal to get up," White explains. "We want them to get up pretty much on their own. During the time the foal is resting, we wash the mare with a mild solution of green soap, paying particular attention to the udders, especially between the quarters. Until this time, we haven't messed much with the mare's bag. We start cleaning up the mare's bag in that time when the foal can't stand, but the mare usually has gotten rid of the placenta (afterbirth). In most cases, the placenta slips before the foal really starts to root to get up."

When the mare is slow to expel the placenta, White folds the wide part of it up and ties it with a twine string so that the knot hangs about hock high. That little added weight usually will cause the placenta to slip. If it doesn't, White usually waits until the next day to call the veterinarian. He says one never should try to pull the attached placenta out of the mare. Doing this can cause damage to the mare's uterus. He adds that, should the mare have a hemorrhaging cord, get the veterinarian as quickly as possible.

Once the foal gets up, White tries to have a clean stall right across the aisle. The mare and the foal are moved to this stall and if the temperature is below 35 degrees, they turn a heat lamp on in the stall.

"We don't bed our stalls too deeply. The little guy has a lot of trouble getting up for the first twenty-four hours or so after he is born, so we give him as much traction as we can, until he has figured out how to get up.

"As soon as the foal gets up and nurses, and we move them to the clean stall, we leave the mare and her foal alone. We observe them, but we don't fuss with them. If the foal has a bowel movement on his own, that's just fine. If he starts to strain and looks like he needs it, we will give the foal a plain, warm-water enema.

"We don't routinely give enemas to our foals. The only reason we would give one would be if the foal is straining and not getting any results or if he has a tendency to ball up. If a foal balls up, we might use a little mineral oil for lubrication. It has been our experience, however, that since we quit routinely giving enemas two hours after birth, we have had less trouble with compacted foals."

According to White, one of the most important things in any foaling operation is observation and people who know what to look for. He said that one of the main problems that occurs early in a foal, Rh incompatibility, won't be fatal if detected as soon as the first signs appear. Rh incompatibility — the foal having a blood type that is antagonistic to that of the mare — has either been occurring with increasing frequency or veterinarians are better able to diagnose the problem.

In a case of Rh imcompatibility, the mare's body manufactures antibodies against the foal. Since the mare's and the foal's blood don't mix before the foal is born, the problem doesn't occur until the foal starts to drink the colostrum (first milk).

"The mares that you know produce these kind of foals are no trouble," White feels. "It's the sleepers that give you

Brood mare manager Harry Schmidt checks weanlings with aid of four-wheel-drive Scout, which saves time (above). Foals at Plum Lane are haltered morning the after being born and are led constantly (left). See text.

fits. If we know the foal is probably going to be an Rh incompatible foal, we put a muzzle on the mare's door and as soon as the foal gets up, he is muzzled. We don't want him to have even one little sip of that colostrum. We usually have some colostrum around or some mare's milk that we have frozen. We use this until we can find a nurse mare.

"We use Foal Lac if we have to. If the mare has a history of really high titers, I don't even try to strip the mare of her colostrum. If her history indicates that she has an Rh factor, but in the 1, 2, 3 low-titer area, we will try to milk this mare up to forty-eight hours and sometimes they will clean up this way. Usually, with an Rh factor mare, I try to have a nurse mare lined up before the mare foals. Occasionally you can get a mare that looks like she has cleaned up, but all of a sudden the foal starts to go downhill; then you have to take the foal away and put him on a nurse mare."

If you have a mare that you don't know to be an Rh factor mare, there are certain signs that appear in the foal that will tell you that things aren't right. Major areas that White's foaling men watch are the insides of the lips and the eyelids of the foal. "If you see any yellowing (jaundice) on the lips or the eyelids, it means that you had better get the foal away from his mama, because her milk is killing him," White says. "To go with the yellowing, the Rh incompatible foal usually has a colicky tendency.

"Another thing that careful observation will indicate is the first sign of joint or navel-ill — swelling in the area of the navel or the front ankles," White says. "Now this may sound silly, but we watch the angle of the foal's pastern in front. Anytime that we get a foal that starts to straighten up this angle over a relatively short period of time, we take a blood count. We don't routinely do blood counts on our foals. We did for a long time, but we didn't really learn anything from them. Sometimes it will help you catch a condition that is masked, but usually it is a waste of money.

"However, if you get a foal that is walking down — walking nearly on his ankles because he is so weak in the pastern — and in less than twenty-four hours he is standing up almost too straight, you had better get a blood count, because nine times out of ten you are going to find his white cell count has gone way down. This sometimes occurs even with the combiotic treatment. And, despite all the care you take, you still sometimes lose a foal for some totally unexplained reason."

White has some advice for people who are inexperienced with newborn foals. "If the foal starts to look a little sluggish, get in the habit of taking his temperature at least every twelve hours. Anything on the low side of 102 is nothing to get excited about. Actually, if you are young or inexperienced with foals, the first few times it doesn't hurt to routinely take the foal's temperature twice a day, even when he looks healthy. This way you have some advance warning when things are going wrong and the extra handling that the foal gets from having his temperature taken doesn't hurt him at all."

White likes to get his mare and her foal out the same day the foal is born unless it is very cold or raining. He doesn't like his foals to get wet before they are about 2 weeks old.

This 2-week-old filly has no qualms about the feed bucket. If the mare objects, she should be tied so the foal can eat.

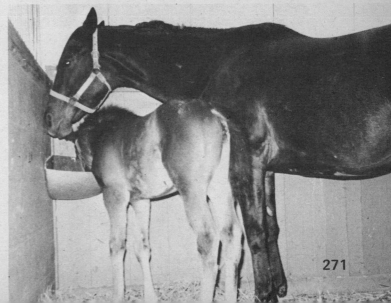

271

FOALING PROCEDURES
Cleanliness is of the utmost importance.
Keep foaling room and barn shed clean at all times.
Always wear clean overalls.
Wash hands thoroughly before each foaling.

PREPARATION:

When mare becomes restless and shows signs of labor, snap her to wall chain; then braid her tail, starting at end of tailbone, double braids back on tail and bandage. No tail-hairs should show.

Wash mare with soap and water and rinse off with quseptic solution. At this time, check to see that mare is not sutured. If she is sutured, call a veterinarian for help. Sponge off mare's udder with cotton and clear water. Turn mare loose.

Muck out stall and remove water-bucket.

Set up table outside stall. Set out navel paint and small cup for applying. Set out tetanus antitoxin and combiotic in syringe. If veterinarian is called, put out bucket containing obstetrical chains in quseptic solution, roll of cotton and plastic soap bottle. Have leather shank and twitch handy.

FOALING:

Leave mare alone as much as possible. When foal first appears, check to be sure both front feet are showing. Check later to be sure foal's nose is between knees. If feet and nose do not appear, call a veterinarian for help! Grasp foal's pasterns and exert pull when mare strains.

Pull only when mare strains!

If foal appears upside down, make mare get up and walk her around stall, then let her lie down. Repeat if necessary. If foal does not right itself, call for help.

When foal's hips have emerged, clear out its nostrils and mouth: make sure it is breathing, and leave. Mare should lie quietly as long as possible. If cord breaks before mare gets up, pull foal around to her head where she can see it. Do not put foal where she will step on it when she gets up.

Apply navel paint immediately after cord breaks. If stump on foal bleeds excessively, squeeze with fingers until bleeding stops. If cord does not break when mare gets up, cut below white line.

Give foal 5cc of combiotic as soon as possible in buttock. Be careful not to hit bone with hypodermic needle.

After mare gets up on her feet, tie after-birth in large knot, so it will hang clear of floor.

Clean out stall thoroughly and re-bed with plenty of straw. Replace water-bucket, filling with water and a quart or so of warm water to take chill off.

When mare drops after-birth, remove from stall and examine horns to be sure no pieces have been retained in mare.

NEWBORN FOAL:

The normal foal will struggle to get up after about 10 minutes. This struggling is important to foal. Leave him alone. Foal should stand alone by the time it is two hours old. If he does not, help him. If foal is still too weak to stand after three hours, call a veterinarian for help.

Some mares, especially maiden mares, will not allow foal to nurse. In this case, try holding mare; sometimes twitch is necessary.

Check foal during night to be sure he is nursing regularly. Examine mare's bag to be sure foal is nursing both sides. If he is not nursing both sides, milk out caked side.

AFTER FOALING:

If mare colics after foaling, give her four ounces of sedative with dose syringe. If this does not quiet her after 30 minutes, call a veterinarian for help. If colic appears more than one hour after foaling, call a veterinarian for help. Be sure foal is out of way. If mare becomes violent, remove foal from stall.

Keep all stalls with foals in them mucked out during night.

If foal is born before midnight, check eye membranes at 2 a.m. and 6 a.m. for sign of yellow coloring. If yellow appears, put muzzle on foal and call a veterinarian for help.

He keeps the mare and the foal in small, individual paddocks — actually portable steel cattle pens — until the foal is about a week or 10 days old. Then they are turned out in small, wooden-fenced paddocks with no more than four other mares with their foals. These paddocks are about an acre to an acre and a half in size. They stay in these paddocks until the foals are about a month old. They then are turned out in a fifty-acre field.

When the foals are 30 days old, they start spending twenty-two hours a day in the field. They only come up for a two-hour period in the morning.

"I feed a pelleted feed that is about sixteen percent protein and everything on the place gets the same feed. I've found that the foals go to the feed bucket and start eating earlier with the pelleted feed than they did when I used a lot of oats and corn. The pellets are from seven to ten percent molasses and I think it is the sweetening that attracts the foals. Some of my foals will start eating when they are only 3 days old.

"When they go out in the fifty-acre field, I have a creep feeder set up near the barn for the foals. I usually start creep feeding my foals in June. By this time, they are usually eating pretty well with their mothers. If you get a mare that is a complete hog at the feed bucket and won't let her baby eat with her, you'll have to tie the mare away from the bucket while the foal eats.

"When the foals are eating from the creep, I like to see each foal clean up about four or five pounds of pellets a day. Now, you might say that I have no way of knowing how much a foal eats when he is creep fed, but you can tell. If all your foals look pretty uniform, they're probably getting enough feed. If one starts to go downhill or doesn't look as good as the others, then you have to start feeding it besides what it gets in the creep feeder."

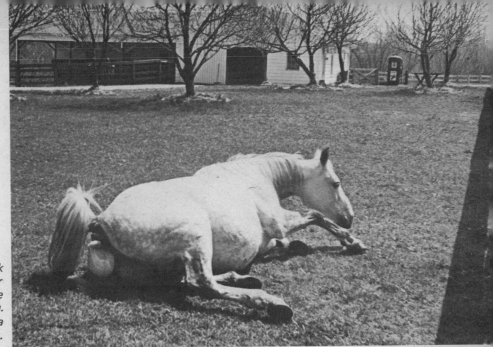

Half-Arab show mare, Clearcreek Cara, begins to foal soon after lying down (right), caught in the eye of photographer John Sheckler's camera. Foreleg emerges (below) as Linda Jones tries to keep the mare down.

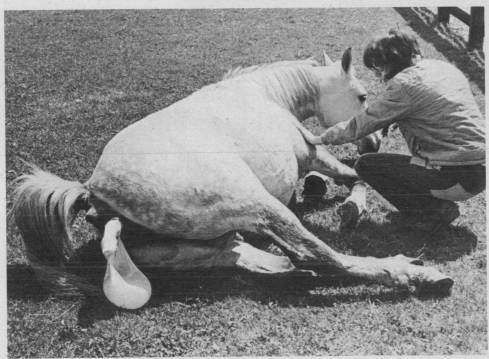

THE MIRACLE OF BIRTH

Delivery almost complete, Ms. Jones squints down toward foal still encased in placental sac. Time of the delivery was unusual — most come at night.

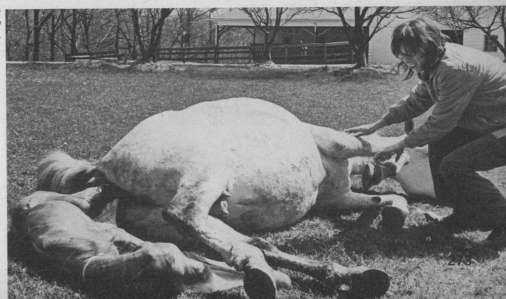

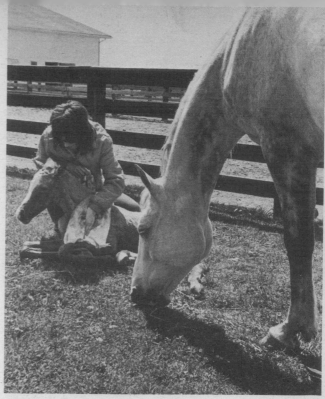

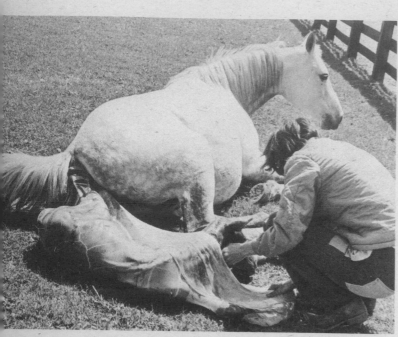

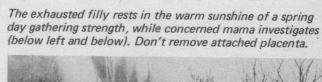

Ms Jones breaks the bag surrounding the foal's face (left), then begins to wipe off filly after total delivery and removal from sac (above). Mare already is up and grazing, something breeders feel shouldn't be done yet.

The exhausted filly rests in the warm sunshine of a spring day gathering strength, while concerned mama investigates (below left and below). Don't remove attached placenta.

Front legs spraddled, young foal struggles to maintain her balance (right). This first attempt, barely an hour after her emergence, was unsuccessful, as are most.

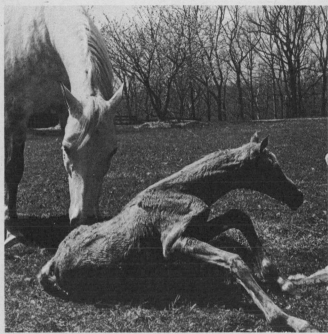

Linda Jones smiles as foal, dubbed Clearcreek Caren, tries again (above). The foal has a great deal to learn!

Success! The leggy filly, appendages planted securely, stands beneath the protecting neck of mother and, within a week, this clumsiness will be only dimmest memory.

CARING FOR THE NEW FOAL

Most trainers agree that no time should be wasted in starting a new foal's education. The following explains some of the popular methods used in handling foals.

One of the first things taught is how to lead, but before you can lead him, he must be caught. It's best to have the mare and foal in a stall or similar small enclosure to do the catching.

In catching the foal, hook one arm under his neck and, if he tries to get away, keep him slightly off-balance by pushing on his hip with your other hand. This gives you a little leverage, so he doesn't take you right off your feet. You can see why it's a good idea to begin catching and haltering the foal right away, rather than waiting until it has become a tough colt or big filly.

After you have caught the foal, rub him all over with your hands and talk to him. Try to settle him down and let him know you're not going to hurt him. Continue restraining him, rubbing gently and talking softly, until you feel him relax, then let him go. You can return later for more of the same.

While catching and handling the foal, keep an eye out for the mare. Sometimes a mare that's normally sweet and gentle will become highly protective. If you aren't really sure of the mare, get a halter on her and have someone hold her when you handle the foal. We know one trainer who learned this lesson the hard way: several broken ribs and a huge bite on the chest!

Some horsemen like to leave a halter on their foals all the time. In some instances, this is probably a good idea; such as when you have a lot of foals and you can't spend enough time with each individual.

Most horseowners, however, only have a few foals to handle and therefore like to braid the lead rope right into the foal halter. With this, they have to put a halter on and take it off the foal each time he's handled. Before long, you're catching and haltering him so often that he gets used to it and the sequence is no big thing.

Many think it's a mistake to lead the mare and just let the foal run loose to follow. Sometimes he will follow and sometimes he won't. You should have a helper and lead both the mare and the foal.

In catching the foal, have the foal halter and lead rope coiled up on your left shoulder. After you have him caught, let it slide down your arm to your hand and put it on him, making sure that it fits him correctly.

The foal haltered, you can begin teaching him to lead by looping the lead rope around behind his rump, just above the hocks. Take a good firm hold on the lead rope, both under the halter and on the end coming around from behind the rump.

Be careful at this point, because sometimes a foal will go over backwards. If this should happen, be prepared to keep his head from hitting the ground by keeping a strong hold on the rope coming from the halter.

Having him in soft ground is a good idea. There are probably a lot more foals than we hear about killed by falling over backwards and hitting the poll on the hard ground.

As you begin to lead the foal, put most of the pull to go forward on his rump. If he comes forward willingly, lead him with as little pressure as possible. Most likely, he will not come willingly and you will have to pull him by the rope around his rump. Stay sharp here as he may pull back, he may lunge forward — or he may come along nice as you please.

One obvious aid in teaching the foal to lead is to have a helper lead the mare ahead of you. The foal will see her and want to follow. Once the foal is beginning to lead without too much resistance, try to get him to shoulder up; that is, walk up beside you, where you are beside his left shoulder. If you begin this work right away, you will find it a great help to have your foal handling well on the halter when you get ready to send your mare back to the stallion to be bred again.

When you do get ready to breed the mare back and you have to trailer the mare and foal, here are a few important things that you should remember as far as trailering procedures are concerned. Some mares, when they realize they are in a trailer without their foals, will tear a trailer — and sometimes themselves — to pieces before you can stop them.

Always have help at trailering time. Some like to take out the center divider of their trailers. However, other horsemen haul mares and foals by merely tying the center divider over to one side. When you are ready to load up, have the trailer in a good spot and have some hay in the manger for the mare.

Most foals, at this age, will have to be put in the trailer. The best way to accomplish this is to have a helper lock arms with you, behind the foal's rump, just above the

A good way to immobilize a frisky foal is demonstrated (above). One hand grasps the dock of the tail, the other encircles foal's neck and weight pushes him off-balance.

hocks. Walk right on up the ramp into the trailer and just stuff him in there. Once he is inside, have your helper stand at his rear and to one side, then hold him in while you load the mare beside him.

With the center divider out, hook the two butt chains together behind the mare and foal. At this point, lock the mare, foal and helper inside the trailer by closing the tailgate and securing it. With the mare now tied, the helper removes the halter from the foal and exits the trailer via the escape door, making sure that the foal doesn't try to go out the escape door, also!

You have to use judgment here. If your mare is bad in the trailer or you suspect that she will be, proceed with caution. Whatever you do, don't endanger your helper!

Do not tie the mare — or any other horse, for that matter — in the trailer until the butt chain is hooked and the tailgate is closed and locked. Keep in mind, too, that more than one foal has dived out over the tailgate. Some trailers are equipped with a high tailgate or even an upper door to prevent this. Most tailgates, however, are not really high enough to prevent the foal from jumping out, if he really tried it.

You can handle this problem with a piece of plywood about two feet wide, at least a half-inch thick and about a foot longer than the trailer is wide. For trailers with ramps, by backing off on the lock nuts, you can open it just enough to slip the plywood in behind it, then tighten them to secure the wood in place. This isn't very fancy, but it does a

good job and, when the foal is big enough to be tied in, like his dam, you can put it aside till next year.

If your trailer is different to this, you will have to find a way to fit the wood above the door. But whatever you do, don't haul your mare and foal without it.

When ready to unload, the proceedings are reversed. Have your helper go in through the side door to catch and halter the foal. Take the plywood off, then untie the mare! Let the trailer gate down and let down the butt chains. Take out the foal then.

There may be times when you would like to restrain the small foal without any hassling around, such as holding him still for the veterinarian. To do this, simply place one hand under his neck and grip him tightly about the tail, right at the dock where it joins the rump. Using this method, you can hold him firmly in place and won't hurt his tail.

After the foal has become somewhat used to being handled and is accustomed to being haltered and led, it's a good time to start handling his feet. If a horse has his feet handled properly from the time he is a little foal, he probably will turn into one of those nice-to-shoe individuals and problems with handling his feet and shoeing will not be apt to show up later.

When you begin to handle the foal's feet, it is a good idea to have someone hold him for you. Start by picking up a front leg. Don't hold onto his leg if he struggles. Through repeated tries, you should be able to get him to let you have his foot just for a moment. Give it back to him and

When catching the new foal, have halter and lead rope coiled over the shoulder, then slip it down slowly to avoid spooking him (left). It then is applied and the foal can be led away or taught to lead using a butt rope around the hindquarters (right).

pat him before he struggles. Move to a back leg, pick it up, then put it down before he has a chance to pull. Go around him once in this manner and let it go for this time.

Come back to the foot raising each time you halter the foal. However, when he has become used to having his feet picked up, hold a foot with one hand and pat on the sole with the other. This little bit of handling and tapping on his feet will be of tremendous value when you have to trim his hooves later on.

Most horsemen don't like to handle a young foal's ears or his nose, except in grooming. He must learn to have them handled eventually, but he will most likely only learn to jerk away from you if you start grabbing for them right off.

When you brush him, use a soft one initially and brush his back to let him feel it and get used to it. Brush his face and all about his head, being careful of his eyes. Be sure to brush in the direction that the hair grows. Don't neglect his legs.

Henry White starts his parasite control program when the foals are 8 days old. "We start this early, because there is some evidence to indicate that the scours a foal gets during foal heat may be due to the movement of strongyles (bloodworms) through the foal. So we give our foals an ounce and a half of thiabendazole. Usually you get another scour period around fifteen to eighteen days and we use the same treatment, except we follow the thiabendazole with milk of magnesia an hour later. If this doesn't stop the scouring problem, we use a drug that is primarily Kaopectate. If that doesn't work, there is always paregoric.

"We start tubing the foals between 6 and 8 weeks. If we don't tube them at that time, we give them about an ounce of thiabendazole per hundred pounds of body weight with a dose syringe. This is up to three ounces. After that, they can't handle it too well with a dose syringe. They spit too

The first step in loading is to shove foal into trailer, not the mare (above). She could panic if separated from foal and destroy trailer or herself! She then is loaded by the helper, who leaves her tied but unties the foal (below).

much out. Once we start tubing the foals, we tube them about every two months from then on.

"The only exceptions to this practice are sick foals. When they get to be yearlings, we worm them for any bots they might have picked up. One of the things we've found that also helps control parasites is rotation of pastures. If you don't let a field get over-horsed, you cut down the available parasites for the foals to pick up. I try to rest a field or two each year for at least 120 days."

White says he leaves his foals' teeth alone, until they are yearlings or older. Then, all he does is check them for sharp edges. "A teething foal will eat about anything he can get his mouth on — fences, straps, gates; sometimes you get a bunch of weanlings in a field and for some reason they will bark a tree, one single tree. They'll pick out a tree and you can put anything you want on it, but nine times out of ten they'll strip it anyway. There isn't much you can do to stop this chewing when they are teething."

It is true that a lot of foals just get dumped out into a pasture and are gathered up as 3-year-olds, sent to the trainer and somehow turn out just fine. There is, however, a lot to be said against this kind of practice. For example, many of these neglected horses grow up with crooked legs when, with a little handling, they could have been trimmed and straightened. Also, when they are hard to handle, it becomes easy to put off worming them.

If you should have an emergency, it would sure be a lot nicer to have all of your horses gentle and handling well. The little extra money you spend to take excellent care of your horses packs a big reward. Needless to say, this goes for your time, too.

Keep in mind, during that awkward age when he is no longer a foal but not yet a horse, that he still needs you. Take care of him and the rewards will keep right on coming.

After the tailgate has been raised, the helper exits via the escape door (below), keeping foal from following! Since foal could jump tailgate, thick plywood board is installed over the top, completely sealing exit (above).

MEMORIES OF DEAR JOHN

As A Fitting Conclusion, Slim Pickens Describes The Curious Bond Between Horse And Horseman

One of the stunts Pickens used in rodeo act was to have Dear John sit on his haunches. Text outlines why the old horse no longer is asked to perform this maneuver.

*M*OST PROFESSIONALS IN the horse business make a point of never allowing themselves to become attached to any individual horse. To start with, it isn't good business, especially if you have an animal that's worth more money than you care to do without. Also, most pros go through so many horses over a period of years that they seldom have an opportunity to become attached to a particular mount. The average trainer, for example, may keep a horse for three months before either selling it — if he owns it — or turning it back to its owner.

But even these seeming professionals have a spot somewhere in their hearts in which a special horse usually finds love that never is shown other animals. It's a little like the spinster who never has been in love; when it happens, it's all the way.

That seems to have been the case with Dear John.

Slim Pickens, cowboy turned actor and a success at both, leaned on the fencepost near Bishop, California, and stared out across the lush green grass to where the Appaloosa horse was grazing. There was a distant, wonderous look that could have veiled a tear.

"This actin' business has been mighty good to me," he said, still staring at the old horse that contentedly nuzzled a clump of grass, "but I'm smart enough to know that I owe a lot of whatever success I've had to ol' Dear John."

Hearing his name mentioned, the horse looked up for an instant, then returned to his grazing.

"I had made all those pictures with Rex Allen," Slim recalls, whenever he discusses the horse, "but when Republic Pictures closed down and we all went our separate ways, they remembered me as nothin' but a comic in series of Western films. I was havin' a tough time gettin' a job and was just about to quit this picture business."

In the interim, however, Pickens had made a film for an independent in which he had been called upon to rope a 1600-pound bull from the old horse. "He was barefoot, too, — no shoes to help hold — but I dabbed that rope around that bull and John set down on him. When the bull hit the end of the rope, we slid a dozen feet. It woulda tipped over any normal horse, but ol' John held him."

From that incident the horse began to develop a career of his own. A Disney producer saw the footage and called Pickens to rent the horse. The at-liberty actor explained that he went with the horse and they had to hire him, too.

"So they hired me to do somethin' just so they could

When Dear John was retired to pasture, Slim Pickens acquired an Appaloosa successor, given to daughter Daryle Ann Lindley. He rides it more than she does (left), with dog for company.

use Dear John," Slim drawls. "That year, the horse made $7600 and I don't recall how I did. You know, that's more'n a lot of high-priced racehorses make in a year."

Pickens had barely started his film career at Republic — and that goes back something over twenty years — when he spotted the Appaloosa in a pasture near a film location in Northern California. He went into a nearby bar and asked the bartender about the horse. As it turned out, the barman was the owner and allowed that the horse was for sale, "if he could make a little somethin' on him."

According to Pickens, "I told him I'd let him make $25 and he said the price would be $150 in that case. I learned later that I'd been had, since he'd only paid $100 in the first place and the reason the horse was on pasture was 'cause ol' John had throwed him a time or two.

"I used him in a picture, while I was trainin' him, and we didn't have no trouble. Then on the second picture, he come apart on me while we was doin' a scene. After that, it took more'n six months of us punishin' each other before we come to an understandin'. After that, there wasn't anything that horse wouldn't do that was in reason. The differ-

While there have been other horses in the Pickens/Lindley brood, none comes close to replacing Dear John.

Pausing in a shady stream for a cool drink, cowboy/clown/actor Pickens and Ms. Lindley recount past events that endear Dear John to them both.

ence between him and a lot of horses is the fact that he knew more about reason than a lot of riders.

"For instance, I've never had him fall with me, no matter what I asked him to do. And I've jumped him over teams of horses, over wagons and over solid stone fences that scared hell out of me, when we were comin' up on them.

"But if John took off, I knew we would make it. If he knew we wouldn't, he'd just quit and not even try. And when he said no, I never tried him a second time. He knew better'n I did what he was capable of handlin'."

One of Pickens favorite stories regarding the old horse involves his daughter, actress/columnist Daryle Ann Lindley.

"She wasn't very old — about 12, I reckon — and had been in a number of horse shows without much success, ridin' a little horse I'd bought her.

"We were at a fair, where I was appearin' with Dear John and, after listenin' to her, I told her I'd get her a horse that would win for her.

"The next day, I took John down to the creek and washed him up, then I clipped some of the hair off his nose and around his fetlocks. I put her saddle on him and led him up for her to get onto. Daryle Ann took one look and began to cry. She didn't figger ol' John could even get entered in a class, but I convinced her to give it a try."

The horse and his rider were entered in an equitation class in which the young rider was required to dismount, then remount. She then was so small that she had to use the saddle strings in pulling herself up enough to get into the saddle.

"Of course, by this time, John was trained to buck on cue," Pickens recalls, "and I figgered if he was gonna respond at all, it would be while she was pullin' herself up like that. I was sittin' in the stands, holdin' my breath, prayin' a little, but nothin' happened. He was a perfect gentleman. In fact, he was so perfect that he walked off with the blue ribbon."

Later in the day, with his own saddle on the horse, Pickens went through the horse's entire bag of tricks, including the bit where he bucks on cue. That night, a little old lady walked up to Pickens, shaking her head.

"Mr. Pickens," she said, "you must have had to look for ages to find two horses as perfectly matched as the one your daughter rode this morning and that outlaw of yours."

Pickens simply smiled at her and nodded. "Yes, ma'am. I sure did."

Although he sounds like he is straight out of the branding corrals of Texas or Oklahoma, Slim Pickens was born something over half a century ago in Kingsburg, California, a cattle running area in its own right. His legal name is Louis Bert Lindley, Jr., and the means by which he adopted the Slim Pickens handle is a story in itself.

He was just 15 years old when he began rodeoing over his father's objections. So word wouldn't get home, he decided to use another name.

"Why don't you call yourself Slim Pickens," another cowboy advised, "because that's all you'll get around this rodeo."

"At that time, during the Depression, I was already six-foot-three and I weighed about 140 pounds, so the name fit. Now, I'm still the same height and weigh about 240. I'm tempted to bill myself as the 'formerly Slim Pickens'."

According to a close friend, movie writer Clair Huffaker, "For the past twenty-plus years, Slim's mingled — or maybe mangled — both rodeoing and acting. According to the all-time rodeo champion rider, Casey Tibbs, Slim is the most loved, famous and daredevil rodeo clown in the business.

"For the uninitiated, clowning is the most dangerous job on the rodeo circuit. Aside from roping, bulldogging and riding maybe 10,000 bucking horses and Brahma bulls, Slim has brought laughter to millions of rodeo fans while risking his life bullfighting and such. Like, for example, when the 2000-pound, killing-mad Brahma tosses its rider and turns to trample and gore the stunned fella, who's that funny-looking guy in the baggy pants and comic makeup who dashes in front of the bull, waving his oversized bandanna? Who does the furious bull take out after? And who leaps hilariously into the barrel just in the nick of time? Who gets the hell knocked out of him, as the furious monster rams and slams against those hopefully stout barrel staves? That's Slim.

"Last year," Huffaker says, "a few well-meaning friends managed to drag Slim to a doctor, just to see if he was really still alive. He still had seventeen broken bones mending and, in his whole life, Slim's only worn four casts." The doctor's final verdict was that Slim was not only alive, but nearly indestructible. The doctor was heard to remark in an aside that it was also fairly possible that Slim's not too overly bright.

In the Air Force during World War II, Slim was riding a bucking horse "just for practice" on a Wisconsin farm, when it fell on him and fractured three vertebrae. That resulted in a medical discharge, but he went right back to the rodeo circuit, where he was discovered by a movie director and won a role in an Errol Flynn Western. From there, he went to Republic Pictures to sidekick for Rex Allen and Rocky Lane.

"It was at Republic that the big work-lack set in and I was farmin' out my horse on condition I work, too," Slim recalls thoughtfully. He was a meany in "One-Eyed Jacks" with Marlon Brando, then his stock shot high when he portrayed the cowboy bomber pilot in "Doctor Strangelove."

Pickens retired — more or less — from active rodeo work in 1964, after he suffered a broken back during an appearance at the Medicine Hat show in Alberta, Canada. But he still does his own riding, roping and looks insulted at the idea of a stuntman doing his chores for him.

There have been other Appaloosa horses in the Pickens — or Lindley — family besides Dear John. For example, Daryle Ann owned a horse that Slim used as a double for his horse on occasion. It was an outstanding jumper and won the young lady a handful of ribbons before it was sold. It was aptly called Little John.

"I was heartbroken about that sale for months and never let him forget it," Slim's elder daughter admits. "Finally, he bought another Appaloosa and gave it to me after he'd done some hard training. Even today, he spends as much time on that horse as I do."

Rex Allen, a friend of more than twenty years, recalls that Pickens retired Dear John from the rigors of movie and rodeo work about the time that he, himself, retired from rodeo clowning.

"He knows this veterinarian, Dr. Joe Hird, up at Bishop who has a lot of pasture, a good barn and a feel for horses," Allen recalls, "so Slim one day hauled old John up there and turned him out. He goes by several times a year to see the old horse, but still has the same trouble he always did. Any of the other members of Slim's family can walk right up to the horse but Slim has a tough time catchin' him."

According to Allen, he was buying some feed one day about three years ago, when Slim happened into the same store and reported that he'd heard from Doc Hird. Feed was short and he had been feeding Old John on pellets, but he was recommending that Pickens bring in some ground alfalfa and molasses, because of the old horse's teeth. Allen volunteered to help Pickens haul a couple of tons of the mixture in his dump truck.

It's possible Slim Pickens could train this Appaloosa in John's image, but he doesn't tour much anymore. Besides, could any horse really take the place of John?

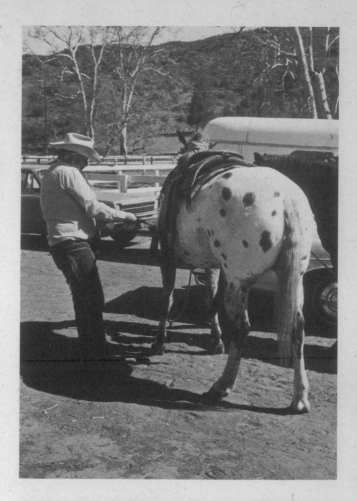

At the mountain ranch operated by the veterinarian, the feed was unloaded, then Pickens led his old film compadre back of the house to look at the horse.

"Pickens told me he hadn't been on the horse in six years and that he hadn't even been able to catch him in three," Allen recalls. "And according to Slim, it took everything short of a bear trap to catch him, if he didn't want to be caught."

They found the horse eating in an open corral, so Allen slipped to the open gate to guard it while Pickens worked the horse into a corner and put a rope on him.

"While I was standing there, Slim swung up on the old horse's back and gave him the cue to buck. This is really two different signals and one has to follow the other, but even after six or seven years, the old horse's feet came off the ground, his head went down, his back arched as he went up in the air in a performance that sent Pickens flying through the air to end up in a pile of humanity that looked for a minute like it might need some more repairing.

"But Pickens picked himself up out of that corral with a big grin, happy at the fact the horse hadn't forgotten. Slim gave the old horse another cue that caused him to sit down, dog style. His rear legs were bunched up under him — or were supposed to be, as I remembered the trick — but this time, one of them stuck straight out. Pickens signaled the horse to get back to his feet.

" 'I'll never ask him to do that one again,' " Slim said. "He had forgotten that old John had developed arthritis so bad in that one leg that he'd even hold it up when he was galloping in the pasture, running on just three legs.

"Doc Hird had tried cortisone treatments, but admitted that in a horse that old, any relief was strictly temporary.

" 'When I take th' rope off, he'll act young enough,' " Slim prophesied. " 'He'll bust out that gate and run clear to the far end of the pasture. He's always afraid I'm gonna load him up to go rodeoing.'

"But Dear John didn't run," Allen recalls. "He just stood there for a minute, then came over and stuck his head over Slim's shoulder. They stood there like that for a long time."

Now, nearly four years later, Slim Pickens looked at the same horse in the same pasture, watching Dear John graze among the yearling colts. Pickens shook his head.

"He ain't gettin' much of that grass," he confided. "His teeth're so worn down that about all he can do is gum it a lot. Fact is, he purty near lives off that ground alfalfa and molasses, with some rolled barley in Winter to give him body heat.

"But he thinks he's grazin' and if that makes him happy, that's all that really matters."

This time the tears had managed to find their way through that faraway look behind which he'd tried to hide them before.

But now Slim Pickens didn't try to hide those tears and he didn't wipe them away in his hardbitten, gruff fashion.

Instead, he just let them well and smiled a little, as though proud that he should cry over an old horse that probably wouldn't last through the next Winter.

This Santa Fe-type saddle is one of Pickens' prized possessions and dates back more than 150 years (right).

The horse ridden by Pickens in this old Republic film
was Little John, a horse used to double Dear John on
occasion. Similar feats were accomplished by older horse, too.

From left: Mrs. Pickens, Daryle Ann, Slim and other
daughter, Maggi Lou, browse through old scrapbooks.
Truly, they all are filled with memories of Dear John.

Address Listings

ASSOCIATIONS FOR HORSE AND HORSEMAN

Alaska State Horsemen, Incorporated, P.O. Box 4-012, Anchorage, Alaska 99509

American Albino Association, Incorporated, Box 79, Crabtree, Oregon 97335

American Buckskin Registry Association, P.O. Box 1125, Anderson, California 96007

American Association of Equine Practitioners, Rt. 5, 14 Hillcrest Circle, Golden, Colorado 80401

American Farrier's Association, P.O. Box 695, Albuquerque, New Mexico 87103

American Horse Council, Incorporated, 1776 K Street, Washington, D.C. 20006

American Horse Protection Association, 3316 N Street, N.W., Washington, D.C. 20007

American Horse Shows Association, 527 Madison Avenue, New York, New York 10022

American Humane Association, P.O. Box 1266, Denver, Colorado 80201

American Morab Horse Association, Box 687, Clovis, California 93612

American Morgan Horse Association, Incorporated, Box 265, Hamilton, New York 13346

American Mustang Association, Incorporated, P.O. Box 122, Berlin, Wisconsin 54823

American Paint Horse Association, P.O. Box 13486, Fort Worth, Texas 76118

American Part-Blooded Horse Registry, 4120 S.E. River Drive, Portland, Oregon 97222

American Quarter Horse Association, P.O. Box 200, Amarillo, Texas 79105

American Remount Association, 20560 Perris Boulevard, Perris, California 92370

Appaloosa Horse Club, Incorporated, Box 403, Moscow, Idaho 83843

Appaloosa Horse Club of Canada, Box 3036, Postal Station B, Calgary, Alberta, Canada

Arabian Horse Club Registry of America, One Executive Park, 7801 Belleview Avenue, Englewood, Colorado 80110

Arizona State Horsemen's Association, 5133 N. Central Avenue, Phoenix, Arizona 85012

California Horse Council, 224 E. Olive Avenue, Burbank, California 91502

California State Horsemen's Association, P.O. Box 1179, Santa Rosa, California 95403

Canadian Girls Rodeo Association, Box 23, Calgary 2, Alberta, Canada

Central Ohio Saddle Club Association, Incorporated, 1330 Cleveland Avenue N.W., Canton, Ohio 44703

Chickasaw Horse Association, Incorporated, Love Valley, North Carolina 28677

Colorado Horsemen's Council, 14405 W. 52nd Street, Arvada, Colorado 80002

Connecticut Horse Council, Holines Road, East Lyme, Connecticut 06333

Empire State Horsemen's Association, 875 King Street, Chappaqua, New York 10514

Equestrian Trails, Incorporated, 10723 Riverside Drive, North Hollywood, California 91602

Florida Horse Council, Room 415, Mayo Building, Tallahassee, Florida 32301

Georgia Horse Council, 2552 Habersham Road, N.W., Atlanta, Georgia 30305

Girls Rodeo Association, 8909 N.E. 25th Street, Spencer, Oklahoma 73084

Half Quarter Horse Registry of America, Rt. 2, Box 67-F, Saugus, California 91350

Horsemen's Benevolent & Protective Association, 600 Executive Boulevard 317, Rockville, Maryland 20852

Inter-County Horsemen's Association, Box 111, Brookfield, Ohio 44403

International Arabian Horse Association, 224 E. Olive Avenue, Burbank, California 91502

International Arabian Cutting Horse Association, 1471 Apache Boulevard, Tempe, Arizona 85281

International Buckskin Horse Association, Box 357, St. John, Indiana 46373

International Rodeo Association, P.O. Box 615, Pauls Valley, Oklahoma 73075

Iowa Horse Council, Rt. 1, North Liberty, Iowa 52317

Junior Rodeo Association, 8473 45th Street, Riverside, California 92509

Kansas Saddle Horse Association, 1209 N. Eighth Street, Kansas City, Kansas 66112

Maine Horse Association, Rt. 1, Box 240, Greene, Maine 04236

Maryland Horse Breeders Association, Box 4, Timonium, Maryland 21093

Massachusetts Horsemen's Council, 117 Grove Street, Upton, Massachusetts 01568

Michigan Horse Council, P.O. Box 494, Lansing, Michigan 48902

Minnesota Horse Council, P.O. Box 292, Long Lake, Minnesota 55356

Mississippi Horse Council, 700 Main Street, Columbia, Mississippi 39429

Missouri Horse and Mule Council, Box 101, Lynn Creek, Missouri 65052

Morgan Horse Cutting Association, RR 1, Box 208, Springfield, Illinois 62707

Morris Animal Foundation, 531 Guaranty Bank Building, Denver, Colorado 80202

National Cowboy Polo Association, 8295 Ralston Road, Arvada, Colorado 80002

National Cutting Horse Association, P.O. Box 12155, Fort Worth, Texas 76116

National Flag Race Association, 309 S. 19th, Mt. Vernon, Illinois 62864

National High School Rodeo Association, 298 S. Oregon, Ontario, California 97914

National Intercollegiate Rodeo Association, Sam Houston State University, Huntsville, Texas 77340

National Little Britches Rodeo Association, P.O. Box 651, Littleton, Colorado 80120

National Reining Horse Association, 1290 Hine Road, Hamilton, Ohio 45013

National Trails Council, 53 W. Jackson Boulevard, Chicago, Illinois 60604

Nevada State Horsemen's Association, 1545 S. Wells Avenue, Reno, Nevada 89502

New England Horsemen's Council, Incorporated, 327 Parker Street, East Longmeadow, Massachusetts 01028

New Hampshire Horse & Trail Association, 322 N. Adams Street, Manchester, New York 14504

New Jersey Horse Council, 310 W. State Street, Trenton, New Jersey 08618

New Mexico Horse Council, c/o Jim McCauley, Corvales, New Mexico 87048

North Carolina Horse Council, Box 308, Zabulon, North Carolina 27597

North American Trail Ride Conference, 1995 Day Road, Gilroy, California 95020

Ohio Horsemen's Council, P.O. Box 302, Lebanon, Ohio 45036

Oklahoma Horsemen's Association, 2525 Northwest Expressway, Oklahoma City, Oklahoma 73112

Oregon Horsemen's Association, Box 257, Coburg, Oregon 97401

Original Half Quarter Horse Registry, Hubbard, Oregon 97032

Pacific Coast Hunter, Jumper and Stock Horse Association, 4401 Keystone Avenue, Culver City, California 90230

Palomino Horse Association, Incorporated, P.O. Box 324, Jefferson City, Missouri 65101

Palomino Horse Breeders of America, P.O. Box 249, Mineral Wells, Texas 76067

Penn-Ohio Horsemen's Association, Incorporated, 4900 Cooper Road, Lowellville, Ohio 44360

Pennsylvania Equine Council, 324 Animal Industry Building, University Park, Pennsylvania 16802

Pennsylvania Horse Breeders Association, 17 W. Miner Street, Westchester, Pennsylvania 19380

Pinto Horse Association of America, Incorporated, P.O. Box 3984, San Diego, California 92103

Professional Horsemen's Association of America, Midland Riding Center, Rt. 1, Midland, Georgia 31820

Rhode Island Horsemen's Association, Incorporated, Box 25, Warwick, Rhode Island 02887

Rodeo Cowboys Association, 2929 W. 19th Avenue, Denver, Colorado 80204

South Carolina Horse Council, c/o Extension Horse Specialist, Clemson University, Clemson, South Carolina 29631

Spanish-Barb Breeders Association, P.O. Box 7479, Colorado Springs, Colorado 80907

Spanish Mustang Registry, Incorporated, Cayuse Ranch, Oshoto, Wyoming 82724

Standard Quarter Horse Association, 4390 Fenton, Denver, Colorado 80212

Texas Horse Council, 5314 Bingle Road, Houston, Texas 77018

Tri-State Horseman's Association, 1722 Tamarach Drive, Long Lake, Minnesota 55356

United Professional Horsemen's Association, P.O. Box 494, Lake Zurich, Illinois 50047

Virginia Horse Council, P.O. Box 72, Riner, Virginia 24149

Washington State Horsemen, Incorporated, 8175 N.E. 150th, Bothell, Washington 98011

West Virginia Horse Council, c/o David Keith, West Virginia Department of Agriculture, Charleston, West Virginia 25305

Wild Horse Organized Assistance (WHOA), P.O. Box 555, Reno, Nevada 89504

Wisconsin State Horse Council, North Main Street, Lodi, Wisconsin 53555

Ysabella Saddle Horse Association, Incorporated, McKinzie Rancho, RR 2, Williamsport, Indiana 47993

TACK & SADDLERY

AAA Engineering & Manufacturing Company, P.O. Box 273, Arcadia, California 91106

Action Company, P.O. Box 541, McKinney, Texas 75069

Armstrong Supply Company, Box 11133, Chattanooga, Tennessee 37401

B&B Leather Company, 2519 The Plaza, Charlotte, North Carolina 28205

Big Horn, 2305 S. Hickory Street, Chattanooga, Tennessee 37407

Billy Royal, 3777 Green Road, Cleveland, Ohio 44122

Bona Allen Saddle & Leather, P.O. Box 829, Fort Worth, Texas 76101

Bronco Products, Box 57, McKinney, Texas 75069

Colorado Saddlery, 1631 15th Street, Denver, Colorado 80202

Court's Saddlery Company, 403 N. Main Street, Bryan, Texas 77801

Custom Made Saddlery Company, 2924 W. Valley Boulevard, Alhambra, California 91803

Equus, P.O. Box 1740, Covina, California 91722

Ervin Quick Bit Maker, 23007 Lyon Street, San Jacinto, California 92383

Fargo Saddlery, Route 5, Lenoir City, Tennessee 37771

Farragut, Incorporated, Lexington Drive, Concord, Tennessee 37720

Fits-Em Company, 3449 S. Harding, Indianapolis, Indiana 45217

Five-A Ranch, P.O. Box 712, Chino, California 91710

Floyd Lariat Company, 240 E. Rosewood, San Antonio, Texas 78212

Les Garcia, P.O. Box 1966, Reno, Nevada 89505

Henly Halter Company, Route 2, Wagoner, Oklahoma 74467

Hollis Bits, Route 1, Beeville, Texas 78102

Horn Saddle Company, Route 2, Box 738, Gresham, Oregon 97030

J.B. Ranch Supply, Box 650, Rapid City, South Dakota 57701

J.R. Saddlery, P.O. Box 834, Ceres, California 95307

Johnson Ideal Halter Company, P.O. Box 208, Eastwood Drive, Aurora, Illinois 60510

Kelly Manufacturing Company, 838 Logan, Middleport, Ohio 45760

Keyston Brothers, 1000 Brannon Street, San Francisco, California 94103

L.C. Tack Supply, 10111 E. 48th Street, Tulsa, Oklahoma 74145

Lookout Saddle Company, 1600 Rossville Boulevard, Chattanooga, Tennessee 37408

Lovins, Bruce Silver Saddle Manufacturing Company, 18 Thatcher Avenue, Alexandria, Kentucky 41001

M&E Manufacturing Company, P.O. Box 1832, Lancaster, California 93534

M&H Products Company, Ellsworth, Nebraska 59340

MacPherson Leather Company, 200 S. Los Angeles Street, Los Angeles, California 90012

Midwest Saddlery Company, 4415 B Drive South, Battle Creek, Michigan 49017

Monarch Leather Goods, RR 3, Vale, North Carolina 28168

S.D. Myres Saddle Company, 5030 Alameda, El Paso, Texas 79996

National Bridle Shop, 815 E. Commerce Street, Lewisburg, Tennessee 37091

National Safety Stirrup Company, 2217 N. Clifford, Las Vegas, Nevada 89110

North & Judd, P.O. Box 1111, New Britain, Connecticut 06052

Ozark Leather Company, P.O. Box 947, Waco, Texas 75703

Partrade, P.O. Box 1886, Chattanooga, Tennessee 37407

Potts Longhorn Leather, 3141 Oak Grove, Dallas, Texas 75219

Ralide, Incorporated, P.O. Box 131, Athens, Tennessee 37303

Rawhide Manufacturing Company, 1009 G Street, San Diego, California 92101

Red Ranger Saddlery, 1600 E. 27th Street, Chattanooga, Tennessee 37404

Redfield Halters, 2668 El Camino Real, Mountain View, California 94040

Remco Specialties of Texas, P.O. Box 44078, Dallas, Texas 75234

Renalde Crockett & Kelly Bit & Spur Company, 1525 18th Street, Denver, Colorado 80217

Ritter Saddletrees, 5034 Alameda, El Paso, Texas 79996

Rogers Saddlery, 105 N. Ballard, Wylie, Texas 75098

Roper's Supply Company, Route 3, Box 349, Ellensburg, Washington 98926

Roy Bit & Spurs, P.O. Box 33, Comfort, Texas 78013

Ryon Saddle & Ranch Supplies, 2601 N. Main, Fort Worth, Texas 76106

Safety K Stirrup, P.O. Box 1157, El Cajon, California

Salisbury Saddle Company, Route 4, Box 102, Longmont, Colorado 80501

San Angelo Die Casting & Manufacturing Company, P.O. Box 984, San Angelo, Texas 75901

Schneider Saddlery Company, 3777 Green Road, Cleveland, Ohio 44122

Simco Leather Company, 1800 Daisy Street, Chattanooga, Tennessee 37405

Sooner Lariats, Incorporated, 2216 S. Rosedale, Tulsa, Oklahoma 74343

Southern Saddlery, 3001 S. Broad Street, Chattanooga, Tennessee 37402

Standard Saddle Tree Company, P.O. Box 367, Vernal, Utah 84078

Stockmen's, Incorporated, P.O. Box 1, Lawton, Iowa 51030

Sylvester Saddle & Leather Company, Route 1, Box 251-H, Zachary, Louisiana 70791

Tack International, 154 Tices Lane, East Brunswick, New Jersey 08816

Tack Room, 153 E. State Street, Westport, Connecticut 05880

Tar Heel Saddlery Company, Route 3, Box 253, Wake Forest, North Carolina 27587

Taylor Tack Equipment, Box 49, Ravalli, Montana 59863

Tex Tan Western Leather Company, Box 711, Yoakum, Texas 77995

Texas Saddlery Company, 4606 River Drive, Amarillo, Texas 79108

Trammel Bits, Incorporated, P.O. Box 792, Albany, Texas 75430

Triple J, Incorporated, Gwinner, North Dakota 58040

Triple-N Saddlery, P.O. Box 6, Bryant, Alabama 35958

Utah Saddle Company, P.O. Box 427, Vernal, Utah 84078

Valley Head Saddlery Company, P.O. Box 143, Valley Head, Alabama 35989

Veach Saddlery Company, 1011 Princeton Road, Trenton, Missouri 64583

Victor Leather Goods, 7350 Adam Street, Paramount, California 90723

Visalia Stock Saddle Company, 10069 Joerschke Drive, Grass Valley, California 95945

Vogt Western Silver, P.O. Box 2309, Turlock, California 95380

Western Saddlery, 1222 E. 38th Street, Chattanooga, Tennessee 37407

Whitey's Halter Company, 2503 Middle Country Road, Centereach, New York 11720

Wofford Leather Company, Box 638, Gainesville, Georgia 30501

Wonder Whip Company, Box D, Fostoria, Iowa 51340

WESTERN WEAR

Allen Manufacturing Company, 3301 W. Alameda, Denver, Colorado 80219

Americraft, Incorporated, 1601 Bassett Avenue, El Paso, Texas 79923

Bailey Hat Company, 2558 San Fernando Road, Los Angeles, California 90065

Bay River Trading Company, 1310 N. 10th Street, San Jose, California 95112

Big Horn, 2306 S. Hickory Street, Chattanooga, Tennessee 37407

Billy the Kid, 100 S. Cotton St., El Paso, Texas 79901

Border House Imports, 126 N. 5th Street, Grand Junction, Colorado 81501

Brill Brothers, Incorporated, 2102 W. Pierce Street, Milwaukee, Wisconsin 53204

Byer-Rolnick, 601 Marion Drive, Garland, Texas 75040

California Leather Garment Manufacturing, 860 S. Los Angeles Street, Los Angeles, California 90014

California Ranchwear, 14600 S. Main Street, Gardena, California 90248

Charmoll, Incorporated, 366 Wacouta, St. Paul, Minnesota 55101

Colt-Cromwell, 11-17 Melcher Street, Boston, Massachusetts 02210

Corral Sportswear, P.O. Box 938, Ardmore, Oklahoma 73401

Cresco Manufacturing Company, 1201 Jacobsen Avenue, Ashland, Ohio 44805

Dickson-Jenkins Manufacturing Company, P.O. Box 628, Fort Worth, Texas 76102

Donnell's of Denver, 1160 Stout Street, Denver, Colorado 80204

Ep-Ro Manufacturing Company, 1250 Broadway, Denver, Colorado 80203

Great Western Leather 123 W. Tomichi Avenue, Gunnison, Colorado 81230

Gross Western Tailors, 4004 Grape Street, Denver, Colorado 80216

Guni & Shanta, Incorporated, 953 E. Sahara, Las Vegas, Nevada 89105

Gwin Manufacturing Company, 321 W. Arizona Drive, Stanfield, Arizona 85272

Handler-Fenton, 224 W. Alameda Avenue, Denver, Colorado 80223

H Bar C Ranchwear, 101 W. 21st Street, New York, New York 10010

House of Morgan, Box 789, Big Spring, Texas 79720

Indian Original, 521 7th Street, Rapid City, South Dakota 57701

J Bar T, 722 S. Los Angeles Street, Los Angeles, California 90012

Kantex Industries, 12113 Johnson Drive, Shawnee, Kansas 66203

Karman Western Wear, 1513 Wazee Street, Denver, Colorado 80202

Lady Wrangler, 1411 Broadway, New York, New York 10018

La Sevilla, Incorporated, P.O. Box 126, Mangham, Louisiana 71259

Lasso Western Wear, 6623 S. Zarzamora, San Antonio, Texas 78221

H.D. Lee Company, P.O. Box 440, Shawnee Mission, Kansas 66201

Levi Strauss & Company, 2 Embarcadero Center, San Francisco, California 94106

Larry Mahan Cowboy Collection, 1100 Montana, El Paso, Texas 79901

Miller Western Wear, 8500 Zuni Street, Denver, Colorado 80217

Mountain Products Corporation, 123 S. Wenatchee, Wenatchee, Washington 98801

Niver Western Wear, 1221 Hemphill Street, Fort Worth, Texas 76104

Pioneer Wear, 1718 Yale Boulevard, S.E., Albuquerque, New Mexico 87105

Pool Manufacturing Company, 1601 S. Montgomery, Sherman, Texas 75090

Prestige-West, 1216 Arch Street, Philadelphia, Pennsylvania 19107

Prior Company, 1133 S. Platte River Drive, Denver, Colorado 80223

Rockmount Ranch Wear, 1549 Wazee Street, Denver, Colorado 80202

Ruddock Manufacturing Company, 1825 Magoffin, El Paso, Texas 79901

Santa Fe Leather, 1900 Chamisa Street, Santa Fe, New Mexico 87501

Schott Brothers, Incorporated, 10 W. 33rd Street, New York, New York 10001

Scully Brothers, Incorporated, 725 E. Washington Boulevard, Los Angeles, California 90021

Seasons Four Sportswear, 323 Alexander Avenue, Tacoma, Washington 98421

Shreveport Garment Manufacturers, P.O. Box 1646, Shreveport, Louisiana 71165

Smith Brothers Manufacturing, 506 N. Howard, Carthage, Missouri 64836

Tem-Tex Corporation, 1531 Wazee Street, Denver, Colorado 80202

Trego's Westernwear, Box 927, Woodward, Oklahoma 73801

Utica Duxbak Corporation, 815 Noyes Street, Utica, New York 13502

Walls Industries, P.O. Box 98, Cleburne, Texas 76031

Washington Manufacturing Company, 224 2nd Avenue N., Nashville, Tennessee 37201

Western Fashions, 1513 Wazee Street, Denver, Colorado 80202

Western Heritage, 319 Forest Grove Drive, Richardson, Texas 75080

Western Trails, Incorporated, P.O. Box 668, Bend, Oregon 97701

Westmoor Manufacturing Company, 212 S. 10th Street, Omaha, Nebraska 68102

Woolrich, Incorporated, Woolrich, Pennsylvania 17779

Wool West, 311 S. Mt. Vernon, San Bernardino, California 92410

Wrangler Western Wear, 2300 Stemmons Freeway, Dallas, Texas 75207

BOOTS

Acme Boot Company, P.O. Box 749, Clarksville, Tennessee 37040

Anwelt Corporation, 1 Oak Hill Road, Fitchburg, Massachusetts 01420

Blue Bell Boots, Apex Street, Nashville, Tennessee 37205

Border Boot Company, 1716 E. Lincoln, Fort Collins, Colorado 80521

Ceder-Crest Shoe Company, Nashville, Tennessee 37202

Champion Boot Company, 317 Mills, El Paso, Texas 79997

Cowtown Boots, 6966 Gateway East, El Paso, Texas 79915

Del Norte Saddlery, 110 W. San Antonio Avenue, El Paso, Texas 79901

DeWitt Boot Company, P.O. Box 9094, El Paso, Texas 79982

Dexter Shoe Company, 31 St. James Avenue, Boston, Massachusetts 02116

Double S Boot Company, 914 Los Ebanos Boulevard, Brownsville, Texas 78520

Durango Boots, P.O. Box 10, Harpeth Valley Industrial Park, Franklin, Tennessee 37064

Endicott Johnson Corporation, 1100 E. Main Street, Endicott, New York 13760

Frontier Imports, 613 N. Stanton Street, El Paso, Texas 79901

Frye Shoe Company, 84 Chestnut Street, Marlboro, Massachusetts 01752

Guni & Shanta, Incorporated, 953 E. Sahara, Las Vegas, Nevada 89105

Hondo Boots, 4458 El Paso Drive, El Paso, Texas 79993

Hyer Boot Company, P.O. Box 191, Olathe, Kansas 66061

Justin Companies, P.O. Box 548, Fort Worth, Texas 76101

Laramie Boot Company, 2009 E. Yandell Drive, El Paso, Texas 79902

Leddy Boots, 6966 Gateway East, El Paso, Texas 79991

Lucchese Boots, 110 N. Broadway, San Antonio, Texas 78205

Ben Miller Boot Company, 215 Leon Street, El Paso, Texas 79901

Navarro Brothers, 213 S. El Paso Street, El Paso, Texas 79901

Nocona Boots, Box 599, Nocona, Texas 75255

Rios of Mercedes, P.O. Box 789, Big Spring, Texas 79720

Sanders Bootmakers, 3023 Durazno, El Paso, Texas 79905

Skinners Quality Boots, 4606 River Drive, Amarillo, Texas 79108

Stewart Boot Company, 2021 E. 14th Street, Tucson, Arizona 85719

Texas Boot Company, Forrest Avenue, Lebanon, Tennessee 37087

Tony Lama Company, 1137 Tony Lama Street, El Paso, Texas 79915

Wolverine World Wide, 9341 Courtland Drive, N.E., Rockford, Michigan 49341

Wrangler Boots, Granada Avenue, Nashville, Tennessee 37206

WESTERN HATS

American Hat Company, 4510 Feagan Street, Houston, Texas 77001

Bailey Hat Company, 2558 San Fernando Boulevard, Los Angeles, California 90065

Bandera Hat Company, 320 S. Lake, Fort Worth, Texas 76104

Biltmore Hats, Incorporated, 139 Morris Street, Guelph, Ontario, Canada N1H 6L7

Burton Belt Company, 508 N. Hoyne Avenue, Chicago, Illinois 60612

Byer-Rolnick, 601 Marion Drive, Garland, Texas 75040

Candy Straws, 2632 Lester Road, Denair, California 95316

Eddy Brothers Hat Company, 414 W. Pico Boulevard, Los Angeles, California 90015

Goorin Brothers, 115 Park Lane, Brisbane, California 94005

Harris Polk Hats, 1409 W. Tanager, Warsaw, Indiana 46580

Henschel Manufacturing Company, 1602 Locust Street, St. Louis, Missouri 63103

International Hat Company, P.O. Box 2174, Benton Park Station, St. Louis, Missouri 63158

Langenberg Hat Company, P.O. Box 17, Marthasville, Missouri 63357

Lone Star Hat Company, 3507 Copelan Drive, San Antonio, Texas 78220

Meier & Frank, 5641 N. Washington Street, Denver, Colorado 80216

Mexican American Hat Company, 2528 Texas, St. Louis, Missouri 63128

Miller Brothers Hat Company, 2700 Canton Street, Dallas, Texas 75226

Miller Western Wear, 8500 Zuni Street, Denver, Colorado 80217

Moore Hat Company, 109 D Avenue, Lawton, Oklahoma 73501

Old Mission Leather, 1335 Walker, San Luis Obispo, California 93401

Ranch Company Western Wear, 920 Washington Boulevard, St. Louis, Missouri 63101

Rhodes Enterprises, P.O. Box 257, Springville, Utah 84663

Rockmount Ranch Wear, 1549 Wazee Street, Denver, Colorado 80202

Stetson Hat Company, 3601 Leonard Road, St. Joseph, Missouri 64502

Stevens Hat Company, P.O. Box 609, St. Joseph, Missouri 64502

Texas Hat Company, P.O. Drawer 619, Laredo, Texas 78040

CHAPS

Allied Western Wear & Equipment, 1716 E. Lincoln, Fort Collins, Colorado 80521

Don Atkinson Saddle Shop, 411 W. 13th Street, Trenton, Missouri 64683

Bar W Manufacturing, 3804 N. Main Street, Fort Worth, Texas 76106

Bona Allen Saddle & Leather, 205 N.W. 7th Street, Fort Worth, Texas 76101

J.M. Bucheimer Company, Frederick, Maryland 21701

Chap-Parel, Incorporated, Box 505, Abilene, Kansas 67410

Colorado Saddlery Company, 1641 15th Street, Denver, Colorado 80210

Colt-Cromwell Company, 11-17 Melcher Street, Boston, Massachusetts 02210

Contract Leather, Route 3, Box 633, East Stroudsberg, Pennsylvania 18301

Conway Saddle Company, 1890 E. Orchard, Littleton, Colorado 80121

DD Leather Products, 1510 Hogansville Road, LaGrange, Georgia 30240

Double A Leather Company, Route 193, Kingsville, Ohio 44048

Fantasy Craft, 713 56th Street, Sacramento, California 95819

Fargo Saddlery, Route 5, Lenoir City, Tennessee 37771

Garza Leather Company, 2903 Expressway, McAllen, Texas 78501

J Bar W Industries, Route 1, Eaton, Indiana 47338

MacPherson Leather Company, 200 S. Los Angeles Street, Los Angeles, California 90012

Miller Harness Company, 131 Varick Street, New York, New York 10013

Myers Saddle Company, 5030 Alameda, El Paso, Texas 79996

New Braunfels Leather Company, 197 S. Seguin Avenue, New Braunfels, Texas 78130

Partrade, P.O. Box 1886, Chattanooga, Tennessee 37407

Perkies, Incorporated, 255 E. Kellog, St. Paul, Minnesota 55101

Robert A. Porter Company, Route 5, Franklin, Tennessee 37064

Rawhides, Incorporated, 216 Danna Laine, Houston, Texas 77009

Rodeo Shop of Fort Worth, P.O. Box 12693, Fort Worth, Texas 76116

Rogue Leather Company, 754 S.W. 6th Street, Grants Pass, Oregon 97526

Service Manufacturing Company, 155 Saw Mill River Road, Yonkers, New York 10701

Simco Leather Company, 1800 Daisy Street, Chattanooga, Tennessee 37406

Smith Worthington Saddlery, 287 Homestead Avenue, Hartford, Connecticut 06112

Tack Room, 153 E. State Street, Westport, Connecticut 06880

Tack International, 154 Tices Lane, East Brunswick, New Jersey 08816

Tar Heel Saddlery, Route 3, Box 253, Wake Forest, North Carolina 27587

Tex Tan Western Leather Company, 100 Hickey Street, Yoakum, Texas 77995

Texas Saddlery, 4606 River Drive, Amarillo, Texas 79108

Udderly Leather Manufacturing, Route 5, Box 154, Antioch, Illinois 60002

Wilco Leather Goods, P.O. Box 726, Charlottesville, Virginia 22902